Practical KDE

Dennis E. Powell

Technical Editor: Bob Bernstein

Contents at a Glance

que®

A Division of Macmillan Computer Publishing, USA
201 W. 103rd Street
Indianapolis, Indiana 46290

Practical KDE

International Standard Book Number: 0-7897-2216-X

Library of Congress Catalog Card Number: 99-64404

Printed in the United States of America

First Printing: December 1999

01   00   99   4   3   2   1

Trademarks

Warning and Disclaimer

Executive Editor
Jeff Koch

Acquisitions Editor
Gretchen Ganser

Development Editor
Hugh Vandivier

Technical Editor
Bob Bernstein

Managing Editor
Matt Purcell

Senior Editor
Susan Ross Moore

Copy Editors
Pamela Woolf
Kate O. Givens

Indexer
Joy Dean Lee

Proofreader
Debra Neel
Pamela Woolf

Team Coordinator
Cindy Teeters

Interior Design
Anne Jones

Cover Design
Rader Design

Copy Writer
Eric Borgert

Layout Technicians
Liz Johnston
Jeannette McKay

Production Analyst
Dan Harris

Contents

About the Author

Dennis E. Powell is an award-winning reporter and writer who has extensive experience in a variety of media for more than 25 years. Beginning in his teens as a newspaper photographer, he went on to such varied duties as daily newspaper police reporter, breaking news reporter for WOR radio in New York, radio network news editor at CBS, and magazine writer on a number of technical subjects. His 1988 article on the Space Shuttle Challenger disaster won national awards and earned him a Pulitzer Prize nomination. He has written for *Forbes FYI*, *Yankee*, *Navy Times*, *Tropic* (the magazine of the *Miami Herald*), the *New York Post*, and numerous other publications. He also wrote the tour books for the last two Billy Joel concert tours.

He has been involved in computers since the early days of the IBM PC. Since the acquisition of his first computer, he has built all his own machines and those of friends, family, and some commercial clients. He is experienced and conversant in DOS, Windows, OS/2, and Linux, and has documented a number of commercial and in-house applications in each of these operating systems. He has employed KDE from its beginning.

He and his wife live on their little horse farm in Connecticut.

About the Technical Editor

Bob Bernstein sat down in front of a TRS-80 in 1981 and wrote a one-player version of Pong in BASIC. He still likes to play with BASIC. Linux has been a preoccupation "since Red Hat version 3.03," but Debian has since won his allegiance. Past careers include working as a land surveyor ("up through the ranks from junior rodman to chief of party") and several years as a licensed mental health counselor. Occasionally he can be found taking a computer science course at Rhode Island College. If marooned on a desert island he would prefer to have available recordings of Debussy's piano music, some of Thomas Merton's writings, and "a reliable source of caffeine."

Dedication

The world is a lesser place for the passing of Father Winston F. Jensen, and in recognition of that fact, to him this book is dedicated.

Acknowledgments

The difficulty involved in trying to make technical information readable—heavens, maybe even interesting!—is matched only by that in keeping track of and properly thanking all the people who made it possible. If I have succeeded in any way in the former, it is due to many people who I will surely insufficiently credit in the latter. The shortcomings in both cases are mine.

But here are at least some of the people without whom the book you are holding would not have been possible.

In my experience every big project has somewhere someone without whom that project simply could not have come to pass; in this book it's Bob Bernstein. He is someone upon whom it is not possible to heap too much praise. From the beginning of my Linux experience, he has endured cheerfully the silliest of questions, has taken hours of his own time to solve problems with programs in which I was interested but he was not, has soothed my late-night outbursts when something didn't go as I'd hoped, and held his temper when failing to do so would have been entirely justified. He is technical editor of this book, which job I can assure you I did nothing to make easy. He is also someone who, through it all, I have come to consider a warm, personal friend and adviser on much more than Linux. We both have our crotchets, but amazingly have never fired them at each other.

Gretchen Ganser, first, joined soon by Hugh Vandivier, were the midwife and, I guess, obstetrician, and it was not an easy birth. They are listed formally as acquisitions editor and development editor respectively, and that's a nice little pair of categories, but they have also been mentors; gentle taskmasters; soothers of raw nerves; patient beyond enumerating; and, I hope despite my manifold annoyances, friends, too. I do not, so far as I know, know any saints and cannot therefore attest to their patience, but if it is as reported, Susan Ross Moore, the project editor, has met that requirement for sainthood. Were I to write another computer book, I would beg for all three of them.

Scott D. Courtney, Caldera's Erik Ratcliffe, and just about everybody in KDE development filled in the multitude of blanks in my knowledge. Likewise Donnie Barnes of Red Hat, who has put me straight on more than a few things in his inimitable fashion (besides being the only person to have an entire *language* in a Linux distribution in his honor). Michael J. DeNigris III, a great programmer whom I shall one day win over to the path of truth and righteousness that is Linux, and John DeRosa, Junior and Senior, have always provided support that was, well, essential, as has

Gerard Koeppel, who writes interestingly about subjects that would not at first catch the imagination. Kari Jackson and Stewart Jenkins each contributed ideas and materials that make this book better.

It is in no way proper to write a book about Linux without major thanks to Linus Torvalds, who not only invented it and became a cyberfolk hero, but who never lost his tremendous humility. And he writes clean code.

My friend William F. Buckley, Jr., is entirely responsible for my addiction to computers, as he is my addiction to sailing. The reader may conclude that he has done no service in the former, but I thank him on both counts anyway.

My wife, Susan, already had my eternal devotion; for putting up with me during the writing of this book she has increased the already enormous degree to which I am indebted to her.

The persons above are responsible for what is good about *Practical KDE*. What is not is mine alone.

—dep

introduction

Early in the summer of 1998, a remarkable event took place. That it was little remarked upon outside a relatively small group of computer users doesn't really matter. For here was the first time that a group of volunteers, working together even though they were spread around the world and many had never met each other, produced a complete, full-featured graphical user interface and accessory applications for a computer operating system. It included system configuration tools, communications applications, games, small productivity tools—everything that one would expect in an expensive commercial GUI, and all with a common interface.

It was as if a group of talented young hackers, in touch with each other chiefly by email, had gotten together and starting from scratch produced Microsoft Windows. (They would be insulted by this, because they believe, not without supporting evidence, that their work is in many ways better than Windows. This book will not undertake that argument and will leave it to the Internet newsgroups. Though I am not writing about Windows, and I'm not writing on a machine running Windows; I guess my vote has been cast.)

Their project was called *KDE* or, more properly, *the* KDE, because *KDE* stands for *K Desktop Environment* (the K doesn't stand for anything), and on that summer morning version 1.0 of it was released.

Here for the first time was a fully integrated GUI for the increasingly popular Linux operating system as well as other, similar operating systems. It was pretty, it was powerful, it was easy to use, and it was free for the download.

A Little History

It is now almost legendary how in 1991 a mild-mannered, modest, and brilliant young computer science student named Linus Torvalds sought to write a clone of the powerful UNIX operating system that would run on a relatively modest computer. Satisfied with what he had begun, he made it freely available to others over the Internet.

They, and he, built upon it. Soon a tight little group of programmers were working on the "kernel" of what came to be known as *Linux*.

No Long I!

Many people, especially Americans, seem puzzled as to the proper pronunciation of Linux. It was inspired by, and rhymes with, the *Minix* program, which was and is a single-user UNIX clone for 80286 and better processors. The *lin* in Linux is pronounced as the *lin* in *linen*. The *ux* is pronounced as the *ucks* in *ducks*. The accent is on the first syllable. *Lin*'ux.

At first the exclusive province of the few skilled programmers who could, literally, hack it, Linux grew and word of it spread. Within a year or two, it had developed a cult; this grew into a movement. Word spread further. More and more people down-loaded it to give it a try. Programmers were impressed. Skilled hobbyists were impressed. Mere users—you and I—saw it as a lot of work for little benefit. It would never be a "desktop" operating system, no matter how powerful it was, until it had a desktop.

In due course, the possibility of a graphical user interface came about with the release of XFree86 for Linux. Also developed by unpaid hackers, it is not a GUI in and of itself, but it establishes the underpinnings for one. Soon the rest of the pieces—called *window managers*—began to appear. These provided windowing functions—resizing, opening, closing; the things you never think much about—but for the most part no applications. They were followed by "widget sets" that allowed the development of graphical applications, which consisted largely of calculators, little text editors, and such public-domain programs from full-grown versions of UNIX as people cared to port to Linux and XFree86.

Your Tax Dollars at Work

Two of the most popular Linux applications, X-FTP and Nedit, were produced at national physics research laboratories, Lawrence Livermore and Fermilab respectively. They remain popular today. You can download them and use them, free of charge, from most Linux application repositories.

The window managers and widget sets grew in both number and quality. There was a wonderful compatibility about it all: Almost any window manager would run almost any XFree86 application. The widget set would have to reside on the local computer or local area network, true, or the program would have had to be *statically compiled* against the widget set. (This means that the program itself contained the widgets, making it larger and a little slower, but it would run.)

Of course, each application would behave in its own way, or at least each widget set would. Some had scroll bars that would scroll down if the left mouse button were clicked, and up if the right mouse button were clicked instead. Others behaved a little more conventionally. The commands rendered by menus were different in both name and behavior, from application to application. What's more (read "worse"), configuring almost everything, from putting an icon on the desktop to changing the background color or image, involved editing a sometimes difficult to find and almost always difficult to understand text file. It was possible to make a very attractive graphical desktop for Linux, true, but the few who could do it were the ones who were so comfortable with the Linux command line that for them it was mostly a stunt. The Linux system administrator whose boss had elaborate and mercurial aesthetic sensibilities certainly earned his or her keep.

As time went on, window managers grew in power but not ease of use. There were the basics—twm, fvwm, the attractive AfterStep, the breathtakingly beautiful Enlightenment that was also breathtakingly difficult to bend to one's will—but the inconsistencies among applications remained. By now, commercial outfits were gathering up all the pieces necessary to put together a working Linux installation. Beyond the *kernel*, the core of Linux, there were all sorts of other things, such as compilers and programming tools, widget sets, development libraries, device drivers, XFree86 itself, applications of both the text and graphical varieties. Then they were burning them onto CDs, which were then sold, generally with some sort of installation program and a little book that would help the user get it all installed. It may seem a little odd, paying $50 or so for software that anyone with a modem and an Internet provider could download for free. But if the user's time was worth anything, in most cases it was well worth the money spent: Imagine traipsing all over the Internet and downloading a gigabyte or so of software!

Even then, as the second half of the '90s began, Linux was quite an achievement. It was the basis of more World Wide Web sites than you would have ever imagined. Had it appeared in its then-current state six or seven years before, it would have been the most amazing thing that anyone had ever seen and would have been immediately adopted all over the place.

But six or seven years earlier the computer buyer would receive a machine with a blank—not even formatted!—hard drive, a box of 5.25-inch DOS diskettes to fit the big A drive, a DOS manual, and whatever other programs were bundled with the system. It fell to the user, then, to plug it all together, fire it up, insert the first DOS diskette to begin an exploration of fdisk, format, and perform the other tasks that would bring the machine to life.

By the mid-1990s, computer buyers didn't need to know anything about computers, and what's more, many didn't *want* to know anything about computers. The fact that they had to plug the carefully labeled pieces together was annoying enough. The things they needed in order to compute were already on the drive. Plug it together, plug it in, turn it on—that was it. The chief user variable was the choice of mouse pad.

Even if a user is interested in learning about computers to the extent that he or she can gain proficiency, inertia is a powerful thing. Nobody is going to blow away the contents of a perfectly functioning hard drive loaded with familiar programs without a very good reason to do so.

Linux, though very, very good and getting better each day, lacked such a compelling reason. Its reputation as being tremendously difficult to use was only partly deserved. People accustomed to DOS and its derivatives would not only bring little useful knowledge with them, they would bring knowledge that in some ways would actually run counter to the way things are done under Linux. Assuming that the user spent the time, learned the commands, and got Linux up and running, what would be gained? What could be done? Painfully little. (Here old Linux hands will disagree, but in terms of the average user, I'm right.) New users were in large measure computer science students and people disgruntled over the apparently moribund status of the once excellent OS/2 operating system. (I'm among the latter.)

In short, Linux was a pain, and anybody who switched to it was likely to switch back to the old "DOSrivative," wishing that the investment in a tape backup unit had been made, so that restoration of the old system would be simpler.

It was with an eye toward this situation that in October 1996 KDE was founded. It was not until 10 months later that developers met in Arnsberg, Germany, sponsored by many organizations with an interest in Linux. Soon, the fledgling project became what amounts to a nonprofit corporation. Having settled upon the QT libraries and widget set published by a company called Troll Tech, a foundation that made sure that QT would be freely available forever was established.

Relax: QT Is Free for You to Use

There was, and to some extent continues to be, debate in the highly political Linux world over whether KDE, because it is built on a proprietary library, can truly be called freely available. The foundation was established to eliminate these concerns, but some people remain suspicious. I can find no reason for them to be.

Code was written, passed around, tested, and incorporated into the grand scheme. On July 12, 1998, KDE 1.0 was released, followed in February 1999 by KDE 1.1.1, which incorporated a multitude of improvements in both the underlying GUI and its native and included applications. KDE in one form or another became either the default desktop or an install option in almost every Linux distribution. Its popularity soared: In just one day in the spring of 1999, more than 34GB of KDE files were downloaded from just one U.S. site. In midsummer 1999, KDE 1.2 was released, which chiefly added improvements and configuration options that enable the user to alter its look and feel.

And that brings us to today.

KDE Is *Not* Windows

The first thing that a new KDE user does, fresh from a DOSrivative system, is double-click on an icon. A new KDE user first notices that there are two copies of whatever program was selected, or else one copy and one error message. The first lesson the new KDE user learns is that to do something in KDE, you need click it only once.

A graphical user interface does make things easier, but it does not necessarily make things easy. For example, if you click on the correct combination of icons and menu items from the default KDE desktop, you will get Figure I.1, the Process Manager.

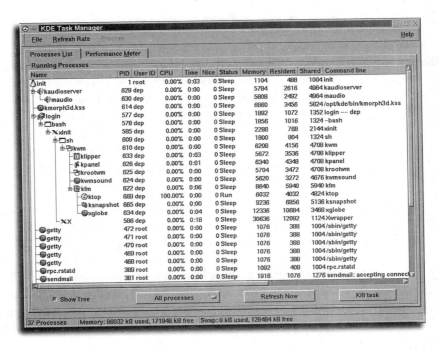

FIGURE I.1
You'll learn later on how useful the Task Manager is.

Or, if you are logged in as root, you see Figure I.2, the Runlevel Manager.

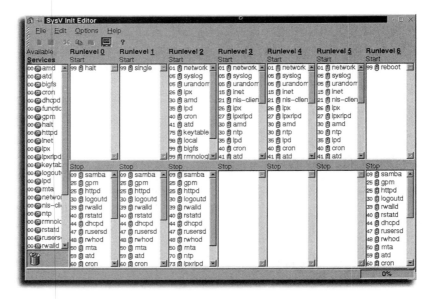

FIGURE I.2

The Runlevel Manager controls which services are available under what in Linux are called run levels. It will all make sense once you've read Chapter 25.

Pretty frightening, isn't it? What *is* all that? Fear not, because you'll find the answers in *Practical KDE*. The idea right now is that point-and-click does not impart understanding. Hence this book. There is another point: While it is possible that you have switched to KDE from some other Linux desktop, the chances are also good that you're new to Linux. Seeing a comfortable-looking desktop, you may be drawn to think that there's nothing to be learned. Nothing could be further from the truth! Don't worry; you can handle it, but it does involve learning many new things. They're not always easy, but they're never insurmountably difficult.

Now, there are some things that this book is not, and it's best to announce them before we go any further. KDE is the subject of this book; Linux is not. Insofar as the functions and capabilities of Linux are addressed through KDE, that connection will be covered. But the installation, configuration, and mastery of Linux (and the other, similar operating systems on which KDE can run) require a serious book of their own. In fact, several such books exist. So, while I hope this book is thoroughly useful to the new Linux user who, after a successful installation, has booted to a colorful and friendly KDE desktop, that user will very likely want to explore other avenues as well in obtaining total Linux proficiency. The experienced Linux hand should find this book useful as well because KDE is much more than a pretty face. In it, both kinds of users should learn practically everything—everything practical—about the exciting K Desktop Environment.

The Future

As in all things related to Linux, the future of KDE is bright. Although the 1.1.x versions discussed here will continue to be supported and improved, the big excitement in the KDE world is anticipation of KDE 2.0 and its associated Koffice suite of applications, which should be released sometime in 2000. This new version will not be compatible in many ways with KDE-1.1.x and will be built on the Troll Tech QT-2.0 library (KDE is currently built on QT-1.42 or QT-1.44). Some people will rush to upgrade, whereas others will, of course, will hesitate to give up their finely tuned systems (tuning will be detailed in the pages that follow) and will stick with KDE-1.1.x until there is a real need to make the change.

Meanwhile, the good people at XFree86.org continue to make improvements to XFree86, and the Linux kernel itself is gaining new capabilities at an ever-increasing rate. If you have hardware that isn't supported, wait a few weeks or write support for it yourself and contribute to the cause. That is, after all, how Linux and KDE came to be.

How To Use This Book

There are really two ways to use this book: Read it and consult it. I am endeavoring to make it possible to read *Practical KDE* from beginning to end without causing your mind to wander too many times to fond thoughts of dental procedures, but I doubt that very many people will begin on the first page and keep it in hand until they reach the index. In fact, even if you set out to read it from start to finish, entire sections will certainly have nothing to do with how you use KDE or your computer, and you might as well skip them. They're not written in disappearing ink; they'll still be here if later you find you need them. Although every chapter will be of use to somebody, few people will need them all. Someone will install KDE for use in administering, say, a Samba server. Someone else will install it because it has a really cool Asteroids game (which it does). Still, some chapters *will* be of universal interest—the installation chapters, if you've not yet installed KDE, and the configuration chapters because even the experienced KDE user will find tidbits of use. These chapters will also be of use to someone upgrading an existing KDE installation because with the new Linux distributions KDE is handled in several different ways.

To ease browsing, each chapter has at its beginning a list of the things it covers.

Unless you read and memorize it, though, you'll probably find that most of the time you pick up *Practical KDE*, it will be to get the answer to a specific question. For this reason, it has been organized so as to be useful as a reference.

In short, you can use this book any way you like. Effort has been made to make its use easy and rewarding, whatever method you choose.

Use the Gray Matter!

One important point: Don't overlook the information in the gray sidebars throughout each chapter. These items will provide tips, shortcuts, warnings, and notes that will make you a master of KDE!

Conventions

We will, in the course of discussing KDE, adopt several conventions, many inherited or outright hijacked from other graphical user interfaces. Chances are good that you know these already or will be able to glean their meaning from the context in which they are used. But just to make sure there is no confusion, it's probably a good idea to list them. Here they are, beginning with a listing of screen elements and an illustration that shows most of them (see Figure I.3).

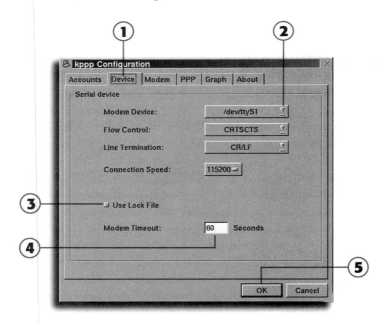

FIGURE I.3

The KDE 1.1.1 desktop. KDE 1.2 looks much the same, though the color depth is greater, providing a richer-looking screen.

① Tabs   ④ Text box

② Drop list   ⑤ Text button

③ Check box

- **Dialog box**—This is any window that appears for configuration purposes.

- **Tabs**—These are located across the top of some dialog boxes. They resemble the tabs atop folders in a file drawer. The important thing to remember is that it's possible, though not likely, to confuse tabs in this usage with the Tab key on your keyboard. Let context be your guide.

- **Drop list**—This is a variable in a dialog box that provides a listing of choices from which you may select one. The list is made visible by clicking on the underlined downward-pointing triangle on the right side of the default item.

- **List box**—This is similar to a Drop list, but rather than clicking on the icon at the right, you scroll up and down using the appropriate triangles until you find the setting you want. This is rarely used in KDE, but is found in some applications.

- **Text box**—This is a place where you must enter information via the keyboard.

- **Radio button**—This is a round button that is selected by clicking it or using the **Tab** key to get to it, and then pressing the **spacebar** or **Enter** key to select it. It will get a dot in its center or change color to signify it is selected. Under the rules of KDE (and GUI programming standards in general), a radio button is used in a listing of possible configurations when one and only one of the possibilities may be selected.

- **Check box**—This is a square button that is selected by clicking it or using the **Tab** key to get to it and then pressing the **spacebar** or **Enter** key to select it. When selected, it turns a darker shade of gray, unless the Draw Widgets in the Style of Windows 95 choice is made in desktop styles. In that case, a check mark appears. Under the rules of KDE (and GUI programming standards in general), a check box is employed in a listing of possible configurations when more than one of the choices can be selected. (This convention is not always observed, however, and there are places where the choices offered by check boxes are mutually exclusive.)

- **Text button**—This is a button that contains text and that, when clicked, does what it says. The ones you will encounter most contain text saying Help, Default, OK, Apply, and Cancel, usually (but not always) in that order.

Additionally, some conventions we will employ in the text itself to make examples and other information stand out. For instance, there will be places where a listing of programming code, a shell script, or even an ASCII text configuration file will be shown. When we do that, it will look like Listing I.1.

Listing I.1   Sample Code Listing (The /etc/xinit/xinitrc Script for Caldera Open Linux 2.2)

```
1  #!/bin/bash
2
3  XAUTH=$HOME/.Xauthority
4  MKCOOKIE=/usr/bin/mcookie
5
6  touch $XAUTH
7
8  for host in localhost $HOSTNAME $HOST; do
9       xauth add $host/unix:0 . `$MKCOOKIE`
10      xauth add $host:0 . `$MKCOOKIE`
11 done
12  exec Xwrapper -auth $XAUTH :0
```

And that pretty much covers it.

System Requirements

We are all familiar with unrealistic claims for software: notations on the box that say "80386 processor and 4MB RAM required, Pentium III 500 and 128MB RAM recommended." Well, okay, maybe not *that* bad, but clearly there's a difference between the theoretical and practical minimums. In that this is not *Theoretical KDE*, we'll deal here in the practical minimums: what you need to have in order to actually do useful work. The requirements are not excessive, and the chances are good that your computer more than meets them or can be made to do so at very little expense.

Hardware

For all practical purposes, you will need a Pentium processor (or its equivalent; I've had great success with AMD chips), the faster the better; 64MB of RAM (more helps, too); and a hard drive with at least 100MB of available storage on a Linux (ext2) partition.

The greatest likelihood of a problem is with your video card. (Fully one-third of the questions and problems posted to KDE mailing lists and newsgroups are video card related, with the rest spread about equally among modems, network cards, and everything else.) Whether your video card is supported is not up to KDE; it is determined by the support or lack thereof in XFree86. It is a good idea to check the hardware compatibility list posted on the Web site of the vendor of your Linux distribution to make sure your card is supported. Alternatively, you can check at the XFree86 site, http://www.xfree86.org. The biggest problem seems to be with the very newest, cutting-edge, 3D cards. If a manufacturer makes specifications available to the XFree86 Organization, it is a quick and relatively simple matter to add support for it. If the manufacturer does not, though, it's a time-consuming and difficult process of backward-engineering and could take months.

The next greatest likelihood of a problem is with your modem. For some reason—greed, insanity, or a combination thereof—a few years ago some manufacturers began producing not-quite modems, labeling them as modems and selling them to the unsuspecting. These things do not contain all of the processing power that a real modem has, instead passing it off via a software interface, to the computer's main processor. The net effect is that they work, if that's the word, with Windows only. Sadly, the vast majority of internal modems made today are these atrocities. If you bought a computer in the last three or four years and it came with an internal modem, you are almost certainly a victim. The only solution is to replace your not-quite modem with the genuine article. As of this writing, the contagion has not spread to external modems, so your best bet is with one of those (which also have front panels that provide useful diagnostic information, making them a better idea anyway).

Network cards also can cause some trouble, especially the "plug-and-play" variety. Again, it's wise to check your Linux distributor's Web page to find out whether yours is supported.

Sound cards, if you use them, are pretty well supported but can be difficult to set up unless they are mainstream, jumper-set, ISA-bus cards.

Except for the base system requirements, all of the possible trouble spots listed are from the Linux system itself, not KDE. But because KDE administers and uses all of these things, it's possible to blame KDE for a more fundamental incompatibility. It's best to check everything out ahead of time and to avoid anguish and head scratching (to say nothing of intemperate midnight posts to the newsgroups!) later.

Software

The software that you need to have before beginning a KDE installation is modest: Linux (or an equivalent UNIX or UNIX-like operating system); XFree86 (or one of the commercial equivalents that will be discussed later in the book); and the QT-1.42 or, better, 1.44 libraries from Troll Tech, which are available almost anyplace you would get KDE itself. If your Linux distribution has KDE, it has QT and XFree86 as well. Otherwise, it can all be downloaded from the locations listed in Appendix A, "Finding the Latest KDE and Its Applications."

And that's that. So, let's get to work!

Toolkit

"By his tools can the workman be told."

I searched all over for a quote that said words to that effect and, finding none, I was forced to make up the one above. It will do. In the early days of personal computing, it was customary for articles and magazines to list the software and hardware that were used to construct the article or publication, even as some books devote a page to the history of the typeface employed. This was a good idea, and I herewith propose to contribute to its revival.

Practical KDE was written on a fairly basic desktop machine running an AMD K6-2 processor at 400MHz with 1MB of L2 cache and 256MB of RAM.

It was written entirely in the word-processing program of StarOffice 5.0 or 5.1, with files saved in Microsoft Word 97 format for transmission to the (otherwise entirely enlightened) people at Macmillan who require that format. StarOffice has improved vastly in stability in the version shipped with Caldera OpenLinux 2.2, on which it was run during the construction of this book.

Screenshots were made with KSnapshot and saved in BMP format. I then used GIMP to convert them to the required (and much smaller) PCX.

All this was done atop a succession of KDEs. Very early work was done in KDE 1.1, followed soon by 1.1.1, which gave way to weekly builds of pre-betas of KDE 1.1.2, and finally, KDE 1.1.2 itself, which is where things will stay until the urge to explore arrives and I tackle the pre-betas of KDE 2.0, which promises to be breathtakingly good. But that is the subject for another book, another edition.

One note to the reader: Experiment! Try it out! It is a simple thing to back up your nice, safe, working KDE and to download the source code for KDE and build your own custom version. Chances are it will go without a hitch, but if it doesn't, you will have learned something—if nothing else, some questions to ask and areas for additional learning—and you can restore your old version. But if—no, *when*—it succeeds, you will have a sense of power over your computer unlike anything you've ever experienced. You will have gained a valuable skill, and will no longer be at the mercy of the prebuilt software about which others have made all the important decisions. Remember: When you are marveling at the vast knowledge of the Linux and KDE gurus, which admiration is certainly deserved, don't forget that there was a time when they, too, were starting out.

part

I

INSTALLATION

Installing KDE

If KDE Came with Your Linux Distribution

Getting KDE On Your Own

It can come as no surprise that before you can run KDE, you must install it. If you are new to Linux, this can be more than a little daunting because you have probably already seen absolutely nothing that you recognize. The file extensions are different: where are .exe, .com, and .bat files? How can you tell what is a program and what isn't? In fact, where *are* the programs? There's not even a C:> prompt! *Where am I?*

Then there are the files that you *can* find: things that end in strange Martian extensions like .tgz, .rpm, as well as stuff like "Greatprogram-3.3.1-LINUX-i586.tar.bz." *What's with all the dots? What am I supposed to do with this stuff?*

Actually, the fundamental notions, as you will soon see, are pretty easy to understand. So relax, ignore that growing "what-did-I-get-myself-into" sense of panic, and read on. You'll have it mastered in just a few minutes. We will be dipping into the Linux command line a little bit here, but far from being frightening, it will cause you to say "Wow!" and "That's cool!" and even feel a little bit smug. You'll see.

If KDE Came with Your Linux Distribution

Most current Linux distributions come with KDE and install it when you install Linux itself. In this case, depending on the distribution, you are likely to boot to KDE immediately after putting Linux on your hard drive. It should look like Figure 1.1, or close to it.

FIGURE 1.1
The default KDE desktop is so configurable that it's unlikely yours will look like this for long.

This chapter is devoted to bringing you to this happy point, so if you've already achieved it, you're ahead of the game. This doesn't mean, though, that you should ignore what follows. You'll want to upgrade KDE at some point, and you may well want to compile a version of KDE especially suited to your own system. In those cases, you'll be back.

There's a chance, too, that you'll be using a distribution that won't go at once to the KDE desktop.

Some Distribution-Specific Notes

Because of varying interpretations of Linux standards, variation among things allowed by those standards, and frankly, variations among the things that distributors find convenient, KDE finds itself by default in different places depending on the Linux distribution. There is sense in removing the KDE included with the distribution and downloading new KDE from the KDE ftp site (ftp://ftp.kde.org or one of its mirrors) and installing it to /opt/kde. Here's where the distributions put KDE unless you force them to do otherwise.

SEE ALSO

➤ *I have more on placement of KDE in Chapter 35, "Upgrading to the Latest KDE Version," page 629.*

Red Hat Linux 6.0

In several places, Red Hat 6.0 is considered the most "cutting edge" of the distributions and blazes its own trail. The area of chief interest at the moment is the fact that it comes equipped with three different window managers and desktop programs: KDE, Gnome, and AnotherStep. It also comes with a program called Switchdesk, which enables you to move freely among these, though you can't run them all at once. The KDE included with Red Hat 6.0 is version 1.1.1pre2, which is a beta version, so there's some sense in upgrading to 1.1.1 or 1.2 as soon as you're comfortable with KDE. Previous versions of Red Hat did not contain KDE at all, so if you are running one of these, you will have to download and install KDE.

Caldera OpenLinux 2.2

Caldera's Linux makes more extensive default use of KDE than does any other distribution and is aimed at stability for serious business use. In fact, the installation program is based on the same programming tools and libraries as is KDE itself. When you boot the default Caldera OpenLinux 2.2 system, you are greeted by the KDM graphical login screen, which takes you directly to KDE. Caldera 2.2, however, is shipped with KDE 1.1, so you will want to upgrade as soon as you feel competent to do so, which is to say after you've read this chapter.

Debian Linux

Debian has the reputation of being the "purest" Linux distribution and is typically used by very serious Linux hackers. No version of Debian comes with KDE. The bad news is that this means you will need to acquire it on your own; the good news is that if you're running Debian, you probably know how to do this (though I'll explain how anyway). In the spring of 1999, Debian announced a collaboration with KDE.org and Canada's Corel (maker of the famous CorelDRAW and now the WordPerfect and WordPerfect Office Suite programs) to create a new Linux distribution. Corel Linux includes several custom features, so its KDE differs from the standard distributed versions. If you're running any of the several current versions of Debian Linux, you can find KDE for it in DEB file format on the KDE ftp site and its mirrors.

SuSE 6.1

This German distribution, popular throughout Europe and making inroads elsewhere in the world, includes both KDE and Gnome. You can set the default at installation and change it later.

Linux Mandrake 6.0

The Mandrake people offered a distribution with KDE before anyone else. The distribution consists of an enhanced Red Hat Linux with KDE, Gnome, and GnuStep desktops, though KDE is the flagship. The Mandrake Web site (www.linux-mandrake.com) notes that once people try KDE, they stick with it.

Slackware Linux 4.0

One of the first Linux distributions, Slackware 4.0 defaults to KDE 1.1. As with Caldera, an upgrade is in order, though 1.1 works perfectly well.

Other, Older Distributions, and "Nibbleware"

A great many Linux users, perhaps the majority, don't have the latest distributions, and many of those have engaged in the practice of *nibbleware*. This is simply gradually upgrading an older distribution in bits and pieces as new and interesting capabilities appear. (The change from Linux 2.0.3x to 2.2x has been so widely accepted with so many people upgrading the kernel and associated packages, that it might better be called "chompware.") If you are among these users, you have KDE only if you downloaded and installed it. If you haven't yet, the next section is for you, as well as those who need or want to upgrade.

Getting KDE On Your Own

You can acquire KDE in two forms: compiled binaries and source code. Within these categories, though, are subcategories (especially among compiled binaries) for specific Linux distributions and for other operating systems, such as the various Sparc Solaris releases, Alpha, PPC, BSD, and the various flavors of UNIX.

The compiled binaries are pretty much ready-to-run programs: all you need to do is install them. With source code, the program is still in the form of text files and scripts that can be read with any text editor, altered by the user who has programming skills, patched to fix bugs, and optimized for a particular computer—not just a particular operating system, but the actual specific computer itself. The trade-off is that compiling the source code and making it into binary files takes more time than does getting and installing the binaries. It's also a little more complicated because there are more commands to learn and more things that can go wrong.

If you're new to Linux and to KDE, you will probably want to go with compiled binaries at first. Though KDE is remarkably easy to compile and install, it is probably no one's idea of a good place to begin learning about compiling source code.

In any case, the place to begin is at the KDE Web site, `www.kde.org`. By all means feel free to browse the site, but when you are done, click the **Download** link. You will be encouraged to choose a mirror site, which is a good idea for two reasons: it reduces congestion at the KDE site, and it usually results in a quicker, cleaner download for you. Although some of the mirrors lack the very latest developmental code and programs that aren't really ready for release, they all have what is called the *stable tree*. This is the collection comprising KDE and KDE applications that have been deemed ready for release.

When you have chosen and connected with the mirror of your choice, you need to dig down through the directories until you are at /pub/kde/stable. (For instance, on the KDE site itself, the URL is `ftp://ftp.kde.org/pub/kde/stable/`.) Here you will have the opportunity to choose 1.1.1 or 1.2. If you want an attractive, high-color desktop, choose the latter. Its hardware requirements are slightly more stringent, but on most systems, the performance difference won't be something you'll notice.

Having made your choice, the next stop is the subdirectory labeled /distribution. Here you are given a choice of package formats: DEB, RPM, PKG, or TAR.

Compiled Binaries: RPM and DEB

For our purposes, you will be interested in the RPM or DEB subdirectory: DEB if you are using Debian Linux, RPM if you are using any other Linux distribution. (PKG is for Solaris, and TAR is something we'll get to when we discuss source code.)

In each of these subdirectories, you'll find more subdirectories. In the case of RPM, it contains specially built binaries for specific Linux distributions. In the case of DEB, it has packages built for different versions.

About Your C Libraries

I won't spend much time on it, but it is worth noting that in 1999 very big changes took place in the Linux world at a very fundamental level. The part that most excited most users was the release of the 2.2.X kernel, two years in the making. This added a great deal of support for newer hardware and was a wonderful development. It could also be compiled with the EGCS compiler, removing most people's last reason for having the old GCC compiler on their machines. (If you don't understand the last sentence, you needn't worry.) The part that most excited programmers and applications developers was the arrival of *glibc-2.1*.

In the beginning of Linux, there was libc, which was the set of C language libraries used by the Linux kernel and applications. (Those coming to Linux from the DOSrivative world can think of it as being a kind of grand master .dll.) It was good, but it had its limits. It wasn't as extensible as developers liked. Some modern niceties, such as multithreading, were all but impossible to implement under it. It needed improvement, and so glibc was developed. Like many software projects, it wasn't especially stable at first, and most Linux distributors didn't embrace it (and upgrading on your own was a real bear). With its 5.0 version, Red Hat became the first major distribution to embrace glibc. Red Hat paid a price for its boldness, too. There were stability and compatibility problems at first, though these were gradually resolved. Improvements were made to glibc, but these hacks were never particularly standardized. This resulted in the selection of C libraries that were called glibc-2.0.7 but weren't the same and were incompatible in some ways. Most distributions stuck with libc, now libc5.

Not until the arrival of glibc-2.1 was there a version with which distributors could be happy. Current Linux distributions are built on glibc-2.1.

Why should you care? Because this is why KDE has so many different compiled binaries. Many people are perfectly happy with their older, libc5-based systems, which are stable and in many cases quite elaborate. (When you visit a Web site, the chances are good that you're connected to an older Linux system. Upgrading everything to a new distribution isn't something undertaken lightly.) Whereas most modern distributions can happily run libc5-based applications, those applications lack the advantages of the more powerful glibc, and an libc5 system simply doesn't run anything built against glibc.

So, in the DEB subdirectory you will find subdirectories for the libc5 (Hamm) distribution, and the glibc (Potato) one. (Who names these things?)

Alas, in the RPM subdirectory you are stuck with glibc, which contains subdirectories for a variety of distributions. Pick yours if you are running a glibc distribution. (If you are libc5, you have to "roll your own": compile it yourself. We'll get to that.) When you select the subdirectory for your distribution, you get—that's right—

another subdirectory, offering either i386 or source. Choose the former. (No, your computer isn't an Intel 386 machine, and you feel a little bit insulted. Don't. The 386 is the lowest common denominator, which means that these RPM binaries will work on your machine. Later on, if you want to experiment with optimizing KDE for your machine, you can compile.)

Get Files That Match!

It is possible that multiple versions of essentially the same thing reside in the /i386 subdirectory. These are *build levels*, which means that the packages were put together by different people or at different times or both. Although packages from different build levels might work together, it really isn't a chance that you want to take. Therefore, make sure that the packages are *identical* after the first part of the name, which we'll get to now.

The /1.1.1/distribution/rpm/Caldera-OpenLinux-2.2/i386 subdirectory contains this:

```
kde-1.1.1-col22.md5sums.gz              456 bytes  Mon May  3 07:49:00 1999
kdebase-1.1.1-1-col22.i386.rpm          6127 Kb    Mon May  3 07:49:00 1999
kdebase-1.1.1-3.i386.rpm                6118 Kb    Tue Jun  8 21:02:00 1999
kdebase-1.1.1-5.col22.i386.rpm          6116 Kb    Fri Jun 25 16:09:00 1999
kdebase-opengl-1.1.1-1-col22.i386        128 Kb    Mon May  3 07:49:00 1999
kdebase-opengl-1.1.1-3.i386.rpm          128 Kb    Tue Jun  8 21:03:00 1999
kdebase-opengl-1.1.1-5.col22.i386        128 Kb    Fri Jun 25 16:20:00 1999
kdegames-1.1.1-1-col22.i386.rpm         2258 Kb    Mon May  3 07:49:00 1999
kdegraphics-1.1.1-1-col22.i386.rpm      1155 Kb    Mon May  3 07:49:00 1999
kdelibs-1.1.1-1-col22.i386.rpm          1733 Kb    Mon May  3 07:49:00 1999
kdelibs-devel-1.1.1-1-col22.i386.rpm     225 Kb    Mon May  3 07:49:00 1999
kdelibs-doc-1.1.1-1-col22.i386.rpm       566 Kb    Mon May  3 07:49:00 1999
kdemultimedia-1.1.1-1-col22.i386.rpm     769 Kb    Mon May  3 07:49:00 1999
kdenetwork-1.1.1-1-col22.i386.rpm       2978 Kb    Mon May  3 07:49:00 1999
kdesupport-1.1.1-1-col22.i386.rpm        340 Kb    Mon May  3 07:49:00 1999
kdesupport-devel-1.1.1-1-col22.i3         78 Kb    Mon May  3 07:49:00 1999
kdetoys-1.1.1-1-col22.i386.rpm           171 Kb    Mon May  3 07:49:00 1999
kdeutils-1.1.1-1-col22.i386.rpm         1361 Kb    Mon May  3 07:49:00 1999
korganizer-1.1.1-1-col22.i386.rpm        716 Kb    Mon May  3 07:49:00 1999
```

Frankly, it's a little embarrassing. It's such a mess, with several files of different build levels that aren't in complete KDE file sets, but it can be sorted out. (Caldera users be grateful: The Red Hat subdirectory isn't just worse, it's *much* worse. On the other hand, the Red Hat subdirectory contains RPMs for QT, for which the Caldera user must visit the Caldera site, ftp://ftp.calderasystems.com.) Perhaps by the time you read this, the directories will have been cleaned up a bit, but in case they haven't…

Here are the files you need:

- qt-1.44
- kdebase
- kdebase-opengl (if running 3D graphics appeals to you)
- kdegames (why not?)
- kdegraphics
- kdelibs
- kdelibs-devel (not essential, but you want them)
- kdemultimedia
- kdenetwork
- kdesupport
- kdetoys (entirely optional, actually, but a small download)
- kdeutils
- korganizer (optional, but a valuable program)

A good rule of thumb is to go by the date because files put up on the same date will probably work together (in this case, they certainly do).

It is worth noting, too, that you are likely to find current RPMs (or DEBs) for your particular Linux distribution on the distributor's ftp site, in the /contrib directory. This is especially true if the KDE version you seek has been out for at least a few weeks. It sometimes takes that long for the RPMs to be built and contributed.

Once you have downloaded the necessary files, installation is relatively simple: As root, use the RPM command from the command line:

```
rpm -i filename —prefix=path
```

Now, the KDE files need to be installed in a particular order: qt, kdesupport, kdelibs, kdebase, after which you can install the other packages in any order you want.

If you are upgrading an existing KDE installation, the command is

```
rpm -Uvh filename —prefix=path
```

They, too, need to be installed in the order listed above, though you probably won't be upgrading your QT libraries.

Once you've run this command on QT and all the KDE RPMs, KDE is installed on your hard drive.

> **Where Does KDE Go?**
>
> It has never been entirely clear where KDE's files should reside. In the early days, RPMs were built to put KDE in /opt/kde, whereas if it was compiled from a tarball, it went to /usr/local/kde.
>
> Nor did it especially matter, so long as KDE's binary directory (/kde/bin) was in the path statement in either /etc/profile or ~/.bash_profile, preferably the former. (The ~/, by the way, means the user's home directory, and the dot in front of bash_profile means that it is a hidden file.) It was good for the user to know where KDE was because when upgrading it's a good idea to make a copy of it elsewhere for backup purposes, in case something goes wrong.
>
> With Red Hat 6.0, another possibility emerged. Red Hat puts KDE under /usr, meaning that what used to be in /kde/bin is now in /usr/bin, what used to be in /kde/lib is now in /usr/lib, and so on. This is in keeping with a reasonable interpretation of Linux standards, but it can also make backing up before an upgrade one royal pain because lots of non-KDE files are in those directories, too. Red Hat 6.0 users are wise to keep copies of their previous RPMs around in case a reinstall is necessary. Everybody else should go ahead and put KDE in /opt/kde and prosper. You can also use /usr/local/kde, but the reasons for doing so aren't compelling.

Debian users will, of course, use DEB files (unless some love of adventure causes them to employ the Debian *alien* program to allow the installation of RPMs by converting, which might be a good idea if for some reason DEBs were not available). As with an RPM install, you must be logged on as root or superuser in order to install the DEB packages. The fundamental syntax is:

```
dpkg —install filename
```

However, with the *apt* front end for dpkg, you can install the entire batch of KDE DEB files at once, presuming they are in the same directory and you have changed to that directory, to wit:

```
apt-get install kde*
```

Whereupon KDE is installed on your Debian system.

Installing from Source

If you're new to Linux, you may not believe it, but trust me: sooner or later you will succumb to the need or desire to compile your own programs. Trust me on this, too: after you've done it, you'll wonder why you waited so long. Compiling software on your machine—"rolling your own" in hacker idiom—will give you a sense of power and accomplishment that few other things in computing can match. But there's more: you will have access to applications for which no prebuilt binaries exist. You will have access to the newest stuff: there's always a lag time of a few days or a few weeks before somebody takes the not inconsiderable trouble of putting together RPMs and DEBs. When you compile your own programs, you can make changes to cause the results especially to suit your system. You can also apply patches that fix annoying bugs without waiting for a whole new version and actually alter the code to fit the way you work. It's not difficult, either. Now how much would you pay? Well, it's all free!

In fact, there's every likelihood that when you installed Linux you also installed just about all that you'll need to compile KDE, and if not, most of the things you will need are on your Linux CD:

- **EGCS**—The current C and C++ compiler. Later versions of GCC will work, too, though EGCS is recommended. If you haven't already, install every EGCS package on your distribution CD except those that have "static" in their names because you don't need those. (They make "statically linked" binaries that are bigger and slower. You don't need them unless you are building KDE for use on a machine that doesn't have enough of Linux installed to make it very useful at all.)

- **AUTOCONF**—The automatic configuration utility.

- **AUTOMAKE**—The utility that automates much of the compilation.

These items aren't KDE-specific. You'll need them to compile just about anything. There are, of course, some things you need just for KDE:

- **QT-1.44**—These are the QT libraries on which KDE is built. You can get QT as source code, but this is one instance where downloading the compiled version, as well as the development version QT-devel, from your Linux distributor is a good idea. While much of the QT distribution is primarily of interest to developers, it makes good sense to get the full package because you are likely one day to be interested in using, say, Kdevelop. Make sure to get QT-1.44. Although QT-2.0 has been released and will be the basis for KDE 2.0, it is incompatible with KDE 1.X. The source contains all of QT, but you need to download individual files if you get compiled binaries. The binary files you want are:
  - **qt-144**
  - **qt-devel-1.44**—Necessary if you're compiling KDE
  - **qt-doc-html-1.44**—Necessary if you do any development
  - **qt-examples-1.44**—Unnecessary but useful

- **qt-opengl-1.44**—If you want to use 3D effects
- **qt-tutorial-1.44**—Again, useful for programmers

SEE ALSO

➤ *For more info on Kdevelop, see Chapter 36, "Programming for KDE," page 639.*

- **BZIP2**—It is extremely likely that you already have this compression program on your machine. If you don't, it's available on the KDE site as well as almost any place that has a Linux file repository.

- **KDE source code**—You'll find this in the same place as the RPMs or DEBs for your distribution, though you want to go to the /source subdirectory. Download everything that ends in *tar.bz2* with the possible exception of kdesdk, which is the KDE software developers kit that you probably won't need. Don't download anything that ends in *.lsm* because those are merely small descriptive files about the packages of the same name (*lsm* stands for *Linux Software Map*).

When you are done, you should have these files in your KDE download directory:

- kdeadmin-1.1.1.tar.bz2
- kdebase-1.1.1.tar.bz2
- kdegames-1.1.1.tar.bz2
- kdegraphics-1.1.1.tar.bz2
- kdelibs-1.1.1.tar.bz2
- kdemultimedia-1.1.1.tar.bz2
- kdenetwork-1.1.1.tar.bz2
- kdesupport-1.1.1.tar.bz2
- kdetoys-1.1.1.tar.bz2
- kdeutils-1.1.1.tar.bz2
- korganizer-1.1.1.tar.bz2

(This assumes installation of QT from RPM or DEB, and KDE 1.1.1. Obviously, the files for KDE 1.2 would be the same, except that they would say *1.2* where these say *1.1.1*.)

The entire download totals about 17MB, so it will take a while, especially if undertaken over a slow connection or during peak use hours. It's a fine thing to do when suffering from insomnia or early on a weekend morning.

Two Useful Linux Tricks

Although these aren't exclusive to KDE, two little Linux features make the compilation process easier.

The first is filename completion. If you are in the directory containing your downloaded KDE files and want to manipulate one of the files, say, copy it someplace, you can enter the command, a space, and begin to type the filename followed by a **Tab**. For example, if you type

```
cp kdes
```

and then press **Tab**, it becomes

```
cp kdesupport-1.1.1.tar.bz2
```

If more than one file is in the directory with the letters you typed, you will hear a beep. Pressing **Tab** again will list them for you. An example would be *kdeg*, which could be kdegames or kdegraphics. You may add the necessary letter to distinguish them, and press **Tab** again.

The second is the capability to scroll among commands. Pressing the **Up** arrow key lets you return to the previous command that you typed. Pressing it again lets you go to the one before that, and so on. You can edit these commands, so instead of typing a complex command followed by a filename, you can press the **Up** arrow and **Backspace** over the filename to execute the same command on a different file. You can still use the **Tab** key to complete filenames here, too.

Additionally, most shells in common use—meaning the one you are probably using if you have no idea what a shell is—emulate these other conventions: **Ctrl+A** moves to the beginning of a line, and **Ctrl+E** moves to the end.

Having obtained all these files, it's now time to build KDE. While you can do this in several different ways, this is the simplest and most straightforward in keeping with Linux standards. In all the commands listed, you enter the command and press **Enter**.

Building KDE

1. Log in as root or su to root. (At a command line full screen or in a terminal window, type **su** and press **Enter**. When prompted, give the root password.)

2. Copy the kde files from the directory into which you downloaded them to /usr/local/src:
   ```
   cp ~/dirname/*.* /usr/local/src
   ```

3. Change to /usr/local/src.

4. Because bzip2 can use wildcards, you might as well unzip them all at once, though, if you would rather do them one at a time, you could replace the asterisk with the full filename:
   ```
   bzip2 -d k*.bz2
   ```

5. You might go ahead and open the resulting .tar files one after another before beginning compilation. I open them as I compile them as an added check of what is done and what isn't. The choice is entirely up to you, but if you do just one at first, it should be kdesupport. You must make and install the packages in this order: kdesupport, kdelibs, kdebase, and then the others in whatever order you choose.

```
tar xvf kdesupport-1.1.1.tar.bz2
```

6. The `tar` command will have created a directory, in this example/usr/local/src/kdesupport-1.1.1/. Change to this directory and configure the package:

```
./configure
```

Where Do You Want Your KDE to Go Today?

You might wish to employ some options with the `configure` command. The most common of these is `prefix`, which allows you to specify the directory into which KDE will ultimately installed:

```
./configure --prefix=/opt/kde
./configure --prefix=/usr/local
./configure --prefix=/usr
```

The last of these would preserve the structure of a Red Hat 6.0 system. It is also possible (and sometimes necessary, if you have multiple compilers installed), to specify the host:

```
./configure --prefix=/opt/kde --host=i586-pc-linux-gnu
```

I will discuss other options shortly.

---

7. `configure` will chug along for up to a few minutes and will then return you to the command line. Look to make sure that it didn't bomb out with some error. (This almost always is due to the lack of one of the compiling tools and which can be remedied by installing the package that the error says is missing.) As it runs, many messages will scroll past. Here is the screen output for the configuration of kdesupport-1.1.1. As you can see, the host type was automatically detected. Also, though it reports the compiler as gcc, EGCS was employed:

```
[root@localhost kdesupport-1.1.1]# ./configure —prefix=/opt/kde
creating cache ./config.cache
checking host system type... i586-pc-linux-gnu
checking target system type... i586-pc-linux-gnu
checking build system type... i586-pc-linux-gnu
checking for a BSD compatible install... /usr/bin/install -c
checking whether build environment is sane... yes
checking whether make sets ${MAKE}... yes
```

continues...

...continued

```
checking for working aclocal... found
checking for working autoconf... found
checking for working automake... found
checking for working autoheader... found
checking for working makeinfo... found
checking for a C-Compiler...
checking for gcc... gcc
checking whether the C compiler (gcc  ) works... yes
checking whether the C compiler (gcc  ) is a cross-compiler... no
checking whether we are using GNU C... yes
checking how to run the C preprocessor... gcc -E
checking for a C++-Compiler...
checking for g++... g++
checking whether the C++ compiler (g++  -s) works... yes
checking whether the C++ compiler (g++  -s) is a cross-compiler... no
checking whether we are using GNU C++... yes
checking how to run the C++ preprocessor... g++ -E
checking for ranlib... ranlib
checking for ld used by GCC... /usr/i386-linux/bin/ld
checking if the linker (/usr/i386-linux/bin/ld) is GNU ld... yes
checking for BSD-compatible nm... /usr/bin/nm -B
checking command to parse /usr/bin/nm -B output... yes
checking whether ln -s works... yes
checking for object suffix... o
checking for g++ option to produce PIC... -fPIC
checking if g++ PIC flag -fPIC works... yes
checking if g++ supports -c -o file.o... yes
checking if g++ supports -c -o file.lo... yes
checking if g++ supports -fno-rtti -fno-exceptions ... yes
checking if g++ static flag -static works... none
checking if the linker (/usr/i386-linux/bin/ld) is GNU ld... yes
checking whether the linker (/usr/i386-linux/bin/ld) supports shared
➥libraries... yes
checking command to parse /usr/bin/nm -B output... yes
checking how to hardcode library paths into programs... immediate
checking for /usr/i386-linux/bin/ld option to reload object files... -r
checking dynamic linker characteristics... Linux ld.so
checking if libtool supports shared libraries... yes
checking whether to build shared libraries... yes
checking whether to build static libraries... yes
checking for objdir... .libs
creating libtool
checking for AIX... no
checking for minix/config.h... no
checking for main in -lcompat... no
checking for main in -lcrypt... no
checking for the third argument of getsockname... socklen_t
checking for dnet_ntoa in -ldnet... no
checking for dnet_ntoa in -ldnet_stub... no
checking for inet_ntoa... yes
checking for connect... yes
checking for remove... yes
```

```
checking for shmat... yes
checking for killpg in -lucb... no
checking for X... libraries /usr/X11R6/lib, headers /usr/X11R6/include
checking for Qt... libraries /usr/lib, headers /usr/lib/qt/include
checking if Qt compiles without flags... yes
checking for moc... /usr/bin/moc
checking for dirent.h that defines DIR... yes
checking for opendir in -ldir... no
checking for ANSI C header files... yes
checking for size_t... yes
checking whether time.h and sys/time.h may both be included... yes
checking for stdlib.h... yes
checking for string.h... yes
checking for sys/file.h... yes
checking for unistd.h... yes
checking for fcntl.h... yes
checking for sys/types.h... yes
checking for memory.h... yes
checking for malloc.h... yes
checking for errno.h... yes
checking for io.h... no
checking for sys/time.h... yes
checking for stdarg.h... yes
checking for stddef.h... yes
checking for gettimeofday... yes
checking for snprintf... yes
checking for tempnam... yes
checking for sysent.h... no
checking for main in -ldbm... no
checking for main in -lndbm... yes
checking for rename... yes
checking for ftruncate... yes
checking for flock... yes
checking for bcopy... yes
checking for fsync... yes
checking for getopt... yes
checking for working alloca.h... yes
checking for alloca... yes
checking for off_t... yes
checking for st_blksize in struct stat... yes
checking for strerror... yes
checking for stdin... yes
checking if the compiler supports function prototypes... yes
checking for gcc option to accept ANSI C... none needed
checking for function prototypes... yes
checking for working const... yes
checking for inline... inline
checking for bool... yes
checking for gethostname... yes
checking for dlopen in -ldl... yes
checking for shl_unload in -ldld... no
checking for main in -ljs... no
configure: warning: you should get yourself a js distribution.
kdesupport contains only a small part of it.
For this have a look at http://www.ngs.fi/js/
```

…continued

```
checking for ANSI C header files... (cached) yes
checking for errno.h... (cached) yes
checking for float.h... yes
checking for limits.h... yes
checking size of int... 4
checking size of long... 4
checking for srand48... yes
checking for drand48... yes
checking for sleep... yes
checking for usleep... yes
checking for lstat... yes
checking if inline works... yes
checking if struct stat has st_blocks... yes
updating cache ./config.cache
creating ./config.status
creating Makefile
creating jpeglib6a/Makefile
creating giflib30/Makefile
creating mimelib/Makefile
creating mimelib/mimelib/Makefile
creating uulib/Makefile
creating js/Makefile
creating gdbm/Makefile
creating rdb/Makefile
creating QwSpriteField/Makefile
creating config.h
[root@localhost kdesupport-1.1.1]#
```

As you can see, a lot of system checking is done. Also, a file called Makefile is created in the /usr/local/src/kdesupport-1.1.1 directory. This is the "recipe" for the compilation that follows.

Then type

```
make all
```

8. Don't be surprised when this takes awhile. Indeed, on a slower system with limited memory, it could take more than a half hour. And don't be alarmed by the occasional warning message. All is well unless the compile bombs with a message beginning with ERROR. In this case, look at the line or two just before the error to see what failed to work. Chances are you'll have no problem, especially if you are using a recent Linux distribution and have installed all the compilation tools.

9. If you are doing all this from a terminal window in KDE (or in another desktop and window manager), now is the time to exit not just the terminal window but KDE itself. It is usually a bad idea to install a new version of an application while the old version is running. (In my experience, it's best when compiling to get out of the X Window System entirely and do it all from the console. It keeps you from accidentally breaking KDE, and it frees memory, making the compilation

go faster.) If you have to exit the terminal and KDE, become root or superuser again if you aren't already, change to /usr/local/src/kdesupport-1.1.1 (or the directory of whatever package you're currently compiling), and type

`make install`

This is really the most satisfying part of the whole compiling procedure, as you watch the files that you have just built from source code (that's what `make all` did) move to their proper places on your hard drive. This won't take very long at all.

10. Repeat the previous steps for kdelibs, kdebase, and the other packages in the KDE distribution. Don't restart an older version of KDE during the process. Remember the magic Up arrow, especially if you have a longish `configure` command. You can press the **Up** arrow a few times and be back to it, press **Enter**, and you've issued the command without risking a typo.

Congratulations! You have just built and installed KDE!

The Annoying GIF Problem

Without remedial action when compiling the QT libraries, you will end up with a desktop unable to display graphics files in the .gif format. This is a problem because KDE itself uses .gif files.

This happens because the owner of the compression algorithm used in .gifs has not put that algorithm in the public domain, so under the free software rules it cannot be encoded into QT or, therefore, KDE by the programmers of either.

But you can put it in yourself, if you are a programmer or are willing to hack the code. To do this, you need to download and open the QT source code in /usr/local. You then need to add mv qt-1.44/ qt. Within the resulting /usr/local/qt-1.44 directory, go into the /include subdirectory, open the file named qt_gif.h, and change this line:

`#define QT_BUILTIN_GIF_READER 0`

to this

`#define QT_BUILTIN_GIF_READER 1`

You then have to recompile and reinstall QT; full instructions are included in the source code. It is actually fairly easy.

Fortunately, Linux distributors that support KDE typically do this for you in their binary packages, but, unfortunately, not always.

Compiling for Power and Speed

You can employ several options to optimize KDE for your particular computer. We've already looked at the `prefix` and `host` options, but there are others. They, too, are added to the command line, and reduce code size, memory footprint, or both. The syntax varies, so I deal with them individually here.

Disabling debug

Linux programs (indeed, most programs for any operating system) contain code designed to make it easier to sort out the problem if something goes wrong. KDE is no exception to this rule. You can greatly reduce this code, which is seldom used, by adding a parameter to the `configure` command:

```
./configure --disable-debug
```

If you have not done this when you compiled, you can do much the same thing later by using the `strip` command (as root or superuser):

```
strip /opt/kde/bin/*
```

What does this give you?

- Reduced code size, which might be a concern if you are using an older, smaller hard drive
- Faster load times (there's less to load), which is especially noticeable if you are using an older machine with a smaller, slower hard drive

Disabling `exceptions`

Exception handling is something not used by KDE 1.X, but if you are using the EGCS compiler, the compiler doesn't know this and builds it in anyway. The way to disable it is to use a compiler flag for the C++ compiler portion of EGCS, like this:

```
./CXXFLAGS='-fno-exceptions' configure --prefix=pathname
```

You lose nothing, and you gain a substantial reduction in the amount of memory that KDE and its applications use.

Pentium

Unless told otherwise, the compiler picks the lowest common denominator and compiles code for an 80386-class processor. This runs just fine on 386s, 486s, the various enhanced 486s, and Pentiums. But if you have a Pentium-class machine (a Pentium, Pentium-MMX, Pentium II, Pentium III, or one of the AMD K-2 or K-3 CPUs), you can optimize KDE for it at compile time by adding the `-mpentium` flag:

```
./CXXFLAGS='-mpentium -fno-exceptions' configure --prefix=pathname
```

This works without the `-fno-exceptions` flag, but there's no reason to keep exception handling, so why do it?

The -O Flag

The letter *O* reduces code size and speeds execution of the compiled code if followed by the number *2* on Pentium-class machines:

```
./CXXFLAGS='-O2 -mpentium -fno-exceptions' configure --prefix=pathname
```

The trade-off is that it takes longer to compile with this option set, and more memory is used during compiling. If you are low on memory, this could involve a lot of swapping to disk, which causes the process to take still longer. It *is* worth the trouble, but be warned: it isn't something to undertake if you need your machine for something else 15 minutes from now. Some packages on some machines can take hours to compile.

So then, if you want to reduce the system resources required by KDE, you can employ some or all of the methods I've mentioned when you're building KDE from source. And, as you've seen, you can stack the options so that for minimum code size and memory usage, you would do this:

```
./CXXFLAGS='-O2 -mpentium -fno-exceptions' configure --prefix=pathname
--disable-debug
```

There are two things worth noting here. One is that the single-quote character (the apostrophe on your keyboard) is needed to offset C++ flags, which are called by `CXXFLAGS=`.

The other is how useful the Up arrow key is in a situation like this. You will be compiling as many as 11 packages to build the entire KDE distribution, and if you can type the line quoted above 11 times without making a mistake, you're better than most. With the Up arrow, you can scroll back through your commands until you find this behemoth, and then press **Enter**.

If you want to be extremely methodical with your compilation and have time to do it, it's a good idea to compile with no options other than `--prefix=`, just to make sure that you have a good download and KDE works. Then you can recompile with the options listed. If the result doesn't work, you need to experiment to see which option gives your system indigestion.

Now, let's get it running.

chapter

2

Starting KDE

Basic Look-and-Feel Control

A Few Common Problems and Their Solutions

It's all well and good to have KDE happily installed on your hard drive, but there's not much point unless you can actually *use* the thing, is there? Here is where we make that come to pass. You'll also learn about KDE's evolving use of *themes*, which let you adapt the look and feel of your new Linux desktop to suit your tastes or to resemble some other system more closely with which you are familiar and comfortable. We'll also deal with a few of the problems that can arise and knock them back down again.

Many modern Linux distributions (such as Caldera OpenLinux 2.3, Mandrake Linux, and Corel Linux, to name three) default to KDE, so when you have installed Linux and reboot, you automatically get KDE. These distributions don't contain the latest KDE version, however, which means that you probably want to upgrade, if not immediately then later. You can, of course, add KDE to distributions that deprive you of it. I have discussed this in passing in Chapter 1, "Installing KDE," and I discuss it in detail in Chapter 35, "Upgrading to the Latest Version," but I want to include some of the information that follows.

The first thing you do after installing KDE and before using it is to add the /opt/kde/bin directory to the PATH statement in /etc/profile.

(This assumes that KDE is in fact installed in /opt/kde. For Red Hat 6.0 users you need do nothing because KDE's binary files have been plopped down in /usr/bin, which is or should be on the PATH already. For those who have put KDE in a directory other than /opt/kde, the pathname should be adjusted accordingly.)

As root or superuser, open an editor either in the existing desktop or on the console. Then open /etc/profile. You see, near the top, a line that looks like this:

```
PATH="/bin:/usr/bin:/usr/local/bin:/usr/X11R6/bin"
```

Add the KDE binary path, to wit:

```
PATH="/bin:/usr/bin:/usr/local/bin:kdepath/bin:/usr/X11R6/bin"
```

You should substitute the actual KDE directory, such as /opt/kde or /usr/local/kde for *kdepath*.

The quotation marks need to be there. There are no spaces anywhere in the line. In addition, the exact placement of the KDE entry isn't critical. Bear in mind, though, that the system searches the directories for a command or file in the order in which they are listed in the PATH line. Therefore, in the unlikely event that there is a KDE file with the same name as one in, say, /bin, and KDE is placed before /bin in the PATH statement, that file would be opened when the one in /bin was called, which could cause all sorts of trouble. Generally, it's a good idea to put the KDE pathname at or near the end of the PATH statement.

If You Use a.out Binaries

On very old Linux installations, the ones that still employ a.out binaries exclusively, you need to modify the **LD_LIBRARY_PATH** statement. Such systems are relatively rare nowadays. If you have one, you know you have it; if you are in doubt, you don't. Modifying **LD_LIBRARY_PATH** isn't something to be done lightly, because if it isn't done correctly, a world of trouble can result. Because of differences among older Linux distributions, consideration of this must remain beyond the scope of this book.

Console Editors

If you haven't installed a console-mode editor, you are pretty much stuck with *vi*, which has the lone advantage of being on every Linux and UNIX system in the world except mine. I deleted it and made a symbolic link called *vi* to an editor I like. I would highly recommend that you get and install Pico. Some also love GNU-Emacs, which has rightly been described as more a religion than a program. In any case, and no matter which one you choose, it's important that you get and learn a console editor. It *will* save you.

SEE ALSO
➤ *For more information on Pico, see Chapter 34, "A Couple of Must-Have Programs," page 617.*

For most Linux installations onto which KDE is newly added, the way to make it the default desktop is to go to a command line (either in console mode or a terminal window) as root or superuser, and type:

`/opt/kde/bin/usekde`

This makes KDE root's default desktop, meaning that the startx command starts KDE and its window manager. Users can do the same thing to make KDE their desktop.

What happens is this: usekde is a script that saves any files in ~/ named .Xclients, .xsession, or .xinitrc and replaces them with versions of its own that start KDE and its associated programs. Time was, all you needed to do was make a text file containing the lone word *startkde* and save it as ~/.xinitrc, and all would be well. The next time you started the X Window System, there would be KDE. This is still true for some Linux distributions, but for newer versions it's more complicated than that.

The startkde script is still employed, but on some systems—Caldera and Red Hat's newest distributions, notably—it isn't enough, and running it by itself produces unexpected results, with parts of KDE starting atop a non-KDE window manager, for instance.

Window Managers and Desktops

In Linux the terms *desktop* and *window manager* are often incorrectly used interchangeably. They aren't the same thing. This is the pecking order of the Linux GUI (see Figure 2.1):

The X Window System itself simply makes it possible for graphical applications to run. It handles the job of making sure that the signals sent to the video card are the correct ones. This is typically XFree86, though commercial replacements are available.

The Window Manager is a layer that does for software what the X Window System does for hardware. It creates a situation where applications run under a defined set of rules in an expected and enforceable fashion. The KDE distribution provides a window manager, *kwm*, optimized for use with KDE. KDE also works with other window managers, but some features (such as setting desktop colors from a KDE menu) aren't available.

The Desktop is a set of applications running atop all this. This can be something as simple as a glorified graphical menu program with few if any native applications (programs that exhibit the same characteristics as does the desktop itself), or a full desktop system, such as KDE, Gnome, or, to a lesser extent, the small and excellent XFce.

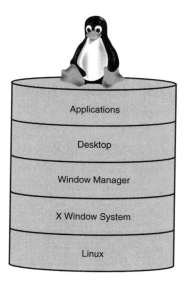

FIGURE 2.1
The layers piled atop Linux to create a desktop with applications running are like the layers of a cake. If this were a real cake, the presence of the penguin would not be sanitary—if it were a real penguin.

So what do you do with a newer distribution, where KDE may be installed by default, but startx doesn't make it appear? That depends on the distribution.

Caldera OpenLinux 2.2 provides two desktop/window manager combinations, twm and KDE with kwm. KDE is the default, as is a fully graphical login, which I discuss in the next chapter. When you log in, you are taken to KDE, unless you have upgraded KDE, in which case you receive an error message I discuss later in this chapter. If you have disabled graphical login, you type **startx** at the console to get twm. To get KDE, you type **kde** (in either case, followed by pressing **Enter**). By the way, twm is pretty sparse. Figure 2.2 shows the default twm desktop in Caldera 2.2.

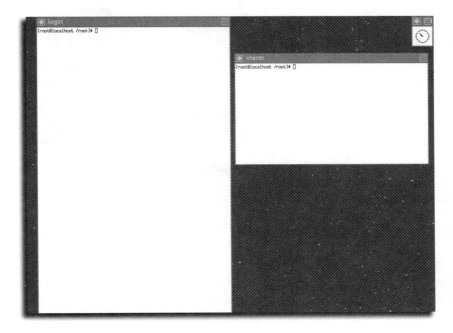

FIGURE 2.2
twm provides the most basic of desktops.

Red Hat 6.0 installs several window manager/desktop combinations. The default brings one to the attractive Gnome desktop and the Enlightenment window manager (see Figure 2.3). Also installed are KDE and kwm, AnotherLevel and its window manager, AfterStep and its window manager, and others.

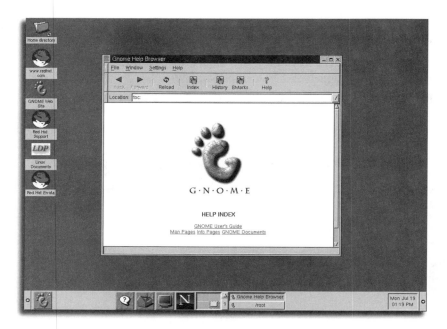

FIGURE 2.3
If you have obtained a Red Hat or Mandrake distribution, you have the choice of Gnome (shown here), but you can easily switch to KDE. When upgrading, you may want to remove all the installed window managers and desktops, and put KDE in /opt/kde.

Included is a program called switchdesk that enables the user to move freely among the three. You can use this from within Gnome to go to KDE (or to AnotherLevel). To invoke it, open a terminal window, type **switchdesk**, and press **Enter**. You may now choose KDE. Restarting the X Window System brings you your new choice.

Some Red Hat 6.0 users have sought to re-engineer the default desktop situation. They download KDE packages from KDE instead of using the beta versions shipped with the product. They then uninstall KDE and, perhaps, some or all of the other desktops and window managers, thereby recovering considerable disk space taken up by rarely or never-used desktops and window managers. Then they install the new version.

Why Uninstall the Old Version?

The new version can be installed atop the old version. Upgrading does not *require* such Draconian action as deletion of the existing one. To eliminate redundant and unused window managers and desktops, though, uninstallation is needed. If you're upgrading, you might as well put KDE into /opt/kde.

In this case, it makes sense to go ahead and install KDE into /opt/kde, instead of /usr, where Red Hat puts it. Remember to change the PATH statement in /etc/profile to reflect KDE's new location. For Red Hat 6.0, you also need to change the KDE directory in /etc/profile.d/kde.sh.

Why /opt/kde?

In the interest of full disclosure, I think and have argued strongly that KDE ought to be in /opt/kde. Doing so causes no harm and makes certain things much easier. Others have argued equally as strong to the contrary. My chief concern is that when one upgrades KDE, as happens from time to time, it is much easier to back up the old version—as a guard against something going wrong with the new installation—if it is isolated in its own directory.

Other distributions vary, though most default to KDE.

Basic Look-and-Feel Control

A relatively recent innovation in Linux desktops is the use of *themes*. These can be something as simple as a set of colors for the desktop and its widget set (window borders and the like) or as complicated as a combination of colors and actual behaviors that change almost everything about the way you interact with your desktop. Themes have been evolving, becoming increasingly elaborate. There is even work underway toward setting a themes standard that would allow them to be transferred from one window manager/desktop combination to another.

It was not until KDE 1.2 was released that a theme manager was included in the distribution. Before that, the KDE user who didn't want to download and install developmental versions of the KDE theme manager was given, essentially, two modest choices. The first was the default, as seen in Figure 2.4.

The second makes Apple Macintosh users feel more at home. It provides a menu bar at the top of the screen (in Figure 2.5, it is beneath the taskbar, which can be relocated, as I will discuss in due course). This menu bar provides the menus for whatever application currently has focus.

FIGURE 2.4
The default theme is KDE's own native look and feel.

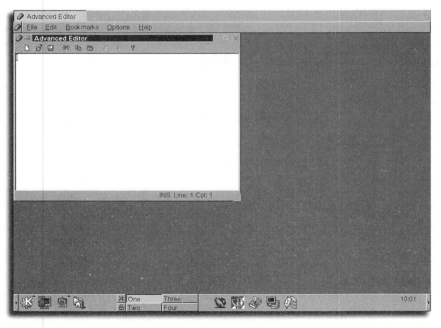

FIGURE 2.5
An Apple Macintosh-style menu bar is also a configuration option with the basic KDE package.

Beginning with KDE 1.2, though, a far broader selection was possible. (With 1.1.1, a theme manager was available for download, as were some themes, but 1.2 was the first time it became part of the distribution itself.)

I will be dealing with KDE's Theme Manager and how it can change a multitude of things about your system, from how it looks to how it behaves, and even how it sounds, later in the book. And I will describe a world of other configuration options in Part II, "Customizing the K Desktop," beginning with Chapter 5, "Making the K Desktop Your Own." For now, I thought it a good idea to give you a little taste of themes with the two (well, two and one-half) provided because they are easy to invoke and can increase your immediate comfort with the KDE desktop.

It is as simple as this: Click on the **K Menu** button; in the resulting menu click **Settings > Desktop > Style**, as depicted in Figure 2.6.

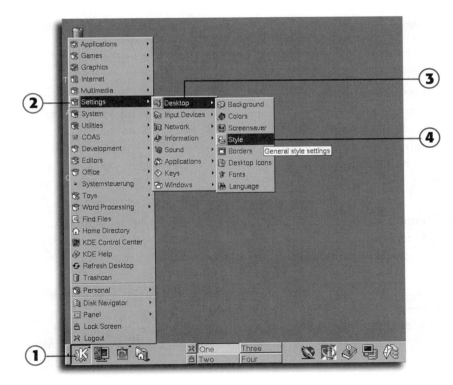

FIGURE 2.6
Use the K Menu to navigate to the Style selection screen.

① Click on the **K** first.

② Then click **Settings**.

③ Then click **Desktop**.

④ Finally, click **Style**.

Clicking on **Style** renders the configuration window, shown in Figure 2.7.

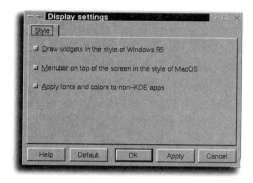

FIGURE 2.7
The Display Settings dialog box lets you choose among the two and one-half style-like functions it offers.

There are several buttons (or check boxes, as you will see) any or all of which you may select. Checking none gives you the default KDE look and feel.

- **Draw widgets in the style of Windows 95** changes a few small features of the desktop, though not their functions. For instance, if you select it, you will note that the button turns gray, as if depressed. Now click on the **Apply** button. See? It turned into a check box instead of a button. Were you to keep this setting and click on **OK**, all such buttons in KDE and its applications would become check boxes until you reopened the Display settings dialog box, unchecked the box, and saved the new setting by clicking on **OK**. This is the one-half of which I spoke.

- **Menubar on the top of the screen in the style of MacOS** produces the effect seen in Figure 2.3. Some people absolutely love it, while others cannot imagine how it could improve things. Experiment to see what you think.

Playing with the Mac OS Style

Try the second option with multiple applications open in windows, moving from one to another. This is one of the two styles of which I spoke, the other being the default (which can be reacquired by clicking on the **Default** button.)

- **Apply fonts and colors to non-KDE apps** would be a good idea if all non-KDE apps were willing to be ordered around. Netscape products in particular tend to misbehave when this button is pushed (or checked), and such features as being able to tell which mail or newsgroup articles you've read by a change in font weight disappears. There are reports that this setting displeases XEmacs as well. People tend to select this item because it sounds nice, forget they've selected it, and then are very puzzled when Netscape and some other applications exhibit unexpected behavior. For that reason, it's probably a good idea to keep it unselected.

That's just a small taste of the configurability of KDE, but it's a taste that allows you to make big changes (especially if you're coming to KDE from the Macintosh world). We will soon go full-bore into customization. But first...

A Few Common Problems and Their Solutions

There are four common errors when one starts KDE for the first time, and each is easily solved. I will present them in decreasing order of apparent importance.

Cannot connect to X server

This is an error message received by users of Caldera OpenLinux 2.2 who have used XF86Setup to configure their graphics cards, as is commonly done. It happens when you try to start KDE (or another window manager or desktop; the conflict is with XFree86) from the console and receive this error instead of a desktop. The solution is to log in as root and, using that console-mode text editor I keep harping about, modify /etc/X11/xinit/xserverrc so that it now says this:

```
#!/bin/bash

XAUTH=$HOME/.Xauthority
MKCOOKIE=/usr/bin/mcookie
touch $XAUTH

for host in localhost $HOSTNAME $HOST; do    xauth add $host/unix:0 .
'$MKCOOKIE`    xauth add $host:0 . `$MKCOOKIE`
done

exec Xwrapper -auth $XAUTH :0
```

After which, you can log out as root, log in as yourself, and start KDE by typing **kde** and pressing **Enter**.

KDE Starts, But Applications Won't

This isn't a common problem, but it is common enough. It happened to me! I would still be digging around for a solution but for an email from Roberto Alsina in Santa Fe, Argentina, who told me the permissions on my /tmp directory were improperly set. He was right, and it took but a few seconds at the command prompt to fix it. There is no way in the world that I'm going to explain Linux permissions here, so if you are encountering this problem, you must do as I say and be content with its fixing the problem. Log out of KDE and log in as root (if you are using KDM, do so in failsafe mode) and at the command prompt type this:

```
chmod 1777 /tmp
```

and press **Enter**.

Fonts Are Too Small

This isn't an error message but an observation. If you are running KDE at a screen resolution of 1,024×768 pixels or more, you may decide that the screen fonts are simply too tiny to be useful, unless you get right down on the screen and squint. You may have even poked around and found where you can make them larger, but they look just awful: all boxy and pixellated. Here's the trick. Your /etc/XF86Config file lists typefaces displaying at 75dpi before it lists those that display at 100 dots per inch. This is fine if your display is 800×600 pixels or less, but those letters get mighty little at higher resolutions. What's the solution? Reverse their order. Edit the first uncommented section, **Section "Files"**, of /etc/XF86Config so that it changes from the default example listed first below to the new example, listed second. (If you are using a version of XFree86 that supports True Type fonts, you can move its line to the very beginning, too, right after RgbPath.)

```
Section "Files"
    RgbPath     "/usr/X11R6/lib/X11/rgb"
    FontPath    "/usr/X11R6/lib/X11/fonts/75dpi"
    FontPath    "/usr/X11R6/lib/X11/fonts/100dpi"
    FontPath    "/usr/X11R6/lib/X11/fonts/misc"
    FontPath    "/usr/X11R6/lib/X11/fonts/75dpi:unscaled"
    FontPath    "/usr/X11R6/lib/X11/fonts/100dpi:unscaled"
    FontPath    "/usr/X11R6/lib/X11/fonts/misc:unscaled"
    FontPath    "/usr/X11R6/lib/X11/fonts/Type1"
    FontPath    "/usr/X11R6/lib/X11/fonts/Speedo"
    FontPath    "/usr/share/ghostscript/5.10/fonts"
```

```
Section "Files"
    RgbPath      "/usr/X11R6/lib/X11/rgb"
    FontPath     "/usr/X11R6/lib/X11/fonts/100dpi"
    FontPath     "/usr/X11R6/lib/X11/fonts/75dpi"
    FontPath     "/usr/X11R6/lib/X11/fonts/misc"
    FontPath     "/usr/X11R6/lib/X11/fonts/100dpi:unscaled"
    FontPath     "/usr/X11R6/lib/X11/fonts/75dpi:unscaled"
    FontPath     "/usr/X11R6/lib/X11/fonts/misc:unscaled"
    FontPath     "/usr/X11R6/lib/X11/fonts/Type1"
    FontPath     "/usr/X11R6/lib/X11/fonts/Speedo"
    FontPath     "/usr/share/ghostscript/5.10/fonts"
```

Wrong charset

This error appears all over the place with some versions of KDE and some configurations. It is utterly harmless and can be ignored without any risk to anything whatsoever. It disappears in KDE 1.2.

KDM for a Totally Graphical System

Many people believe never having to look at the command line is a good thing, and with KDE this is possible through use of an included program called *KDM*. (If you're keeping score, it's part of the kdebase package.) This chapter guides you through enabling KDM, describes the reasons why it isn't always a good idea, and leads you through disabling KDM. That sounds amusing, and in a way it is, but there are good reasons for all of it.

Those who use the Lizard to install Caldera Open Linux 2.2 have KDM enabled by default. When you reboot after the installation, that graphical login is KDM. Alas, others have to enable it just to take a look. Because it appears before the user is logged in and has access to applications, there's no real way to make a screenshot of it! This means that my description will have to do.

On a background of a color of your choice, a color gradient of your choice, or a bitmap of your choice, with either attractive but slow fancy accoutrements or speedy ordinary ones, there is a dialog box containing a greeting, little bitmaps of the users of the system with their usernames, a small square logo bitmap, text boxes into which the username and password are entered, along with buttons, a list box, and a menu across the bottom. These are Session Type (a list box), Go, Cancel, and Shutdown (which renders a menu). It is tremendously configurable, as you'll see. For instance, if for some reason you desire to do so, you could put little scanned-in pictures of the users as the bitmaps that appear with their usernames. You can change the greeting to a company slogan and the logo to the company logo. You can make the pictures of users and their names disappear entirely. (This is a smart thing to do from a security standpoint, if you are sure all the users can remember who they are without a photograph of themselves or other mnemonic aid. They'll have to remember their passwords anyway.)

You can set up KDM to launch a console session or even other window managers and desktops! It really is pretty cool if graphical logins are your heart's desire.

Setting Up KDM

Let us begin with an assumption: KDM isn't already running on your machine, and neither is xdm, which is a similar but less versatile graphical login manager. How do you tell? Well, when you start up your computer, if after booting it presents a purely text screen with a line that says login:, and, if after entering your username and pressing Enter it presents you with a line that says password:, you aren't starting graphically. You are starting in *run level 3*. This is good. If these things aren't true, we'll get to you in a minute, in the next section, "Configuring KDM."

Log out, and then log back in as root. At the command prompt, type `kdm` and press **Enter**. If all is well, you'll be able to appraise the accuracy of my description of KDM. You will see a bitmap of an orchestra conductor, and under it the word *root*. You will also see bitmaps of little heads, resembling the mapped model heads used by the phrenologists of a century ago to determine by shape of head whether a person was a criminal. There is one of these for each user of the system, accompanied by the user's name, which is good, because you won't be able to tell by the picture unless the user resembles the late horror movie star Rondo Hatton. Click on **root** and the word `root` appears in the text box labeled Login. Click on the little head above your username, and your username appears in the text box. In either case, the cursor jumps to the Password text box, where you can enter it. Do this (either root or your username). Press **Enter** or click on **Go**. You should be taken instantly to KDE as if you had logged in normally and typed the command that starts KDE for you. It will actually be a little quicker than what you're used to because the X Window System will already have been started to bring you KDM.

For extra points, now log out of KDE. Without KDM, you're dumped at a command prompt, still logged in as you. Some people find this reassuring. Others find it terrifying. With KDM, you won't find it at all because you'll be logged out! You'll be back at the KDM screen, and to do anything you'll need to log back in.

The K Menu

On the panel at the bottom of the KDE default screen is an icon of a letter *K* atop a mechanical gear. This is the main KDE menu of applications in the KDE distribution, plus other applications that you have installed. It and its desktop mates are described in detail in Chapter 4, "An Introduction to the K Desktop." It is referred to hereafter as the *K Menu*.

Now you know that KDM works. This is an important check because the next thing you'll do is set up your system so that it boots directly to KDM. If for some rare and obscure reason it doesn't work, you have more problems than you can gracefully handle. Go ahead and log in as root. Then click on the big letter *K* on the panel at the bottom of the screen. (The K is in an icon atop a gear: the KDE logo.) This makes a menu appear and at its top is the word **Applications**. Click on it to get a submenu. Click on either **Advanced editor** or **Text editor**; it makes no difference which. When the editor opens, click on **File > Open**. You will see a screen that lets you click around to choose a file. If you want to use the mouse, click on the **...** to go to the top-level directory. Then click on **/etc**, and use the arrows or scrollbar at the bottom to take you to **inittab**. Double-click on it, or single-click to highlight it, and then click on **OK**. If you're quicker with a keyboard, in the text box at the bottom labeled Location type: `file:/etc/inittab` and press **Enter**. Either way, /etc/inittab opens and looks like Figure 3.1.

51

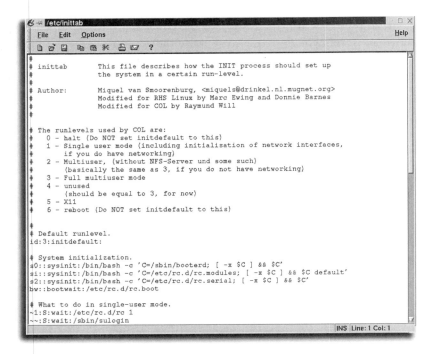

FIGURE 3.1
The Kedit editor is good for altering configuration files such as /etc/inittab.

Take a look at it because you are certain to learn some things about Linux you didn't know before. Of particular interest is the top part, which specifies what the different run levels mean. This is one of the things that varies depending on the age and distribution you are using, though the trend is toward run level 3 for multiuser console mode and run level 5 for graphical mode, X11. First thing, save it as **/etc/inittab.orig** using the **File > Save As** menu items. (You now have to use **File > Open** again to get to /etc/inittab instead of /etc/inittab.orig.) After you've browsed—don't touch anything!—return to the top. The very first line that isn't "commented out," which is to say preceded by a #, is this:

```
id:3:initdefault:
```

Change it to this:

id:5:initdefault:

See what you've done? You've told Linux that instead of booting into console mode, you're booting into X11—graphical—mode. You've changed a 3 to a 5—nothing more. If your distribution uses different numbers to bring this about, change from the multiuser console mode to the X11 mode by changing the corresponding number. The top section of /etc/inittab may—and probably does—contain descriptions of the different run levels for your distribution.

You have one other thing to do. Using **Edit > Replace**, change all instances of xdm to `kdm`. This tells Linux which graphical login manager you want to use. Save the file, log out of KDE, and do an orderly shutdown and reboot. You will be at the KDM login screen. (Debian Linux uses a different method of controlling its run levels and invocation of a graphical login program. Consult documentation provided by that distribution if it is the one you use.)

Backing Up Configuration Files

Throughout this book, when I ask you to back up a configuration file that you are about to edit, I will suggest that you give it an extension of .orig. The reason for this is that if you use the .bak extension, it will likely be overwritten later by some program that modifies the file and saves the original as *whatever*.bak. It is useful to keep a pristine copy of anything you change, for three reasons:

- So you can restore it if your changes break something.

- So you can look at it as your Linux knowledge grows to see and better understand the changes you made.

- When someone asks you how you performed some miracle and all you remember is that you changed a file in, say, /etc, the presence of an .orig file next to a file will tell you that it's one you changed, so you don't have to shuffle through them all.

The .orig is entirely arbitrary, though whatever extension you choose should be consistent. If .octopus is more to your liking, there is no reason in the world why you couldn't use it as an extension.

Configuring KDM

It is truly amazing—and a credit to its talented developers—how thoroughly configurable KDM is. You can make it look pretty much however you want and make it do pretty much whatever you want—even launch window managers and desktops other than KDE.

These wonders are brought to pass through an item on the K Menu. Click on **Settings > Applications > Login Manager**, and you will get what you see in Figure 3.2.

FIGURE 3.2
You have to be root to use the Login Manager.

This is because you're logged in as a mere user. Log out and log back in as root, use the K Menu to get to the same place, and you'll see what's in Figure 3.3.

FIGURE 3.3
The Login Manager provides page after page of customization options.

Here you may specify a "greeting string," which is whatever will appear in large letters at the top of your KDM dialog box. A good rule of thumb is that if it is too long to fit in the box so that you can see it all at once, it's too long to be used here. This can vary, though, because you'll be able to adjust the typeface and font size later on. Still, don't be too loquacious: nobody likes a chatty login screen. A company name is appropriate. On the next line you can point to a logo. Clicking on the logo itself allows you to choose among the ones in the directory specified. If your company logo is square or round, you could put it here. You can also choose widget style. The choices are *Windows* and *Motif*. Choose Motif unless you've chosen a Windows theme for KDE (see Chapter 2, "Starting KDE"). Consistency is important when using a GUI. Choose a language: KDE will surprise you in the number of languages it supports. Then click on the **Fonts** tab, if the defaults aren't to your liking, and see what is depicted in Figure 3.4.

Clicking on the **Change font** button gives you a choice of typefaces and sizes. The drop box to its right lets you specify the KDE screen element you want to change. The box below it all gives you a preview of the changes you are proposing. Knock yourself out. If you make something that turns out to be really ugly, you can click **Cancel** now or **Default** later, after you've tried it out, to get back to where you started. When you've created your masterpiece, click on the **Background** tab for the next level of modification, as shown in Figure 3.5.

FIGURE 3.4
You can select the typefaces you use in KDM, and their sizes, on the Fonts tab.

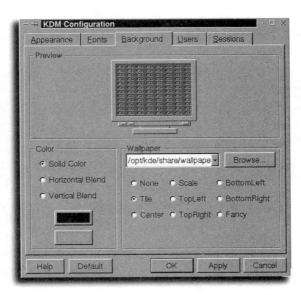

FIGURE 3.5
This part of KDM setup lets you choose colors or bitmap backgrounds for your login screen.

This is where the KDM developers did themselves very graphically proud and also demonstrated that KDM is a KDE application. All that happens here is that you specify the background on which the KDM dialog box appears. Don't underestimate this if, for instance, you are a company that deals with customers who are likely to see this screen because some very imaginative and strikingly elegant effects are possible. On this tabbed page, the preview is at top (along with a little representation of the monitor, its base and control buttons, and even a little green LED to show that the monitor is on). The bottom half is devoted to things that change the preview image and the actual image it represents.

You can choose a single solid color. If you don't like the one offered, click on the button that contains the sample to get the KDE color editor. There, you may choose from a number of standard colors or pick a custom color. If you do the latter, it is a good idea to add it to the custom colors by first selecting a blank space in the custom color palette, the rows of blank spaces in the color palette, and then clicking on the button that lets you save the custom color. This way, you can employ it later in your color scheme to create a consistent, unified effect.

For a classy, interesting, or flat-out garish effect, you could choose one of the two blend options: horizontal or vertical. The former lets you choose a color that appears at the left side of your screen and one that appears at the right. The two are blended, one into the other, across the screen. The former provides the same effect except the change takes place from top to bottom.

Developing Good Taste

Hint: Bright green to purple looks just awful. Deep blue at top and bright red at bottom looks like the sky a few minutes after sunset. Indulge yourself in the chief danger of this configuration option, which is trying out different combinations.

You can also choose a bitmap graphic as wallpaper. Unless the **No wallpaper** choice is selected, the wallpaper selection overrides your colors if the wallpaper is tiled or scaled. Your wallpaper choices include any of the almost ridiculously profuse ones provided in the KDE distribution, plus any that you add, which can be in .jpg or .xpm formats. If you have bitmaps of your own, put them in the /kde/share/wallpapers directory. When scaling a bitmap so that it fills the screen, remember that there's a big login box smack dab in the middle. This isn't the place for the portrait of the company president. Otherwise, you can experiment with placement by using the radio buttons and looking at the preview. When you are happy, click on the **U**sers tab, shown in Figure 3.6.

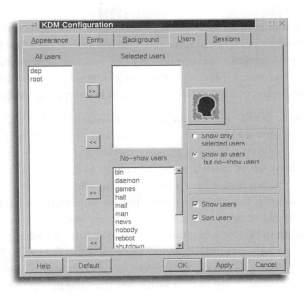

FIGURE 3.6
The <u>Users</u> tab lets you determine whether usernames will appear on the login screen and, if so, which usernames and which bitmap is associated with each.

This tab doesn't let you add or remove users for the system itself, but it does let you specify who shows up if users are depicted at login as potential phrenology subjects. A lot of interesting stuff happens here that is perhaps best illustrated by an example.

On the left side is a listing of all the users of the system. Let's say that you work at a company with a vast number of users on the system but only a few who meet in your office with the public. They are the ones whose faces appear in advertisements and for whom you've sprung the extra money to get their pictures printed on their business cards. As customers walk to their cubicles, they pass computers with the login screen visible. Glancing around, they will see those familiar faces on the login screen, reinforcing the advertising and continuing to present those public faces. Ah, but how to bring this about?

First, you click the radio button at right center, **Show only selected users**. Then, click on the usernames of the users you want to depict, and click on the arrow box pointing from **All users** to **Selected users**, which puts the chosen ones into the selected users box. (It's probably a good idea to encourage publicly depicted persons to choose usernames that aren't goofy, because the username will be visible, too. So, if the company's president logs in as "poopiepie" because that's what his wife calls him, it might be a good idea for him to demonstrate his sentimental affection in some other way. Customers are otherwise likely to be unimpressed.

Now comes the cool part. By highlighting a username in the **Selected users** box and clicking on the head icon, you can replace it with something else! And this something else can include a digital picture—perhaps the very one on their business cards or television or newspaper advertisement. Of course, for this to look good you need digital photographs of all the selected users, or else it will look as if you have space aliens on the staff.

There are a couple of reasons why the nifty arrangement set forth above would be a very bad idea, and it would be wrong not to mention them. The first and less important one is that if you have many people meeting the public (or decide to check the **Show all users but no-show users** radio button), you could end up with a login screen that looks like a page from a high school yearbook. The other and potentially critical one has to do with security. If your system contains any information you don't want made available to the world at large, and if there is even the slightest chance that an unauthorized person might gain access to a machine when no one is looking, anything that lists usernames is a very bad idea indeed. Why? Because if this feature is disabled, in addition to trying to figure out a password, the cracker would also have to correctly guess a username. The likelihood of doing both is much less than the likelihood of guessing just one. To enable this security feature, uncheck the lower right check boxes as shown in Figure 3.7. Sadly, the little pictures go away with the usernames.

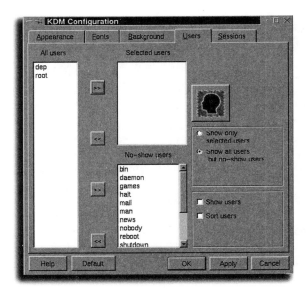

FIGURE 3.7
For maximum security, uncheck the boxes to eliminate the display of usernames.

Users Who Never Log In

You should notice a box labeled **No-show users**. Linux gives user privileges to a number of system functions. This box demonstrates that they are there, but they aren't required to log in.

When you have established the user configuration you need, click on the **Sessions** tab (see Figure 3.8).

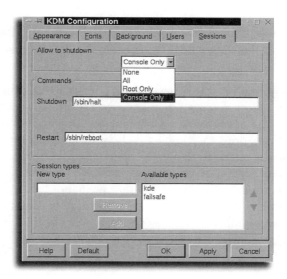

FIGURE 3.8
The shutdown and reboot commands, as well as the kinds of sessions KDM will launch, are configured on the final **Sessions** tab of the Login Manager setup.

Here is where you set some privileges for functions provided by KDM, and to some extent specify what those functions are.

At the top is a drop box in which you choose who can shut down the system. This is of particular use if multiple terminals are running off a single machine. Sharp words will be exchanged if somebody shuts down the whole system while a coworker is finishing up a report that took hours. The text boxes below the drop box specify the commands that Shutdown and Restart the system. If you have a "green" machine, for instance, some options don't just halt the system but also power it down, if you have these features compiled into your kernel.

The Kernel

The Linux kernel brings together the ideas of the freshest and cleverest young minds in the computing world. They have provided features almost beyond the imagination of we mere mortals. These features are beyond the scope of this book, but you are encouraged to learn as much as you can about the options available in the Linux kernel, which is remarkably flexible. Some of these require that you compile the kernel yourself—"burn a kernel" in the vernacular—but so long as you are painstaking, it really isn't at all difficult. Fortunately, the documentation necessary to perform a kernel burn is provided with the kernel source code. Just be sure to read it all and follow the instructions *exactly*.

The bottom portion of the screen is devoted to the session types available from KDM. The default choices are **kde** and **failsafe**. The latter provides a rescue mode in case KDE for some reason fails to start, but you can add more.

Using KDM to start different window managers and desktops is more complicated than anything heretofore discussed. Frankly, it isn't for the novice, but anyone familiar with Linux and scripting can do it. Having said that, the variations among the way modern Linux distributions are handling X11 configuration files and the variations among the commands required to start different window managers and desktops preclude a discussion of it here, beyond noting that it can be done. The documentation provided with your distribution, the KDM documentation, and the instructions for installing and starting other window managers and desktops combined will enable you to modify the Xsession file in a subdirectory of /etc/X11 (this is one of the variations), and the systemwide xinitrc file to accommodate such additional setups as you desire.

Using KDM

Having dealt with the installation and configuration of KDM, it's finally time to use the thing. Let's begin by doing an orderly shutdown of the system for a reboot, and rebooting.

You'll be greeted by the KDM window, configured as you chose. If you did not disable the depiction of users, they (or the chosen few, anyway) appear in all their glory. If you are among them, you can click on your icon and see your username entered on the appropriate line. If not, if you'd prefer it to clicking on your picture, or if you decided not to list users on the KDM screen, just type in your username and password. Then click on the button labeled **Go**. You are instantly transported to KDE.

You can do other things at the KDM window. By clicking on the **Session Type** drop box, you can choose from among the window manager/desktop combinations you have installed. The default list is **kde** and **failsafe**. The latter opens a little terminal window where it may be possible to fix something that is broken and that prohibits logging in to KDE. You must choose this after you have entered your username and password; otherwise, it will change back to kde. The **Go** button will take you to your choice.

The **Cancel** button returns all fields to their condition when KDM was started, which is to say no user chosen and no password entered, with KDM configured to launch KDE.

The **Shutdown** button renders a subsidiary dialog box not unlike the one produced when one selects **Shutdown** from the **Start** menu in Windows 9X. The radio buttons give you the choice of shutting down the computer entirely, shutting down and restarting (rebooting), restarting the X server you are using, or going to console mode (useful if you are upgrading an X server, all of XFree86, or KDE itself). The specific commands invoked by the Shutdown and Restart choices, as previously noted, can be edited in the $\underline{S}$essions tab in the KDM configuration dialog box.

Why Not to Use KDM

Although KDM is attractive and very reliable, all sorts of things can cause the underlying software to become misconfigured or corrupted. This can make restarting the computer problematic, to say the least. Examples include a poorly executed upgrade of XFree86, a reinstallation of KDE that uses a directory different from the one on which it was initially installed, or a badly edited configuration file. Fixing the problem is beyond the scope of this book but can involve booting Linux in single-user mode and, from the command line, attempting to find and repair whatever is wrong, which can be a time-consuming and frustrating task. But at least you can get into the system and attempt to undo whatever you did. Begin with your last system change.

Let me note: This is unlikely, but it has been known to happen, and with sufficient frequency that it is worth mentioning.

The solution, of course, is to do none of the above and, if your system defaults to KDM (or, for that matter, XDM, the program on which KDM is based), to undo it. This requires editing /etc/inittab and finding this line:

```
id:5:initdefault:
```

Change it to this:

```
id:3:initdefault:
```

Now you've told the system to boot into run level 3, which is multiuser console mode. You won't use KDM (or XDM) at all. (Again, if your distribution uses different numbers to specify the different run levels, you want to change the number from the one that specified an X11 default to the one that defaults to the standard multiuser console.)

You may want to review the contents of /etc/lilo.conf as well, and if there is a line that says something on the order of vga = 274, remove it. Then the entire boot sequence will take place in console mode, with no reliance on any graphical subsystems. It also allows the entire boot sequence to be written to screen, where some system problems might make themselves apparent. This is of no use to users who don't have to maintain their own systems, but it is helpful if you are the diagnostician and maintainer of the system.

Editing /etc/lilo.conf

Be *extremely* careful when you edit /etc/lilo.conf because errors can result in a system that won't boot at all. Back up the original /etc/lilo.conf to /etc/lilo.conf.orig so that you can back out if there's a problem and look for the error without that growing sense of panic.

After you've changed /etc/lilo.conf, still as root, from the console or in a terminal window type **/sbin/lilo** and press **Enter**. Watch carefully for any error messages. If they occur, look at your new /etc/lilo.conf before rebooting, fix the problem, and rerun /sbin/lilo; otherwise, your machine may not reboot. If you can't find the problem, restore your backed-up lilo.conf and run /sbin/lilo to return to the original state of affairs. You can then fix /etc/lilo.conf to remove the offending line at your leisure. You probably should read and understand the lilo man page before you experiment too extensively, but this procedure should be safe.

When all this is done, the system goes through its boot procedure and end up at a console screen that looks like this:

```
localhost.localdomain login:
```

There, you (and other users) enter the appropriate username, press **Enter**, and are prompted for a password, which you type in followed by another **Enter**, and a command prompt results. You or the other user then must type the command that starts the X server, your window manager, and your desktop (typically **startx**, but **kde** for Caldera 2.2), and press **Enter** again.

It's slightly more complicated, but it is somewhat safer.

chapter

4

An Introduction to the K Desktop

Presuming that all has gone according to plan so far, you are able to get to the KDE desktop pretty easily: either automatically through KDM or by using the startx or kde commands after logging in. In this case, you are greeted by a screen something like the one shown in Figure 4.1.

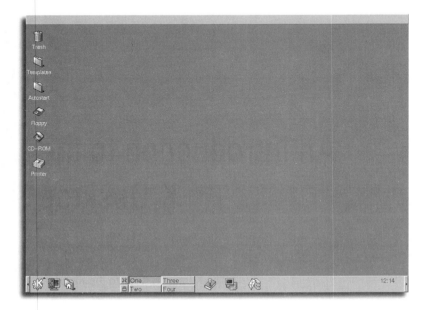

FIGURE 4.1
The default KDE desktop.

It looks pretty friendly, doesn't it? But if you start clicking on icons and buttons, it won't be long before you find things you don't understand, especially if you are new to Linux. This chapter is heavily illustrated because the desktop is easier to show than it is to talk about.

Play Around—But Not as root!

You should feel free to explore the desktop, but unless you like to walk a tightrope without a net, do it as a user, not root. That way, you won't be able to do much that you can't undo. This doesn't mean that you should play fast and loose with Delete commands, but there is little that you are likely to do that can't be undone. Not so if you are logged in as root. The illustrations in this chapter are from a root screen only because nothing has been changed from the default.

A Tour of the Desktop

The best place to start is to identify the various screen elements. The bar across the top is the *taskbar*. When applications are running, reference to them is made here, and from here you can bring them to the foreground, restart minimized applications, and even close running programs. Across the bottom is the *K Panel*. All KDE functions are available here, plus anything that you choose to add. (I discuss customization in great detail in Part II, "Customizing the K Desktop," which begins with the very next chapter.) The other screen elements, many of which are located on the K Panel, are identified in Figure 4.2.

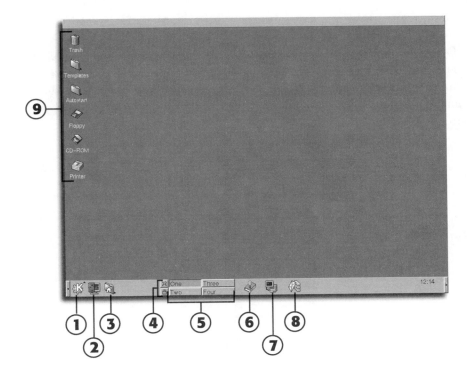

FIGURE 4.2
The screen elements.

① K Menu button

② KDE Control Center button

③ KFM (the file manager) button

④ Logout and Screen Lock buttons

⑤ Desktop Switcher buttons

⑥ KDE Help Center button

⑦ KVT (a virtual terminal) button

⑧ K Mail button

⑨ Default desktop icons

The K Panel—Keys to the Kingdom

Items 1 through 8 in Figure 4.2 are located on the K Panel, which you are probably assuming is the center of action in KDE—and if you are, you're right. Let's take a quick overview of the default K Panel items:

They Look like Icons and Taste like Icons, but...

I should note right now that items on the K Panel are buttons, not icons. There is a difference. *Buttons* on the K Panel behave in the same way as buttons that say, for instance, Apply or Cancel. *Icons* are representations of actual files or links to files.

1. The **K Menu** button opens, unsurprisingly, the K Menu as illustrated in Figure 4.3. This is the chief place where you launch applications in KDE. There are a few programs directly on the K Menu, but most are in submenus (and sub-submenus, and in a few cases even sub-sub-submenus), signified by the stylized arrows next to the K Menu items.

FIGURE 4.3
Click on the **K Menu** button for access to installed applications.

2. The **KDE Control Center** button offers instant access to the entire range of KDE configuration options. Clicking it opens the KDE Control Center (see Figure 4.4), which uses the familiar hierarchical tree where you gain access to the possibilities for each part of KDE. It is the chief tool you will use in Part II of this book.

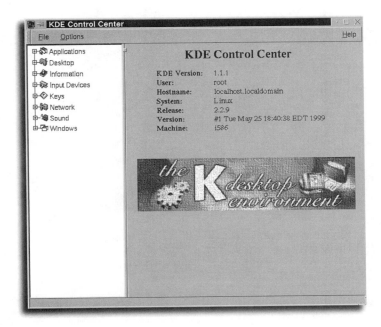

FIGURE 4.4
The KDE Control Center button is the gateway to a panoply of configuration possibilities.

3. **KFM**, the K File Manager, has a button on the K Panel, too, and it is one that you will use frequently. In addition to its use as a file manager, it is also a Web browser and full-featured ftp client. It's also the subject of two chapters all its own: Chapter 10, "Navigating *Everything* with KFM," which deals with its use as a file manager, and Chapter 24, "Using KDE for Other Internet Functions," which tells how it is used for online work. Its most basic state is shown in Figure 4.5.

4. The **Logout** and **Screen Lock** buttons, stacked one atop the other, do pretty much what you would expect. The **Logout** button logs you off of the system entirely if you are using KDM or another graphical login manager. Otherwise, it simply closes the KDE and X Window System session and leaves you at a command prompt, still logged on to the machine. The **Screen Lock** button instantly starts your chosen screensaver (or blanks your screen if you have selected no screensaver) and requires your password for you to open it again.

FIGURE 4.5
KFM is a file manager and so much more.

Locked Out!

Many KDE users who try to use the Screen Lock as a user (as opposed to root) discover that it is impossible to get back in again. You move your mouse and a password screen pops up. You enter your password and press **Enter**. It cogitates a moment, and it pronounces the attempt a failure. All you can do is press the **Alt+Ctrl+Backspace** key combination, which, if you are running KDM, takes you to the login screen. If you aren't running KDM, it takes you to the console, still logged in as you, so anyone can type **startx** or **kde** and be back at your now unlocked desktop. What to do?

As root, at the command prompt change to the /kde/bin directory wherever KDE is installed (/usr/bin for Red Hat 6.0) and type **chmod u+s kcheckpass**. This runs the kcheckpass program SUID, which means all users can use it as if they were the superuser, which in turn means that you, the user, can use it to unlock your screen.

Beware, though. If you aren't using KDM, anyone can still use **Alt+Ctrl+Backspace** to close down KDE and the X Window System, and restart KDE, and have access to your desktop. So if you're leaving your desk and don't want it to be easy for anyone who has a little skill to have access to your machine, it's best to log out entirely, leaving the machine at a login prompt.

5. The **Desktop Switcher** allows you to move freely among two to eight "virtual" desktops. These are the equivalent of extra monitors on which different applications can be running, and they do much to reduce screen clutter. The default number is four, and you go from one to another by clicking on the corresponding button.

6. The **KDE Help Center** button opens general KDE help. It is in HTML, and the help center is a browser that allows you to move through the help system as if you were online, though much, much faster. Figure 4.6 shows the opening page.

FIGURE 4.6
The KDE Help Center provides lots of information in a comfortable browser setting.

7. **KVT,** the K Virtual Terminal, provides a command prompt, which is extremely useful in Linux because many functions, such as compiling applications, are most quickly and efficiently done there. Additionally, it allows you to run many text-based console-mode applications on your desktop. When you click its button on the K Panel, you see Figure 4.7.

SEE ALSO

➤ *I have more about KVT and its sister applications, the Mini-CLI and Konsole, in Chapter 11, "Using the Command Line in KDE," page 257.*

8. The K Mail button opens KDE's powerful email program. Figure 4.8 shows a quick peek at it.

SEE ALSO

➤ *For more information on using Kmail, see Chapter 22, "Kmail for Quick Communication," page 461.*

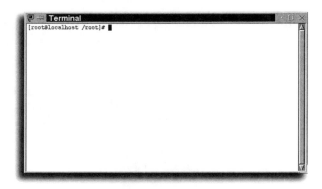

FIGURE 4.7
KVT provides what amounts to a small console-mode terminal on your graphical desktop.

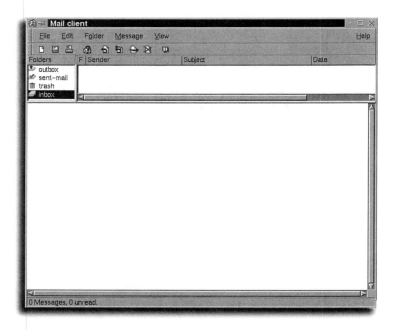

FIGURE 4.8
K Mail is your email connection with friends, family, and associates throughout the world.

K Panel, like the rest of KDE, is extremely configurable. You can add applications to it, remove applications from it, and move applications around on it. You can change its location and its size, you can hide it—just about anything you want.

SEE ALSO

➤ *To find out more about using the K Panel, see Chapter 7, "Making a Super K Panel," page 175.*

Disappearing Act

At each end of K Panel, you'll find a small, crosshatched button with a little black triangle pointing off the screen. Push this and K Panel "rolls up" into the little button, whose triangle changes direction. Push on it again and K Panel is restored. When it is minimized in this way, it adds a little box with three icons to the upper-left corner of the screen. These icons are for the K Menu, the KDE window list (think of it as a task manager), and the KDiskNavigator, about which there is more later in this chapter. The K Panel stays on top of whatever applications may be running under it full screen or in that part of the screen.

Desktop Icons: Useful Shortcuts

Several icons are placed on your desktop by default. They vary depending on the Linux distribution you are using and whether you added KDE to your Linux system yourself. The ones that are always present are the Trashcan, the Templates folder, and the Autostart folder. Pictured here, too, are icons for your floppy drive, CD reader, and printer. You can add and remove icons as suits your taste and needs. A bit about the default icons: All three represent folders—in this case subdirectories of the ~/Desktop directory, but they can be moved.

Trashcan

The first, the Trashcan, is somewhat but not entirely like the trashcans found in some DOSrivative operating systems. In Linux, "delete" means gone forever. It does in KDE, too. If you are in doubt about deleting a file, you can drag it to the Trashcan (or right-click the file's icon and select **Move to Trash**), and it will move to the Trashcan directory. You may at a later time click on the **Trashcan** and view its contents and move any file you want to keep back to where it belongs. The Trashcan folder is similar to other folders (see Figure 4.9) but its Edit menu contains an item allowing you to empty the Trashcan. Choose it and all the files in the Trashcan are assigned to oblivion.

The chief difference between KDE's Trashcan and those from elsewhere is that you must specifically move a file to it. Deleting a file doesn't automatically put the file in the Trashcan; in fact, it's gone forever.

Templates Folder

The Templates folder contains items that you will use frequently or not at all: there seems to be little middle ground. This has a lot to do with whether a user wants a desktop populated with icons. In any case, clicking on it opens the folder depicted in Figure 4.10.

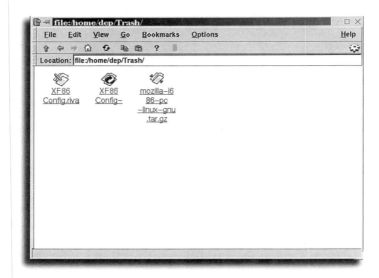

FIGURE 4.9
In most respects, the Trashcan is a directory of files you think—but aren't certain—you want to delete.

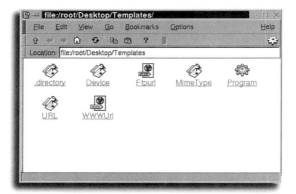

FIGURE 4.10
The Templates folder quickly allows you to create desktop links to applications and files of many sorts.

To use these templates, drag the icon for the chosen file type to the desktop and, in response to the small menu that pops up when the icon is dropped, choose **Copy**, not Move. Then, by right-clicking the icon and selecting **Properties**, you can assign the program or function desired to it.

Two Approaches to Templates

If you are working on a big report in a particular application, you can either make an icon for that program with the filename of your report as a parameter, or set the file type of your file to open the program automatically with the file in it. Either way, you can use a template.

SEE ALSO

➤ *You'll discover much more about working with templates in Chapter 8, "Adding Applications to the Desktop," page 191.*

The Autostart Icon

The Autostart icon opens a folder (see Figure 4.11) in which you may drag icons for any applications that you want to start up when you start KDE. It is, at first, empty.

FIGURE 4.11
If you have any non-KDE applications that you want to have started every time you use KDE, the Autostart folder is the place to put links to them.

Too Many Autostart Programs!

Many times a user will try out a little program, decide that it ought to run all the time, and drop it into the Autostart folder. Then, the next time that user starts the system, two copies of the program are running!

The problem is that when KDE is restarted, it restarts any KDE applications that were running at the time it was closed. If a copy is in the Autostart folder, it starts that one, too. The difficulty is in determining which applications meet this qualification and which ones don't. Here's how you do it. Start all the applications that you want to have running all the time. Then click on the **Logout** button on the K Panel. If you receive no error message in the form of a box saying that applications are present that won't restart, all the applications you are running will automatically restart. If you are treated to the error box, you know which of your selected programs need to be dropped into Autostart.

The icons representing disk drives, when clicked, open KFM windows showing the contents of the diskette or CD, if any, in the corresponding drive. Basically, it saves you from having to click all the way up to /mnt to get access to these devices. You can create similar icons for hard drives, partitions on hard drives, directories, or even individual files if you want.

Printer Icon

The **Printer** icon, though often not created by default, is potentially very useful if drag-and-drop functions are your cup of tea. Clicking on it opens the K Printer Queue program (see Figure 4.12).

FIGURE 4.12
Click on the **Printer** icon to see what print jobs are queued.

To print a file, simply drag it to the Printer icon and drop it thereon.

This assumes that the file is in a format that the printer or the Linux PostScript emulation, Ghostscript, understands, which isn't an assumption that you can always make. The Printer icon can sometimes require some tuning. If you decide that it is simpler and more reliable simply to print from the application that created the file, you won't be the first.

The Nifty RMB Menu

But wait, there's more! Right-clicking the desktop produces a menu, as shown in Figure 4.13.

FIGURE 4.13
The desktop right-click menu provides instant access to functions for which you might otherwise have to dig.

Let's quickly and briefly run down the desktop RMB menu:

■ **New** renders a submenu (see Figure 4.14) that duplicates the functions of the Templates folder.

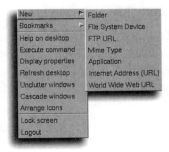

FIGURE 4.14
The RMB New menu allows you to create new desktop objects.

■ **Bookmarks** allows you to edit your KFM bookmarks file.

SEE ALSO

➤ *You can find out more about bookmarks in Chapters 10, "Navigating* Everything *with KFM," and 24, "Browsing and Other Trhings Internet," pages 225 and 493.*

■ **Help on desktop** opens the Desktop section of the KDE help system.

■ **Execute command** opens KDE's miniature commandline interface (also known as MiniCLI), where you may enter a command to execute. The MiniCLI is actually far more versatile than you might think.

SEE ALSO

➤ *I cover the MiniCLI more fully in Chapter 11, "Using the Command Line in KDE," page 257.*

■ **Display properties** starts the Display section of the KDE Control Center.

SEE ALSO
➤ *Display properties is explained beginning in Chapter 5, "Making the K Desktop Your Own," page xx.*

- **Refresh desktop** does just that: It cleans up any "artifacts" left behind by a wayward application. For instance, it repaints the desktop.

- **Unclutter windows** attempts to rearrange the windows on your desktop so that you can at least see a little bit of each one.

- **Cascade windows** tries to put open windows in an order so that at least the title bar of each is visible.

- **Arrange icons** repositions the icons on your desktop so that something else isn't covering them up and they are evenly spaced for a neater look.

- **Lock screen** performs the same function as the lock button on the K Panel.

- **Logout** performs the same function as the logout button on the K panel.

The Taskbar Is More Than a List

In the upper-left corner of the desktop (by default) or across the top of the screen (where you'll put it) is the taskbar. It lists running applications and a great deal more. I exhaustively explore its configuration options in Chapter 7, but a good look at it now is useful. Its appearance with three applications running is illustrated in Figure 4.15.

SEE ALSO
➤ *For more on configuring the taskbar, see Chapter 7, page 175.*

The actions available for use with the taskbar are configurable. By default, clicking on a running application there brings it to the front and gives it focus (and restores it if it is minimized). Double-clicking on its taskbar button (or clicking with the middle button, if you have a three-button mouse or trackball) minimizes it, and right-clicking produces a menu, as shown in Figure 4.16.

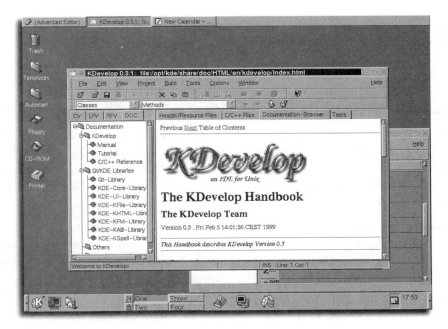

FIGURE 4.15
The taskbar here shows three running applications: the Advanced Editor, KDevelop, and KOrganizer. The parentheses show that the Advanced Editor is minimized; the depressed taskbar button shows that KDevelop has focus.

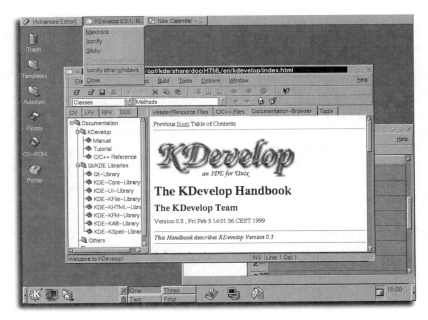

FIGURE 4.16
The taskbar has its own RMB menu, which allows you to manipulate running applications from outside the applications.

In addition to being positionable on the screen, you can hide the taskbar from view except when the mouse pointer is bumped against the corner or edge where it resides.

Virtual Desktops to Make Your Monitor Bigger

It is possible, even easy, to have so many applications open that they are stacked one atop the other. When this happens, moving around among them is difficult. This is especially true of applications such as Netscape and StarOffice, which you are likely to want to run full screen. For this reason, window managers and desktops in Linux have traditionally offered *virtual desktops*.

These in effect extend the screen in order to make it many times bigger than it is—up to eight times as big, though four is the default. The four buttons on K Panel, labeled **One**, **Two**, **Three**, and **Four**, provide one way of navigating among these.

If you are new to this idea, you can best demonstrate it by opening an application… any application. Then click one of the Desktop Switcher buttons to change to a different virtual desktop. As you can see, it's blank. There, open a different application. Now switch back, again using the Desktop Switcher, to the first. It's still there. Let's say you're in the middle of a complicated project, with several applications open and set up just so. You are interrupted by something else, just want to take a break and check your email, or look on the Web for the answer to a problem that has just come up. You can pop over to a different desktop, do your new tasks there, and return to your project later.

It really requires no setup; it's there by default. But you can do a couple of things to make it a little more convenient.

One thing that many people find extremely annoying is that the virtual desktops might be installed in such a way as to make them all but seamless: You move from Desktop One to Desktop Two merely by bumping your mouse cursor against the right side of your screen and leaving it there for a few seconds. If you are over against that side, performing some task, you might all of a sudden be surprised and horrified to see your open applications suddenly disappear. They haven't—you've just switched to a different desktop. No real harm has been done, but it certainly breaks your concentration!

Fortunately, when we begin to customize the K Desktop in the next chapter, I'll show you how to fix the problem of disappearing applications and offer some other useful customization ideas.

The K Panel Buttons and the Pager

The Desktop Switcher buttons on the K Panel are sometimes called "the pager" because many Linux desktops contain an application of that name that does much the same thing. True pagers typically contain a very small view of the applications running in each desktop, as a reminder of what is where. The buttons on K Panel don't do this. To further complicate the issue, a small utility called the Desktop Pager, located in the K Menu's System submenu, performs this function, displaying the icons of running applications in each desktop. The K Panel buttons do have one aid to navigation: The button of the current desktop has a darker look, as if it has been pushed.

You should know a couple of things about virtual desktops. You will notice in all applications running under KDE—even non-KDE applications—a little widget that looks like a pushpin next to the miniature application in the upper-left corner of the application window. If you click on this, the application becomes *sticky*. This means that if you have pushed this button the application persistently follows you around from desktop to desktop.

You will also notice that as you move from desktop to desktop, the taskbar continues to show applications running in all windows. If you click on an application that is running on a different desktop, the application isn't brought to the current desktop. Instead, you are returned to the desktop where it is running.

Finally, if you have KDE-native applications running across several virtual desktops when you shut down KDE, they all reopen when you restart on Desktop One. This can be quite a surprise. On the other hand, it can remind you that you had these applications running all over the place, perhaps forgotten, consuming system resources.

Zooming Around with KDiskNavigator

A relatively new arrival to the KDE desktop is *KDiskNavigator*, which can make your life a lot easier. It is illustrated, albeit in a fairly extreme form, in Figure 4.17.

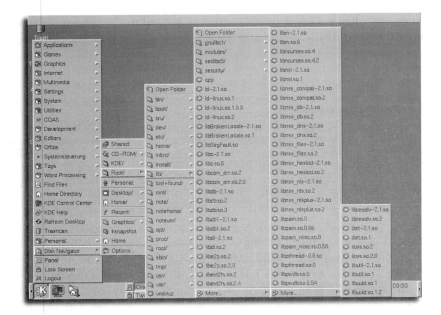

FIGURE 4.17
KDiskNavigator takes you to recently and frequently used locations on your computer.

KDiskNavigator is the only K Menu item that we'll look at in this chapter because when K Panel is minimized, it is one of the few things that remains and because it really is a desktop kind of program.

The fundamental notion behind KDiskNavigator is that in an elaborate hierarchical file system such as Linux's, you can access the places you want to visit on your computer more efficiently than by climbing up and down the directory tree. (A tree has its root at the top, by the way; it might actually make more sense if it were displayed upside down.) KDiskNavigator (hereafter referred to as *KDN*) seeks to shorten the distance between two points: where you are and where you want to go, not today but right now.

To view KDN, click the **K Menu** button and rest your mouse pointer on Disk Navigator. When it appears, you'll see that it is divided into several sections:

- **Shared** provides access to the files and resources on the machine that all users use.
- **Personal** takes you to your local desktop and your home directory.
- **Recent** provides shortcuts to the applications you most recently used.
- **Options** lets you configure KDN.

The first three sections give you access to your entire drive, drives mounted on other machines networked to yours, and even sites on the Internet, though there probably are better ways of navigating the Web. KDN, as its name states, is mainly for getting around on the local machine or network.

With KDN visible, you can move the mouse pointer up and down KDN, noticing the places, signified by one of those little stylized triangular arrows, where a submenu pops out. If the directory is a big one, the bottom item is More and resting the mouse pointer there spawns another menu, possibly with another More at its bottom, and so on. Clicking on any item does whatever clicking it in KFM would do:

- Launch it if it is a program
- Open it in an editor, if it is a test file to which you have read access
- Go to it in KFM, if it's a Web bookmark and you are online

At the top of each submenu is an item labeled **Open Folder**. Clicking on this launches KFM at the specified location, where you may view, move, copy, or delete files (depending, of course, on the permissions associated with the files). If you hold the **Shift** key while clicking on **Open Folder**, a kvt terminal opens at the specified location—no need to change directories.

There's /Root, and Then There's /root

One of the few anomalies in KDE—calling it a mistake would probably not be too strong—is the use of the word *root* in association with directories. The top-level directory of a Linux system, what users are accustomed to calling the root directory, is generally signified in the Linux world as /. That's all—just a single forward slash. It's not really called anything, except maybe the top-level directory. From a command prompt, you would change it by typing **cd /** and pressing Enter.

In KDE's tree views, both in KFM and in KDN, this top-level directory is called /Root. No big deal, except that the root user—the superuser—has a home directory. It is called /root. This can be confusing, especially to new users coming from the DOSrivative world, where filenames aren't case-sensitive.

It also explains why there's a /root directory under the /Root directory, and why, if you are logged in as root, you can open KFM or KDM and see a directory called /Root, which is /, and a directory called Home (or worse, My Home) that is actually /root.

This is KDE, so it must be configurable. In KDN, you do the configuration through the **Options** button at the bottom of the KDN menu. Clicking on it produces a dialog box like the one in Figure 4.18.

FIGURE 4.18
KDN's Options dialog box lets you change the appearance and behavior of KDN.

The only complicated part of this dialog box is found behind the **Edit Personal** and **Edit Shared** buttons. (By the way, you cannot edit the Shared section unless you are logged in as root.) To add an item to one of these KDN sections—say a file or directory in which you frequently work—click on the appropriate Edit button. A KFM window opens. Click on **File > New > Internet Address (URL)**. (I know, it doesn't make any sense to me either, but it works, even if it isn't exactly intuitive.) This is illustrated in Figure 4.19.

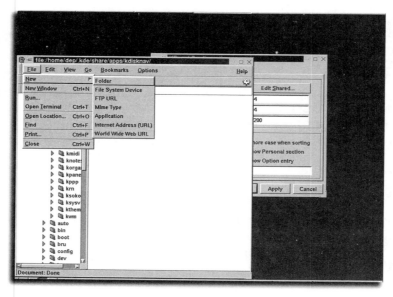

FIGURE 4.19
Choose **Internet Address (URL)** to add an item to KDN.

When you do this, a dialog box appears, as shown in Figure 4.20.

FIGURE 4.20
This is where you name the new item on your KDN menu.

Delete the letters *URL* and replace them with the name you want to give your KDN menu item. In the example we're going to use here, we will create a menu item for the directory containing the manuscript of this book. I'll call it—why not?—*KDEBOOK*, as you can see in Figure 4.21.

FIGURE 4.21
The new entry, KDEBOOK, is entered where URL used to be.

Then click **OK**. Another dialog box appears, as shown in Figure 4.22.

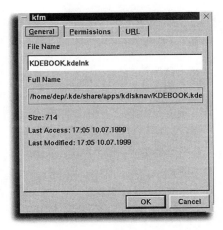

FIGURE 4.22
You now need to make changes in the soon-to-be-familiar KFM Properties dialog box.

Now you click on the **URL** tab, changing nothing in the first two tabs. The sparse URL page is shown in Figure 4.23, but it won't be sparse for long.

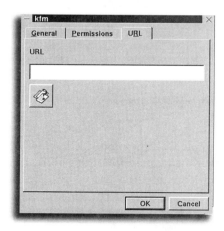

FIGURE 4.23
Here you specify what file or directory you want your new KDN entry to open.

You need to tell KDN what you're talking about and what icon to use. In the URL box, type `file:` followed by the full pathname to the program or directory you want to be able to open from KDN. In this example, it's `file:/home/dep/kdebook/mss/`—no spaces (see Figure 4.24).

FIGURE 4.24
Type **file:** followed by the full pathname. No spaces allowed.

Then, to select an icon for your new KDN menu item, click on the icon with the question mark atop it, just below the URL window. Suddenly another window appears, containing all the available icons. Because this is a folder and I want to open it, I've selected an open folder icon (see Figure 4.25).

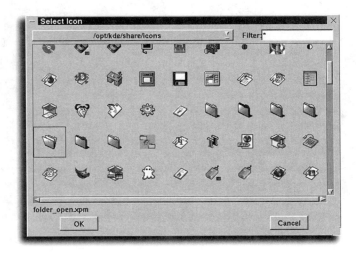

FIGURE 4.25
Clicking on the icon beneath the URL box reveals scads (a non-technical term) of available icons. Select one by clicking on it, and click **OK**.

After you've selected your icon, click **OK**. You are returned to the KFM dialog box. Click **OK** there, too. Close KFM. If you want to add other items, repeat the process. If you want to make other KDN changes (the possibilities are described below) make them, and then click on **OK**. Your new item is now on the KDN menu, as witnessed in Figure 4.26.

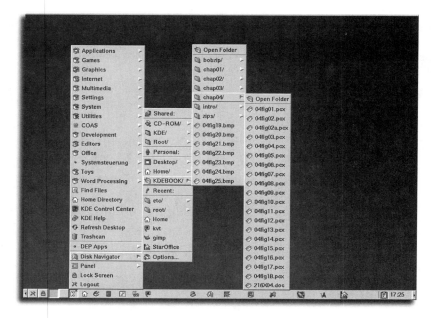

FIGURE 4.26
The new KDN item, in all its subdirectoried glory!

You might have thought by now that I'd forgotten the rest of the items in KDN Options. I haven't. Let's take another look at that Options dialog box, shown in Figure 4.27.

FIGURE 4.27
Now we'll look at KDN's other options.

The things you can change are

- **Max recent folder entries** lists by default the four folders you've most recently opened. Change the number if you like, but keep it within reason or KDN can become impractical. (In which case, please petition the publisher and maybe you can arrange for us to whip together a book called *Impractical KDE!*)

- **Max recent file entries** lists the documents or applications you've most recently opened. Again, the default is four and again, you can change it.

- **Max files in a single folder** sets the threshold for an error message to the effect that there are too many files in the folder to get to it through KDN. Why is such a setting necessary? Because some directories would take forever to load— /dev comes to mind. You might not want to wait. If you don't mind, change this value to a higher number.

- **Show dot files** toggles the display of hidden files, which in Linux are hidden by giving them a dot as their first character.

- **Ignore case when sorting** lets files and directories appear in alphabetical order, irrespective of the case of the first letter in the item's name. Otherwise, the items whose names begin with capital letters appear first, in alphabetical order, followed by the ones whose initial letters are in lowercase. Linux is highly case-sensitive, so the convenience achieved by employing this option may be over-shadowed, because every other Linux application behaves differently. Consistency, in this case, isn't foolish.

- **Show Shared section** (try to say *that* three times quickly!) toggles the display of the Shared section in your KDN menu.

- **Show Personal section** toggles the display of the Personal section of your KDN menu.

- **Show Recent section** toggles the display of the Recent section of your KDN menu. This is useful if you don't want anyone else to be able to determine what you've been doing. When it is off, the little database of recently used programs and files isn't updated, so turning it back on starts with a clean slate, so to speak.

- **Show Option entry** toggles the Option item at the bottom of the KDN menu, which is how you got to this dialog box. If you "unpress" this button (or uncheck this box, if you're using the Windows 95 widget emulation), how are you supposed to be able to make changes? Easy. Right-clicking the **K Panel** anywhere that there isn't an icon produces a small menu, the first item of which is Configure. This produces a dialog box, the last tabbed page of which is the KDN Options page.

- **Terminal application** lets you specify which terminal program starts when you hold the **Shift** key and click on the **Open Folder** item at the top of a KDN directory listing. The default is kvt, though you could choose konsole, xterm, or Aterm, to name a few.

SEE ALSO

➤ *kvt and konsole are KDE applications and are detailed in Chapter 10. The others are non-KDE applications, so to learn about them, you need to consult the documentation that comes with them.*

When you are all done, click **OK** to save the changes you've made. It's a good idea to log out of KDE and then back in to make sure all the changes have been enacted.

For those who are old Linux hands and who feel better editing a text file to configure an application, you can do this with KDN. The file you need to open is ~/.kde/share/config/kpanelrc. Go to the section that begins [kdisknav].

What's this ~/ Thing?

If you're new to Linux, you've probably encountered pathnames that begin with ~/ and you've probably wondered what in the world that is, though these may not have been the exact words you used. What it means is the current user's home directory. You can use it at a command prompt to specify the directory. For instance, if I wanted to copy a file to my home directory, I could type

```
cp afilesomeplace.txt /home/dep/
```

Or, I could type

```
cp afilesomeplace.txt ~/
```

The result would be the same either way.

This section looks like this:

```
[kdisknav]
MaxNavigableFolderEntries=200
MaxRecentFoldersEntries=4
ShowDotFiles=on
RecentFiles=/usr/opt/kde/share/applnk/Home.kdelnk,/usr/opt/kde/share/
  applnk/Utilities/kvt.kdelnk,/usr/opt/kde/share/applnk/Graphics/
  gimp.kdelnk,/home/dep/.kde/share/applnk/StarOffice.kdelnk,
RecentFolders=//etc,//root,
MaxRecentFilesEntries=4
Terminal=kvt
IgnoreCase=off
```

As you can see, you can change just about anything here except the addition and deletion of items. It's probably a bad idea to try to edit the Recent entries themselves, though you can certainly change the configuration number of the ones kept and shown. You can add some further configuration items here, although KDN is in a period of change and this varies from version to version. It would be best for you to consult the documentation with your version (click the **Help** button in the Options dialog box) to learn what you can and can't do with the version you have.

Careful with that Text Editor!

A lot of configuration files contain lines that seem to go on forever. Depending on your choice of text editor, these may be wrapped for easy display. Depending on how your text editor does this, though, it can end up breaking the file and keeping the application from running because some editors don't just wrap the line for display purposes; they actually insert a carriage return. The application does not expect this and chokes. Therefore, it's important that you make certain your editor of choice doesn't do this. If in doubt, turn off word wrap entirely. You'll need to use the scrollbar to get to the ends of some lines, but your edits won't ruin the file.

part

II

CUSTOMIZING THE K DESKTOP

Making the K Desktop Your Own

The default KDE desktop is certainly attractive and exciting when you start it for the first time. For many Linux users, it is the long-awaited answer to many, many prayers. Nevertheless, we computer users don't waste much time before having thoughts that begin, "I sure wish I could…"

Well, with KDE, chances are you can. This chapter begins a section that tells you how. First, the easy stuff. In the first part of this chapter, we will be using a KDE configuration program called *kcmdisplay*, though we'll never type its name and its name will never actually appear onscreen. (If you want, though, you *can* start it at a terminal window command prompt by typing `kcmdisplay` and pressing **Enter**. Of course, because you need the X Window System to be running for kcmdisplay to work, you can't run it from the console. And again, you never need to type its name in order to get its full utility, as you shall see.)

Spicing Up the Background

Neutral blue is nice, but it isn't everyone's favorite. The talented KDE programmers realized this—in due course you'll begin to wonder if there's anything they *didn't* realize—and allowed for a multitude of wonderful effects and images. The default desktop, Figure 5.1, works.

The quick and easy way to bend the background to your will is to find a place on the desktop not occupied by an application and click the right mouse button. Among the choices is **Display properties**. Click it and you get an elaborate dialog box, as shown in Figure 5.2.

Before we begin changing things, let's amble around this first tab, labeled **Background**. In the upper-left corner is a section called Desktop. We now discover that each of the virtual desktops available under KDE can have its own discrete background, independent of all the others. If you find One, Two, Three, and Four (indeed, up to Eight) a little ordinary, you can rename the desktops to whatever you would like to call them by clicking on the **Rename** button and typing in your new choice. Remember that these names will appear on your K Panel. Labeling one "Games" and another "Boss Key" probably wouldn't be a very good idea for a machine at work. In any case, select the desktop that you want to modify here; in this example we'll use One.

FIGURE 5.1
The default KDE desktop is meant to be improved upon. Moreover, it cries to be improved!

To the right of Desktop is an image of a little monitor where you can preview your choices in a general fashion. Complex textures or bitmaps don't always display perfectly in so small an image, but there's a way—we'll get to it—to preview those as well.

Beneath Desktop is the Colors section, where you may choose a solid color or any of several variations on two colors for your desktop background.

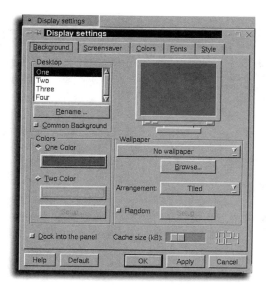

FIGURE 5.2
You can customize much in your KDE desktop with the Display Settings dialog box.

Low Memory? Keep it Simple

Your display choices consume varying amounts of memory and in some low-resource systems can actually reduce system performance. Anything more than the choice of one color requires that a copy of the entire desktop be kept in memory, and for high-resolution systems at high color depths, this can be considerable. If you make elaborate desktops for each of your virtual screens, each of these is kept in memory, too. If you have 128 or 256MB of RAM, go ahead and knock yourself out, unless you plan on running lots of big programs at once. Otherwise, it's something to keep in mind. If you discover that your system slows down after you've created your desktop masterpiece, it might be good to set your sights a little bit lower, literally.

To its right is the Wallpaper selection section. Here you can select from a wide array of wallpaper images that came with your KDE distribution or from images (in .jpg or .xpm format) that you supply yourself. (If you want to provide your own, copy them into your /kde/share/wallpapers directory.) We will be returning to this section later in this chapter and spending some time here.

At the bottom right is a button that allows you to **<u>D</u>ock into the Panel**. If you choose this, the Display settings dialog box minimizes itself into K Panel when you close it.

Finally, a slider determines the amount of memory that will be set aside to cache your desktop. The range is from 128 to 5,120KB. The more complicated your desktop—lots of colors, big bitmaps—the more memory you want to employ in this way. Experimentation is the best way to determine the best desktop performance without taking away memory needed for applications.

Across the bottom are buttons that will become familiar to you as you configure KDE:

- **Help** is pretty self-explanatory: It opens the KDE help system to the topic of the current dialog box.

- **Default** returns you to the system defaults for the items covered by the current dialog box. It's great for fixing something you've inadvertently broken.

- **OK** applies the changes you've made and closes the dialog box.

- **Apply** applies the changes you've made but doesn't close the dialog box, which is useful for full-scale previews.

- **Cancel** undoes any changes you've made since you opened the dialog box.

Setting Background Color Effects

Selecting a single-color background is simplicity itself: Click the **<u>O</u>ne Color** button and, if the color you desire isn't displayed in the color bar beneath that button, click it. You are transported to the color palette, where you can pick the color you want or create a custom color. (If you select a custom color, click one of the blank color boxes to select a location for your new color before saving the color.) Click **OK**, and then on **Apply** to see if you still like it. If you do, click **OK**, and you're done.

For a two-color background, click—you guessed it!—the **<u>T</u>wo Color** button. Now you select not just the first color but the second as well, with the preview window in the little monitor showing what you have so far, as shown in Figure 5.3.

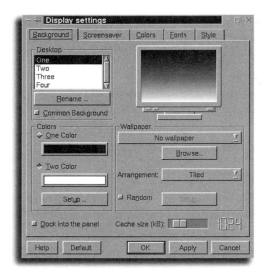

FIGURE 5.3
Click the **Two Color** button to select colors for several interesting effects.

The default effect is a blending of the two colors from top to bottom. If you'd like to try something else, click the **Setup** button, which renders the dialog box shown in Figure 5.4.

FIGURE 5.4
Click the **Setup** button to explore two-color effects.

As you can see, in addition to the default you have several other possibilities. **Blend colors from right to left** does just that (see Figure 5.5). You'll notice that there are no options to blend colors from left to right or bottom to top. To achieve these effects, simply reverse the colors you have chosen in the color selection bars.

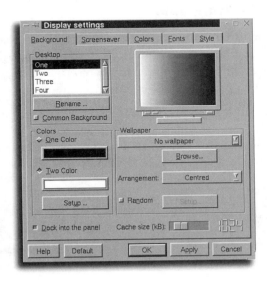

FIGURE 5.5
After selecting a color blend, it is displayed on the preview "monitor."

Other effects are possible, in the form of patterns achieved by clicking the **Use pattern** button and selecting from the **Pattern name** box. A small preview window shows how this will look, as you can see in Figure 5.6.

FIGURE 5.6
When you select a pattern, a little preview box shows what you have wrought.

When it all looks the way you like, click **OK** twice. You've produced a two-color effect, which experimentation will demonstrate can be extremely elegant or really garish and awful. It's all up to you.

Bitmap Backgrounds: Wallpaper

Colors are nice, and certainly they are efficient, but rare is the computer user who doesn't sometimes want to make the image on the monitor a little, well, *different*. The easiest way to do this is through the use of bitmapped graphics, either displayed as images or tiled for a pattern or texture effect.

Dozens and dozens of these are included in the KDE distribution, and you can add your own as well, by copying your graphics files in .xpm or .jpg format into the /share/wallpapers directory of your KDE directory. You can then see them by clicking on the **Wallpapers** drop box in Display settings, as shown in Figure 5.7.

Your Own Private Desktop Bitmap

If you don't want your desktop bitmap to be available to everyone, you may click the <u>B</u>rowse button and go to the place in your ~/ directory, or elsewhere, where the graphic file is kept.

When using bitmapped backgrounds, it's a very good idea to click **Apply** to get a sense of the actual screen effect. The preview window is simply too small to give an accurate picture of the resulting desktop. You can always try something else if you don't like the applied desktop.

Many of the supplied bitmaps are texture effects, but there are other possibilities. For example, I've cleaned up a little bitmapped copy of my company logo, so that it will merge with itself seamlessly. It makes a decent background, as shown in Figure 5.8. But that picture shows, too, an error I made.

I kept a two-color setup, even though I am using a tiled bitmap. This means I'm keeping an image in memory, the two-color screen, that I'll never see. It is simply throwing away memory. If you use a tiled bitmap, make sure you select **<u>O</u>ne Color**. It's an easy mistake to make, and one not easily noticed. But it will cause your Linux system to begin to swap to disk that much sooner, and using the swapfile slows the system considerably.

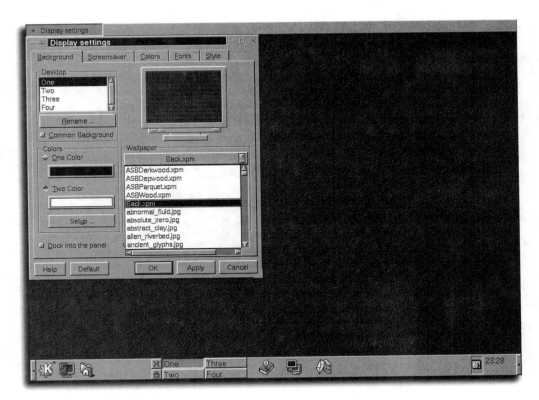

FIGURE 5.7

The Wallpaper drop box lists scores of included background bitmaps, plus any you have added yourself. In some cases, the preview screen shows more of a tiled effect than does the actual background when applied. As a result, some previews that look terrible make gorgeous desktops. If in doubt, apply it and judge its appearance on the desktop.

Of course, you can do things with bitmaps other than tile them. A big image that doesn't fill the screen, if tiled, would look terrible. The KDE designers, of course, provided for this, as you will see if you click the **Arrangement** drop box (see Figure 5.9).

You can have a high old time for yourself, trying out the different effects. Again, use of the **Apply** button is helpful here. If you scale a tiny bitmap to the full screen, for instance, the effect may not be the same as that in the preview window, and you may well decide to try something else.

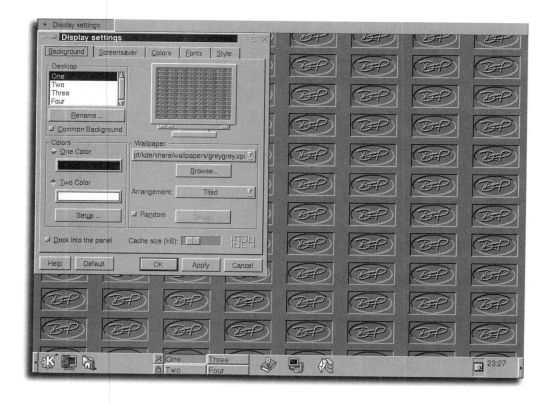

FIGURE 5.8
There's a resource-wasting mistake in this picture. Can you pick it out?

The use of a two-color background here isn't necessarily needlessly wasteful. It does use more resources, but with some of the wallpaper arrangements, at least you'll be able to see where you've spent that memory. Figure 5.10 shows an example.

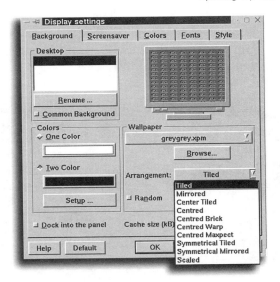

FIGURE 5.9
The **Arrangement** drop box offers numerous choices for manipulating bitmap backgrounds.

FIGURE 5.10
A combination of two-color background and centered bitmap can create a pleasing effect, albeit at a cost in memory.

Here I've chosen a two-color—black-to-white—background, and a scanned color photograph of one of my wife's horses. The effect is that of a picture frame. I clicked **OK** and got the desktop shown in Figure 5.11.

FIGURE 5.11
The finished desktop, with centered bitmap and top-to-bottom blended colors. Not bad, eh?

As you can see, the possible combinations are not quite infinite, but certainly extensive. It's easy to get carried away or to spend hours trying out different arrangements.

If You Can't Make Up Your Mind

Programmers use the term *feature creep* to describe a phenomenon perhaps unique to them. It applies to any feature added to a program not in response to some actual need, but simply because the programmer has figured out how to do it. KDE is full-featured but not excessively featured. Still, if there is anyplace that it comes close to feature creep, it's with the **Random wallpaper** feature. This rotates among the bitmaps in a list, changing the background at predetermined intervals. In my experience, KDE users set this up, use it for a little while, mostly to see if it works, comment upon it, and turn it off, never to be started again. It can be startling to be in the middle of something, perhaps with several applications open in windows, and have the background change suddenly, with no further prompting from you, every few minutes.

If you want to try it out, which you probably do, here's how.

Click the **Random** button. Then click the **Setup** button, which will have become active—no longer grayed out—when you chose random mode. This opens a dialog box like the one in Figure 5.12.

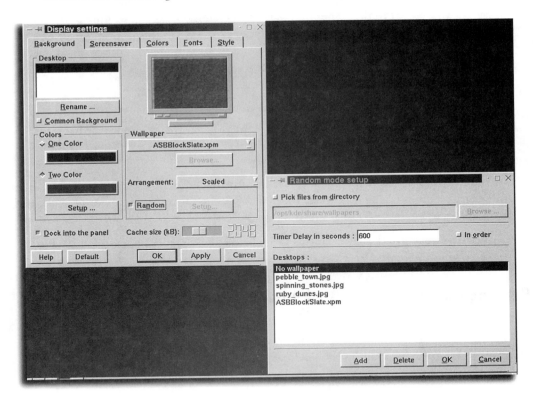

FIGURE 5.12
The Random Setup dialog box lets you choose the bitmap wallpapers that are displayed and how frequently they are changed.

At the top of this dialog box is a check box labeled **Pick files from <u>d</u>irectory**. If you choose this, the desktop rotates among all the files in the specified directory. If you choose this option, it's a good idea to preview all the files in the directory to make sure none look really terrible. You could also create a directory in which you put the background wallpaper you want to use in this way, then use the **<u>B</u>rowse** button to navigate to it. If you are old-fashioned, you could just type in the pathname of the directory containing the bitmaps you want to use.

You could also create and use a list of wallpapers that the random background program will use. To do this, uncheck the **Pick files from <u>d</u>irectory** setting. The Desktops list now becomes ungrayed. Three bitmaps are already listed, topped by **No wallpaper**. To add a bitmap, highlight the **No wallpaper** listing and click **<u>A</u>dd**. Then, returning to the still-open Display settings dialog box, choose a bitmap. When you return to the Random mode setup dialog box, the new bitmap has been added, replacing the second instance of No wallpaper. Do this over and over until your list contains all that you want it to contain. You can delete entries, of course, by highlighting them and clicking on **<u>D</u>elete**.

There are two additional settings: Timer Delay in seconds and In <u>o</u>rder. The former is a text box into which you can enter the frequency with which your desktop changes. The default is 600 seconds, or once every 10 minutes. The latter, if checked, causes the backgrounds to rotate through the list in the order listed, rather than at random.

When you've set all this up to your satisfaction, click **OK**. When returning to the Display settings dialog box, make sure you click the **<u>D</u>ock into the panel** check box, or the random desktop program won't work.

And if you are wondering what this little doodad is doing in a book called *Practical KDE*, you are right: There's nothing practical about it.

Running Applications as Backgrounds: Cool Stuff

This isn't (yet) practical either, but I like it. Several applications exist chiefly to provide backgrounds that, unlike colors or bitmaps or even bitmap switchers, actually *do* something. Right now, the things they do are limited: an animated fish tank, a program that tried to make your screen look like a fireplace as it consumes much of your processor's power, an animated globe that if properly configured shows those in windowless offices whether it is dark outside. This is an area where more and more development is likely to occur, perhaps to the point of producing something useful. In the meantime, it can produce a cool effect.

Of these programs, only one has been optimized for KDE. It is XGlobe, Thorsten Scheuermann's excellent port of the venerable XEarth program, developed by Kirk Lauritz Johnson. It is downloaded and compiled—perhaps you can find a compiled binary, but it builds so easily it's hardly worth much of a search—and then run. If you give it the `-kde` command line option, it becomes the background for all virtual screens without using any more memory. If you are running it, you can kill the kbgndwm task, which is redundant if XGlobe is running. This will save a little dab of memory. Because there are frequent updates to Xglobe, whose interactions with KDE vary, be sure to check the documentation that comes with the version you are using.

SEE ALSO

➤ *See Chapter 12, "Managing Linux System Functions with KDE," if you don't know how to kill a process in KDE, page 271.*

If a live application background is what you want, it is set up as a program, not as a background. Begin by going to the Display settings dialog box and turning off two-color and wallpaper settings. You don't need them, and they will just consume memory. Click **OK** to close the dialog box; you're done with it. Then start the program that you would have as a background to make sure it works on your system. Open and close a few programs. Switch virtual desktops. If all is well, no little "artifacts" left on your screen from the programs, or in your programs from the screen, you can create a .kdelink for it and copy it into your Autostart folder. Then it starts every time you start KDE.

SEE ALSO

➤ *To learn about .kdelinks, see Chapter 9, "Working with Themes," page 211.*

To get a sense of how a live background might look, here's XGlobe (see Figure 5.13) running on a highly customized desktop from which all icons have been removed and in which both the taskbar and K Panel have been set to hide themselves (all of which we'll learn how to do later in this chapter). This desktop is set to update itself every 20 minutes.

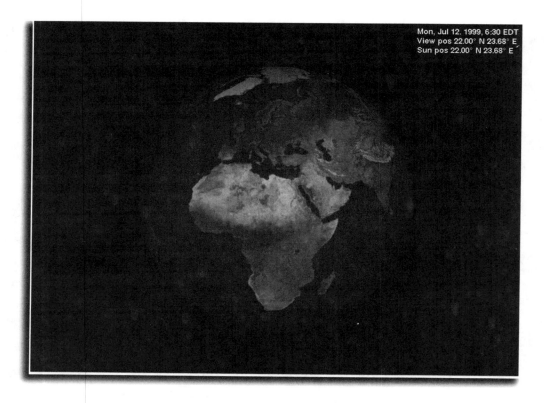

Mon, Jul 12, 1999, 6:30 EDT
View pos 22.00° N 23.68° E
Sun pos 22.00° N 23.68° E

FIGURE 5.13
XGlobe running on a KDE desktop in which everything else has been hidden. It's all there for you to use, you just don't see it.

Selecting a Screensaver

Screensavers came into wide use in the old days of single-color text-mode terminals, where over time the phosphors in the cathode-ray tube would be altered by the constant display of characters in the same places. Though modern monitors are said to be much less vulnerable to this kind of damage, screensavers have become a standard part of almost every operating system and user interface, and in this Linux and KDE are no exceptions.

The Console Screensaver

If you are using a console-based login, you can conduct an experiment: Don't start KDE. You'll see that in a few minutes your Linux screen automatically blanks. The Linux screensaver isn't invoked when the X Window System is running, so Linux GUIs have to provide their own screensavers if the screen is to be blanked or some other screen life-extending program is to be used.

You can invoke KDE's screensavers through the **Screensaver** tab of the Display settings dialog box (see Figure 5.14).

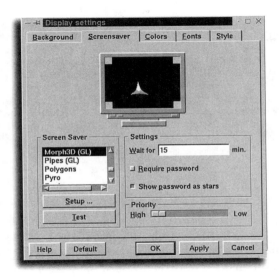

FIGURE 5.14
Use the **Screensaver** tab to configure your KDE screensaver.

At the top of the **Screensaver** tab there is a preview "monitor," but if you look closely, you'll find a difference between this preview and others we have seen: this version contains little gray boxes in the corners. If you click one of these boxes, a little menu appears with three settings:

- Ignore
- Save Screen
- Lock Screen

This menu allows you to set what happens if the mouse pointer is rested in the corresponding corner for five seconds or more. If you choose **Ignore**, nothing happens. If **Save Screen** is selected, the screensaver is invoked. If **Lock Screen** is picked, the screensaver starts, but you won't be able to return to your desktop without entering your password.

SEE ALSO

➤ *About the password function, see the sidebar, "Locked Out!" in Chapter 4, on page 63.*

The section at the lower left of the **Screensaver** tab is where you make your choice of screensaver module, where you decide how it will look.

Standard or OpenGL?

If you have the Mesa GL libraries installed and have compiled OpenGL support into your QT libraries or if the precompiled ones you installed have this support, you will see several screensaver modules that use this standard in the list. If you don't have this support, the 3D screensavers won't have been built when you compiled KDE. Depending on the type and speed of your processor and the type and speed of your video card, these three-dimensional screensavers can be striking or slow and silly-looking. The ones that use the OpenGL support are listed among the others, but their names are followed by **(GL)**. It is possible to install precompiled KDE atop QT libraries that don't support OpenGL; in this case, the GL screensavers appear, but they won't be good for much. Actually, unless you have really fast hardware, they're not good for much anyway.

The only one whose name gives you any sense at all of its appearance is **No screensaver**, which simply blanks the screen after the specified amount of time. The others have names, but any connection between the names and their actions is sheer coincidence. You can click one after another, looking at the preview "monitor" to narrow down the list of those that interest you. Most of the screensavers are configurable, which means that you can greatly alter their appearance by clicking the **Setup** button. The contents of the Setup dialog box vary depending on the screensaver being configured. For instance, the Banner screensaver moves a word, phrase, or slogan of your choice across the screen. **Setup** is where you choose the size, typeface, color, and contents of the message. If you are a programmer, you might be darkly amused by the Black Screen of Death screensaver, which emulates many mortifying system crashes. It merely runs the preview "monitor" through the various horrifying messages that it presents.

NEW
VERSION 1.1.2 Users of the newest version of KDE may be delighted by the Matrix screensaver, which has become very popular among those who regularly download and build developmental versions of KDE.

When you've pretty well settled on a screensaver and configuration, you can click the **Test** button to try it out. (Actually, you can do this for any screensaver module at any time in the process, but it's a good idea to do this before finalizing your decision because some of the screensavers, notably the OpenGL ones, are likely to be somewhat different in speed and appearance than they are in the preview "monitor.") Then you move the mouse or press any key to come back to the **Screensaver** tab.

The Settings section is where you determine the general behavior of your screensaver irrespective of which one you've chosen. In the **Wait for ___ min.** text box, you enter the time, in minutes, that your keyboard and mouse are to remain inactive before the screensaver kicks in.

Beneath the text box where the threshold time is set are two check boxes. The first is **Require** password. This turns the screensaver, even when invoked by timeout, into a screen lock, and you can't get back to your desktop and applications without entering your password. The second, **Show password** as stars, determines what is echoed to the screen when you enter your password. If it isn't selected, nothing is echoed at all, which means that if you lose track of where you are in your password, you might get an error and have to start all over again.

Finally, the Priority section determines where the screensaver falls in the application's pecking order. The default is High, which is fine if you don't typically have much going on when your mouse and keyboard are untouched for a period of time. If, however, you regularly do complicated and lengthy calculations or compile programs in terminal windows, these processes could slow down if the screensaver comes on while they are underway. (In my opinion, which isn't by any means universally held, you might as well leave the X Window System entirely to compile software. It frees up system resources, and the compile goes that much faster in many cases.)

Setting or Building a Color Scheme

In the Display settings dialog box you can set the appearance of all your KDE native applications and the appearance of some aspects of other X Window System applications running under KDE. This is done on the **Colors** tab (see Figure 5.15).

At the top of the tab is a sample window that shows all the various widgets whose colors can be changed. It serves as both a preview and a guide to their names.

At the lower left is a listing of prebuilt Color Schemes that came with your KDE distribution. You can click through them and, if there's one that you like, you can click **OK** and you're done. But perhaps you want to modify one, tune it a little. Or maybe you want to build one from scratch. In that case, click the **Add** button. When you click this button, you'll be prompted to name your new scheme, as demonstrated in Figure 5.16.

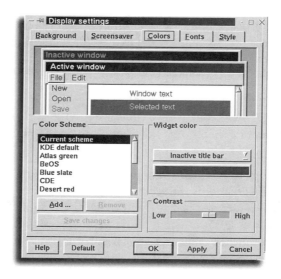

FIGURE 5.15
Click the **Colors** tab to change the display colors of your KDE widgets.

Give It a New Name

You can modify the existing color schemes under their own names. If you get unexpected results—as you very likely will when editing schemes for the first time—you can ruin the scheme with no way to restore it unless your memory is very good and you can undo what you've done, item by item.

FIGURE 5.16
The **Add** button prompts you for a name for your new color scheme.

As you can see, the currently selected scheme is the starting point for your artistic endeavors, so it makes sense to look around for the existing scheme that is closest to where you hope to end up. You can now begin to recolor your widgets. (That's what it is, though I'd hate to be the one who says, "Don't bother me right now—I'm recoloring my widgets.") This process is enabled by selecting the target widget from the drop list in the Widget color section (see Figure 5.17), and then clicking on the color bar beneath the selected screen element.

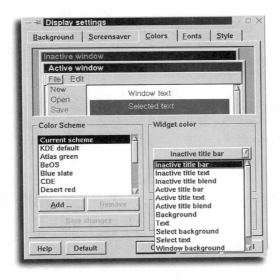

FIGURE 5.17
Use the drop box to select the screen element you want to change.

Clicking the color bar produces the **Select color** dialog box (see Figure 5.18), where you do just that. The 24 standard System Colors appear in the upper-left part of this dialog box; if you want one of those, just click it and then click **OK**. If your tastes are more exotic, you can go to the color palette at upper right and click a spot, whereupon that color will appear in the little box below the palette. If you like, you can hold down a mouse button as you zoom around the palette, watching the changes in the preview box until you get the hue and shade you like. If you are a graphic designer and know the numeric values for the color you want, you can type them right in to the text boxes. This is also something useful in a business where multiple machines are to be configured consistently.

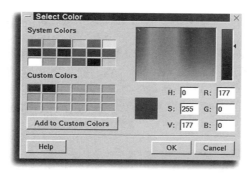

FIGURE 5.18
The Select Color dialog box is used in KDE when a color selection needs to be made.

Don't overlook the vertical bar next to the palette. It determines the brightness of your selected color. You can click anywhere on it or use the mouse to slide the pointer up and down until the color is just right.

After having gone to all this trouble, there's a good chance you might want to employ your hard-won color, or a variation on it, elsewhere. To do this, you can save it as one of the 24 possible Custom Colors. First, click a blank space in the Custom Colors section, which starts out with 24 blank rectangles. (If they're all full, pick one you're not excited about anymore, because it will be overwritten by the new color.) If you don't do this, then the color will go into the first rectangle, erasing whatever is currently there. Once you've selected the proper rectangle, click **Add to Custom Colors**. Then click **OK**, and you'll be taken back to the **Colors** tab, where you can see how the change looks. Repeat this for each widget you want to recolor.

> **Don't Go Hogwild!**
>
> Try to be a little restrained when setting widget colors. If you set the Background to black or white, you'll end up with a desktop that is all but unusable. If you pick loud, garish colors, you'll end each day with a headache (though I know someone, otherwise sane, who uses purples and greens exclusively, together on the same big screen). Remember: you have to live with it!

When you've made all your changes, click **Apply**, and if you still like what you've done, click **OK**.

You Can Change Your Desktop Fonts, Too

In addition to the colors on your desktop and the background, you have a choice of typefaces and font sizes for the items and labels that are part of your KDE desktop. Bring this about by clicking on the **Fonts** tab in the Display Settings dialog box, resulting in the dialog box in Figure 5.19.

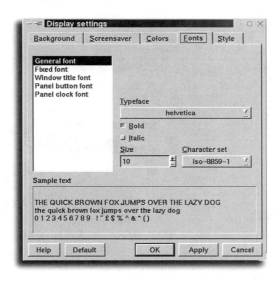

FIGURE 5.19
The **Fonts** tab lets you change your onscreen typefaces.

The Difference Between Fonts and Typefaces

With the coming of the computer age, the word *font* has come to be greatly misused, employed when the word *typeface* is meant. The name of the kind of type is the *typeface*; that typeface in a particular size is a *font*. Helvetica and Times are typefaces. Helvetica 12pt. is a font. The KDE **Fonts** tab is one of the few places in computing where the distinction is properly made.

Changing the typeface and size for a particular screen element is as simple as can be: First, select the screen element you want to alter. Then click the **Typeface** drop box (see Figure 5.20).

115

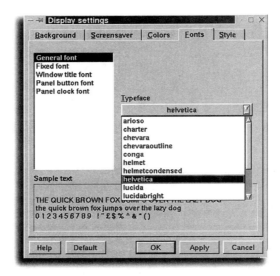

FIGURE 5.20
To pick a new typeface, click the **Typeface** drop box.

Your selection will be previewed in the Sample text window at the bottom of the dialog box. To select **Bold** style, **Italic**, or both, click the appropriate check box. Repeat to suit your heart's desire.

Though it isn't of use to most users, especially the ones in the United States writing exclusively in English, you may select a different **Character set**. The available character sets vary depending on the typeface chosen. To change the **Character set**, click the drop box (see Figure 5.21).

You should take note of some important considerations and caveats when changing the display of characters on your desktop. First, it's probably wise to make note of the changes that you've made and what the original values are. Some changes that seem like a good idea later cause problems when a particular application chokes on them, or when there isn't enough room to display the selected font at full height. Additionally, not all typefaces have a full set of screen fonts, so a change in size may not be reflected in a change in the sample text display. Finally, you may need to restart KDE to see all your changes take effect. If you forget to do this, no real harm is done, but you might be very surprised the next time you start KDE.

You can always undo all your changes by clicking the **Default** button, even after you've saved them.

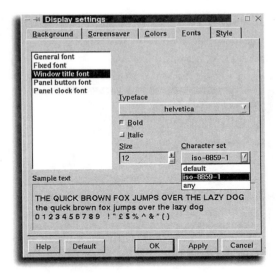

FIGURE 5.21
Change the **Character set** employed on your desktop by clicking the drop box. Not all typefaces support multiple character sets.

Setting System Styles

I covered the final tab of the Display settings dialog box, **Style**, in Chapter 2, "Starting KDE," but we'll look at it again here. As you can see in Figure 5.22, it offers but three choices, though they are wide-ranging in their effects.

- **Draw widgets in the style of Windows 95** doesn't change the behavior of anything, but it does change the look. The most obvious place is in check boxes themselves. If this box is selected, check boxes get little check marks in them when chosen; if it isn't, they adopt a Motif-style button look, and when chosen look as if they were pressed.

- **Menubar on the top of the screen in the style of Mac OS** removes the menubar from the top of the applications you are running and places the menubar of the active application—the one that currently has focus—at the top of the screen.

- **Apply fonts and colors to non-KDE apps** may or may not apply fonts and colors to non-KDE apps because some non-KDE apps don't go along with the program. In some other cases, checking this box can reduce the functionality of non-KDE applications. And how well it works can depend on what choices you have made on the **Fonts** tab. In short, it can be a little flaky. Unless you're adventurous, it's probably best to leave it unchecked. If you do check it, you'll need to restart KDE to get the full effect.

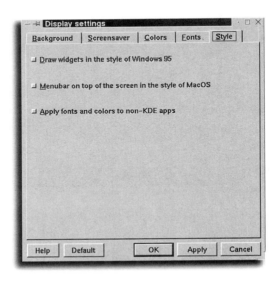

FIGURE 5.22
The **Style** dialog box sets look-and-feel elements for all of KDE and in some cases outside it.

Careful with that Default Button!

Clicking the **Default** button in any of the five Display Settings screens sets all five of them to the defaults, which include Windows 95 styles and Applying colors and styles to non-KDE applications. So you want to reset the defaults only if you've horribly broken something and want to start from scratch.

A World of Other Settings: KDE Control Center

We have heretofore been using the Display settings dialog box, which we've gotten at by right-clicking the desktop and choosing **Display properties** from the resulting menu. There is another way to gain access to it and many, many other KDE system settings. It is the KDE Control Center, which is placed by default on your K Panel and is also available on the K Menu. As you will see, it contains many of the things we've already covered, a lot of new stuff, and some stuff that doesn't seem to belong there at all. Its mild-mannered opening screen is what we see in Figure 5.23.

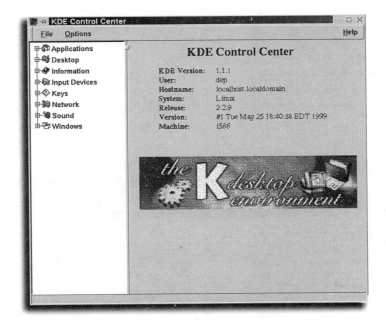

FIGURE 5.23
The KDE Control Center is the locus for vast configuration possibilities. Fortunately, the defaults are fine for most things.

The Control Center can be a little confusing. No matter how little or how great your experience with computers, with Linux, or indeed with KDE, some things are in the Control Center that you *know* are there and remember seeing, but when you look for them, they cannot be found. Some things are not where you would guess they belong. With luck, and your exploring abilities, this part of the chapter will lead you to your objective.

The opening screen tells you a little about the versions of KDE and Linux that you are running:

- The version of KDE
- The user who is logged into the current session
- The name of the host computer
- The operating system that is running (KDE works for many versions of UNIX, not just Linux, and there has even been talk of a port to OS/2, though I've seen no evidence of development work in that direction.)
- The release number of the operating system
- The date and time that the kernel was compiled
- The type of machine for which it was compiled

119

A tree view on the left shows the broad areas in which the Control Center holds sway. Separating the two frames is a movable bar. You can adjust how the window is divided by clicking and dragging it by the small box at the top of the line separating the two parts. You can open any of the broad categories to behold the goodies within by clicking on the small box containing the plus sign at the category's left, or by double-clicking on the category's name. Doing so doesn't open any of the revealed choices. To do that you must click the name of the item you want to inspect or, perhaps, alter.

Figure 5.24 demonstrates this, as is the fact that pretty much everything in the Control Center can be reached through means other than the Control Center.

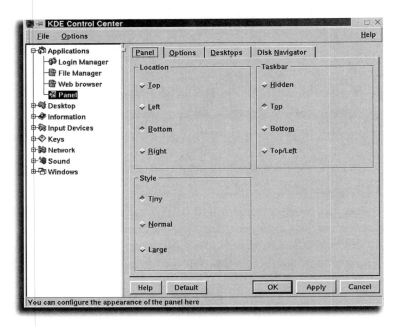

FIGURE 5.24
The Control Center isn't the only way to get to configuration options. Of the items listed under Applications, configuring the Login Manager was discussed in Chapter 3, the File Manager will be configured in Chapter 10, the Web Browser in Chapter 24, and part of Panel configuration—the Disk Navigator—was handled in Chapter 4, all without resort to the Control Center. But here it's all in one place.

The way you set up K Panel on your machine has a great deal to do with how useful you find it. When it's tuned to the way you work, it's indispensable, and when it's not, you'll find it in the way. The first tab of the Control Center options, **Panel**, lets you choose the locations of its two main elements, K Panel itself and the taskbar, as well as the size of K Panel. A **Tiny** K Panel reduces its height, and therefore the screen space it takes, by half, and doubles the icons you can fit on it. You are already familiar with the **Normal** size because it is the default. The **Large** size is probably useful only in special circumstances.

About the Screenshots

The screenshots in this section are from my working machine, which has a 17-inch monitor running at a resolution of 1024×768. I mention this because the selections I've made are shown in these pictures and are the ones I find most useful for a screen of this size at this resolution. My opinion isn't unanimously held, though it should be; feel free to experiment and see that I'm right!

Options, the second tab of the Panel configuration, is shown in Figure 5.25.

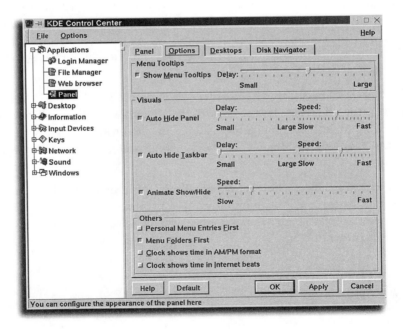

FIGURE 5.25
The **Options** tab, perhaps more than any other single page of settings, determines how convenient K Panel, and therefore in large measure KDE itself, will be.

Menu Tooltips, located at the top, is where you decide whether you want the little yellow bubble help items to appear over K Panel icons and K Menu entries and, if you do, how long you want your mouse pointer to rest atop the icon or menu entry before they pop up. If you want them, click the **Show Menu Tooltips** check box and drag the slider with your mouse to specify the delay.

Next is **Visuals**. Only experience can convince you how very important these settings are. The first of these settings is **Auto Hide Panel**. It is highly recommended. The panel disappears except for a line of a pixel or two except when your mouse pointer is at the edge of the screen where the K Panel resides, whereupon it appears. The **Delay** and **Speed** sliders let you select how long it sticks around before disappearing again, and how quickly it does so (or pops back into view when revisited) respectively.

Auto Hide Taskbar and its sliders do for the taskbar what the corresponding settings did for the K Panel. Again, I highly recommend this. You will bump into both it and the K Panel from time to time as you control other applications, but if you set them to disappear quickly, it's really no bother, and you recover a useful quantity of screen in the bargain.

Animate Show/Hide is a totally cosmetic setting. If it is enabled, the Auto Hidden screen elements seem to slide from their hiding places; otherwise, they just appear, poof. The slider controls how long this slithering from the deep takes to accomplish. It's annoying if set too long, at least for Tiny and Normal K Panels, the only available sizes of the taskbar.

The final section is **Others**. The first two items have to do with K Menu behavior, whereas the other two have to do with the appearance of the clock that shows up at the right end of the K Panel. We will deal in detail with the first two in Chapter 6, "Customizing the K Menu." The clock settings will give us quite enough to handle just now.

The first of the clock choices is **Clock shows time in AM/PM** format. If you don't check it, the clock will be in military (24-hour) time, and 1:00 p.m. will be 13:00. You will think that I am making up the second choice, but I'm not. It's **Clock shows time in Internet beats**, which is to say clock ceases to show time at all.

A Solution in Search of a Problem

It seems that the Swatch company, maker of popular and trendy wristwatches chiefly of plastic, dreamt up the idea of dividing the day into 1,000 equal parts, with the day starting at midnight at Swatch headquarters in Switzerland. If you select this item, you will never again have to wonder how many thousandths of a day it has been since it was midnight in Switzerland. (I told you you'd think I was making this up.) Perhaps the idea was to sell Swatches to those who are interested in knowing, instead, what time it is, now that their computers won't tell them anymore. What the Internet has to do with it is anyone's guess. We can only imagine that later versions of KDE will include as clock options the rate of increase of the national debt or running totals of how many sandwiches have been sold by leading hamburger vendors.

Not only does Swatch propose to replace something that has worked without the slightest complaint for more than 500 years (namely, the measurement of time), the company also decides to render hours, minutes, and seconds obsolete. Why not just divide the earth into thousandths? You'd need to do that, because for navigational purposes there is a connection between hours, minutes, seconds, and longitude. And, of course, they'd have to relocate the sun, which is exactly one minute of arc. To enlarge it to be one Internet beat would require it to be almost 1.5 times its current size. Swatch has arrived at a marketing effort that would kill all life on the planet!

For the Swatch company's weird explanation of how they hope to do for time what Esperanto did for language, and details of a wristwatch that shows Internet beat time (a good choice for the soon-to-be-unemployed-due-to-habitual-tardiness) see www.swatch.com.

Enough Internet beats spent on that foolishness. Next tab.

The **Desktops** tab, shown in Figure 5.26, deals with the virtual desktops, the functions of which we've explored in earlier chapters. The slider labeled **Visible** lets you select the number of virtual desktops. The range is from two to eight that appear on the K Panel. The **Width** slider lets you decide how much Panel space they'll take. This is irrespective of the width required for fully displaying the names, if any, you give them in the text boxes corresponding to each virtual desktop in the top part of the tab. To put it another way, if you set the width too short, the names are truncated to fit that width. On a Normal-sized K Panel, the virtual desktops are tiered two-high, whereas on a Tiny panel they're in a row, single-file.

Eight Virtual Desktops Not Enough?

If for some reason—I can't imagine what it would be—you find a need to have more than eight virtual desktops, you can configure KDE to allow as many as 32 of them! In a text editor, open ~/.kde/share/apps/config/kwmrc and scroll to the line that begins NumberOfDesktops=. Following the equals sign, put in the number of desktops you want, up to a maximum of 32. Save and close the file, and then close and restart KDE. Now you have all the desktops you could possibly want.

The **Disk Navigator** tab (see Figure 5.27) will be familiar to those who read Chapter 4, "An Introduction to the K Desktop." It appears here as a reminder that if you disabled the **Show Option Entry in Disk Navigator**, you can get to it on the **Disk Navigator** tab.

CHAPTER 5 Making the K Desktop Your Own

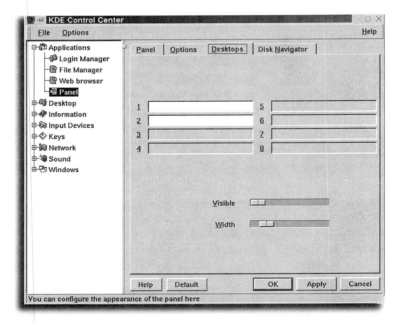

FIGURE 5.26
You can specify the number, names, and K Panel width of the virtual desktop buttons on the **Desktops** tab.

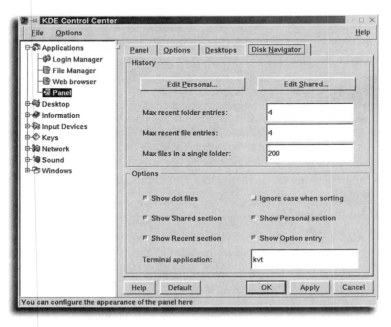

FIGURE 5.27
You can configure the **Disk Navigator** from the Control Center as well as the **Options** entry on the KDN itself.

The next general section in the KDE Control Center is **Desktop**. In that we devoted the first half of this chapter to many of these items, albeit launched in a different way, we will look at only the items that aren't duplicated in the **Display settings** dialog box. The first of these is **Borders**, which is shown in Figure 5.28.

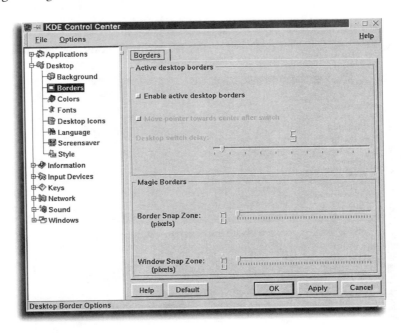

FIGURE 5.28
The **Borders** tab determines what happens when the mouse pointer or an application gets near the edge of the screen.

The first section, Active desktop borders, lets you decide whether resting your mouse pointer against the edge of the screen will cause a jump to the next virtual desktop at that edge, and if so, how long the pointer must sit there before the change takes place and what happens immediately afterward.

To enable this kind of screen navigation, click the check box next to Enable active desktop borders. If you choose not to do this, you can still navigate among your virtual desktops by using the buttons on K Panel. If you do check this box, the next two settings become available for configuration. The first is Move pointer towards center after switch. This prevents the mouse from accidentally resting against a border when you walk away from your desk, switching to the next desktop, where it would still be resting against the edge, and switching that one, too, after a little while, in the fashion of a traffic light. The slider, Desktop switch delay, lets you choose how long the mouse pointer is at the screen's edge before the jump to a new virtual desktop takes place. The units are in seconds.

125

The bottom half of the **Borders** tab is Magic Borders. If you set a value for the **Border snap zone**, anytime you drag a window to within the specified number of pixels of the screen's edge, it is sucked over to be flush with the edge. Similarly, if you set a value for **Window snap zone**, anytime you drag a window to within the specified number of pixels of another window, it is sucked over to be flush with the edge of that window.

The next Desktop item not explored earlier is **Desktop Icons**, shown in Figure 5.29.

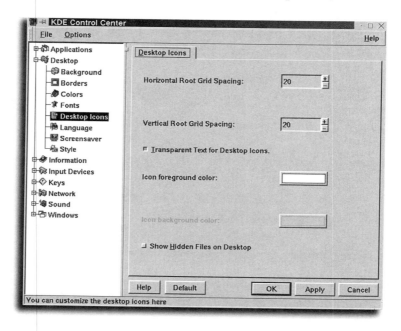

FIGURE 5.29
The spacing and appearance of icons you keep on the Desktop are set in the **Desktop Icons** tab.

The Horizontal and Vertical Root Grid Spacing values specify a virtual grid to which desktop icons snap. This can produce a neat, organized appearance. The **Transparent Text for Desktop Icons** check box determines whether the text that identifies those apparently not-so-intuitive icons appears on a background that is the same color as the screen itself. If you check it, the icon text appears to be directly on the desktop background. If you don't check it, you can specify a uniform background for icon labels in the Icon background color color bar below. The Icon foreground color color bar allows you to select the color of icon label text. By fiddling with these controls, you can make the icon text entirely invisible if you want.

Getting Rid of Desktop Icons

Some people, and I'm among them, would just as soon have a desktop uncluttered by icons, completely free of them. You can do this in KDE, though it isn't documented. For most systems, all you have to do is open your ~/.kde/share/config/kfmrc file in a text editor such as Kedit. (Note that this is a file in the hidden .kde subdirectory in your home directory.)

Find a section that begins with `[Paths]`. It will say something like this:

```
[Paths]
Trash=/home/yourhome/Desktop/Trash/
Desktop=/home/yourhome/Desktop
Templates=/home/yourhome/Desktop/Templates/
Autostart=/home/yourhome/Desktop/Autostart/
```

Remove the `/Desktop` from the `Trash`, `Templates`, and `Autostart` lines, and those icons will no longer automatically appear on your desktop. If there are other icons listed in this section in this way, do the same thing. *Do not change the line that begins* **Desktop**=!

You will now have to delete the icons from your desktop manually, but when you restart KDE they won't come back. They will be generated in your home directory instead, where you can use them if you need them but now off the desktop.

If you compiled KDE from source code, you may need to add these lines to ~/.kde/share/config/kfmrc by hand, because they may not be created automatically.

KDE and its included programs offer menus, help files, and other onscreen text in an amazingly large selection of languages. The **Locale** tab, which is brought to the foreground by clicking the Language listing in the Control Center (see Figure 5.30), is where you determine the language in which KDE will speak to you.

Actually, KDE will speak to you in more than one language if you want. Developed in large measure in Europe where people are typically multilingual, KDE allows, indeed requires, you to set three languages (though all three can be the same language if you like). This way, if a program isn't translated into your first choice, the second is sought; if there's no luck there, KDE looks for documentation in your third choice. You use the list boxes on the **Locale** tab to make your first, second, and third choices.

The Wrong Charset Error

Versions of KDE before 1.1.1 (and even after, in some circumstances) suffer from a little bug wherein every time you exit KDE, or open a virtual terminal, the alarming `Wrong charset! Wrong charset!` message appears on your screen.

If you suffer from this problem, you should know two things. The first is that the message (and whatever caused it to appear, which is still a matter of some debate) can cause no harm and can be safely ignored. The second is that setting all three languages on the Locale tab to the same language usually makes it go away.

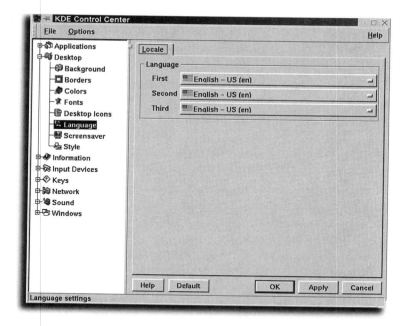

FIGURE 5.30
Choose one, two, or three languages for KDE's menus, icons, and help files on the **Locale** tab.

We've already spent a lot of time on the Screensaver and Style dialog boxes, and there is nothing new in the Control Center iteration of those things, so we'll not discuss them here. The next broad category is Information, and we won't discuss that here, either, beyond wondering what it is doing in the Control Center. It is a comprehensive and useful listing of useful system information, but you can't change or configure any of it.

SEE ALSO
➤ *This information is all available on K Menu's Information submenu under the Settings menu, and I discuss it in Chapter 21, "Sending Email with Kmail," page 443.*

This brings us to Input Devices, the first of which is International Keyboard (see Figure 5.31).

The International Keyboard tab configures a program called KiKbd, which allows you to switch among the different behaviors of various national keyboards. If you use just one keyboard mapping all the time, you can safely ignore this entire keyboard section because you'll probably never use any of the things it does.

To begin, click the **Add** key, which renders a truly vast listing of national keyboards from which you can make a choice. The top keyboard in your list is the default; you can use the **Up** and **Down** buttons to change the order of your list. If you add a keyboard by mistake, use the **Delete** button to make it go away.

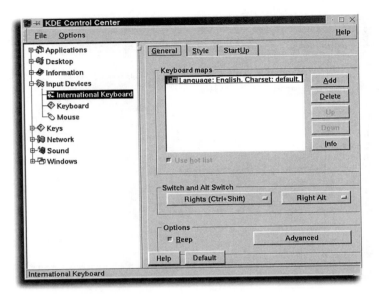

FIGURE 5.31
Yes, keyboards have nationalities, too, and the International Keyboard tab lets you set the one(s) you want to use.

The Switch and Alt Switch settings let you determine what key combination cycles you to the next keyboard on the list. If the **Use hot list** box is checked, this key combination produces a menu of the keyboards on your list. The **Beep** check box causes a system beep to take place when you change keyboards.

Advanced settings will make sense to you if you're accustomed to switching languages, character sets, alphabets, and keyboards, and it will all be the Greek charset to you if you're not. Choosing it produces a dialog box where you can emulate CapsLock within KDE to relieve a problem with the hardware CapsLock in some languages. You can set the switch keys so that, if held for an extended period of time, they will produce the entire world keyboard menu. You can also decide whether changing keyboards applies to the entire desktop, just the current window, or a certain class of windows—which is to say, specific applications. If you choose the last, you may also check a box that will keep the class settings from session to session.

The **International Keyboard Style** tab, shown in Figure 5.32, lets you choose colors for the menus and keys associated with KiKbd. Click the color bar and pick the color you want. You can also change the typeface and size of the characters appearing in KiKbd.

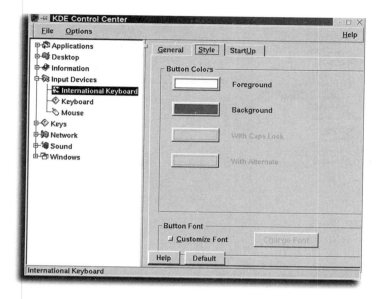

FIGURE 5.32
The **Style** tab uses familiar color bars and lists to let you change the appearance of KiKbd.

Finally, there is the **International Keyboard's Start Up** tab, shown in Figure 5.33.

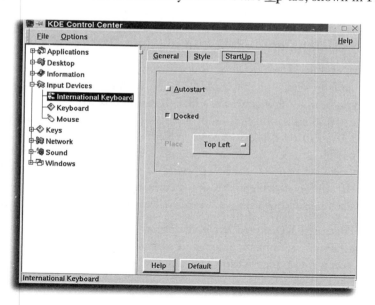

FIGURE 5.33
To start KiKbd automatically, either docked into K Panel or in your choice of screen corners, state your preferences here.

The **Start Up** tab allows you to **Autostart** KiKbd whenever you start KDE. If you want it to dock automatically into the K Panel, choose the **Docked** check box. Otherwise, click the **Place** list box to select the screen corner in which it will make its appearance.

The next input device is **Keyboard**, shown in Figure 5.34.

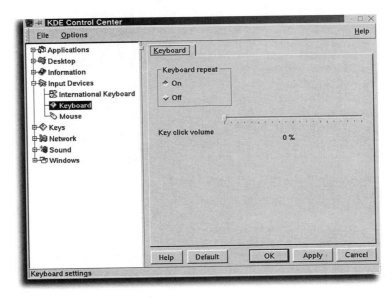

FIGURE 5.34
The **Keyboard** tab is as straightforward as the International Keyboard settings are obscure! Also, the settings might not work.

The **Keyboard** tab offers two settings, and in both cases there's the possibility that your choices won't work. The first, Keyboard repeat, won't work unless you enabled it when you set up XFree86. (Don't worry, you almost certainly did.) Here you can turn it off, and a key, if pressed for a long time, will not fill your screen with the character it represents. The second is Key click volume. For those who miss the days of clacking typewriters, this setting can bring that nostalgic little touch of noise and chaos to the workplace. When this is set, every time you hit a key a click is emitted from your computer speaker. At least, that's the idea. I've never been able to get it to work and don't know anyone else who has. Not that it's something on which one would typically spend a lot of time. If there has to be a nonfunctioning feature, this one is as good as any (with the possible exception of Swatch Internet beat time).

The last of the input devices is **Mouse** (see Figure 5.35). Its settings all work, as long as you have a mouse or other pointing device. If you don't, you can forget KDE because current versions to not allow navigation by keyboard alone even though hotkey combinations are spattered sporadically about the KDE screen.

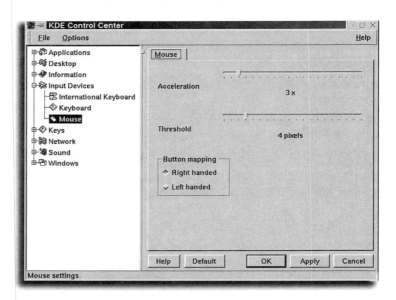

FIGURE 5.35
The **Mouse** tab can make your pointing device much more efficient and easier to use.

How quickly your mouse pointer zooms around the screen is determined by the Acceleration slider. Its behavior is fairly standard: Moving the pointer a short distance at high speed sends it farther than moving it a longer distance at low speed. Working hand-in-mousepad with Acceleration is Threshold, which determines how far the mouse must be moved before Acceleration kicks in. This way, you can edit that bitmap graphic pixel-by-pixel without accidentally sending your mouse pointer into the next ZIP code.

Finally, there is Button mapping. This reverses the functions of the buttons on your pointing device, in case you want to use your left hand for mouse manipulation.

We move next to a section that you will use all the time, or at least sometimes. It is the Keys section (see Figure 5.36).

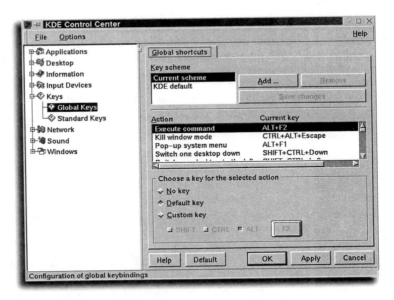

FIGURE 5.36
Key bindings are all changeable in KDE.

The Global Keys tab, labeled **Global** shortcuts on the tab itself, is where keys are bound to actions. It looks a lot more complicated than it is, and it is unlikely that you'll change anything here anyway. What you *will* want to do, though, is learn what the key bindings are. (However, the **Global shortcuts** page is a quick reference when you are at your computer: Just scroll through the list. You'll find some surprises. For instance, did you know that **Alt+F1** produces the K Menu, anytime, anyplace? I didn't until just now. Try it.) Still, there are some things you should know about this page.

First, you'll notice that you can choose a **Key** scheme in much the same way that you would choose a Color scheme. You can also create schemes based on these, or you can start from scratch. (A reason to do this would be if you regularly use programs that have key bindings that conflict with the KDE ones. You could create a custom scheme that changes the KDE hotkeys or turns them off, so that your application would work as expected.) Now, there are two key schemes provided. You cannot change them and you cannot delete them. You *can* make changes and apply them, but they work only during the current session and are gone when you next start KDE. So if you want to make and save changes, you will need to click the **Add** button, where you will be prompted to name your new set of key bindings, which will be based on the scheme highlighted at the time you click **Add**.

One example: Some of WordPerfect's bindings conflict with those from KDE. You could create a Key scheme called "WordPerfect," in which you change the conflicted bindings to something else. You could then switch to it when you plan on using WordPerfect.

To make changes in your new Key scheme, use the controls in the **Choose a key for the selected action** section in the lower half of the screen. Your choices are the following:

- **No key**, which disables the key binding for the selected action
- **Default key**, which adopts the choice made in the scheme on which your new one is based
- **Custom key**, in which you make the choices by clicking on the combination key and regular key of your choice

The **Global Keys** tab deals with generally systemwide bindings, things that are used, for instance, by the KDE Window Manager. To standardize key bindings among KDE applications (or at least many of them), you must move down one category to Standard Keys (see Figure 5.37).

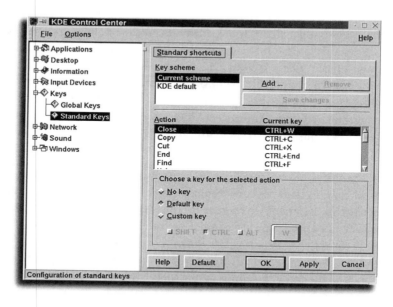

FIGURE 5.37
Standard Keys is to KDE applications as Global Keys is to the KDE desktop. It binds key combinations to actions within KDE's applications.

The **Standard Keys** tab, labeled **Standard shortcuts**, works in exactly the same way as the Global Keys tab. The sole difference is in the actions that are bound. As you scroll through the list, you'll see that these are all things that take place within applications themselves: text manipulation, cursor movement, that sort of thing. Again, you can set up your own scheme if you like, and again you cannot change the two provided schemes, but you can use them as the basis for your customized, renamed ones.

The next major Control Center Category is Network, and it currently contains but a single item, the three-tab Talk configuration.

SEE ALSO

➤ *I fully explain talk configuration in Chapter 15, "Multimedia: Music and Movies," so we won't get into it here beyond noting that this is a route to its options.*

We go therefore, to Sound, where there are two items, the first of which is **Bell**, shown in Figure 5.38.

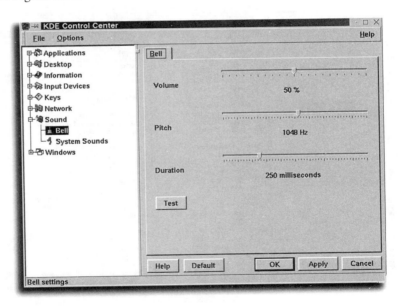

FIGURE 5.38
By careful manipulation of the controls, you can make your KDE system beep, which is certain to get your attention.

The **Bell** is actually the beep that is the only useful sound that little speaker in your computer is capable of making, which it usually does when something has gone wrong. It should, therefore, get your attention, and the KDE settings allow you to make sure that it does. A combination of volume, duration, and frequency can be arrived at that will threaten crystal wine glasses and resonate with the fillings in your teeth. Or you can opt for something a little less painful.

There are three settings to be made:

- **Volume**, which of course is how loud it is
- **Pitch**, which controls the frequency (though it won't go into subwoofer range, nor will it cause the dog to howl)
- **Duration**, which sets the length of time in milliseconds that the sound is emitted

There is a **Test** button that lets you try out the different settings. Generally, the correct setting is the one that when tested evokes a shout of, "Stop it! You're driving me crazy with all that beeping!" from the next room.

The System Sounds tab, shown in Figure 5.39, is labeled <u>Sound</u> on its tab and is where you can assign a little .wav file to very nearly everything you do.

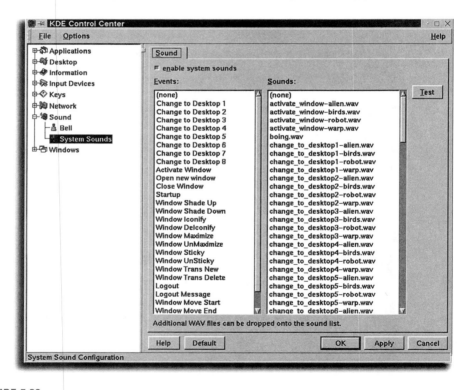

FIGURE 5.39
Madness lies here: You can assign a sound file to just about any action you take in KDE.

Too Much Noise

I was recently in a large office that had hundreds of computers, all with sound cards and speakers, and all with system sounds turned on. The place sounded like a cuckoo-clock factory, and I wondered how they ever got anything done there. After a little while, I learned the answer: They didn't. The point, quite seriously, is that if you assign sounds to everything that happens on your screen, and if you work in an office, don't be surprised if one day after work the person who sits next to you tries to run over you as you walk to your car.

And if you work alone, you'll probably attach a system sound to everything on the desktop at first, but then cut back to just a few things. A constant stream of little jingles and sound effects coming from your speakers is, let's face it, annoying. It's even more so if you work quickly so that you're three actions ahead of the sounds. When you take your hands off the keyboard you are treated to several seconds of what sounds like band practice during an earthquake.

Years ago I had a little .wav file of Darth Vader saying, "You have failed me for the last time," that I assigned to the trashcan. It was very funny...the first time.

System sounds can be fun, but they require the exercise of considerable courtesy. The person at the next desk might be a very skillful driver.

System Sounds differ from the **Bell** in that they require a sound card and speakers to be installed and properly configured or you won't hear them. They also require that the little check box, **enable system sounds**, be checked. You'd be surprised at how many people fail to do this and then wonder why the sounds don't work.

In the section that takes up much of the tab, you assign sounds to actions. It looks as if this has already been done for you, doesn't it? Well, it hasn't. For every action you want to bless with musical accompaniment, you must first select the action in the first column, labeled **Events**, and then select a noise from the second column, labeled **Sounds**. The Test button lets you try out the result. It's a good idea to configure this when no one else is around.

If you have other .wav files you'd like to use, you can drag them from a KFM window to the **Sounds** column, whence they can be assigned to **Events**. (I very much liked the startup and shutdown sounds that came with my copy of OS/2 Warp, so I brought them over and used them in the same places in KDE. They're the only sounds I have enabled, and they're elegant.) For some reason, not all .wav files will work here, though I've never seen an explanation as to why this is. There is apparently more than just one .wav format.

The last general Control Center category, Windows, allows the tuning of a great many desktop attributes. It begins with the **Advanced** tab, shown in Figure 5.40.

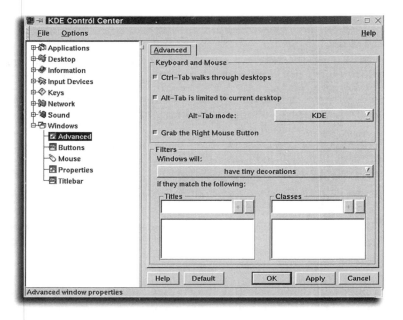

FIGURE 5.40
The **Advanced** tab does a little bit of several different things, from controlling hot key behavior to setting window behavior for certain applications.

There is probably nothing that you'll want to change here until you have become an advanced user. With the defaults, use of the **Ctrl+Tab** key combination cycles you through the virtual desktops, whereas **Alt+Tab** cycles you through running applications, including those on other desktops unless the **Alt+Tab is limited to the current desktop** button is selected. The Filters section allows you to select applications and X classes and assign special properties to them. This involves things that are far, far beyond the scope of this book.

The **Buttons** tab, shown in Figure 5.41, lets you assign buttons to the titlebars of all applications running under KDE. You can decide whether a particular button is to appear at the left end of the titlebar, the right end, or not at all. There can be a maximum of three buttons at each end, so if you assign more than that, the ones chosen first will be replaced by the ones chosen later. The buttons higher in the list appear closer to the center of the titlebar.

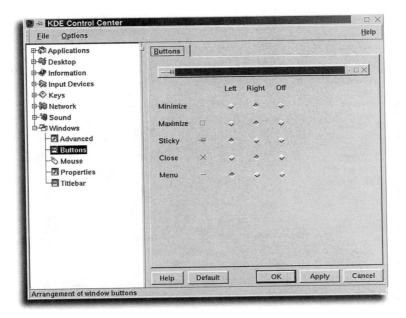

FIGURE 5.41
The **Buttons** tab. The **Menu** button appearance is often different, it being replaced by a miniature icon of the particular application. But clicking on it will get you a menu anyway.

Mouse is a tab that roars, as you can see in Figure 5.42.

It isn't as complicated as it looks. It lets you choose what actions you want to bind to
the buttons on your pointing device, and to those buttons when used with combination keys. Each possibility offers a list box of possibilities from which you can
choose. You are likely to decide that the default is fine, which, absent a compelling
reason to change it, it is. If you do make changes, be sure that you don't eliminate
some essential function. Remember: The Default button is your friend. And if you
have managed to disable your mouse's ability to click it, you can use the Tab key to
navigate to it, and the Enter key to invoke it.

The next tab, called **Properties** in the Control Center list and **O**ptions on its own
tab, controls policies, as you can see in Figure 5.43.

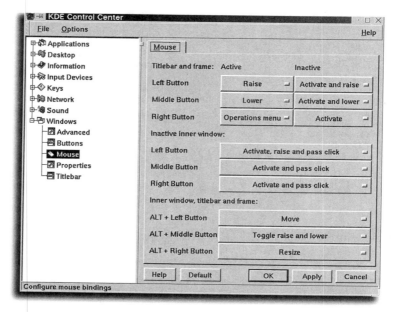

FIGURE 5.42
Looks daunting, doesn't it? Actually, the **Mouse** tab does for the mouse what the **Key Bindings** tab does for hotkeys—that's all.

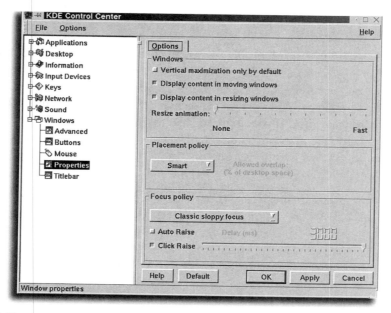

FIGURE 5.43
The window management **Options** tab determines what happens when you move a window or move the mouse pointer over a window.

The first section, **Windows**, sets attributes for application window resizing. If you select the first check box, **Vertical maximization only by default**, when you click the **Maximize** box (wherever you put it in the **Buttons** dialog box, but typically the second button from the right in the titlebar) the window expands to full height but its width remains unchanged. This is just the thing for programmers who like to see as many lines of code as possible or for writers who like to see a whole tab at a time.

The second button, **Display content in moving windows**, keeps the contents of a window instact when you grab it by its titlebar and drag it to a different part of the screen. This of course involves numerous screen repaints and can gobble so much processor capacity that other running applications (or other users on the system, if there are some) can be brought to their knees. It's a high price to pay in efficiency for a little transitory aesthetic pleasure. If this is unchecked, a wire frame lets you know where the window will be, and when you release the mouse button the new window is painted.

The third button, **Display content in resizing windows**, has the same effect and the same shortcomings as does the display of content when a window is moved; in addition, it looks kind of goofy. But it does have a purpose: You can see if you are reducing the size of the window in a way that hides something important, where you might miss it if you don't notice that the window has now sprouted scrollbars. If this is unchecked, a wire frame lets you set the dimensions of the new window, and when you release the mouse button the resized window is painted.

The **Resize animation** slider builds on the weaknesses of the Display contents buttons, allowing them to consume even more of the processor in animating the resizings, particularly maximizations and restorations (returning a window to its non-maximized state by clicking the **Maximize** button in an already maximized window). If the system is heavily loaded, this animation can take place in weird spasms.

The **Placement Policy** section determines where and how applications will open on your screen from among five choices, selected by a drop box:

- **Smart** begins by putting the first application you open in the upper-left corner of your screen, or as close to it as it can without conflicting with other screen elements (taskbar or K Panel; it pays no attention to icons). A second application is placed with minimum overlap. And so on.

- **Cascade** does its best to keep the titlebars of all running applications visible. Its best isn't all that good.

- **Interactive** placement does what it can to keep windows from overlapping by more than the amount specified in the **Allowed overlap spin** button, which becomes ungrayed when this choice is made. If it can't, it puts the window down wherever you click the mouse.

- **Random** placement simply plops the new window down any old place.

- **Manual** placement creates a window that moves around as you move your pointing device and continues to do so until you click one of the mouse buttons. It then drops to the desktop, right there.

So far, we've been dealing with the placement of windows. Now we'll look at what happens when the mouse pointer passes over windows, as determined by the **Focus Policy**, which offers four choices in its drop box:

- **Click to focus** gives a window focus (makes it active, makes it editable, and changes the appearance of the titlebar) when you click inside the window itself.

  This is a tall order if most of the window, all but say that X in the upper-right corner, is obscured by other windows. In this case you can resort to the taskbar or to **Alt+Tab** to cycle through applications until you get to the one you want. A problem can occur if a dialog box or error box from the application has appeared and is now hidden behind it. In this case, the application won't take any input, and you can spend a while scratching your head trying to figure out why. Fortunately, error boxes and dialog boxes that conform to KDE standards all appear on the taskbar, so you can use it to unbury the wayward error message, click **OK**, and be on your way.

- **Focus follows mouse** can be amusing because it can give focus to a window without raising it. If you accidentally jiggle the mouse so that it is now in another window, you can blithely type along, entering text into the wrong application, for quite awhile. Fortunately, there is a way around this, which we'll get to in a minute.

- **Classic focus follows mouse** introduces the possibility of there being no window that has focus, if the mouse pointer is on an unused portion of the desktop. Otherwise, the window that has the mouse pointer has the focus.

- **Classic sloppy focus** leaves the focus in the last focused window until a new window is entered, whereupon it gains focus.

Two buttons are available in this section that can make some of the focus policies a lot more practical. The first is **Auto Raise**, which brings the focused window to the top (though it still doesn't solve the problem of hidden dialog boxes or error messages that require your intervention before you can proceed). Associated with it is a slider that sets a delay before the focused application pops to the top. If you have a very steady hand, you won't need a delay, but when reaching for a scrollbar you occasionally overshoot, it's best to give yourself some time here to get back to where you want to be. The other button is **Click Raise**. This allows you to bring a window to the top by clicking anywhere in it; normally, you have to click the titlebar to raise it. **Click Raise** does nothing new if you have **Click to focus** set as your policy.

The final stop on our tour of the KDE Control Center is the tab entitled **Titlebar**, as shown in Figure 5.44.

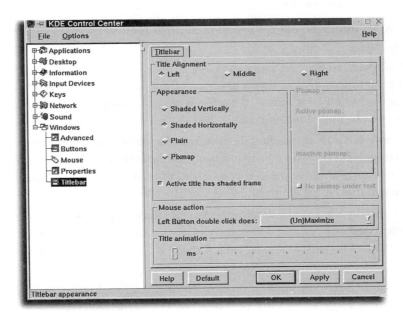

FIGURE 5.44
You may wonder why the **Titlebar** tab isn't part of the Desktop section. Me, too.

This tab is just plain fun. The **Title Alignment** buttons let you determine whether the title in the titlebars of your applications will be at the left of the titlebar, in its center, or flush right.

The **Appearance** section lets you do cool things with the titlebar, such as establish a color gradient from top to bottom or from one side to the other. You can elect to give the active titlebar a three-dimensional effect by clicking on the **Active title has shaded frame** check box.

Some of the classiest effects can be achieved by using a bitmap background for the titlebar. If you have selected the **Pixmap** check box in **Appearance**, the controls in the Pixmap section of the tab become active. You can select bitmaps for the active and inactive phases of your titlebars here. You can also check the box that prevents the bitmap from extending under the titlebar text. For a prettier effect, it's better to go back up to <u>C</u>olors in the **Desktop** section of the Control Center and pick colors for your active and inactive titlebars that contrast with your chosen bitmaps. It's a good idea to accentuate the contrast a little less for the inactive titlebar, so you'll be able to tell them apart more easily.

The Mouse action section lets you decide from a drop list what you would like to have happen when you double-click the titlebar of an application. The choices are

- **(Un)Maximize** maximizes a windowed application and windows a maximized application.

- **(Un)Shade** rolls up an application like a window shade into its titlebar, leaving just the titlebar visible. If you have several applications with which you've done this stacked on your screen, the effect is that of a wallpaper store, with the rolls ready to be pulled out and cut.

- **Iconify** is a little misleading, because it doesn't reduce the application to an icon. Instead, it makes it disappear and banishes the lone remnant of it to the taskbar. It minimizes it, the same as if you clicked upon the little dot button in the titlebar, third from the right unless you moved it.

- **(Un)Sticky** renders the application Sticky, which is to say it now appears in all virtual desktops, or, if it was sticky already, unsticks it, leaving in whatever virtual desktop it currently occupies, even if that isn't where it started out.

- **Close** pretty well speaks for itself. With this selection, double-clicking on the titlebar of a running application closes it. If it is an application that asks for confirmation, confirmation will be sought; otherwise, it's history, same as clicking the X button in the upper-right corner.

One item remains: **Title animation**. This abomination slides the title of the program, program plus loaded file, anything that it thinks ought to be in the titlebar, back and forth across the titlebar in instances where the window is too small for the whole titlebar contents to be displayed. It is no doubt well-intentioned, but it is also very distracting. Don't believe me? Use the slider to set the speed of this animation to a non-zero value and see for yourself. Just remember that this is where you come to set the value back to 0 to turn it off. You'll be back.

That's it for the Control Center and for the greater variety of desktop customizations. You should now be well-armed to make the desktop whatever your imagination can conceive. Now we'll see what mischief we can inflict upon the K Menu.

chapter 6

Customizing the K Menu

Appfinder: Doing Most of the Work for You

Sorting It All Out with kmenuedit

Making Systemwide Changes

The icon on K Panel containing the big letter *K*, with a gear behind it (if you are using the normal or large setting) or just by itself (if you have your K Panel set to tiny) is the first step on the path to all the applications you have installed. You already know this.

For a while it's likely you'll be very happy with it. But if there is a bit of the tinkerer in you (and, in that you use Linux and KDE, there probably is), it won't be long before you notice little inconveniences that make you wish that K Menu were organized a little differently, or contained some things it doesn't, or didn't contain some things it does. There must be, you think, a way to change it around.

You're right. There is. And that is the subject of this chapter. Here we will explore the strategies for making your K Menu more useful and the means of bringing those plans to fruition.

When first you fire up KDE, chances are your K Menu will look something like the one in Figure 6.1.

FIGURE 6.1
The default K Menu is good. In this chapter, we'll make it better.

Going down the menu, you should note that stopping on any entry that ends with a little triangle pointing to the right spawns a submenu, and many of these submenus have sub-submenus, and at least in some distributions (notably in the COAS menu in Caldera Open Linux 2.2) there are sub-sub-submenus. It is all organized in a very hierarchical fashion, with applications assigned to categories that more or less reflect their functions, though there are probably a few with which you might take issue. For instance, were you to download and compile KDevelop, the wonderful IDE (integrated development environment) for KDE, you are likely after installation to look for it in the **K Menu > Development** subdirectory. And you are likely to be disappointed because it won't be there. It will have placed itself in **K Menu > Applications** instead.

SEE ALSO

➤ *I sing the praises of KDevelop in Chapter 31, "Using DOS Applications with dosemu," page 587.*

K Menu Nomenclature

There being no established way of specifying paths in K Menu, and it being overly bulky to say "**click K Menu**, click **Settings**, click **Information**, and click **Memory**," a bit of shorthand, adapted from Internet newsgroup usage, shall here be adopted as of now. The above directions will be shortened to this:

K Menu > Settings > Information > Memory.

That's simple, right? In fact, we'll use it for all menu items that lack a reason for a different kind of explanation, for instance, **Edit > Find in Page**, or **File > Open**.

To some, putting KDevelop in applications makes perfect sense, while to others it doesn't. You can put it wherever you want.

Appfinder: Doing Most of the Work for You

Depending on your Linux distribution, the version of KDE you are running, and how you installed KDE, when you install it a program called Appfinder on K Menu (and $KDEDIR/bin/kappfinder on your hard drive, where $KDEDIR is your kde directory), may or may not have automatically run. You will be able to tell by whether K Menu contains non-KDE applications that are on your system.

If it didn't run automatically, you can add applications by clicking **System >**
Appfinder while you are logged in as root or superuser (see Figure 6.2). A database
of popular Linux applications is searched and when an application is found, its
parameters—whether it is supposed to run in a terminal window, for instance—are
entered. It is then added to K Menu in a place that may or may not make sense to
you. Don't worry about the location just yet because soon we'll be moving things
around. Appfinder takes from a few seconds to a few minutes to run, depending on
the speed of your system, the size and fullness of your hard drive, and how many
applications you have installed.

If you forget to run it as root, it puts the applications it finds, annoyingly, in a submenu labeled Default. When you compile the kdebase package, kappfinder runs as
part of the compilation process.

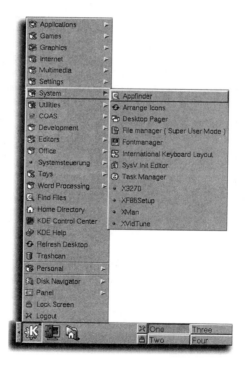

FIGURE 6.2
You can find Appfinder in the System submenu of K Menu.

If you are running an early version of KDE, say 1.0 or the 1.1.1 pre2 version that
shipped with Red Hat Linux 6.0, running Appfinder after it has already been run
could produce duplicates of applications in your menu. This isn't difficult to clean

up, but it is certainly time-consuming, so it's good to check and see whether applications such as xv (in the Graphics submenu) have already been placed in K Menu. Another way to check is to click the Personal (sometimes User) K Menu item to see what's in there. If it is well-populated, Appfinder has been run, as is the case in Figure 6.3.

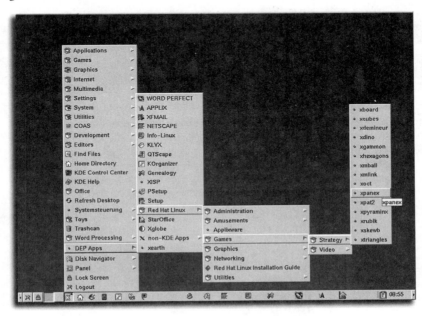

FIGURE 6.3
Appfinder is pretty thorough at finding installed applications, isn't it? This is my user directory, all sprawled out.

If you are a careful viewer, you'll notice an inconsistency in Figure 6.3. While there is a Red Hat Linux listing, there is also, in the main K Menu, a COAS listing, meaning that Caldera Open Linux must also be installed. How can this be? Simple: I have parts of both on my hard drive.

Sorting It All Out with kmenuedit

While Appfinder goes a long way toward automating the K Menu configuration process, there is no way that the good people at kde.org can possibly arrive at a set of routines that will read your mind and decide where you would like applications to be put. (It would have to be running all the time, anyway—people change their minds!) Therefore, they have done the next best thing. They have created an application called *kmenuedit* that makes the job of adding, moving, and deleting applications in K Menu a trivial task.

---

kmenuedit from the Command Prompt

For reasons unknown—to me, anyway, and to everyone I've asked about it—on some installations of KDE attempting to edit menus in the usual way, from **K Menu > Panel > Edit Menus**, produces an error saying that kmenuedit isn't installed, even though it is and in many cases the user used it just five minutes ago.

Rebooting solves the problem, but there's a less extreme measure that can be taken. Open a terminal window, kvt or konsole, type `kmenuedit`, and then press **Enter**. The program will start and run just fine.

To start kmenuedit, choose **K Menu > Panel > Edit Menus** (see Figure 6.4).

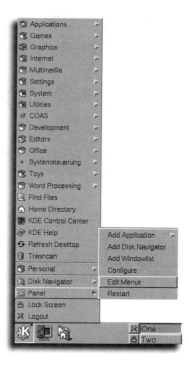

FIGURE 6.4
The path to kmenuedit is straightforward, as long as you remember that K Menu is part of K Panel.

The result will be a screen very much like the one in Figure 6.5.

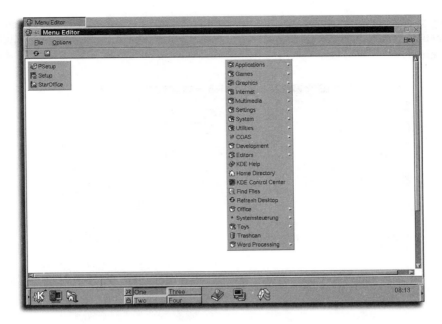

FIGURE 6.5
In kmenuedit, the personal (left) and the systemwide (right) menus are separate.

What happens next has much to do with whether you are logged in as root or as a user.

Changing Your Personal Menu

We'll begin by editing the Personal menu. Logged on in the username you customarily employ when working in KDE, open kmenuedit.

Don't Log In as root Unless You Have to

If you've made it this far in Linux, you probably know that you should log in as root only when you have some specific systemwide task to perform; otherwise, you should be a regular user. If you don't know this, well, now you do.

In this demonstration, we'll use my own KDE desktop as an example. We'll begin with a little housekeeping. When I installed Caldera Open Linux 2.2 on this machine, I kept some Red Hat Linux applications, but I moved them to other locations so the Red Hat submenu is no longer necessary. Though I could delete the whole thing at once, why not take it apart a little bit at a time and learn about kmenuedit as we go along? Figure 6.6 shows the Red Hat submenu opened down several levels.

FIGURE 6.6
To open a submenu in kmenuedit, click it; to close the submenu, click it again.

Select the item you want to modify and right-click it. (Clicking the left mouse button on it does nothing.) You should get the menu shown in Figure 6.7.

Because we'll have to do it at some point and it might as well be now, let's look at the menu items and what they do. The first, **Change**, produces the dialog box illustrated in Figure 6.8.

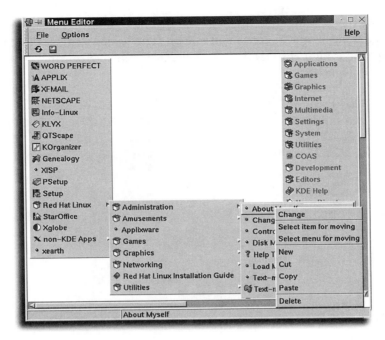

FIGURE 6.7
If you click an item and nothing happens, try again, this time using the *right* mouse button. You'll get a menu that lets you manipulate the item.

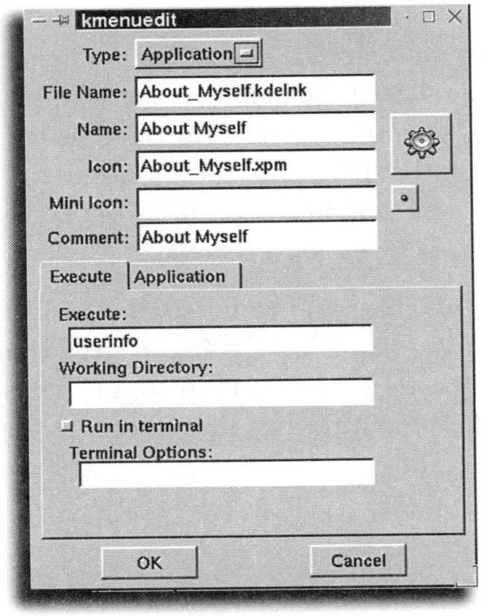

FIGURE 6.8
The Change dialog box will become very familiar to you as you manipulate K Menu items.

This is where you set up the parameters K Menu uses in executing applications, and we will have much, much more about it anon. The second item is **Select item for moving**. Choosing it changes the mouse pointer from an arrow to a large plus sign, as shown in Figure 6.9.

FIGURE 6.9
Clicking **Select item for moving** changes the mouse pointer into a plus sign until it is clicked again somewhere else. That appears to be all it does, however.

Sadly, this "feature" does nothing more, nor does the item that follows, Select menu for moving. After you've selected the item or menu, there's no facility for completing the move. Perhaps it will be implemented someday (the last item in the kmenuedit help file is "5. To do," and that page contains a lone entry, "rewrite KMenuedit"). But it doesn't matter because you don't have to do anything special to select an item or menu in order to move it, as we shall soon see.

The next RMB (right mouse button) menu item is **New**. Clicking it creates an entry in the current menu named EMPTY. It also spawns the dialog box you saw in Figure 6.8, though now, as you see in Figure 6.10, the fields are empty, literally and figuratively. Again, we'll explore this fully in the coming pages.

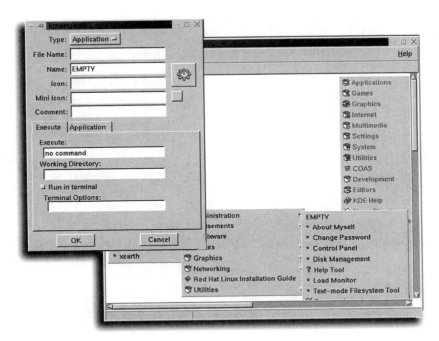

FIGURE 6.10
The New dialog box awaits information that will let you create a K Menu entry, and a menu placeholder named EMPTY.

Cut removes the current item and places it in the clipboard. In Figure 6.11 you can see that the top menu item, About Myself, has been removed.

Copy puts a copy of the item in the Clipboard, but keeps the original intact.

Paste inserts the item that has been placed in the clipboard *in front of* an item selected elsewhere (or in the original place, if you Cut by mistake), as seen with About Myself in Figure 6.12.

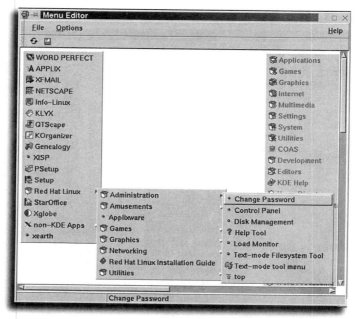

FIGURE 6.11
The top item in the menu has been Cut...

FIGURE 6.12
...and now Pasted, and thus relief from those late-night identity crises has been made two submenus closer.

The last item on the RMB menu is **Delete**, and if it is exercised on a single item the item just disappears. But if it is employed while an entire submenu is selected, it throws a confirmation box, illustrated in Figure 6.13.

FIGURE 6.13
It's easy to click an entire submenu and then delete it accidentally. This confirmation box encourages you to take a second look.

Moving Items and Menus

You can move items and menus around with the Cut and Paste commands, but why bother with all that when there's a much easier way? In kmenuedit, you can simply drag items and even whole menus from one place to another. Take a look at Figure 6.14 and see for yourself.

FIGURE 6.14
You can drag a copy of a menu item—or a whole submenu—with the mouse to a new location. In this case, it's the xeyes application, which is why it is the lone application floating in space attached to nothing.

When you release the mouse button, a Copy of the item is added to the bottom of the menu where you released the mouse button (see Figure 6.15). You can then go back and delete the original.

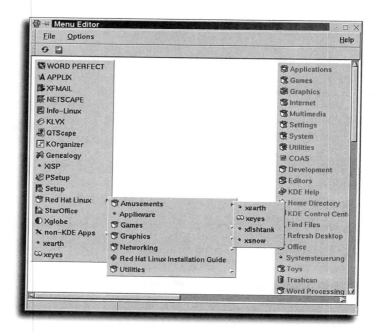

FIGURE 6.15
The dragged menu item, either a program or a submenu, will appear at the bottom of the menu where it is dropped.

As I said, all the items in the Red Hat submenu have been sent to other locations; I want to be rid of the entire submenu. I selected it, clicked the **RMB**, and clicked **Delete**, getting the expected confirmation message in Figure 6.16, and the result in Figure 6.17.

FIGURE 6.16
The Red Hat submenu has, as you've seen, a multitude of sub-submenus. If I click **OK**, it's all gone forever. Will I?

FIGURE 6.17
You betcha! And the Red Hat submenu is history.

It might be that you want to move an item from one subdirectory to another subdirectory that's not higher up in the tree. Can you have two submenus open at once in kmenuedit? (You can't in K Menu.) Take a look at Figure 6.18.

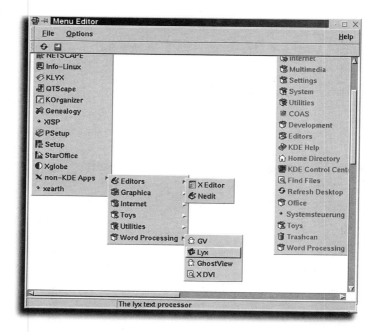

FIGURE 6.18
You can have multiple submenus at the same level open at once. Here, I'll move the Lyx document processor.

In fact, you can have any (or all, but it gets a little messy) submenus, sub-submenus, and so on, open all at once. And you can drag and drop from anyplace to anyplace within your Personal menu when you're logged in as yourself (see Figure 6.19).

Adding Applications from Scratch

Now that we've figured out how to move applications and menus around K Menu, it's time to add one that doesn't already exist. It might be something so new that it's not in the Appfinder database yet. It might be something you wrote yourself or that you wrote especially for your business or organization. It might be an existing application with new parameters, such as a spreadsheet program preloaded with a specific, commonly visited file, or a non-KDE program you've just installed. (Most KDE applications now insinuate themselves into K Menu as part of installation.) You already know part of it: Pick the place above which you want to have the new entry, right-click, and select **New**. You will get the contents of Figure 6.20.

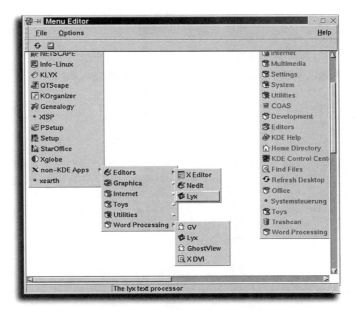

FIGURE 6.19
Lyx has now been copied to its new location. I can leave copies in both places, or I can go back and delete the original or, if I've changed my mind, the copy.

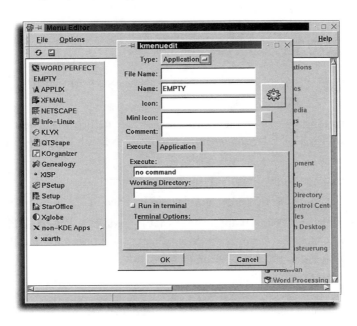

FIGURE 6.20
RMB > New produces an EMPTY entry and the means of filling it.

Let's pause for a second to look at the list box that's produced when you click **Application** (see Figure 6.21).

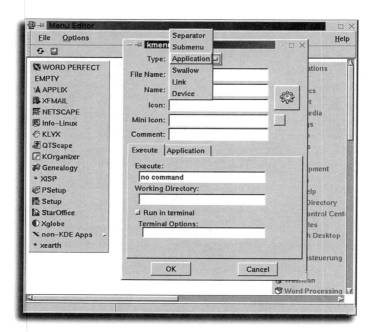

FIGURE 6.21
Yes, you can add more than just applications to K Menu.

The new item can be any of several kinds of objects you encounter in KDE and Linux:

- **Separator** is simply a line that appears across the menu at the point currently occupied by EMPTY. This is useful if you want to break up the menu into categories.
- **Submenu** creates a new submenu in the menu structure.
- **Application** is a program to be run directly by clicking the menu item.
- **Swallow** is a special kind of application that is "swallowed" by K Panel when it is running. The clock is one, as is the MoonPhase toy. These are typically configured other than by hand, but the possibility is provided for here.

- **Link** is where you can put a WWW URL on your K Menu, though you need to be online for the menu entry to be of any use; you'll find it makes more sense simply to bookmark the URL instead.

- **Device** is an actual physical device that is part of your computer. If you wanted to do so, you could create a Drives subdirectory and use this setting along with the information for each drive in your machine to populate it.

In this case, we're adding the popular Nedit editor. As a result, I've filled out the dialog box as shown in Figure 6.22.

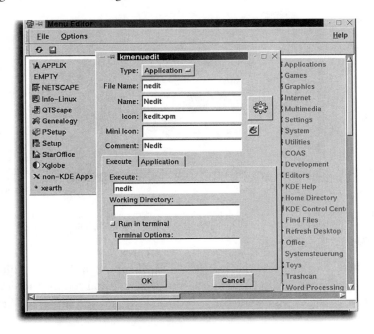

FIGURE 6.22
The first page of the Nedit menu setup screen.

You could imitate what I've done here, and you probably wouldn't go too far astray. But you want to know what these fields mean, right? Well, you should.

The first line, File Name, contains the name of the .kdelnk file you are creating. You are safe in putting in the name of the application with or (as in the illustration) without the .kdelnk suffix, the result is a .kdelnk file anyway.

SEE ALSO
➤ *What is a .kdelnk file? Chapter 9, "Working with Themes," (page 211) tells you all about them.*

163

Then comes the Name of the program as you want it to appear in K Menu. This is followed by Icon and Mini Icon that you access by clicking the box containing the gear, which is the default KDE icon. The default is used unless you specify an icon, and if all the icons look the same, it pretty much defeats the purpose of having them in the first place, doesn't it? Clicking it produces a window of all the available icons (see Figure 6.23). Pick one and click **OK**. Generally the Mini Icon comes along at no extra charge.

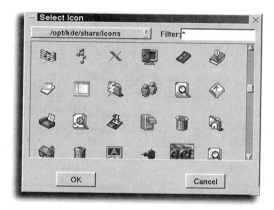

FIGURE 6.23
Pick from among the listed icons to get rid of the default gear icon. Unfortunately, most of the provided icons already have a purpose. Fortunately, you can use an icon editor later on, when you have nothing better to do, to modify one of these or create one of your own.

The Comment line is where you specify what will appear in the little yellow bubble-help things that show up if you rest your mouse pointer on the menu item for awhile, if you have it enabled. (And sometimes, according to newsgroup reports, even if you don't.)

So far you've created a menu item, but you haven't told it what to do. You begin to give your entry meaning with the Execute line in the Execute tab. In its simplest form, you simply type the command to be executed, in this case nedit. If the command isn't in your PATH variable, you'll need to enter the full path to it or create a symbolic link to it in a directory that is on your PATH. (This is basic Linux, beyond the scope of this book, as is what you should do if you are using a shell other than bash. If you don't know, you're probably not.)

This is where you can do a little creative thinking to bring about some remarkably practical results. If you are working on a project that consists largely of one file opened in a particular application, chances are you can add the filename to the command and give the whole thing a unique name and icon. (Don't forget to change the **File Name** entry.) When you click that menu entry, up pops your file in its proper program. This is especially useful if you have set up KDE so that other files of that type open in a different program.

This illustrates that the Execute line should contain any command line options you want to use when you run that program—from that menu item. You can have multiple menu items for the same program, each with a different set of command line parameters, so long as you make sure each has a discrete File Name entry. For instance, I have several versions of XGlobe from which to choose, depending on whether I want to see the Earth as viewed from space at a point above Connecticut, from the Sun's point of view, with place markers turned on, and so on. My mood determines which one I run on any given day. The one I use most frequently has this in its **Execute** box:

```
xglobe -kde -mag 0.75 -mapfile earth.gif -ambientlight 25 -wait 600 -nomarkers
```

Just so you know, this means execute the xglobe program (which is in /usr/local/bin, so it's on my PATH) optimized for KDE at a magnification of 75 percent of full screen using for its surface the contents of graphics file earth.gif with the light on the dark side of the earth 25 percent as bright as the sunlit side (though absent a setting telling it so, I don't see the dark side anyway) updated every 600 seconds and without any place markers.

If the program requires a Working Directory to be specified, you may do so in the box of that label. Most don't.

If the program is a console application, you need to check the **Run in terminal** box. If there are any command line options that need to be set for the terminal window before it runs your application, you can specify them in the **Terminal Options** box.

If You have an Earlier Version of KDE

In the early days of KDE, the default behavior was for the **Run in terminal** box to be checked, so a terminal window would show up even when you didn't need it. But if you closed it, the window containing the program you did want would close, too. There was a lot of head scratching before we mere users figured out what the problem was and that the solution was to go to kmenuedit every time this happened and uncheck the box.

You might think that you are now done, and in most cases you are. But there's a little more here that the advanced user can employ to good advantage. It's on the Application tab, shown in Figure 6.24.

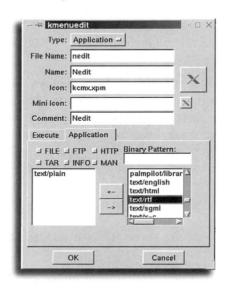

FIGURE 6.24
For advanced users only: Here you can associate your application with a particular type, or several types if you want (and the app agrees).

The Application tab lets you associate particular types of files, binary patterns, what-have-you with the application that you have just menuized. In the illustration, the text file type was found in the list on the right, and the < arrow was clicked to associate it with Nedit.

I don't typically use this tab at all because for me it's just as easy to right-click the icon of a file not associated with a particular application, click **Open with**, and specify an application. There's less chance of breaking something.

Or You Can Drag and Drop

After having brought you through all of this—it was for your own good; you'll thank me when you get a little bit older—I shall now provide an alternative method of adding applications to the K Menu.

Drag 'em to the menu in kmenuedit and drop 'em there. Really. I shall prove it. Let's start with Figure 6.25.

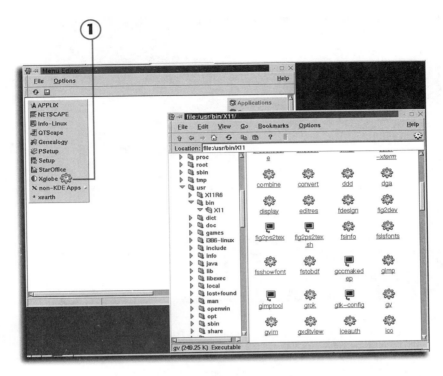

FIGURE 6.25
Pick your program from the KFM file list to begin the quick method of adding to K Menu.

① The gear icon appearing in the menu is the item being dragged.

For purposes of this quick demonstration, I'll put the gv program, which allows you to view files in Adobe PostScript and Acrobat formats, on my Personal menu. I pick it up by clicking it with the left mouse button *and holding the button down* as I drag it to the menu, where, in Figure 6.26, I drop it.

That's all well and good, I can hear you thinking, but surely this simple action cannot have provided enough information in the settings for the program to do anything useful, right? Wrong. Let's look, by clicking the RMB on the new gv item and selecting **Change**. Figure 6.27 tells the tale.

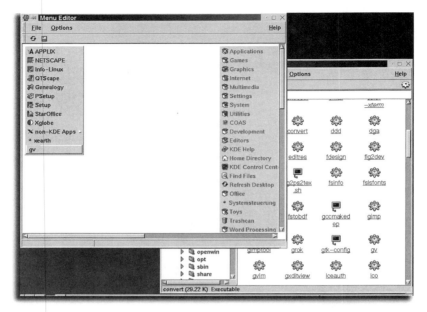

FIGURE 6.26
When you've dragged the desired program to the desired menu, release the mouse button. No matter where you are in the menu, the item goes to the bottom (as is the case with gv here).

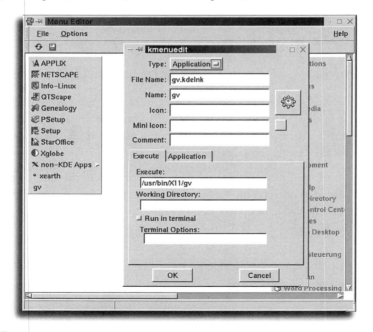

FIGURE 6.27
The mere act of dragging and dropping of the program onto the menu fills out everything essential for a working K Menu item.

All you have to do—and you don't even *have* to do this—is pick an icon and maybe a little bit more descriptive name and enter a comment for bubble help. This is very cool indeed and almost makes up for that Swatch Internet beat clock silliness of the last chapter.

Having made all the changes you care to make, you must save your Personal menu, which is achieved by clicking **File > Save** in kmenuedit. Before you do that, though, there's a nice little item under the **Options** menu, namely **Change Menunames**. If you select this item, shown in Figure 6.28, you can move from the default menu name, Default, to something else.

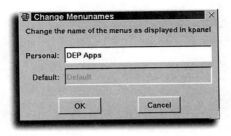

FIGURE 6.28
Even if it is the default, Default, is a poor choice for a name of a menu on which you have worked long and hard, so change it.

After you have carefully crafted your Personal menu, making it contain all your hopes and dreams, it seems kind of a shame to relegate such magnificence to mere submenu status, which of course it is when you click **K Menu** on K Panel (see Figure 6.29).

If you remember all the details from the last chapter—and you may not, because it is a long chapter chock full of details—you'll remember that somewhere there was told of a check box someplace that had something to do with "Personal first" or something like that. Right you are!

Follow this route: **K Menu > KDE Control Center > Applications > Panel > Options** tab, made famous by the Internet beat thing. In the same section, at the bottom of the page, are two items of interest to us now (see Figure 6.30).

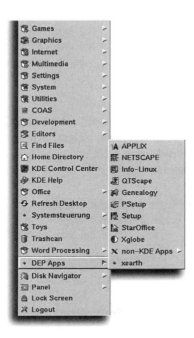

FIGURE 6.29
All that work and all I got was a submenu entry! Ah, but this, too, can be changed.

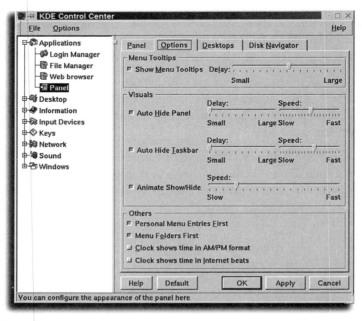

FIGURE 6.30

Checking the **Personal Menu Entries First** and **Menu Folders First** check boxes moves your Personal menu up in the KDE world.

These two items are **Personal Menu Entries First** and **Menu Folders First**. The first one changes K Menu around so that your Personal menu is what appears when you click K Menu, and everything else is a subdirectory. The second one is supposed to (but doesn't yet) put any Personal menu entries that are submenus at the top of your Personal menu. Together, they do this to K Menu (see Figure 6.31).

FIGURE 6.31
Now who's laughing? Your Personal menu is on top, and the old K Menu entries are in a submenu with the name Default.

Yes, your old K Menu is still there (see Figure 6.32).

FIGURE 6.32
See? Rest your mouse pointer on default and there's the old K Menu.

Making Systemwide Changes

So far we've dealt merely with changes to your Personal menu, which is a good place to start because anything you break there can probably be fixed without too much trouble. Now it's time to move into the big leagues: Making changes in the original K Menu that affect all users on the system.

You may have noticed the lack of reference so far to the K Menu that was on the right in all of the illustrations that showed kmenuedit. If you have been editing your Personal menu, you may also have noticed that all the entries on the menu on the right were "grayed out," and there was nothing you could do with them.

As root, that menu isn't grayed out anymore and you can do with it as you want.

The principles and actions are all still the same. You do everything the same way, just on a different menu with broader consequences.

If you wanted, you could just log in as root and incorporate all your Personal stuff into the main K Menu. Everybody on the system would then be able to use it, providing you had all the permissions properly set (for applications and files residing in your ~/ directory, for instance).

This all depends on the kind of system you are using and who else uses it. And while this section has to do with systemwide changes in K Menu performed as root, it's a good place to consider a general menu strategy if more than one user is on your system, or if several associates or family members have accounts.

K Menu Everywhere

Last chapter we learned that you can press Alt+F1 anytime you're in KDE and cause the K Menu to appear. Here's another trick that's even neater: You have a file, probably empty, ~/.kde/share/config/krootwmrc. If you do, open it in an editor, say Kedit. If you don't, you can open the editor to an empty file. Either way, type these two lines:

```
[MouseButtons]
Left=Menu
```

Then, save the file (and if it did not exist previously, save it as ~/.kde/share/config/krootwmrc).

Now, next time you start KDE, clicking anywhere on the screen that isn't otherwise occupied will produce K Menu.

For example, if you have family members of varying ages and interests all of whom use the computer, each with his or her own username (account), you might want to make the main K Menu, that goes to everyone, relatively sparse, to avoid confusion and to keep inquisitive little mouse clicks from going where they oughtn't. In such cases, Personal menus that come up first with the applications a child might use would make sense.

Or you might be administering a Linux system that's used in a small office. The games are quite a temptation; so is the Internet. You can tuck these safely away from the main K Menu and make them available to users who won't overdo it or, in the case of the Internet, need access.

Very likely you can move some system administration tools from the main K Menu without harm and with some reduction of clutter. Many of these can be executed only by root anyway. The entire System and Settings submenus, for instance, can be moved from the main menu to root's Personal menu. (Oh yes, root has a personal menu, too.)

There are some potential pitfalls, of course. You don't want to remove configuration tools until all the desktops are configured. You don't want to delete anything from the main K Menu without first copying it to root's personal menu and making sure it works. You need to plan the menu structure of your system. And if you do move things, you need to remember where you put them because online help and sources such as this book won't be able to guess where you put the program being discussed.

That having been said, one of the great strengths of Linux is that it is a multiuser system. KDE builds on that fact admirably, providing tools to make the most if its system administration. The point is that skillfully and thoughtfully used, kmenuedit when run as root can make use of the computer more rewarding, more productive, and safer for all.

SEE ALSO

➤ *We'll look at system administration in some detail in Chapter 12, "Managing Linux System Functions with KDE," page 271.*

chapter 7

Making a Super K Panel

Putting K Panel and the Taskbar
Where You Want Them

Controlling the Behavior of the
K Panel and Taskbar

K Panel Icons for One-Stop
Application Launching

Somewhere on your screen, probably at its bottom, is what to me is KDE's secret weapon. It is the K Panel, and you can make it do things that users of other desktops and operating systems wish they could do but can't. In this chapter, we shall uncharitably rub their noses in it, because we'll exploit K Panel to the max.

Actually, I misspoke a little. I gave the location of what KDE users think of as K Panel, but really, the name belongs to four discrete parts. We've dealt with two of them already, and in this chapter we'll see what we can do with the other two. The four parts are

- **Disk Navigator**, whose acquaintance was made in Chapter 4, "An Introduction to the K Desktop."
- **K Menu**, the subject of Chapter 6, "Customizing the K Menu."
- **K Panel**, the item whence applications can be launched and docked.
- **Taskbar**, which was introduced in Chapter 4, but which we'll exploit further here, at least in some ways.

Having already used the names in the preceding list and having now nodded to the fact that they are all technically K Panel items, let us agree to call them henceforth by the names in the list.

Putting K Panel and the Taskbar Where You Want Them

Several configuration issues involve K Panel and the Taskbar, the first of which is positioning. Let's explore the possibilities.

Figures 7.1–7.5 show the KDE desktop with the Taskbar and K Panel.

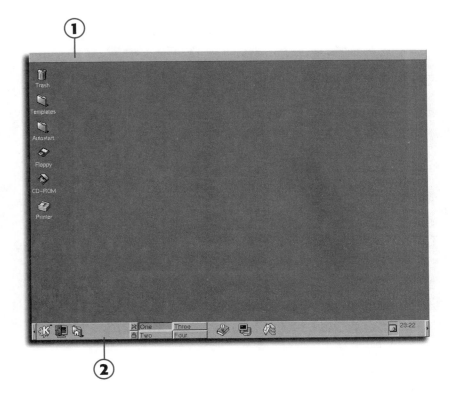

FIGURE 7.1
The default KDE desktop with the Taskbar at top and K Panel at bottom.

① Taskbar

② K Panel

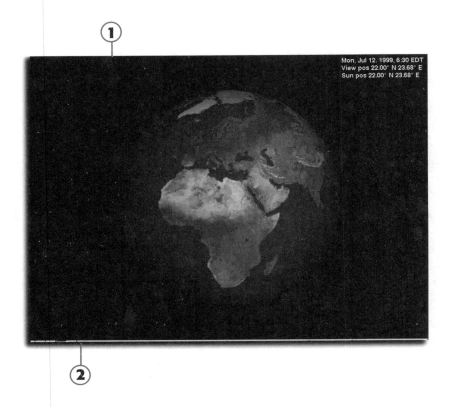

Mon, Jul 12, 1999, 6:30 EDT
View pos 22.00° N 23.68° E
Sun pos 22.00° N 23.68° E

FIGURE 7.2
A highly customized KDE desktop. The thin line at top is the Taskbar, and the thin line at bottom is K Panel.

① Taskbar

② K Panel

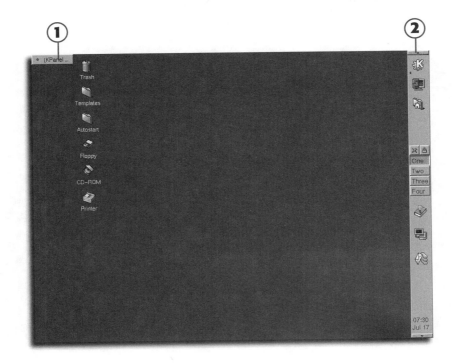

FIGURE 7.3
Here the Taskbar has been placed in the upper left, and K Panel on the right, with the Large style set.

① Taskbar

② K Panel

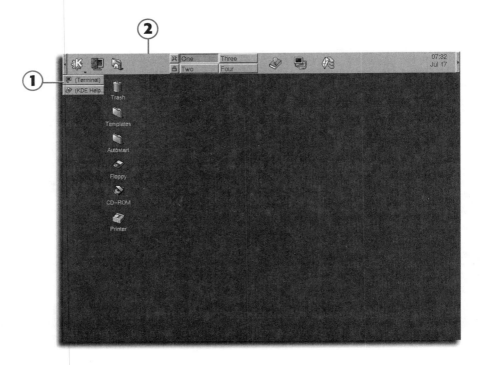

FIGURE 7.4
Now K Panel is at top, the Taskbar is in the upper left, and the icons have been rearranged so that none will be hidden.

① Taskbar

② K Panel

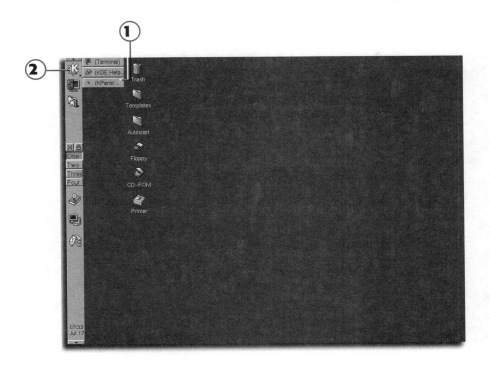

FIGURE 7.5
The same arrangement as that in Figure 7.4, with two exceptions. K Panel has been moved to the left, and the Normal style has been set.

① Taskbar

② K Panel

There is really a reason for all this. Figure 7.6 shows another option.

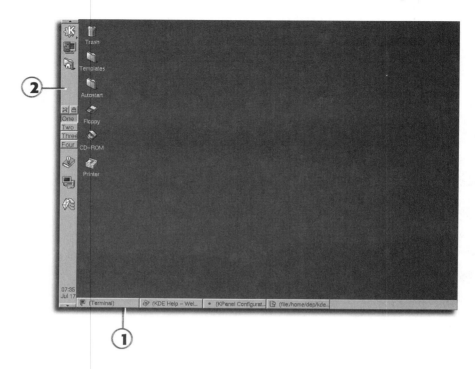

FIGURE 7.6
Now the Taskbar has been moved to the bottom of the screen.

① Taskbar

② K Panel

And you can see one more option in Figure 7.7.

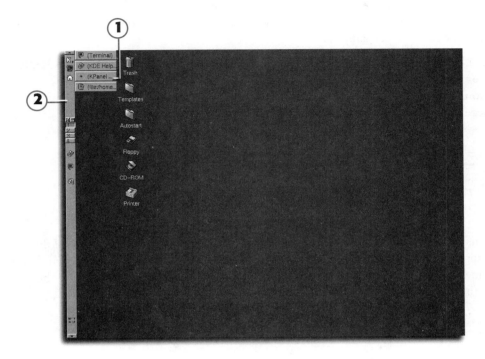

FIGURE 7.7
This is the same arrangement found in Figure 7.5, but the Tiny style has been chosen. Not all the possibilities are attractive.

① Taskbar

② K Panel

As I said, there *is* a point to all this. There are two, really: the obvious one, that K Panel is readily configured, and the slightly more obscure one, that these images can serve as a reference as you decide how you want to configure your own K Panel. It's like a book of carpet samples.

You have three paths to the configuration of K Panel. The first is **K Menu > KDE Control Center > Applications > Panel**. The second is **K Menu > Panel > Configure**. The third and easiest is to right-click on a part of the panel that is not occupied by something else, which renders a menu, as seen in Figure 7.8.

FIGURE 7.8
To customize K Panel, start by right-clicking on an empty place in the panel, and then select **Configure**.

This renders a dialog box, shown in Figure 7.9, which lets you select many of the things we've seen. At top left is where you choose the location of K Panel; you do the same thing at top right for the Taskbar. The bottom left is where you choose the size of the K Panel display.

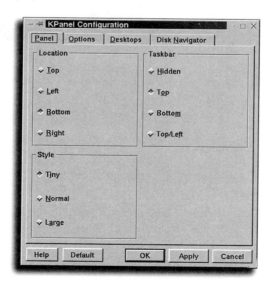

FIGURE 7.9
Choose the size and location of K Panel and Taskbar from the first page of the KPanel Configuration screen.

You will note that among the choices for Taskbar is Hidden. If you make this choice, you in essence do not have a Taskbar. Does this mean that switching among applications that have been minimized, or even learning which applications you have running, is no longer possible? Nope. If you've made this choice, press **Ctrl+Esc** to get a list of applications currently running. You can switch among them from this dialog box.

Current Session

Alas, there is no way to make a screenshot of the dialog box, which is labeled Current Session, but it's also very uncomplicated. Click on the application you want, and then on the button labeled **Switch to**. The only other controls in the dialog box are **Logout** and **Cancel**. Occasionally, if an ill-behaved application has made the desk top seem unresponsive, you can employ this method to get out of KDE, after which you can reenter it. This happens so rarely that I cannot find anyone who has ever had to employ this method, but it's there as a possibility if you need it.

Controlling the Behavior of the K Panel and Taskbar

Those neat desktops that have the K Panel and Taskbar readily available but not always visible are within your grasp. You can also control the manner in which they appear and turn off the "bubble help," those little yellow boxes that appear if your mouse pointer tarries too long on a K Panel item. This is all done from the **Options** tab page (see Figure 7.10).

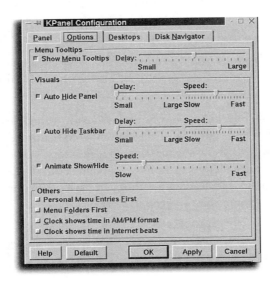

FIGURE 7.10
The behavior of your K Panel and Taskbar are determined by the settings you make on the Options dialog box.

The first choice is **Show <u>M</u>enu Tooltips**, and if you check this box, you get bubble help. If you make this choice, you can use the slider at right to specify how long your mouse pointer must rest on an item before the help bubbles up.

The next two items are **Auto <u>H</u>ide Panel** and **Auto Hide <u>T</u>askbar**. Selecting one or both of these causes the respective screen element to shrink to a thin line at the location you chose on the **<u>P</u>anel** tab page. Moving the mouse pointer to it then causes it to appear.

Next to each of these two items are two sliders. The first, **Delay**, lets you set how long the element sticks around after the mouse pointer leaves it. With the slider all the way to the left, the screen element disappears as soon as the mouse pointer moves away. The second, **Speed**, sets the manner of its departure—whether it's instantly zapped or rolls up in a leisurely fashion. Experiment to find the combination you like. As you use KDE with a variety of applications, you'll probably return to this section to do some fine-tuning.

For instance, occasions occur when the menubar of an application buries itself beneath a Taskbar set to remain constantly onscreen at the top of the screen. This is irritating and, while there are ways around it, why bother when you can set the Taskbar to disappear?

Animate Show/Hide lets you decide how you would like the appearance/ disappearance of these screen elements to take place. This is an eye candy item.

I have discussed the section labeled **<u>O</u>thers** in Chapter 5, "Making the K Desktop Your Own," and it has nothing to do with what we're doing now, so we shall cheerfully skip it. It's not the KDE developers' finest hour, or thousandth of a day, anyway.

How many virtual desktops would you like? Well, your choices are from two to eight in multiples of two, and you make your choice on the **<u>D</u>esktops** page (see Figure 7.11).

The oddly named **<u>V</u>isible** slider determines how many virtual desktops you have. As you slide it to the left and right, you see the numbered text boxes become inactive and active respectively. If you want to name your desktops, you can do so in the text boxes. The **<u>W</u>idth** slider then lets you make enough room in the K Panel buttons for your poetry to be visible. Remember that you have other things competing for space on K Panel, so you'll want to keep it short.

SEE ALSO

➤ *You can make more desktops, up to 32 of them, if you think you really need that many. To learn how, see "Eight Virtual Desktops Not Enough?" in Chapter 5, starting on page 93.*

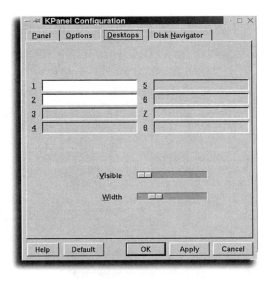

FIGURE 7.11
Here you tell KDE how many virtual desktops you want, what you want to call them, and how they should look on K Panel.

The final page of **KPanel Configuration**, **Disk Navigator**, is considered in detail in Chapter 4, and there is no need to go over it again here.

When you are happy with your settings, click **Apply** and, if everything looks good, click **OK**. Your settings are now in place.

K Panel Icons for One-Stop Application Launching

When you install KDE, some icons on K Panel, when clicked, immediately launch the applications to which they belong. There's no need to go diving through a zillion layers of menus and submenus in K Menu. If you are like most computer users, you do 90 percent of your work in 10 percent of your applications, which are probably not the ones put on the panel by default. So it's a good idea to remove those items you don't want and replace them with the ones you use daily.

There are two easy ways to bring this about. The recommended method is selecting **K Menu > Panel > Add Application**, as shown in Figure 7.12.

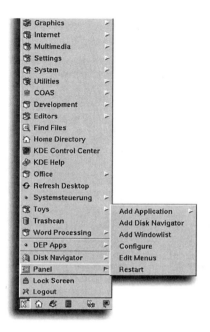

FIGURE 7.12

Begin the process toward adding programs (or whole subdirectories, if you want) to K Panel by going to **Add Application**.

Clicking **Add Application** offers you what looks like K Menu (see Figure 7.13). Click on the item that you want to add to the panel and presto-change-o, it's there.

Before we go on, let's note a difference between the Add Application display and K Menu. You'll notice that at the top of each subdirectory in the Add Application menu there is an item that is the name of the submenu itself. Click on it, and the whole submenu is transported to K Panel. In this way, if you are so inclined, you can array the subdirectories across K Panel. If you have created submenus that contain, for instance, applications with specific files as command-line options, it might not be a bad idea to add the subdirectory to K Panel.

There is another way to add applications to K Panel: Drag and drop from KFM. Open the file manager, find the application, and drag it to K Panel. Voilà!

Once you place an item on K Panel, you can move the application icons around and configure them to make them more convenient to use.

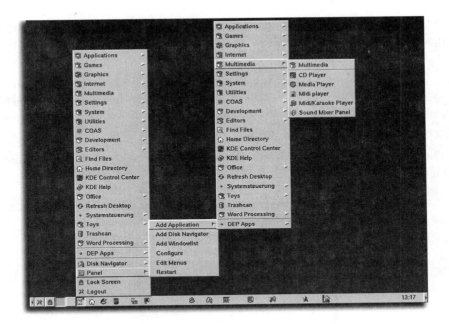

FIGURE 7.13
The **Add Application** image of K Menu differs in one important way: It lists the names of the submenus in the sub-menu listing, but there's a reason why.

Figure 7.14 illustrates the menu you get when you right-click an icon on K Panel. As you can see, you have three choices.

FIGURE 7.14
Right-clicking an icon in K Panel produces a menu for that item.

The **Remove** choice is straightforward: Make that choice and the icon disappears from K Panel. We'll get to **Properties** in a minute. Right now, though, let's talk about **Move** because it can be a little flaky.

When you click **Move**, you must return the mouse cursor to the icon in question, where it changes shape, becoming a four-headed arrow (or a kung-fu throwing star, or a treasure map symbol—anyway, it changes shape). You can then slide it back and forth along K Panel to reposition it. If you are undertaking an extensive panel reorganization, you might have to plan it out ahead of time. Move some icons out of the way to make room for the ones in their new locations, and then move the first ones to where you want them to go, and so on. What you do not want to do is accidentally cover up icons with other icons, which can happen.

You can move anything on K Panel except the clock (or Internet beat monitor, if you've made that choice) and items that have been swallowed by the panel, which will always be on the right. The swallowed items usually have different RMB (right mouse button) menus of their own.

The third item on the RMB menu, **Properties**, opens a dialog box, as seen in Figure 7.15.

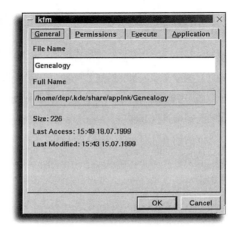

FIGURE 7.15
The Properties K Panel dialog box is a four-tab affair that lets you set up specifications for the program to be launched from the panel.

This is actually the same dialog box that you find for any .applnk file, which conveniently is the subject of the next chapter. Before we leave this subject, however, you should note that you can set up different command-line options for the K Panel icon than you have for the menu item, executable file, or script taken from KFM whence came the K Panel icon. In fact, you can have the same program on K Panel multiple times, each one configured in a different way.

chapter 8

Adding Applications to the Desktop

This chapter chiefly covers something called .kdelnks, though most of the time you deal with them, you won't know them by that name, nor will you need to.

Actually, we've been dealing with .kdelnk files for some time: every time, in fact, that we've set the properties for an application. Some understanding of what they are and what they do is useful to the KDE user, and this chapter attempts to impart that understanding in the matrix of adding application icons to the desktop field itself rather than to a menu or K Panel proper.

Deep in the hidden kde subdirectory in your home directory (~/.kde) is a subdirectory called applnk. Depending on what applications you have installed, it might look something like Figure 8.1 when opened in KFM.

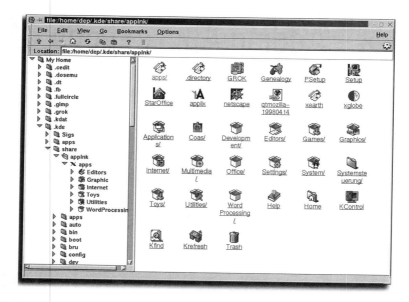

FIGURE 8.1
A typical ~/.kde/share/applnk subdirectory. The icons aren't what they seem.

What Is an Applnk?

If you were to right-click one of the program icons in ~/.kde/share/applnk (there are directory icons as well), and then click the **Open with** menu item and give, say, kedit as the program in which to open the file, you would see something like this:

```
# KDE Config File
[KDE Desktop Entry]
Comment[C]=EMPTY
SwallowExec=
SwallowTitle=
BinaryPattern=
MiniIcon=
Protocols=
Name[C]=Xglobe
MimeType=
Exec=xglobe -kde -mag 0.75 -mapfile earth.gif -ambientlight 25
  -wait 600 -nomarkers
Icon=kmoon.xpm
TerminalOptions=
Path=
Type=Application
Terminal=0
```

Yes. An applnk file, distinguished in that its filename extension is .kdelnk, is a text file. So what do all the lines mean?

If you've followed the preceding chapters, you'll have a faint glimmer of recognition. Those lines seem to coincide with something you've seen before, though maybe you don't quite remember just where. Stay tuned: the mystery will be solved, right after this.

The Properties RMB menu item on one of these applnks might be instructive, and in that we're here anyway, let's take a look. Figure 8.2 starts us off.

FIGURE 8.2
The **General** tab of an applnk file's Properties doesn't tell us anything unexpected.

The **<u>P</u>ermissions** tab, likewise, is fairly standard (see Figure 8.3).

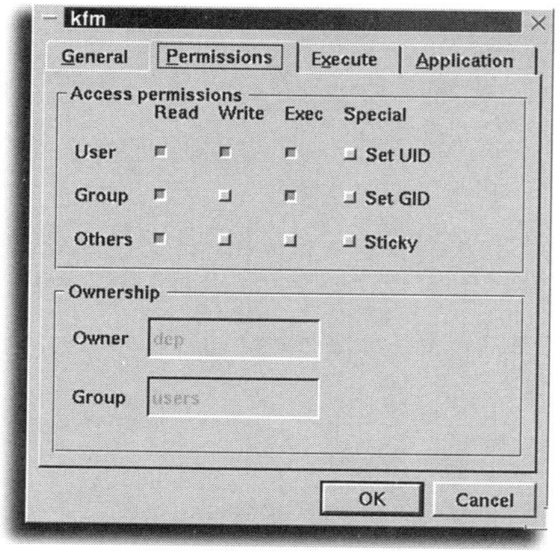

FIGURE 8.3
Hmmm. It's executable, and we know it's a text file, so it must be some kind of script.

The **E<u>x</u>ecute** tab doesn't usually appear in the Properties menu of a file, even an executable one. Perhaps we can learn something there (see Figure 8.4).

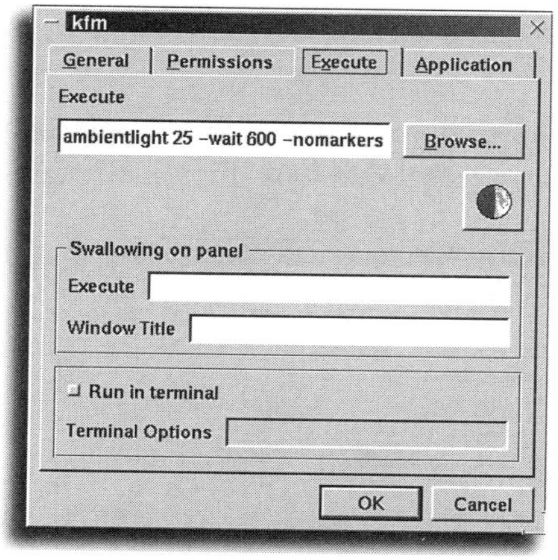

FIGURE 8.4
Now we're getting somewhere!

The **E<u>x</u>ecute** tab contains an Execute box, which seems to be a surrogate for a command line. There is a <u>B</u>rowse button, where you can search for the application to be executed. There is a place, as we've seen, where an icon can be selected. There are places to specify the parameters if the application is one that can be swallowed by K Panel. And—now things are starting to look familiar—a check box appears where applications that must be run in a terminal window are specified, along with any special attributes that that terminal must bring with it.

Finally, there is an **Application** tab, shown in Figure 8.5, where a comment and program name, as well as file associations, can be set. This is looking *very* familiar.

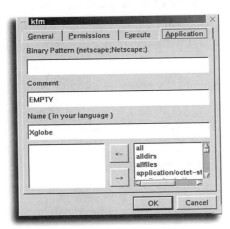

FIGURE 8.5
Where have we seen something like this before? Why, when we've been adding items to K Menu and K Panel!

Well, now! It seems that when adding files, directories, applications, whatever, to K Menu and K Panel, those fancy tabbed graphical screens are generating text files that run as scripts by KDE to set the parameters of the program's operation under KDE, and how KDE reacts to the program. We've already seen that much of this is automatically generated when, for instance, you drag and drop a program, directory, or other file to K Menu or K Panel.

Text Files and Linux

In almost every window manager and desktop for Linux, control of appearance and function is determined by one or more text files. Some are extremely complex shell scripts, whereas others are simple text listings of parameters that are then interpreted by the window manager or desktop and as necessary passed along to applications. KDE is no different. Its configuration files, including those related to the launching of non-KDE applications, are simple text files that can be edited in an editor, if you are sufficiently familiar with their format. Where KDE differs from many desktops is in the elaborate graphical means whereby you don't ever have to use an editor to write these files. Often, it's simply a matter of filling in the blanks, as is the case with the creation of .kdelnk files. The applications themselves may have configuration files, which aren't necessarily standardized, but which are often text files, too, generated when you set the options for the program within the program itself. For KDE applications, these are kept in ~/.kde/share/config.

An applnk file, then, is a text file that sets the configuration parameters for an application to be run under KDE. It is normally generated through a graphical configurator but may be edited with a text editor, if you know what you're doing. The *lnk* in their names suggests that they are link files, but they are nothing like the hard and symbolic links familiar to the Linux user.

Application Access with Applnk Files

We have already seen how applnk files are created for adding applications, directories, or files to K Menu and K Panel. They can also be added to the Desktop itself. Here's how.

Right-click the desktop, and select **New** (see Figure 8.6).

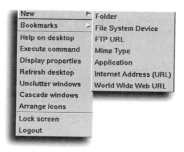

FIGURE 8.6
The RMB New submenu lists the kinds of applnks that can be added to the desktop. For this demonstration, we'll set up a new Application.

By selecting **Application** from the submenu, you get the dialog box shown in Figure 8.7.

FIGURE 8.7
The RMB **New > Application** item renders a default filename that can be changed now or later.

The program we're adding to the desktop is Ssystem, an interesting OpenGL solar system simulator. So we'll name it now, as shown in Figure 8.8, though we could change the name later if we wanted. It's just that until then, the desktop icon would be called Program.

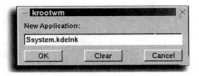

FIGURE 8.8
The program's name is added, but the extension isn't changed.

Clicking **OK** does two things: It adds an icon (the KDE default gear) to the desktop, and it opens a dialog box (see Figure 8.9).

FIGURE 8.9
Though an icon has been added to the desktop, it won't do anything until we fill in the blanks.

The **General** tab presents nothing to do, so we'll move on to the **Permissions** tab (see Figure 8.10).

FIGURE 8.10
Because I want to be able to execute this program, I've checked the **Exec** check box. The permissions here are simply a graphical way of setting the familiar Linux permissions.

Having the **Permissions** tab specified that we want to be able to execute the program, it is useful to tell KDE what we want to be able to execute, which is set on the **Execute** tab, shown in Figure 8.11 and Figure 8.12.

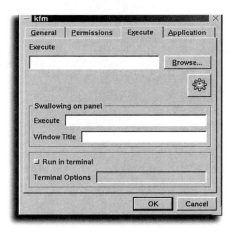

FIGURE 8.11
The **Execute** tab arrives blank, so KDE doesn't yet know what program is to be run. We fill in the blanks.

FIGURE 8.12
The commands to start the program are entered in the Execute text box. And an icon is selected from among those displayed when the icon that contained the default KDE gear is clicked upon.

The **Execute** tab requires the name of the file to which the icon refers. If the file is somewhere specified in the /etc/profile PATH= line, the full pathname isn't required; otherwise, as here, it is. If the executable file you are calling isn't on your PATH variable, you will need to provide a fully qualified pathname.

Is It on Your PATH?

Okay, so you've downloaded a program and installed it. Is it in your **path**? Here's how you find out:

1. Open a terminal (konsole or kvt) and type its name, usually in lowercase— the documentation with the program can help in this regard—and of course press **Enter**. If the program runs, it's on your PATH variable.

2. If you receive an error message that the command was not found, you need to figure out where it was installed. Still in the terminal, type **find** and the command name. This takes awhile, maybe a few minutes if you have a big drive with lots of software, because your entire hard drive is being searched. In due course, a listing of files containing the command you entered is listed. Scroll through these to find the right one (if the program is named, say, *edit*, you will have a lot of lines to inspect, but the right one will be fairly apparent). Make note of the full pathname.

3. Now type the full pathname at the terminal's command prompt. The application should run. If the file is specified somewhere in the /etc/profile PATH= line, the full pathname isn't required; otherwise, as here, it is.

The **Application** tab can—but here doesn't—need much information, but it can use a little user input, as you can see in the before-and-after images, shown in Figures 8.13 and 8.14.

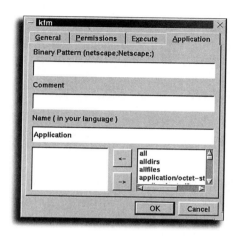

FIGURE 8.13
If you want the "bubble help" to say anything about this icon, you'll need to provide it in the Comment text box. If you want it to be called something other than Application, you'll need to name it here...

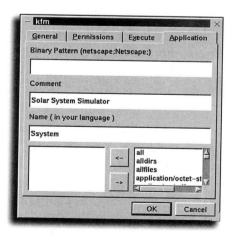

FIGURE 8.14
...which we've done for Ssystem. Then click **OK**.

After you've filled everything out and clicked **OK**, the proper icon, with the proper name, is displayed on the desktop (see Figure 8.15).

FIGURE 8.15
The configuration complete, the selected icon appears on the desktop, presumably able to launch the chosen application.

Ah, but does it work? Let's see Figure 8.16.

FIGURE 8.16
Success! Clicking the icon launches our application, Ssystem.

Nice, but there are other ways of arriving at this place.

Using Templates

Your default KDE desktop includes a folder named Templates. It contains a different way of arriving at the result I just illustrated. How are the template files employed?

Clicking the **Templates** folder renders a KFM window containing the folder's contents (see Figure 8.17).

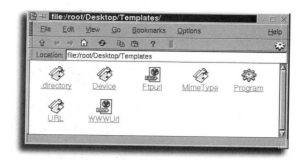

FIGURE 8.17
The Templates folder contains the makings of several different kinds of .kdelnks.

To make use of a template, drag it to the desktop and drop it there. You will be given a little menu, as shown in Figure 8.18.

FIGURE 8.18
Select **Copy** to put a new application template on the desktop.

Choose **Copy**. You don't want to Move the template itself to the desktop, and creating a Link to it would merely assign the attributes you are about to give the new icon to the original, in Templates, which you don't want to do. (This is a standard KFM menu, so it contains items of no use in this context.) You will receive in exchange for your efforts an icon on the desktop identical to the one in Templates, right down to its name (see Figure 8.19).

FIGURE 8.19
The template is copied to the desktop.

You could probably figure out what to do next, but let's go over it anyway.
Right-click the new icon, which gives you the menu shown in Figure 8.20.

FIGURE 8.20
The new icon has an RMB menu, just like any other icon in KDE. For our purposes right now, **Properties** is the choice
of interest.

Click **Properties** to receive the dialog box pictured in Figure 8.21. Look familiar?

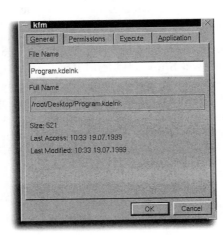

FIGURE 8.21
And here we are at a blank properties dialog box.

You will notice a difference between this procedure and the one listed previously. When the desktop's **RMB > New** menu was employed, there was no dialog box in which the new desktop icon was named, so you have to name it here. Remember to preserve the .kdelnk extension. Then proceed as before. Pretty simple, eh?

Using .kdelnk Files for Total Control

This is where things get really cool. Because .kdelnk files are just that—files—you can manipulate them in pretty much the same way you can manipulate other files. This opens a world of possibilities.

For example, let's say that you, having plopped an icon for Ssystem down on your desktop, suddenly decide that while you like the program (and you should—it's great), you don't use it in the course of your work, so you don't want it so prominently placed as it is when it is a desktop icon. (Go through your K Menu and count up just the applications that are part of your KDE distribution. Imagine what your desktop would look like if they were all iconized on the desktop!) You could right-click on the icon and select **Delete**, and that would be that. But then the Ssystem.kdelnk file would be deleted, and with it would go your work in configuring it. You don't hate the thing, you just want to bury it a level or two. What to do?

Easy. Open KFM, the file manager. (If you have **View > Show Tree** enabled in KFM, this is a little easier, but this is by no means necessary, and we'll figure out how to do it both ways.) Then open your Desktop folder. There you will see the .kdelnk file for every icon that appears on your desktop (see Figure 8.22). If you have **View > Show Tree** enabled, you will also see your ~/ files displayed down the left side of the window.

Now, move up the tree on the left until you find your **~/.kde** directory. (For this, you will need to have **View > Show Hidden Files** checked.) When you find it, click on the little triangle to its left, not on its name. Now a listing of subdirectories will open on the left, but the Desktop directory will still be displayed on the right. Click the triangle next to **Share** to show still more subdirectories. Click the triangle next to **Applnk** to drape down its subdirectories, and on the triangle next to **X_apps** to display—all the subdirectories located in your Personal K Menu! (see Figure 8.23)

SEE ALSO

➤ *If this all seems confusing, you might want to take a look at Chapter 10, "Navigating Everything with KFM," page 225, which is about the file management functions of KFM.*

FIGURE 8.22
The Desktop directory contains the links for icons on the desktop.

FIGURE 8.23
In tree view, you can stretch out directories to show all the subdirectories they contain. At the bottom of the ~/.kde/share/applnk/X_apps chain are the submenus in your Personal K Menu.

Now, depending on where you want the application to appear in the hierarchy of your Personal menu, simply drag the icon from the Desktop directory and drop it on the subdirectory where you would like it to reside. The choices in the illustration (see Figure 8.24) are /applnk, /X_apps, or one of the subdirectories thereunder. Because we don't want to bury Ssystem too far down the line, we'll put it in /applnk.

FIGURE 8.24

When you drop the icon on the target folder, you will be given this familiar menu. In this case, we have decided to Move the applnk, though we could just as easily choose **Copy** to have it in both places. Again, Link isn't a choice we would like to make.

Click **Move** and the icon disappears both from the Desktop directory and from the desktop itself. Where did it go? If you look immediately in your **K Menu > Personal** directory, you won't see it because you have to restart K Panel (**K Menu > Panel > Restart**) before the change becomes visible. But when you do, you see what is shown in Figure 8.25.

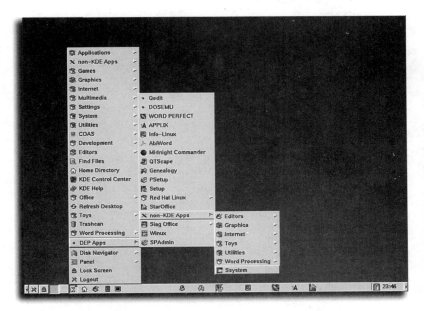

FIGURE 8.25
And there it is, gone from the desktop but now on the menu.

Before we move on—and there's much more to see—let's look at how this is done if you don't have your KFM **View > Show Tree** option checked. All you need to do, really, is open two KFM windows, one containing ~/Desktop and the other showing the directory that is your target for the Move (see Figure 8.26). Simply drag the icon from the first to the second.

This ability to drag and drop works both ways. If an application that you would like to have on your desktop has a menu item in K Menu, you can drag its .kdelnk file to your ~/Desktop directory and drop it there. If you no longer want it to appear on the K Menu, and if it's in your **K Menu > Personal menu**, you can choose **Move**; otherwise, choose **Copy** or **Link**. (You cannot Move the item if it is elsewhere in K Menu unless you are root, but you can **Copy** and **Link**.)

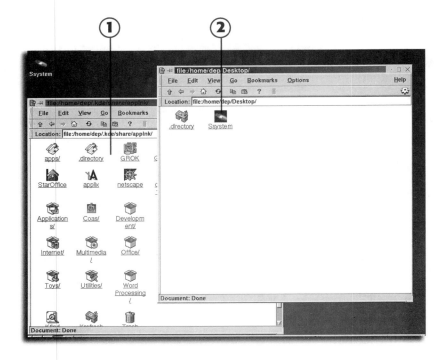

FIGURE 8.26
You can drag the icon representing the .kdelnk file from one KFM window to another.

(1) We're dragging the Ssystem icon from this KFM desktop...

(2) ...to this one.

Copy and Link

It's time to detail the difference between the Copy and Link menu items. If you **Copy** a .kdelnk (or any other) file or directory, you are making a duplicate, discrete instance of it. If you **Link**, you aren't making another one but instead a pointer to the first. In most respects, the two behave identically. But when you **Copy**, you can make changes to the new file you make without the original being affected, and vice versa. If you change a link (or the file to which the link refers), you have changed its contents or behavior in both places.

Systemwide Use of .kdelnk Files

If you are the system administrator, you can make wonderful use of .kdelnk files to add items to the K Menu that all users receive—and even to add icons to the desktops of users.

Let's begin by adding an item to the K Menu for all users. This is done in the same way as described previously, but for two differences: you must be root, and you must copy (or move) the .kdelnk to the proper directory. That directory, as we see in Figure 8.27, isn't in any ~/.kde directory but in the directory where KDE itself is installed.

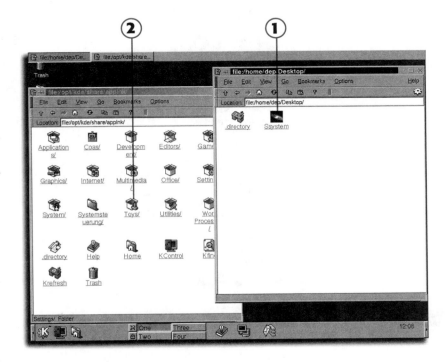

FIGURE 8.27
You can copy or move the .kdelnk file from a user desktop to the systemwide K Menu just as easily as you can copy it from the user's desktop directory to a Personal menu. The trick is for the root user to put it in the /share/applnk file in the systemwide KDE directory.

(1) This time we're dragging the poor Ssystem icon from the Desktop folder...

(2) ...and dumping it in the Toys folder.

In this case—we're still dragging poor Ssystem all over the KDE universe—the only submenu that seems appropriate is Toys because Ssystem isn't a graphics application or a Game. (I probably should create another directory, Science or Astronomy or some such, to hold application .kdelnks such as this one.) So I drag the .kdelnk to

Toys. Now, when I log out of root, log in as myself, and look at K Menu, I see Figure 8.28.

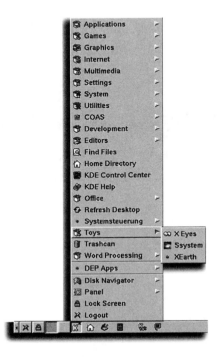

FIGURE 8.28
Now Ssystem is an item on the systemwide K Menu.

Adding icons to the desktop systemwide is a little murkier because different Linux distributions that include KDE set up the default desktop in different ways. One way that works no matter what the distribution is simply to copy the .kdelnk file to every ~/Desktop directory throughout the system.

chapter

9

Working with Themes

It is necessary at the start of this chapter to admit a prejudice: though they can be attractive, I think desktop themes are pretty much a waste of time. Eye candy. A coat of paint. Window dressing, literally. I shall, however, devote myself heart and soul to casting aside this opinion and treat them as if they were practical, but they're not. And surely the most ardent devotee of themes would admit that they are not essential in any way to the proper functioning of KDE or any of its applications. In short, if you want to skip over this chapter until some rainy weekend when you are bored and want to play around with your desktop, you'll lose nothing by doing so.

Okay, So What Exactly *Are* Themes?

Remember in Chapter 2, "Starting KDE," when we looked at the settings whereby widgets would behave in the manner of Windows 95 (well, *some* of the manner of Windows 95, anyway)? And we discussed how there could be a menubar across the top of the screen that would reflect the menu choices of whatever application had focus in the current session, *a la* the Mac OS? Themes are like those choices on megadoses of steroids. They are graphics, configuration files, and sometimes sounds as well, designed to impart a certain look and feel to your KDE desktop. In some cases they provide relatively accurate emulations of other desktops and operating systems, while in others they are where talented and not-so-talented designers give binary voice to their flights of fancy.

A Program for Automating Theme Selection: kthememgr

Under ideal circumstances, changing a theme would be no more difficult than changing, say, the desktop background bitmap. In KDE 1.x this is close to being realized, but not quite. Though some Linux distributors using KDE as their default desktop did bundle software to make theme changing easier and a few sample themes as well, theme handling up to and including KDE 1.1.1 was abysmal, unless you downloaded and built a KDE program, *kthememgr*, to assist you. kthememgr seems to have been withdrawn from availability for individual download, although it is included in KDE 1.2. Fortunately, at least a few distributions include kthememgr. How do you tell? Follow this procedure: **K Menu > KDE Control Center > Desktop**. If you find an entry called Theme Manager (see Figure 9.1), you're among the fortunate. Or not.

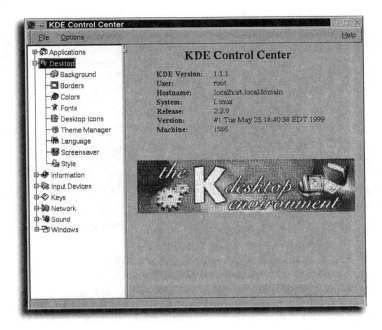

FIGURE 9.1
If you see Theme Manager under Desktop, you have it installed already. Lucky you!

No, not K Theme Manager, kthememgr!

If all this confusion weren't bad enough, there is another program, K Theme Manager, at www.kde.org in the download section. Its exact whereabouts depend on version and stability. The problem is that it doesn't really manage themes. You can't select a theme and install it all of a piece. I am not clear just what the developer of this program has in mind. The name suggests that theme management figures in there someplace. You can download and build it if you want—it's not difficult—but it won't do anything for you that you can't do better through the Control Panel.

Then there is another problem: The one version of kthememgr that did work for KDE-1.1.1 contained a bug that kept it from compiling properly. If you have found this file somewhere (its name is kthememgr.tar.gz), extracted it in /usr/local/src, and have tried to compile it and failed—as you surely will—here's how to fix it.

> **Or You Could Upgrade**
>
> If you don't feel you're up to hacking code and then compiling it, you may skip the rest of this section and spend the time downloading KDE 1.2 instead, if themes are something that puts wind in your sails.

As root, change to /usr/local/src/kthememgr. Then run

```
./configure [followed by -prefix= and whatever other options you like]
```

Then, using a text editor, open /usr/local/src/kthememgr/kthememgr/Makefile. Yes, kthememgr appears twice. Find the file that begins kthememgr_LDADD. It will look like this:

```
kthememgr_LDADD = -lkimgio -ljpeg -lkfile -lkfm -lkdeui -lkdecore
-lqt -lXext -lX11 $(LIBSOCKET) -lpng -ltiff
```

Add **-lz** to its end, to wit:

```
kthememgr_LDADD = -lkimgio -ljpeg -lkfile -lkfm -lkdeui -lkdecore
-lqt -lXext -lX11 $(LIBSOCKET) -lpng -ltiff -lz
```

There is a potential problem here. If your text editor is set to do wordwrap, a carriage return gets thrown in, and the line is split the instant you try to edit it because it is very long. This means that you will have to add a space at the end of every break in the line, and then go to the next part of the line and backspace once to reassemble the parts. This is a pain, but it can be done. Now, if you have installed the latest libtiff and libtiff-devel, zlib azlib-devel, and libpng and libpng-devel, you can change to /usr/local/src/kthememgr and run

```
make all
```

followed by

```
make install
```

and have an even chance or better of actually building the thing.

Using kthememgr

We shall now proceed with the heartfelt hope, wish, and presumption that you have one way or another gotten kthememgr installed on your machine. Following **K Menu > KDE Control Center > Desktop > Theme Manager** gives you what you see in Figure 9.2 (so does typing `kthememgr` in a terminal and pressing **Enter**).

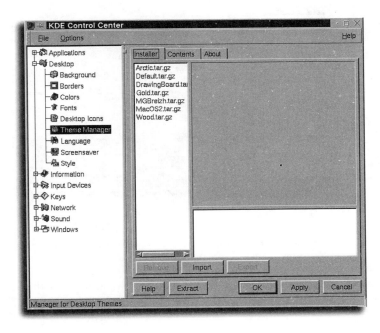

FIGURE 9.2
The first page of the Theme Manager lists the available themes. Unfortunately, the Help button does nothing. It's a work in progress, at least for KDE 1.1.1 and lower.

If you click on one of the available themes, the page gets populated with a preview and information about each theme (see Figure 9.3).

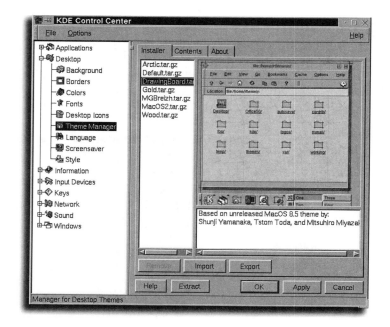

FIGURE 9.3
Here, the popular Drawing Board theme has been selected, and is shown in the preview window. Its talented designers are listed in the box below the preview.

Clicking **Apply** transforms your desktop by causing it to conform with the selected theme (see Figure 9.4).

Don't Click Unless You're Sure!

Caution: There is no way to undo a theme except to replace it with another theme. Once you click **Apply**, you will have a hard slog getting back to your current desktop configuration.

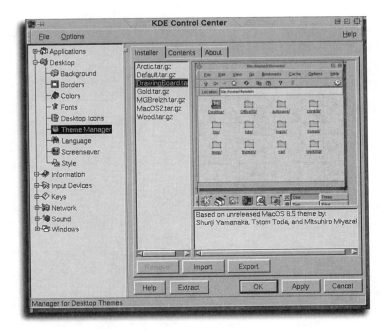

FIGURE 9.4
The Drawing Board theme applied to the desktop.

Themes can be very striking, even if they are not always practical. They change, or can change, just about everything, from the background and colors to the widgets involved in the window furniture to the appearance of icons. Some, though by no means all, themes even change your system sounds. Before we progress, let's sample a few themes, beginning with Figure 9.5. I've opened three sample KDE programs—KFM, Kedit, and Kcalc—to give you a sense of the changes.

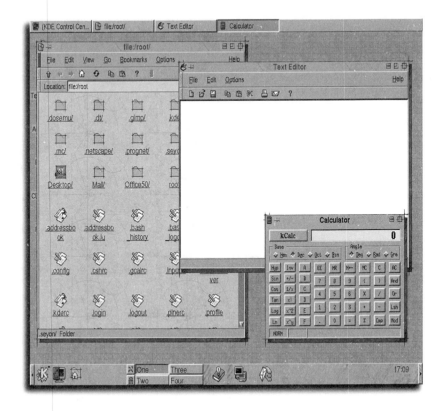

FIGURE 9.5
The Drawing Board theme as it might look in use. Its appearance, as you can see, is strikingly different from the default KDE desktop.

One of the supplied themes is dark and gothic, with finely tooled widgets (see Figure 9.6).

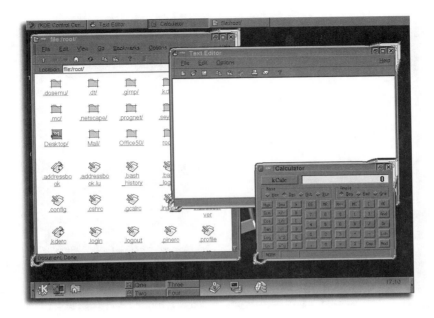

FIGURE 9.6
The MGBreizh theme is a little gloomy, but oh, those widgets!

Another theme is supposed to look like the Mac OS (see Figure 9.7).

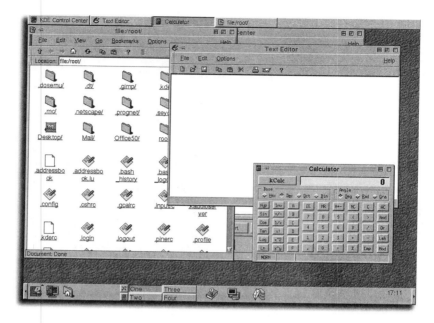

FIGURE 9.7
The Mac OS theme takes things far beyond the standard KDE Mac OS style.

And there is a default theme that is supposed to bring things back to normal (see Figure 9.8).

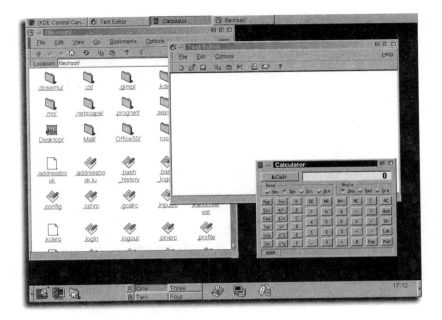

FIGURE 9.8
The default theme doesn't restore KDE to its installation defaults, but at least many things become a little more recognizable.

Enough of that. You get the idea. Clearly, themes go far beyond the other desktop settings available to KDE users, but let's continue now to look at the Theme Manager. The second tab page is Contents, as you can see in Figure 9.9.

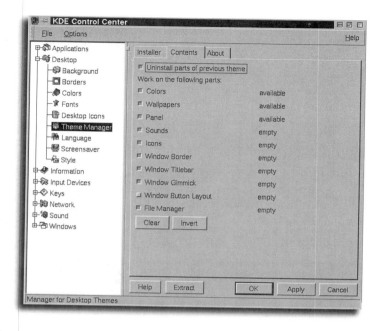

FIGURE 9.9
The Contents page shows what a particular theme comprises and lets you turn elements on and off before applying the theme.

The **Contents** tab lets you see what items are included in a selected theme package before you apply it. You can check and uncheck items that you want or don't want installed. If a particular category is listed as empty, it means that the package doesn't contain that element.

One interesting feature of the Contents page is that by selectively turning elements on and off, you can use your favorite parts from multiple themes to create a custom theme that might be—who knows?—greater than the sum of its parts.

Getting Additional Themes

Of course, the Theme Manager created a whole new area of creative endeavor for programmers, some of whom are actually artists. Themes began to be produced at a breathtaking rate for users to download, look at, and install.

The central repository for themes and information on them is at www.kde.themes.org, which has scores of themes available for download in gzipped tarballs. Once you get them, what do you do?

The easiest thing to do is simply copy them into the /share/apps/kthememgr/Themes subdirectory of your system's master KDE directory. They should then be available. If for some reason you don't want to do that or don't have access to it, you can put them in your ~/ directory somewhere. Then you get to use the Import button on the Theme Manager page of the KDE Control Panel. This is a nice use of the standard code KDE normally uses for **File > Open** functions. Browse to the appropriate place, select the new theme, and click **OK**.

Someday…

Greatly intriguing is the Export button. Though disabled in the KDE 1.1.1 version, it should make theme creation easier, and therefore could make saving the current desktop before you begin experimenting a great deal easier.

Installing Themes the Old-Fashioned Way

Don't.

This was going to be a section that would have gone on and on about how, by the simple task of creating a dozen or more directories, copying all manner of files from tarballs into them, and editing relatively complex configuration text files, you could try out one new theme. By repeating much of that process, you could then try out another, and so on. You could also throw away your computer and get an old manual typewriter or communicate with friends in the neighborhood by flashing your room lights off and on in Morse code. It would make just about as much sense.

If themes are that important to you and you do not have a version of KDE that has the Theme Manager installed, download KDE 1.2 and either install the compiled binaries or compile it yourself. Then you will have quick access to many themes in less time than it would take to install just one.

Now let's get on to something with some meat.

chapter
10

Navigating *Everything* with KFM

The default K Panel carries an icon that looks like a little house. If you rest your mouse pointer on it, the bubble help tells you that This folder contains all your personal files. True enough. But to stop there would be to say that an Indy race car is a device for bringing about the combustion of gasoline. That's because much of what you want to do with KDE, you'll do with KFM. Want to copy a file, move a file, or gaze upon the contents of a file? KFM is the tool you'll use. Want to go to a Web page or download a file by ftp? It's KFM again. KFM is a simple-looking application, and it is simple to use. But simplicity must not be confused with a lack of power: In many ways, KFM *is* KDE.

Your desktop itself is an extension of KFM, as are the default icons (Trashcan, Autostart, and Templates) that appear there. So you've already been working with KFM, though not under that name. You will discover that KFM deals with objects on the local computer, on the local network, and on the Internet in largely the same way, though the Internet stuff won't be handled until Chapter 24 "Browsing and Other Things Internet."

SEE ALSO

➤ *For more information on the Internet and KDE see Chapter 24, page 494.*

In this chapter, you'll fully explore all the functions of KFM and I'll show you how to use it to perform the tasks you do practically every day. We'll begin with configuration, dive into file management (the functions that give KFM its name), and then move to remote file transfers and a little about Web browsing.

Configuring KFM

Click on that little house icon and, if you are logged in as a user, you'll see the contents of your home directory (minus any hidden files or directories) in icon form. It's pretty much like the iconic representations of directories under the graphical user interfaces for other operating systems. (If you are logged in as root, you'll see root's home directory.)

This is the default, but you can change it. If you like the look of the Microsoft Windows Explorer, you can change it to resemble that program. If you prefer a view that provides information about each file and directory in the fashion of the old Norton Commander, you can bring that about, too. Before you get into making those changes, make sure that you have a sense of KFM's general behavior. The default KFM window is shown in Figure 10.1

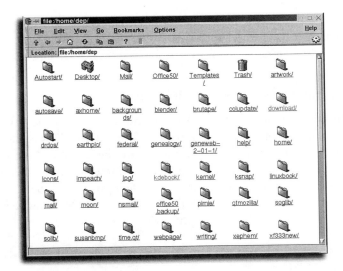

FIGURE 10.1
Clicking on the little house on the K Panel renders the basic KFM window of the ~/ directory.

At first, there's little remarkable about the KFM window. It displays a relatively standard menubar, a toolbar of icons most of whose functions can be guessed (and that offer bubble help if you've enabled it), and a window full of icons. Directories employ the now nearly universal folder metaphor, while the icons for particular files vary depending on the kind of file it is: executable, text file, source code, and so on. At the bottom is a status bar; and unless you have a lot of things in your home directory, it will do its business and its contents (in this case, the word *Working*) will disappear before you notice.

Clicking on a directory icon opens the directory. Clicking on a file icon performs a function based on the kind of file, the mime type, it is. *Mimetype?* Isn't that some sort of Internet convention? You bet. As I mentioned, KFM acts on the local computer as it does on the Internet. This means that items on the Internet won't be handled entirely as you might expect, but the same holds true for items on the local machine. This is demonstrated by the line beneath the toolbar that contains text in the same way that browsers have a line on which URLs can be manually entered and that displays the current URL. If you've used other Web browsers, you probably know that instead of http: or ftp:, you can enter a fully qualified pathname to a file or directory and see that file's or directory's contents in the browser. If you have ever tried it, you also probably know that you would not be very interested in using a Web browser to manage your files.

KFM is different, though. To it, your local hard drive is like a Web site, and Web sites are like your local drive. Yet KFM has features that allow you to configure it depending on the tasks you want to perform so that it will be best suited to those tasks.

Let's look at the things that facilitate file management.

This means jumping directly to the **View** menu. If you fancy the Windows Explorer style of file management, you'll want to click **Show Tree**. This renders a tree view of the current directory, your home directory, down the left side of the window. The triangles next to each listed directory can be clicked to expand that directory. Clicking on the directory itself displays its contents in the right side of the window. In short, it behaves pretty much in keeping with the behavior of the Windows Explorer. Figures 10.2 and 10.3 show how this is brought about.

Seeing the Tree Through the Forest of Icons

The tree view is always there, but when it is not selected, it is not displayed. You can get to it anytime by moving your mouse pointer to the left side of the KFM window. Just before it becomes a single-arrow sizing icon, it becomes a double-headed arrow. When it does, if you hold the left mouse button down and move the mouse pointer toward the interior of the window, the tree appears. This can be useful on-the-fly and, as you shall see, even when online.

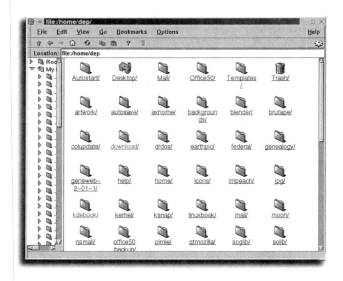

FIGURE 10.2
You can drag a tree view from the left side of the KFM window by pulling the double-headed arrow towards the center of the window.

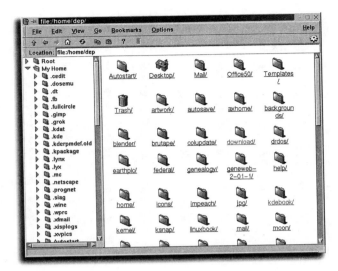

FIGURE 10.3
The tree view completed. You can pop into tree view anytime you want, without having it enabled in the View menu.

There's more to consider in the **View** menu. Linux, as you probably know, has a great number of hidden files and directories, distinguished by a dot (.) preceding the file or directory name. In your home directory, these contain either configuration files for applications that generate them in ways other than direct text-file editing (though they are almost always text files); or files that are used internally by the corresponding application, but that are specific to your particular use of the application. (For instance, your Netscape bookmarks file, an HTML file, is hidden in a directory named .netscape.) Yet for a multitude of reasons, you may want to see these files and directories and open, view, and perhaps edit them. In some cases, particularly when upgrading programs or removing them, you might want to delete the files they have placed in your home directory. (A good example is WordPerfect. Upgrading from the free downloaded version to the commercial version requires deletion of the .wprc directory. This is tough to do if you can't see the files and directories!) So **Show Hidden Files** is something you'll want to have checked, if not all the time then at least occasionally. There's a lot to be seen, as Figure 10.4 demonstrates.

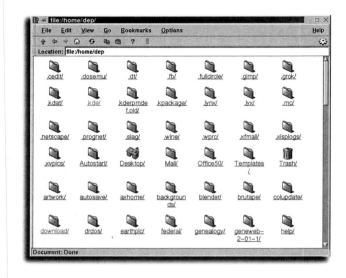

FIGURE 10.4
Lots of files and directories are hidden in your ~/ directory and with **View > Show Hidden Files** enabled, you'll be able to use KFM to get at them.

You may be more comfortable with a window that, instead of showing rows of icons with their names beneath them, displays additional information about the files.and directories. In this case, you want to click **Text View**. The result (see Figure 10.5) is a vertical table of the files and directories in a form not unlike that produced by the ls -l command in a terminal. The file or directory name is followed by its permissions, ownership and group, size, and creation time and date. You can still click a directory or file to open it and you can still employ tree view.

The **View** menu also offers **Short View**, which renders small icons with the file or directory name on the right. Its advantage is that it can display more files or directories in a window of a given size, and some people find it prettier (see Figure 10.6).

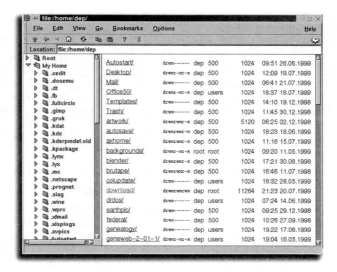

FIGURE 10.5
It's hard to believe, but <u>V</u>iew > <u>T</u>ext View represents the same contents as the other views you've employed.

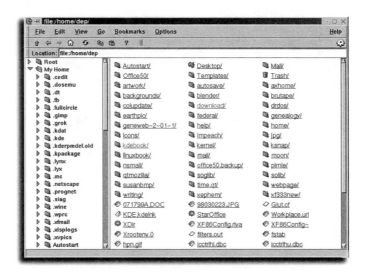

FIGURE 10.6
<u>V</u>iew > <u>S</u>hort View offers maximum value for your screen space.

Where's My Directory?

Sooner or later, every KDE user clicks on a directory and, instead of getting a listing of the files therein, is treated to an HTML page. This is because the user has saved a file named index.html in that directory. The workaround is to uncheck **HTML View** in the **View** menu. Now all the files, even index.html, will be displayed normally as icons. If you want to look at index.html, click it. It will open in HTML mode within KFM. You can then rename or delete it as its contents suggest. This typically happens when someone seeks to save a page of instructions from the Web, and the page's author has named the page "index.html."

For really effective file management, you want to make one quick configuration change. In tree view, the tree contains three items: Root, My Home, and Desktop. These remain no matter what navigation you do on the right side of KFM, where the file and directory icons appear. To fix this, click **Options > Configure File Manager**, and then the **Other** tab. Check the **Tree view follows navigation** box. Then, of course, click **OK.** Because the change is now set for this instance of KFM only, you want to click **Options** and **Save Settings**. Now you've set up KFM so that the tree view will readily display more than the three initial directories (see Figure 10.7). Even if you do not normally use tree view, you want to make this change, for reasons that will soon be apparent.

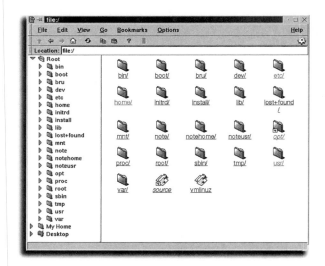

FIGURE 10.7
One setting that makes KFM universally more useful is **Options > Configure File Manager > Other > Tree view follows navigation**.

Copying and Moving Files and Directories

There are several ways of copying and moving files and directories with KFM, and each has its own special purpose. If you learn them, you'll be able to do pretty much anything efficiently.

The simplest method is to right-click the icon of the file or directory you want to manipulate. This highlights it and gives you a menu (see Figure 10.8). You can then select **Copy**. The file is not copied into memory at this point, but instead a temporary link to it is made in memory. Using the arrow icons on the toolbar, you can move around on your drive and when you get to the place you want the file to go, select **Edit > Paste**. If moving the file is what you had in mind, you need to go back and delete the original. To copy multiple files, use the left mouse button to draw a box around them; Then either choose **Copy** from the **Edit** menu or select it from the RMB menu. Again, if you want to move the files, you need to return and delete the highlighted items after you've successfully pasted them elsewhere. If you want to copy or move multiple files that are scattered among files you don't want to relocate, you can hold the **Ctrl** key and click the target files with the left mouse button to select them.

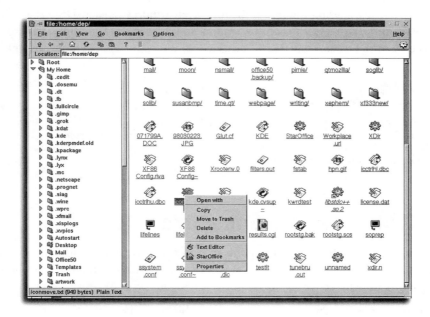

FIGURE 10.8
The RMB menu for each icon in KFM offers choices for manipulating the selected file or directory.

Caution

Make sure you have successfully copied the files before you delete them. There is no "undelete" function in Linux. To be extra-safe, instead of deleting the files, choose **Move to Trash** from the RMB. Then, if it turns out that the files have become corrupted in copying or you deleted before you pasted them, you can recover them from the Trashcan.

This isn't the most efficient way of doing things, though for a file or two it doesn't take too much time, and it *is* easy.

An alternative is to open a second instance of KFM and use the arrow icons to navigate to the target directory. Then, using the left mouse button, drag and drop the file(s) or directory or directories to their new location. Be sure to keep the left mouse button pressed as you select and drag the file. If you click first to select, you'll simply open the file or directory. The advantage to this method is that when you drop the icon or group thereof on the target, a miniature menu appears. You are then asked whether you want to copy the selected item, move it, or create a symbolic link pointing to it and place the link in the target directory.

A third method is useful if you have a tree view. Remember, you can always create a tree view by dragging the tree in from the left window border. Drag the item or items from the right section of the window and drop it or them onto the target directory in the tree. Again, you'll be asked if you want to copy, move, or link.

Jumping Around On Your Hard Drive

The browser-style arrow icons on the toolbar are of use if you're moving a directory or two. As you know, it's a long way from your home directory to the top level directory of your Linux installation. This is where the Location text box is useful. Type in **file:/** and press **Enter**, and you're there! You'll note that in tree view, your home directory is still available on the left.

Using KFM's Powerful Super User Mode

All this is just fine, but what's the point in being able to navigate all over creation if, because of Linux security protections, you can't move files into directories outside your home directory?

Actually, there are many good reasons to be able to navigate the local drive and network drives, even if you can't alter directories or files when you get there. One is that you can run executable files when you get to them, and many Linux programs are not ones that you want to put on menus. Another is to read documentation and configuration files that aren't located in your home directory.

But sometimes you need to change configurations or move files outside your home directory. (The most frequent of these is when you want to put a source tarball into /usr/local/src, extract it, and read or perhaps modify its configuration script or Makefile before compiling and installing a new program.)

Traditionally, you would open a terminal window, type **su** to call superuser mode, type in the root password, and conduct the file manipulations from the command line. This can certainly be efficient if you know the commands for the shell program you're using.

Don't Ignore the Command Line

You really should learn the terminal commands anyway, because one day they will save you. It's difficult to memorize them, though. So at minimum you should print out the command reference for whatever shell you're using. Your Linux distribution almost certainly installed it on your drive, in the usr/doc or /usr/local/doc directory. Keep the printout where you can find it. Over time, you'll become more and more familiar with its contents.

In KDE, there's a way to put KFM into superuser mode. From the Kpanel's K menu, select **System**, and then **File manager (Super User Mode)**. You'll be given a login window, where you must give the root password.

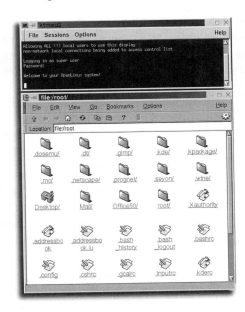

FIGURE 10.9
The login window, at top, begins **File manager (Super User Mode)** by prompting you for root's password. Your reward for entering the correct password is the KFM window at bottom, which has full root privileges.

Enter the root password. (If you are not administrator of the system, sorry, you're out of luck. You'll need to get the system administrator to perform these tasks for you.) Now a new copy of KFM appears, with full write access to the entire system. You can perform all of KFM's file manipulations everywhere.

Caution

This KFM window has all the privileges of the root user, which means that you must be extremely careful in what you do. With KFM in your home directory, the worst you can do is make your life difficult. In Super User Mode, you can literally destroy your system. Even deleting files to the Trashcan can render your system nonfunctional and make getting to the Trashcan to restore them difficult. Moving an important configuration file can have the same effect. So don't use KFM in Super User Mode unless you know what you intend to do, know that it is safe to do, and know how to get out of any situation you might inadvertently create. Nobody likes reinstalling Linux or booting from a floppy and poking around in hope of undoing damage.

Viewing Files with KFM

If you click on any icon in KFM, something happens. What that something is depends on the file type. If the file is executable (a program, signified by a KDE gear icon), the program runs. Often, if it is a part of another program or a console-mode (text-based) program, nothing visible happens, and there is no evidence of its ever having run and generated an error or anything else. Don't click on program icons unless you know what they are. If you want to find out, open a kvt or konsole window, change to the directory containing the executable file, and run it there. Then, at least, you'll see what message it returns.

All files, even executable ones, can be viewed in KFM. You can see their contents.

Text files, tarballs, and, conditionally, RPM files are the easiest: just click on them. In the case of text files, they open in Kedit and, if they are in a directory to which you have write permission, they can be edited and saved with the edits intact. If you don't have write permission, you can still edit the file, but you'll need to save it in a directory in which you do have permission, such as your home directory. Click on a tarball and, after a short wait and probably a little chugging by your hard drive, you have a window containing a directory. Click on the directory icon, and you will see all the files that make up the tarball. From here, all the file manipulation tools that are yours with other files are available. You can copy files to other locations, for instance, or edit them. You can even add files to the archive (*tar*, as you may know, stands for *tape archive*). This is true whether the file is a simple tarball, with a .tar extension, or a gzipped tarball, with a .tar.gz or .tgz extension. If the tarball is not source code but instead a compiled binary, you can learn from its structure where to put it before extracting it to make sure that all its parts go into the right places.

RPM (Red Hat Package Manager) files are a unique and wonderfully conceived kind of Linux file. Typically they are compiled binaries, though sometimes there are source RPMs. While RPMs are beyond the scope of this book, it's useful now to note that when you install them, they put files in all the right places so that they are of full use. Sometimes it's a good idea to know ahead of time what they will do. Although incompatibilities in Linux are not common, they are becoming more frequent with new shared program libraries, widget sets, and the like. What's more, if the RPM contains a program, you want to know what you need to do to access this program. In late 1998, a brilliant young programmer named Paulo Castro wrote a thing called KPackViewer that, when installed, lets you get a full sense of RPMS in KDE. Part of the installation provides the .mimelnk files (a specialized .kdelnk) necessary to look into RPMs from within KFM. If you have it installed (and if you don't, get it and install it), clicking on an RPM fires up KPackViewer, and you can see everything in the RPM. Another program, KPackage, specializes in the handling of packaged files of many types, including the extremely powerful .deb files used by Debian distributions.

Taking RPMs to the Redline

To learn everything about RPMs, read *Maximum RPM* by Ed Bailey from Sams (ISBN: 0-672-31105-4).

Indeed, all the file types for which there are .mimelnks will open in their appropriate programs when clicked from within KFM. This is not necessarily a good thing.

What?

Let me offer an example. A German company, Star Division, has produced an excellent office suite called StarOffice. It is big and powerful, and its installation program offers an option for integration with KDE. This integration is good for one thing: It builds .kdelnks for some file types that override the existing ones. Normally, clicking, say, a .jpeg file would open the K Image Viewer, which, because of its very specific nature, loads quickly. The .jpeg file would appear in the Image Viewer in just a couple of seconds, and you would be able to look at it. But after the installation of StarOffice, clicking on that .jpeg loads StarOffice in all its glory and scores of megabytes. On a very fast machine it can take 30 seconds or more. This is annoying—all this sound and fury is so you can view a little postage stamp of a graphic. It is enraging if you want to look through all the icons in the directory.

Ah, but all is not lost. If you right-click on the icon, you are given a menu that lists all the programs that have .mimelnks for that kind of file. You may choose the one specific to your needs (see Figure 10.10)

When KFM Doesn't Know What to Do

There are files for which there is no .mimelnk. These are displayed in some cases as text files, but a question mark appears atop them. In other cases, you might receive a dialog box asking you what application you want to use to open the file; type in the application name. And in some cases, there is an error message saying that the mime type is unknown. In such cases, click **OK**, select **Open with**, and when prompted, specify an application in which to view the file.

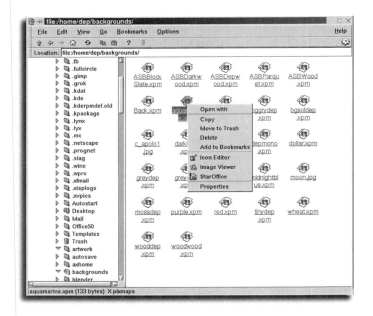

FIGURE 10.10
If KDE catalogues multiple applications as being able to handle a particular file, they are all listed on the RMB menu of that file, with the default application at the top. If you click the icon, that's the application KFM will use to open the file.

Click one of these icons, and you receive a window asking you what program to use to display the contents of this file. There is no default, but Kedit is a good place to start. If you haven't yet created a .kdelnk for, say, files from your favorite word processor and you have forgotten that you made this file with it, there's a good chance that combing through it in Kedit will remind you.

To view executable files, right-click the icon. Choose the program you want to display the contents. If you feel like it, you can look at a compiled program (or a core dump) in WordPerfect. More likely, you will choose the K Hex Editor. It probably won't show you anything useful, either, but at least it's the proper application.

Copying Distant Files: KFM for FTP

As you've seen, you can jump to any place on your local drive by typing `file:` followed by the fully qualified pathname in the Location text box beneath the toolbar in KFM.

Moving KFM's Elements Around

The Location text box, the menubar, and the toolbar all *float*, that is you can move them around the KFM window using the crosshatched bar at the left. Click it and, holding the left mouse button down, drag it to wherever you want. The Location text box and the toolbar can *dock* down the left side of the window vertically. This is practical for the toolbar and impractical for the Location text box. Feel free to experiment. The changes don't become permanent unless you click **Options > Save Settings**. You can drop them outside the KFM window, too, but this is a very bad idea because it will create clutter and confusion later if you save them.

You can do much the same thing, if you are online, on distant drives. And thus you gain the beauty and simplicity of KFM for FTP.

Try this: Go online. Open KFM. In the Location text box, type `ftp://ftp.kde.org` and press **Enter**. In a few seconds (unless the server is full, in which case you will receive an error that says your password is no good, which actually has nothing to do with it), you'll see the contents of the KDE Organization's FTP site. Click on the "pub" directory icon. Now you can explore.

Notice the look of the icons. Some look like text files on your local drive. Click on one, and pretty soon you'll have your local Kedit open with the contents of the remote file.

Now, for fun, try this: Drag open the tree view in KFM if you haven't enabled it by default. Select a directory in which you'd be willing to receive a file. (Your home directory will do if you have no dedicated download directory.) As you explore, you'll surely find a program that interests you. Drag it over to the directory on your local drive that you've decided will work for downloads. Release the button there.

The online KFM view varies depending on whether the site is arrived at by HTTP or FTP (see Figures 10.11 and 10.12)

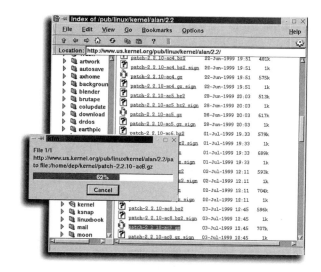

FIGURE 10.11
When you're ftp'ing a file (in this case, new Linux kernel source code), a progress box appears. It appears when you're copying a file from one place to another on your local disk, too, but may come and go in a flash.

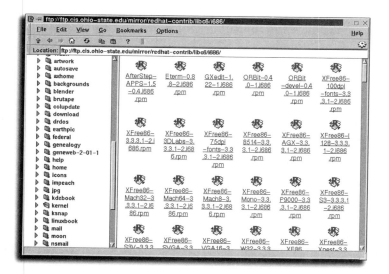

FIGURE 10.12
At some sites the view is a list, whereas at others, pure FTP sites instead of HTML pages that resemble FTP sites, you will see an icon view. You can drag and drop in either case.

Surprised? You get the same miniature menu that you would receive if you were copying a file locally. Obviously, **Copy** is the only reasonable choice, so select it, and watch as the file is copied to the local drive.

You've probably guessed by now, but I'll mention it anyway. You can select whole groups of files and drag them as a group. Unlike some FTP programs, KFM won't try to download all the groups in parallel at 50bps, but instead lines them up to be downloaded one after another serially. KFM reestablishes the FTP connection at the end of each file, so if it's a busy site, you may receive a lockout error—that old `your password is no good` error—at some point during the batch download. Just try again, dragging the files that haven't yet come across to your machine.

The use of remote directories is not entirely identical to that of local ones. For instance, right-clicking the mouse on a distant file won't give you anything useful. Neither does pointing KPackViewer at a remote package, for instance. It won't tell you what's inside. Someday maybe it will, and it would be tremendously useful for it to work that way, but not now.

Using KFM to Browse the WWW

I explore this topic in much greater depth in Chapter 24, but some discussion of it is good here, because it helps you understand the idea behind KFM. Everything in KFM is a URL. This is difficult to conceptualize, but it's not especially new. If you have Netscape installed, fire it up and type in `file:` followed by the fully qualified pathname of your home directory. You'll see a listing of directories and files, not unlike the ones you've seen if you've ever used Netscape for FTP. The difference in KFM is in the *way* it's all done, which is why KFM is good for file management and Netscape isn't.

We've seen how a file called index.html displays an HTML page if it exists in a directory, if the directory is opened in KFM, and if KFM is in **View > HTML View** mode (see Figures 10.13 and 10.14).

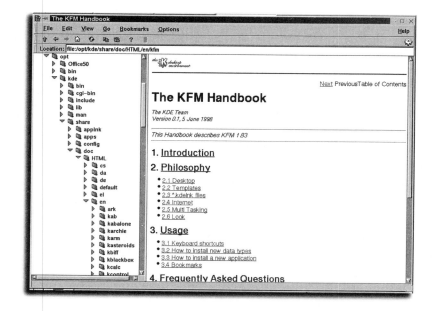

FIGURE 10.13
These are views of the same directory, which happens to be part of the KDE documentation. In the first, **View >
HTML View** is turned on...

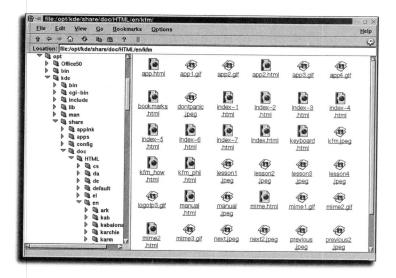

FIGURE 10.14
...while in the second it is off.

Knowing this and knowing how you can dive into an FTP site by entering `ftp://` and the location of the FTP site, you can probably guess what comes next. Yup, you can type `http://` and the location of a Web site, and it displays in KFM in most of its glory. *Most of?* Well, Java isn't supported yet, but forms are. Well, they're iffy, but you can navigate around the Web with KFM fairly well.

Why Keep Two Sets of Bookmarks?

If you have Netscape, you can use its bookmarks, which are kept in a file called bookmarks.html in the hidden .netscape directory in your home directory. If you don't want to navigate to it each time you go online, put a link to it in your home directory. Then, when you go online you can open KFM, click on the bookmarks file, and from the links there, go wherever you want. This is pretty nifty, really. To be cooler still, you can put a link to this file on your desktop and when you are online; click it to open KFM with the bookmarks loaded, ready for navigating.

Coolest of all, you can navigate to your ~/.netscape/bookmarks.html file in KFM, and click **Bookmarks > Add Bookmark**. Now it is on the Bookmarks menu for further use.

If you have a printer set up to work in Linux, you can even print a Web page from within KFM. Simply go to **File > Print** to spawn the print dialog box shown in Figure 10.15.

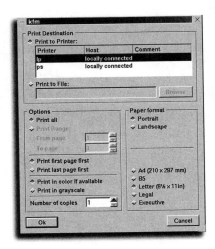

FIGURE 10.15
You can select the print spooler to employ in printing Web pages, the contents of FTP sites, and even directory contents.

Note, though, that the default paper size is A4, not U.S. Letter, so you'll likely need to change that check box before printing.

KFM's Key Bindings

KFM simplifies a number of functions by the use of key bindings, what you may have come to call "hotkeys" elsewhere. Table 10.1 tells what they are and what they do.

Table 10.1 KFM Key Bindings	
To Go	Press
Back in History	**Alt+Left**
Forward in History	**Alt+Right**
One directory up	**Alt+Up**
Open a file/directory	**Return**
Open a pop-up menu for the current file	**Esc**
Move among the icons	**Arrow keys**
Select/Unselect file	**Space**
Scroll up fast	**Page Up**
Scroll down fast	**Page Down**
Scroll right (on WWW pages)	**Right**
Scroll left (on WWW pages)	**Left**
Scroll up (on WWW pages)	**Up**
Scroll down (on WWW pages)	**Down**
Copy selected file to Clipboard	**Ctrl+C**
Paste files from Clipboard to current directory	**Ctrl+V**
Select files by pattern	**Ctrl+S**
Open a terminal in the current directory	**Ctrl+T**
Find files	**Ctrl+F**
Close window	**Ctrl+W**

KFM Command Reference

This section goes menu by menu, across the KFM menubar, describing all the choices and what they do. You probably won't need this very often, but if something has you really flummoxed, you may find the answer here.

Table 10.2 The File Menu

Function	What It Does
New	Renders a submenu that lets you create a new folder object or one of any of the other .kdelnk types. In each case, you are prompted to name the new object.
New Window	Opens another copy of the current KFM window, which is useful if you want to drag and drop files from one to the other or view multiple files at once. You can navigate in both windows, each independent of the other.
Run	Gives you a miniature command-line interface, whence you can run a program.
Open Terminal	Opens a Konsole window.
Open Location	Prompts you for a file, directory, or other URL. Its behavior is identical to that of the Location text box below the toolbar.
Find	Starts the Kfind applet and searches mounted drives for a file of a particular name.
Print	Opens the print dialog box seen. You can print anything you see in the KFM screen, even directory listings.
Close	Ends the KFM window session.

Table 10.3 The Edit Menu

Function	What It Does
Copy	Does not actually copy the highlighted item(s), but instead marks them for copying.
Paste	Inserts the item(s), marked by the Copy command into the current directory. If a file or directory of the same name already exists, you will be prompted to choose an action (see Figure 10.16).

FIGURE 10.16
You can't copy a file onto itself and if you make the attempt, KFM asks you what you have in mind.

continues…

Table 10.3   Continued

Function	What It Does
Move to Trash	Puts the selected item(s) in the Trashcan. If you have removed the file by accident, you can get it back from the Trashcan.
Delete	Erases the file. There is no turning back. If there is any doubt in your mind, use the Trashcan instead.
Select	This is an extremely useful command. It prompts you for a filename or wildcard operator, so, for instance, you could type ***.txt** or **egcs*** and all the files meeting the criterion would be highlighted so that you can perform the actions you want.
Select all	Selects everything in the current screen, whether it is a directory, an FTP site directory, or a Web page.
Find in page	Prompts you for a text string that will be sought within the current page, be it a directory listing, FTP listing, or Web page.
Find **n**ext	Jumps to the next instance of the text string you defined in **F**ind in page.
Mime Types	Takes you directly to your ~/.kde/share/mimelnk directory, giving you a chance to view, modify, or create new mime types.
App**l**ications	Opens your ~/.kde/share/applnk directory and gives you access to your applications and their settings or a place to enter a new application.

Table 10.4   The **V**iew Menu

Function	What It Does
Show Hid**den Files**	Displays the hidden (so-called *dot*) files and directories in the current window.
Show Tre**e**	Enables the tree view on the left side of the KFM window.
Show **Thumbnails**	This is useful if the directory being explored contains graphics files. It presents very small images of those files, which is usually more useful than the filename. For instance, Figure 10.17 shows a thumbnail view of a directory containing some of the graphics used in this chapter.

Twiddling Your Thumbnails

Be forewarned: If you have a directory containing hundreds of images, it can take seemingly forever for all the thumbnails to be generated. Once this is done, though, the display is very quick thereafter because the thumbnails are stored in a hidden subdirectory, /.xvpics, so new thumbnails need to be generated only for newly added images.

Function   What It Does

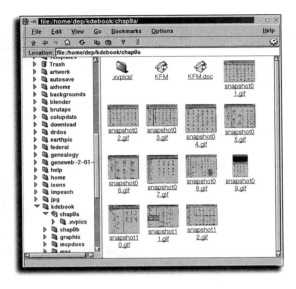

FIGURE 10.17
With the **View > Show Thumbnails** option selected, you can look at tiny preview images of graphics files in the specified directory.

HTML View

This means, really, nothing unless you are browsing the Web, in which case you will want it enabled, or you have directories containing files named index.html, in which case you won't.

Icon View

This is KFM's default view. It shows files, directories, and other objects as icons. To learn more about a particular file or directory, right-click on it and from the resulting menu, select **Properties**. This produces a dialog box (see Figure 10.18). From here you can determine file size and learn other things about the object selected. You can also rename a file by typing in a new name for it. Clicking the **Permissions** tab goes to a second page, see Figure 10.19. This lets you change the permissions and ownership of a file graphically.

continues...

Table 10.4   Continued

Function	What It Does

FIGURE 10.18
Clicking the RMB on an icon renders a dialog box full of information about the icon to which the dialog box refers.

FIGURE 10.19
The **Permissions** tab tells you who can do what with the file and, if you have failed to gain access, one possible reason.

Text View	Provides a view of the current location similar to that produced by an `ls -l` terminal command. You can still perform all functions on the files and directories listed, but it provides the information that you would otherwise need to open the Properties dialog box to learn.
Long View	This is identical to **T**ext View except that a miniature icon precedes each file or directory listed. This provides a visual clue as to what actions can be performed on each particular entry.

Function	What It Does
S̲hort View	Renders the miniature icon and filename, but no other information about the files or directories shown (see Figure 10.20). It is useful in locations that contain many files and directories.

FIGURE 10.20
S̲hort View provides a different way of looking at files and directories, which you can manipulate as you would in any other view.

Rel̲oad Tree	Rescans the tree currently used. If you have added directories or subdirectories during the KFM session, they won't be reflected in the tree view until you reload the tree.
R̲eload Document	Rescans the directory or location currently displayed and updates it. This is useful if, for instance, you have opened a tarball and want to view its contents. These changes won't be visible until you reload the document.
Rescan B̲indings	Performs the function on application bindings that the last two menu items perform on the tree view and the current document respectively, and updates them to reflect any changes made since the KFM window was opened initially. If you've added an application for a particular mimetype, it will now appear on the RMB menu for files of that mimetype.
V̲iew Frame Source	This is useful for HTML documents. When selected, it opens the editor and displays the HTML source code of the particular frame selected in the current HTML page. You can then save it to a file on the local drive, copy it, mail it, or do whatever you would do with any other text display.

continues…

Table 10.4 Continued

Function	What It Does
View Document Source	This is useful for non-framed HTML pages. It otherwise behaves exactly as does View Frame Source.
Document Encoding	Lets you change the character set used in a particular document. This is of use if the document you are viewing looks like gibberish and you're certain it's not supposed to. (Compiled binaries, for instance, always look like gibberish, no matter what character set is chosen.) If you have received a file that uses Cyrillic or Greek characters, it can therefore display them properly. Being able then to read it is beyond the scope of KFM; you'll have to learn the language yourself.

Table 10.5 The Go Menu

Function	What It Does
Up	Takes you up one level in your navigation of the local, network, or distant drive, in the same way that clicking the Up arrow on the toolbar would do.
Back	Takes you to wherever you were right before you came to where you are now. It duplicates the function of clicking the Left pointing arrow on the toolbar.
Forward	Essentially undoes the function of Back. It returns you to where you were before you decided to come back to where you are now. It duplicates the function of the Right pointing arrow in the toolbar. If it is grayed out, it means you haven't been there yet, so you can't return to it.
Home	Takes you to your home directory.

The listing below these menu commands shows all the places you've been in the current KFM session. Clicking any of them takes you directly to that location. This is useful not just for Web browsing but for hopping around your local hard drive as well. If the listing doesn't show anything, it means you haven't gone anyplace yet.

Table 10.6 The Bookmarks Menu

Function	What It Does
Edit Bookmarks	Opens a new KFM window showing the contents of your ~/.kde/share/apps/kfm/bookmarks directory. Here you can delete or edit bookmarks that represent locations on the Web or on your local drive.

Function	What It Does
Add Bookmark	Automatically creates a bookmark file of the current location. If you have Netscape, you can bookmark *its* bookmarks file and be able to use it in KFM, though you cannot add to it or remove items from it with the Add Bookmark or Edit Bookmarks menu items.

Following these two menu items is a listing of all the URLs bookmarked by you in KFM.

The Cache Menu

The items on the **Cache** menu vary depending on the build level of your KFM. In some versions, they will be found under the **Edit** menu and the **Options > Cache** menu.

Table 10.7 The Cache Menu

Function	What It Does
Show History	Renders an HTML page listing every place you have been since the browser cache was last cleared (see Figure 10.21). There is a cache for each user, determined by his or her user number.

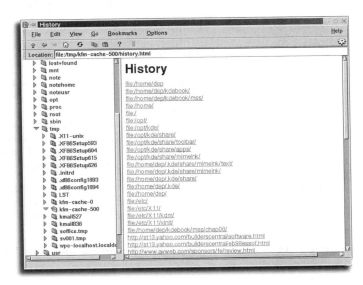

FIGURE 10.21
The **History** file lets you retrace your steps, even if you have gone offline, and in this respect differs from many browsers.

continues...

Table 10.7 Continued

Function	What It Does
Show Cache	This is actually useful because the items in your browser cache are made available for your use. Follow the instructions at the top of the cache display (see Figure 10.22).

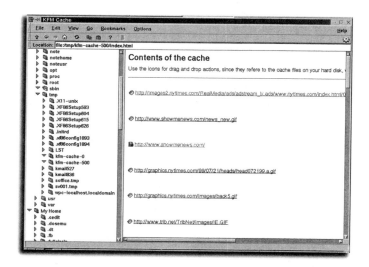

FIGURE 10.22
You may need to use the scrollbar at the bottom of the window to view everything for a particular Cache file item.

Function	What It Does
Clear Cache	This is potentially an extremely important menu item because it has distinct security concerns. If someone else is using your account or has managed to hack the /tmp directory, that person can see where you've been and what information you've used. Clearing the cache removes the ability to make use of the items in your browser cache. It also makes sure no one can tell what you've been up to, which is important in a time when industrial espionage can be a real threat.
Always look in cache	This is an item that checks cached information before reloading it from its source. When selected, it can greatly increase the loading speed of frequently visited Web pages, because all the associated graphics and so forth are stored locally in your cache.
Never look in cache	Increases load times but is useful for URLs that change frequently.
Always save cache	Makes sure your browser cache is stored when you close the KFM window. It is, as noted earlier, a potential security issue.

Function	What It Does
Never save cache	Eliminates security concerns, but means that any speed increase gained from having information stored is useful only if you return to once-visited pages in the same session in which they were initially opened. Again, this makes the most difference when you are browsing the Web. Local files load pretty quickly in either case.

Table 10.8 The Options Menu

Function	What It Does
Show Menubar	Toggles the menubar off and on. A moment's thought will raise a question, the answer to which is this: To turn it back on, right-click anywhere in the KFM window that it not an icon or text listing. The first item of the resulting menu is Show Menubar.
Show Statusbar	Toggles the line at the bottom of the KFM window that displays information about the file or directory over which the mouse pointer currently rests, or that describes the state of affairs when a directory or Web site is being loaded.
Show Toolbar	Toggles the toolbar in the KFM window. If you use it, keep it; if you don't, it frees up a little bit of space on your screen to toggle it off.
Show Location bar	Toggles the text box that displays the current URL and into which you can type a URL that you want to become the current URL. If you never use this, you might as well turn it off, though it can be a useful to keep around. Of course, with all these settings, you can switch back and forth on-the-fly.
Save Settings	Makes whatever changes you've made to the new default behavior for KFM. If you do not select this after you've made changes, the changes only apply to this window in this session.
Save Settings for this URL	Lets you adopt a slightly or totally customized view of KFM for a particular URL. This allows you to make the most of particular sites or drive arrangements without changing KFM for everything. To make use of it, a setting must be changed in KFM itself, which we're about to get to.
Configure File Manager	Opens a dialog box that lets you customize much of KFM's appearance and behavior (see Figure 10.23). You can select typeface and size here, as well as the character set to use. By clicking the appropriate tab, you can select the colors you want to have displayed to signify various attributes of the files and directories you display (see Figure 10.24). The **Other** tab is explained in Figure 10.25.

continues...

Table 10.8 Continued

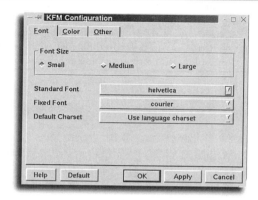

FIGURE 10.23
The Configure File Manager dialog box lets you choose how you would like the file manager functions of KFM to behave.

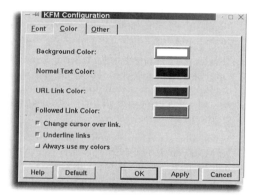

FIGURE 10.24
The **Color** tab lets you distinguish the status of the various items displayed by KFM.

Function   What It Does

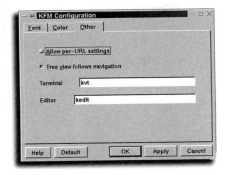

FIGURE 10.25
You can choose your favorite editor and text editor, among **Other** things. You'll
find some potentially important settings under the **Other**. One is a check box
that allows you to save settings on a URL-by-URL basis, which is necessary if
you intend to employ the **Options > Save Settings for this URL** menu item. The
other is the **Tree view follows navigation** check box, which greatly increases
the utility of the tree view. The default terminal program is Konsole, but you can
use kvt or xvt or any other virtual terminal that you like and have installed.

Configure Browser   Allows you to establish settings that are specific to the Web browsing
                               functions of KFM. The first tab is for proxy information, the second is
                               for the handling of HTTP URLS, and the third is for *user agent*
                               programs. These are programs that you want to start from within KFM
                               when online, such as a non-KFM FTP agent. The fourth tab lets you
                               choose how you want to handle *cookies*, those little files that Web sites
                               like to put on your machine for good or ill.

Using the Command Line in KDE

As is true of any operating system, there are times when the Linux user wants or needs to use the command line. These times vary from individual to individual. Some are faster at installing RPMs from the command prompt than they ever would be using a graphical package manager. Some would no sooner think of editing a configuration file with anything other than vi than they would jump off the roof. I don't know any quicker way to upzip and untar a gzipped tarball than the `tar xvfz` command. And if there is a graphical front-end for a compiler that provides for all the options users might typically employ, I've never heard of it, nor can I imagine it.

KDE offers three command-line options to the user (four, really, but one is outside KDE):

- **Konsole**, the new, improved terminal emulator. It has many improvements on older virtual terminals, but until recently it was not utterly reliable.

- **kvt**, said by many in the KDE development community to be thrown together, is on its way out. It is not feature-rich, but it always seems to work.

- **MiniCLI**, the miniature command-line interface, is a quick pop-up window into which you can type a command. Ideal for some things, it is ill-suited to many others.

- **Leaving KDE**, either by closing it or switching to another Linux terminal, is extreme, but it always works. And for some functions, such as upgrading KDE itself, nothing else will do.

We shall, then, explore each of these in turn, with an eye toward which is best-suited for a particular task. Mastering these different command-line interfaces goes a long way toward maximizing the efficiency of your KDE experience.

Slick and New: Konsole

Beginning with KDE 1.1 (it seems so very long ago, those dark ages of January 1999), a second terminal emulator was made part of the KDE distribution. It was called Konsole. It dumped core a lot at first—blew up and left its remains for autopsy in a "core" file—but when it ran, it ran character-mode applications very well. It was announced that this would be the replacement for the venerable Kvt (in KDE terms, it had been around for six months). There were many skeptics. There still are, but the skepticism has faded.

Konsole isn't much to look at, hot off the compiler (see Figure 11.1).

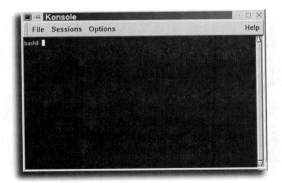

FIGURE 11.1
it isn't very pretty—no X terminal is—but it offers features that make it an attractive choice.

Konsole has features that will knock your figurative socks off. The version included with KDE 1.2, for example, has an interesting File menu (see Figure 11.2).

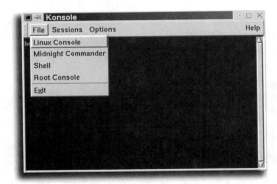

FIGURE 11.2
What file manager figures out you have Midnight Commander (see Chapter 34) aboard or lets you have a root console without typing in **su**?

The great strength of Konsole from the beginning has been its capability to run character mode applications without sending them the wrong signals. Many X terminals, for instance, have a difficult time with Midnight Commander, the excellent file manager. Commands typed in to it would actually sometimes come up in reverse order! But not Konsole, and as if to underline that fact, MC is included on the File menu. And it runs well there, though until some changes are made, the whole business is pretty tiny (see Figure 11.3).

FIGURE 11.3

Here is Midnight Commander in the default, postage-stamp size. Magnifying glass not included.

In an ultimate act of cheek, Konsole not only runs these applications reliably and as they were intended, but even properly and dependably passes along mouse clicks to console applications that support a mouse, whether you have console-mode mouse support installed or not. This is no mean feat in an X terminal. Though several claim it, few deliver it completely. To test it, I clicked **Quit** in Midnight Commander inside Konsole, and I got the result shown in Figure 11.4.

FIGURE 11.4

Konsole passes mouse commands along to applications it is running, without error, which is something very unusual among X terminals.

When I clicked **Yes**, I was returned to the Konsole prompt. To mark text with the mouse, drag the mouse cursor over the text to select it. If the application is mouse-aware, hold the Shift key as you do so. This is a fine set of arrangements, but just the beginning. KFM, you may remember, offers a Super User mode. So does Konsole (see Figure 11.5).

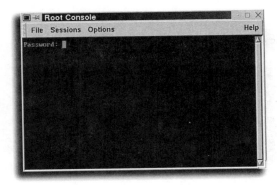

FIGURE 11.5
If you select **File > Root Console**, you are prompted for a password, but then have the run of the system.

Okay, you're right. It's not such a big deal to have a menu item that saves you from the anguish of having to type **su** and press **Enter**. Still, it's a nice touch. Even the tiny default window is good for, say, compiling applications (see Figure 11.6).

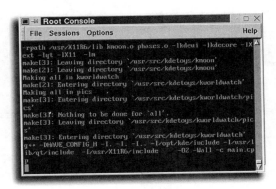

FIGURE 11.6
If you need to do other things while compiling, a small Konsole window isn't an entirely bad idea. You can keep an eye on things while running other apps if you want.

Another interesting and useful feature of Konsole is that it multitasks; a visit to the Sessions menu demonstrates this, as does Figure 11.7.

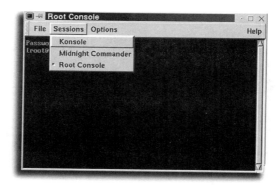

FIGURE 11.7
Konsole's multiple session capability allows you to have several virtual terminal applications open at once. The Sessions menu lets you switch among them.

The Story of Terminals

Konsole has many fine features, but in my opinion the neatest of them is found by clicking the Help > Technical Reference menu item. You will be greeted by a photograph of a VT-100 terminal, the grandaddy of them all, followed by a clear and manifestly interesting discussion and explanation of terminals and terminal emulators (see Figure 11.8). Even if you are not a computer engineer, it's well worth the read, if only to give you a sense of the sophistication of the product that KDE's developers have produced—for free!

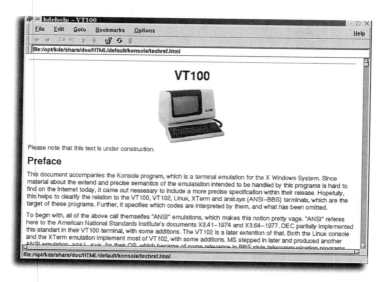

FIGURE 11.8
The Konsole Technical Reference is worth the price of admission. It's a great tutorial explaining what terminals are and how they work, even the virtual ones, like Konsole, that run on your desktop.

You can move freely among the applications running in Konsole. The number of sessions available is greater than the number you are ever likely to need.

But before we go any further, let's configure the thing a little bit with the **Options** menu, see Figure 11.9.

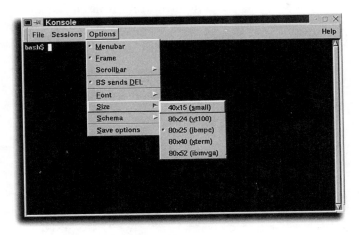

FIGURE 11.9
The Options menu lets you choose window appearance, size of typeface, number of columns and lines displayed, and a color scheme. Remember to **Save options** when you've tailored it to your needs.

It is extremely unlikely that you will have any trouble with selecting the options that you want. The one potential trouble spot, turning off the menubar, is defused by the continuous titlebar announcement. When the menubar is disabled, right-clicking in the Konsole window renders the Options menu. Thus, you can turn it back on (or save your options, if they include the lack of a menubar). If you have titlebar animation enabled in your desktop setup, and if your Konsole window is small, this message slides back and forth, all the time, annoyingly.

Remember, too, that you can alter the size of Konsole by grabbing an edge or corner with your mouse and dragging it to the size you want.

Konsole has a 100-line scrollback buffer, which means you can use the scrollbar, wherever you have decided to put it, to look back over the last 100 lines that have been printed to the screen. This is useful in those long ls -l listings, or when you've used Konsole to launch a graphical application that won't seem to start from the KDE desktop, and you want to see all the error messages. It would be nice if you could adjust the length of the scrollback buffer. One hundred lines aren't enough for some of the mistakes made around here!

The Old Reliable: kvt

The K virtual terminal, or kvt, has been around for a long time, since well before the release of KDE 1.0. It is inelegant and not especially attractive, but it works for most things you would ask a terminal window to supply. As Konsole has become more reliable, kvt has been scheduled for retirement. Like Konsole, it passes mouse commands along to applications that can make use of them, and it is fairly sparse (see Figure 11.10).

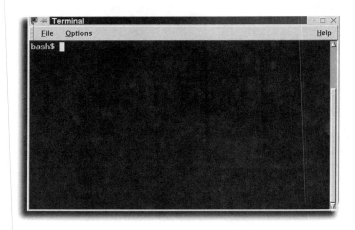

FIGURE 11.10
kvt in all its soon-to-depart glory.

What's more, kvt gets no respect at all from within the KDE community. Here is what its own **Help > About kvt...** screen has to say (see Figure 11.11).

So you really want to run kvt anyway. It's always a good idea to at least glance over the documentation, in the **Help > Contents** file, right? Well, let's see the kvt help system, in its entirety (see Figure 11.12).

You begin to get the sense that the developers at kde.org *really* don't want people to use kvt, don't you? Now that Konsole has achieved a degree of stability that rivals that of kvt, there's really no need to use kvt except in the rare occasion that you find something that refuses to run in Konsole but will work in kvt.

Adieu, kvt.

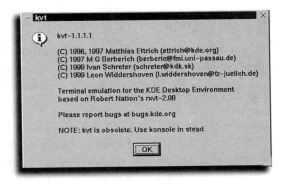

FIGURE 11.11
kvt is unique in that it advises you to take your business elsewhere.

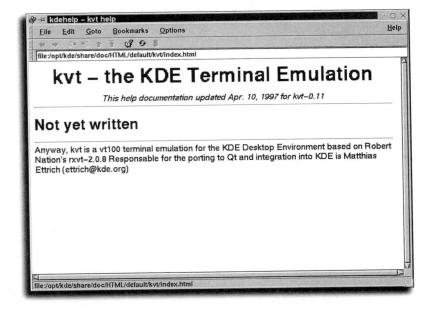

FIGURE 11.12
Nope, and now it never will be. Nor was help ever actually needed in kvt.

Quick Access to the Prompt: MiniCLI

Sometimes it's necessary to execute a quick command: something that doesn't require a whole terminal session to do. Perhaps you want to confirm that the execute string you're putting in a .kdelink is accurate, or maybe you want to start an application that is buried in several layers of menus.

For these purposes and others, there is the MiniCLI: *Miniature Command Line Interface*. (You hear reference all the time in Linux to the cli, which means you should do it from a command prompt.) There are two ways to get to it. The first is to right-click on the desktop and from the resulting menu click **Execute command**. The other is to press **Alt+F2**, anywhere, anytime.

Either way, you will be treated to what you see in see Figure 11.13.

Command:

FIGURE 11.13
The MiniCll provides instant access to Linux commands.

The niftiest use of MiniCLI, though, is in the reading of *man* pages, the first-line Linux documentation. Man pages are normally pretty ugly and unpleasant and all too frequently completely inscrutable. MiniCLI can't help with the content, but it can beautify man pages considerably. For example, this (see Figure 11.14) is how a man page looks in kvt, where the command that summons the page is `man crypt` followed by the **Enter** key.

Ah, but let us do it the modern, scientific way with MiniCLI (see Figure 11.15). Note the colon between the `man` command and the page being sought (in this case, `crypt`).

The result is shown in Figure 11.16. Nice, eh?

The MiniCLI also accepts URLs and attempts to open the location specified. It can't entirely replace the virtual terminal, but what it does it does very well.

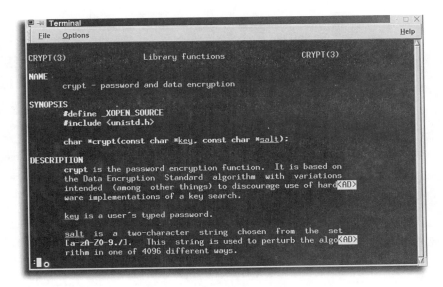

FIGURE 11.14
Man pages look just as bad in Konsole as they do here in kvt.

FIGURE 11.15
MiniCLI provides unsurpassed access to man pages. Just remember that the command here requires a colon, not a space, between the man command and the program or library for which the man page is being sought.

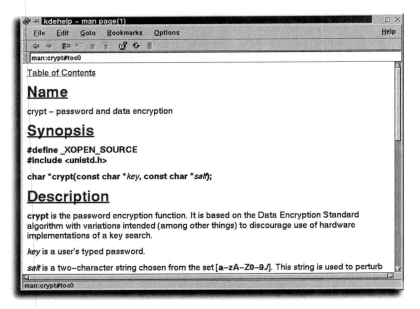

FIGURE 11.16

A man page has been rendered, all nice and graphical, with links that work and a scrollbar. This alone justifies the existence of the MiniCLI in many people's opinion.

part

III

USING THE APPLICATIONS IN THE KDE DISTRIBUTION

Managing Linux System Functions with KDE

Any Linux user is aware of, if not necessarily in love with, the fact that a multitude of processes take place in the mysterious dark recesses of the system. Each is understood by someone but all are understood by few, if any. Most involve the use of alchemy and ingenuity to produce scripts or configuration files. A working system is not to be tampered with (unless it is set up for the purpose of tampering with it), and a non-working system can be as impenetrable as the great questions of the ages are.

The Linux Nine-Hour Rule Has Been Repealed!

I used to believe that all Linux problems, large and small, require exactly nine hours to resolve, and from this formulated the *Linux Nine-Hour Rule*, which says exactly that. With the new generation of Linux distributions, the Nine-Hour Rule is no longer in effect. It has been replaced by the "I don't know; I just did some stuff and then it worked" rule.

In an effort to demystify some of Linux's esoteric inner workings, the KDE developers have built front ends for a number of functions and processes. These do not so much make those processes and functions work to begin with as make them easier, once working, to use and monitor. This chapter is about these KDE applications.

Keeping Track of Virtual Desktops with Kpager

As we have discussed, KDE joins most window managers and desktops in offering multiple "virtual" desktops, which allow you to spread your applications over a much wider area than that delimited by the borders of your screen. You can run from two to eight of these desktops, which you typically access by clicking the K Panel buttons corresponding to each of them.

SEE ALSO

➤ *Actually, you can have as many as 32 virtual desktops. To find out how see "When Eight is Not Enough" on page 123.*

Unlike most window manager/desktop combinations, though, the buttons do not try to display the applications that are running in each desktop. If you have eight virtual desktops and Netscape is running in desktop five and you forget where it is, you can poke around among those buttons for a while before finding it. KDE's effort to solve this problem is Kpager, which you'll find in **K Menu > System > Desktop Pager** (see Figure 12.1).

FIGURE 12.1
Kpager, showing four virtual desktops and the Global desktop. The latter displays all applications that are "sticky," which is to say that have been set to appear on all desktops. In this case, the lone sticky app is Kpager, which has been stretched to abnormal size for easy viewing. StarOffice is running in the first desktop and Netscape in the second, as signified by their icons. If more applications were running in any desktop, all their icons would be displayed.

Kpager is smarter than it looks. You can set it (see Figure 12.2) to show the Global desktop or not, to show its own menubar or not, to display the virtual desktops in one row or two. You can also set it to vary its display from icons to a plain view, which gives the shape of the running applications in each window, to a pixmap view, which attempts to make little thumbnail renderings of the running applications, though, it does not always succeed (see Figure 12.3).

FIGURE 12.2
The **Options** menu provides a surprising variety of Kpager configurations.

FIGURE 12.3
For some reason StarOffice, on desktop 1, does not get rendered in the **Options > Draw Mode > Pixmap** setting. This setting also consumes a tremendous amount of processor resources. The gray bar across each screen, by the way, is Kpager, stretched big for the screenshot. It is sticky and cannot be unstuck, for obvious reasons.

Enough with Kpager's shortcomings. It is very powerful. Right-click on an application, and you are given a list of things you can do to that application. You can resize an application within a Kpager window—and thereby on its virtual screen as well—by clicking and dragging on one of the application's edges if Kpager is in Plain or Pixmap mode. And you can drag an application from one virtual screen to another.

It's easy to drag Kpager from a small size up in the corner to a large size, where application icons will be more visible. Then, when you are done, you can drag it back to tininess once again.

Virtual Terminals

Though not a function of KDE itself, Linux's capability to be a multiuser operating system on a single machine is not as widely known as it should be.

Here's the trick: you can drop out of KDE and into a console—in fact, a half-dozen different consoles all at the same time—and log in as yourself or another user, or even root, anytime you want, without having to close KDE or your running applications. And you can return to KDE and your applications as if you had never been gone.

Simply press **Alt+Ctrl+F?** Where *?* represents a function key **F2** through **F6**, your choice, at the same time. (For instance, **Alt+Ctr+F3**.) This takes you to a console and login prompt. You can log in and do what you need to do: begin compiling a program, for instance. When you are done there, **Alt+Ctrl+F7** brings you back to KDE. You can have multiple console mode applications in various virtual consoles at once, as yourself, another user, or root. Sadly, you can have only one copy of Xfree86 running at any one time, so you cannot have multiple graphical sessions underway on a single computer, keyboard, and monitor.

Manipulating Running Processes with KDE

While Linux is a very robust operating system, it cannot prevent a misbehaving application from keeping system resources, such as memory, if the application misbehaves and refuses to close, doesn't close cleanly, or malfunctions in some other way. For this reason, there are means of killing a running process manually, without its permission and without having to reboot the system. These are a little obscure and daunting to the new Linux user and even to some of intermediate experience. KDE's developers sought to make monitoring and dealing with running processes much easier, if still not easy, by means of a program called *KTop*. (The name will spark recognition among many Linux users: *top* is the console program that does much the same thing.)

You can get at KTop by **K Menu > System > Task Manager**. Doing so produces a window that will look like Figure 12.4 or 12.5, depending on which tab page was being viewed the last time KTop was closed.

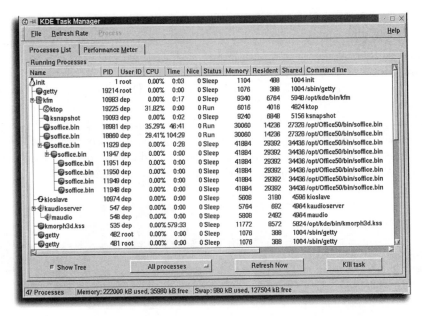

FIGURE 12.4
The **Processes List** shows you all the things that are running on your machine, which is probably far more than you expected.

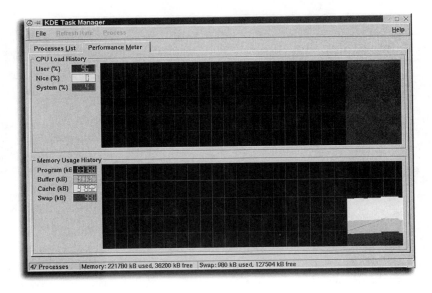

FIGURE 12.5
The **Performance Meter** shows you how your system resources are being deployed. It begins logging when you open KTop, so don't be surprised when it starts out blank.

KTop allows you to select a process and, by right-clicking, renders a menu that lets you kill the task, change its location in the pecking order for system resources, or send it any of several other signals. Some of these functions can be performed only by the root user, and you can only kill applications that belong to you. (You can tell whether you own a process by looking at the User ID column.) Much of the functionality of KTop involves topics that are far beyond the scope of this book. As I said, they made it *easier*, not easy. You can look at the man page for the top application to get a sense of what is going on here, or, for a fuller discussion of the processes and what they mean, turn to a general and comprehensive Linux manual, such as *Running Linux* or *Special Edition Using Caldera OpenLinux 2.2*.

When a Program Stops Responding

From time to time you will likely encounter an application that seems to have locked up. It's a good idea to wait a minute or two, just to make sure it's not in the middle of something. Once you're convinced that it's down for the count, you can haul away its remains with a simple key combination. (This is a famous problem with Netscape. It's not Netscape's fault but instead the fault of the vast army of incompetent HTML and JavaScript programmers who have built some very bad Web pages.)

When a program is dead but not gone, press, at the same time, the **Alt+Ctrl+Esc** keys. You will see that the mouse pointer has turned into a skull and crossbones. Move it to the wayward application and click on it. Poof! It's gone.

Be careful when you experiment with this—I heard those key clicks—because once you click those three keys, everything on your desktop freezes until you click on and kill an application or—and this is the secret few know—click on all three of them again, which makes the mouse pointer of death disappear.

Or so it seems. Forgotten but not gone is more like it. Use **K Menu > System > Task Manager** and look in the **Processes List** to see if it left pieces of itself in memory, as it probably did. When you find a piece of it, click to highlight it, and then click **Kill Task**. To make sure it "took," click **Refresh Now**.

The Kill signal sent to the application is a Signal 15, which is the binary way of saying, "Don't get your coat, don't get your hat, just leave." Once you have selected a process to be sent to its eternal reward, you may want to put it away a little more benignly, which you can do by clicking the **Process** menu and selecting, instead of Sigkill, the more polite **Sigterm**. If the application has the slightest bit of self respect, it will collect its hat and coat, apologize for upsetting you by cleaning up any files it has left around, and depart quietly. The disadvantage is that this doesn't always work. In this case, you can go back and drag out the big gun, **Sigkill**.

It is possible, though not common, for an application to freeze the entire X Window System. If this happens, your lone recourse is to press **Alt+Ctrl+Backspace**. This closes X and KDE—the whole works. You can now safely restart X and KDE and try to figure out what went wrong.

The Performance <u>M</u>eter provides a graphical representation of what your system is up to and how its resources are being used. If you are lucky enough to have a multi-processor (SMP) machine, you receive a separate graph for each processor.

Managing Your Printer

One of the buzz phrases of the 1980s and 1990s was the *paperless office*. The idea was that everything would be on computer, so there was no point in having file cabinets stuffed with papers and printouts. Yes, everything would be on the computer, where it could be found with just a couple of keystrokes. (What's that? Was that a "yeah, right!" from somewhere back in the crowd?) A friend, I remember, got a scanner in hope of eliminating the clutter in his office. Everything went first into the scanner, then the trash. He actually caught himself one day scanning in some junk mail that had arrived the day before. The project, so far as I know, did not last long.

It has not, of course, worked out as promised, at least not yet, though Linux users come closest to the paperless office of any group of computer users. In part, this is because their communications typically happen by email.

The Paperless Manuscript

This book, for instance, will be on paper in my house for the first time when the bound, published edition arrives. Everything else has been done in Linux and sent via email to my editors, who are generally enlightened but who do not have an all-Linux shop...yet.

I have friends, real Linux gurus, who have never hooked up a printer. When I began using Linux, I asked for printer advice and found no one who had ever installed one—not that they couldn't. It had just never seemed a particularly useful thing to do.

And it is in part because connecting and configuring a printer is not as easy under Linux as it is under some other operating systems. (The relative difficulty may be because of the relative unimportance assigned to printers among Linux folk.)

The fact is, though, that printers *are* useful even to Linux users. We all have friends, or perhaps customers, who live in the unconnected dark ages, to whom paper letters must sometimes be sent. When configuring a tricky aspect of Linux, it is comforting to have printed out the man page or HowTo file or ReadMe to serve as a combination guide/security blanket.

Now, having said all that, let me note that while there are graphical ways of setting up your printer, you won't find one in your KDE distribution. Maybe someday, but once you have your printer installed and working under Linux, KDE does provide one or two printer administration tools that make your life easier.

The first of these, the one that is useful to you no matter what printer you kave installed, is *KLpq*. You get to it by going **K Menu > Utilities > Printer Queue**. (If you have a printer icon on your desktop, you get to KLpq by clicking on it.) It is a KDE front end to the printer queue(s) you already have installed on your Linux system. It provides quick access for monitoring print jobs and even changes the order in which they are printed, killing one that has gone astray, and performing other tasks, depending on the permissions you have. It has a busy appearance (see Figure 12.6), but is not tremendously complicated to use.

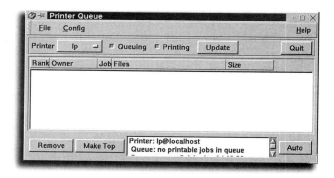

FIGURE 12.6
KLpg, showing the queue for a native PostScript printer with, in typical Linux fashion, nothing queued to print.

When you start KLpq for the first time, you are asked which print spooler program you use. Chances are it's BSD. Try that. If it can't find your spooler, try the others until it finds the one you are using. If it never finds one, you need to revisit your spooler setup.

If you know nothing about your print spooler, you need to revisit the printer setup portion of the installation of your Linux distribution. Most distributions include tools to ease this process, but they may not be highly informative. You may need to crack open the manual to find out what sort of spooler you have, or, you can try various things with KLpq. You're very likely to find it.

After you have found your spooler, the only other configuration option is how frequently you would like the display to be updated. This is set, in seconds, using the slider in **Config > Auto update**. The default is 0, which means it does not update itself unless you click the **Update** button or press the **U** key on your keyboard. The Auto button then tells KLpg to update at whatever interval you specified.

There is every likelihood that you have more than one print spool on your machine. Typically, you have one that sends raw text to the printer, another that filters application printer output (which is usually in PostScript format, and converts it into a form your printer can use), and a third (which is not preceded by a PostScript filter) for use by applications that provide their own printer drivers and wish to speak to your printer in its native language. (The latter applications are usually commercial ones, such as WordPerfect. StarOffice speaks directly to your printer if you have a PostScript printer. Applix products do it all, speaking directly to some printers, to all PostScript printers, and to your print spoolers, which you select when you print.) The Printer list box lets you choose from among them.

The Printing and Queuing check boxes let you select what is displayed.

You can highlight a print job and use the **Remove** or **Make Top** button to delete it or move it forward in the queue. Right-clicking on a print job presents you with a menu with the same two choices.

Another feature of KLpq is drag-and-drop. This is supposed to let you can drag a file icon into the main KLpg window and drop it there (or drop it onto the KLpq icon, if KLpq is not a running application on your desktop), and the file prints. This works about as well as similar arrangements work in other operating systems, which is to say, sometimes. If everything is exactly right—your default queue is the one you want and the file is in a format that your printer (or queue, if it includes a filter) can understand—you might end up seeing your document and learn once again that typos never appear until they are on paper. If everything is not exactly right, you can enjoy page after page shooting forth from your suddenly very fast printer, with one character or one line on each page. This is no fun.

The other printing administration program that might be helpful (which is why I said KDE provides one or two such programs) is the tool for use with Hewlett-Packard LaserJet printers—**K Menu > Utilities > HP LaserJet Control Panel** (see Figure 12.7). If you do not have one of these printers, it will be of no use to you. On the other hand, if you *do* have one of these printers, it will also be of no use to you unless you have one of the latter-day HP LaserJets that have no controls on the printer itself. For those, this application is a replacement for the provided Windows software.

If you have a late-model LaserJet printer (a 5L or 6L, for instance), the LaserJet Control Panel will be familiar to and of interest to you. The rest of us can sit this one out. (By the way, there is no Help button on the LaserJet Control Panel's first two pages. There is one nestled among the controls on the third tabbed page, the one headed Operations.)

FIGURE 12.7
It's pretty, but what does it do? The LaserJet Control Panel is certainly useless to users who don't have LaserJets, and possibly useless to those who do.

Handling CD and Floppy Drives

Another place where Linux is different in a startling and unpleasant way to new users is its way of dealing with CD-ROMs and floppy disks. Because of security issues, these usually cannot be popped into the appropriate drive and read or, in the case of a floppy, written to, as they can in DOSrivative operating systems. To read a CD, you must first put it in the CD reader, and *mount* it, using a console or terminal command like this:

```
mount /mnt/cdrom
```

And you usually must be the root user in order to do even that. This depends on your Linux distribution and the defaults it sets. To change it around, look for information in your distribution's documentation on editing /etc/fstab. Then, when you are done, you must issue another command:

```
umount /mnt/cdrom
```

If you don't, Linux won't let your CD reader give you your CD back. And yes, the command is umount, not *unmount*, something that has puzzled most Linux users at least once. (Actually, most Linux users probably remain puzzled on this score, but at least they learn how to get their CDs out of their machines.)

Mounting a floppy can be even worse:

```
mount -t msdos /dev/fd0 /mnt/floppy
```

The `msdos` part is if the disk is DOS formatted. If it is Linux formatted, it would be `ext2` instead of `msdos`. This is followed later by

```
umount /mnt/floppy
```

And woe to he who yanks a floppy without umounting it!

For some reason, some users think that this is all a bit much. So, some distributions provide various means for automatically mounting and umounting CDs and floppy disks. If you have CD and floppy icons on your desktop, there's a good chance you have such a distribution. The rest of us must be content (as a surprising number of us are) to use the weird commands shown earlier. It makes us seem cool.

But KDE hasn't forgotten the floppy disk user entirely. One of the applications in the KDE distribution is KFloppy, (see Figure 12.8), found at **K Menu > Utilities > KFloppy**.

FIGURE 12.8
KFloppy lets you format floppy disks. That's all.

You can use your KFloppy to format floppy disks. It is a regular formatting machine, offering various sizes (3.5- and 5.25-inch), various densities (High Density and Double Density), and even your choice of formats (msdos and ext2). You can do a quick format or a full format. You can provide a label, let KFloppy provide a label, or leave the disk unlabeled. That is, however, all that you can do with KFloppy.

CD management is an area under active development among KDE programmers, with new applications in the works that catalog CDs, provide a front end to CD writers, and so on. It is useful to check the KDE home page (`www.kde.org`) from time to time to learn about the newest developments.

Hard Drive Management

There are a couple of little KDE tools that do not come with the distribution (in fact, I've seen them only in source code) but that are well worth downloading and compiling in order to help you keep a handle on your hard drive usage.

They are Kdu and KDfree, and they come together in one package along with a program called KSlot that is of use to you only if you have a three-disc CD changer. They all compile together, so unless you want to go fiddling with the code, you get all three at once. They are small, and KSlot will do you no harm if you install them but are not blessed with such a CD reader.

I shall now tell you in excruciating detail how to get and install these programs, and then how to use them. While this is not strictly within the scope of this book, if you have never compiled anything in Linux before, you are going to have to learn sooner or later, and it might as well be now. And this little package compiles very easily, so it is a good first effort. I shall assume that you have a good compiler, egcs, installed, along with such libraries and development packages as are customarily used in compiling programs in Linux. If you don't have these, go get them and do not come back to class until you have. Actually, if you have a fairly modern Linux distribution— anything since the beginning of 1999, certainly, will do—you have these tools, though you may need to install the packages from the distribution CDs.

First thing, log on to the Web and go to `ftp://ftp.kde.org/pub/unstable/apps/utils/` where you will find, down the list, a file called kdu-0.9.3.tar.gz. Download it. Log off the Web. No, don't even check the email; we're waiting on you.

Now, open a terminal and type **su** and press **Enter**. When prompted, type in your root password and press **Enter** again. Then type **cd /[directory containing the downloaded kdu-0.9.3.tar.gz]** and press **Enter**. Now type **cp kdu-0.9.3.tar.gz /usr/local/src** and press **Enter**.

What you've done is obtained the source code and copied it into the directory set aside for source code. Now you'll extract it from its compressed archive.

Type **cd /usr/local/src** and press **Enter**. Then type **tar xvfz kdu-0.9.3.tar.gz** and hit **Enter**. (This gunzips and extracts the files from the tarball.) You will have seen the files go into a directory called /usr/local/src/kdu. Because you are already in /usr/local/src, type **cd kdu** and press **Enter**.

You are called upon now to know the directory in which your KDE resides— /opt/kde, /usr/local/kde or even /usr if you're running Red Hat 6.0. Type **./configure --prefix=[your KDE directory]** and press **Enter**. You can now sit back and watch as your system is searched for all the ingredients necessary for a wholesome and flavorful program. You will see it produce the Makefiles, which are the instructions the compiler will use in building the program.

When it is all done, you'll be returned to the command prompt. Now type `make` and press **Enter**. You can watch the program compile. You may see the word `WARNING:` appear from time to time. Ignore it. In just minutes you will be returned to a command prompt. If instead you see a line that says `ERROR` followed by a number, you do not have all the things you need to compile properly. Unfortunately, the errors can be a little bit obscure. Fortunately, for this application, the likelihood of an error is very unlikely. If you get an error, look at the line above the error line to see what was lacking. Usually, it is a matter of downloading a newer package from your Linux distributor's ftp site. Finally, type `make install` and press **Enter**. You will see lines go zipping by as everything is out into place.

Now, in your terminal window, type `exit` and press **Enter**. You are no longer the superuser, but your terminal window is still open. Type `kdu` and press **Enter**. You will be treated to what you see in Figure 12.9.

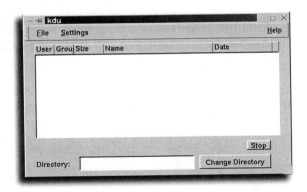

FIGURE 12.9
At first, Kdu doesn't show anything except that you've successfully compiled it.

The Kdu screen is empty because you haven't selected a directory to display. Kdu, by the way, is a KDE front end to the Linux `du` command. It shows how much disk space is being consumed by particular files, directories, and subdirectories on your drive. Let's see, for instance, what a KDE directory looks like (see Figure 12.10).

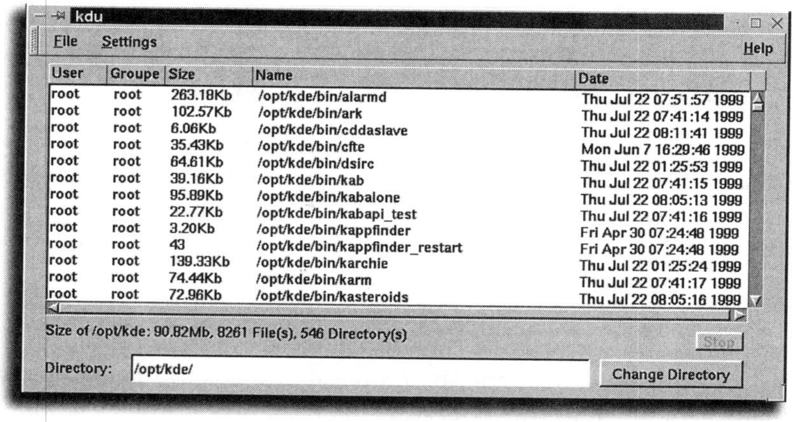

FIGURE 12.10
My /opt/kde directory, which includes several bells and whistles, takes up 90.82MB of hard drive space.

Hey! How'd I do that? Easy. I clicked on **Change Directory**. A listing of the subdirectories in my ~/ directory popped up, as did a drop box at the top of the listing that offered me a choice of /home (~/), /root, and the Root Directory of the system. Because /opt is just off the Root Directory, I chose that, and then /opt, whence I clicked on **kde** and I was there. The system chugged along for a few seconds as it tallied up all the files in the directory and all its subdirectories. Then it gave me the total you see.

As you can well imagine, this is a useful program for hard drive maintenance. When things are getting a little tight, you can see where the offenders are and how much space can be gained by getting rid of a particular file, program, or directory. Of course, you do not want to delete a file, program, or directory the purpose of which is unknown to you.

The controls are extremely simple. The **File** menu lets you change the directory on which you are seeking information or close the program. The **Settings** directory lets you decide what information you want to have displayed in the screen report. That's it.

Now, let's close Kdu. You still have a terminal open, so type kdfree and press **Enter**. *Voilá*! See Figure 12.11.

KDfree, we now learn, lets you know how much space is available on your drive or drives (partitions being viewed as drives). We also learn that I didn't expect Caldera 2.2 to put KDE into /usr/opt with a symbolic link to /opt, so I made a root partition far bigger than anything I am ever likely to use. If things get tight, I'll delete the symlink and make a real directory named /opt, move KDE to it, and put a symlink pointed the other way in /usr/opt. If this doesn't make sense to you yet, don't worry, it will in due course.

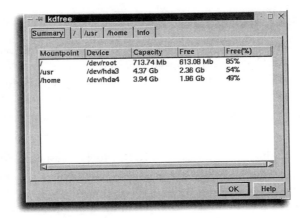

FIGURE 12.11
KDfree looked at all the Linux partitions on my hard drive and told me how much space is available on each, both as
an amount and a percentage of the total partition.

As you can see, I partitioned the drive, using fdisk, to make four primary partitions
(the swap partition isn't shown by KDfree; what would be the point?). But there is
more to be learned about each partition, as you see by clicking the tabs for the individual partitions (see Figure 12.12).

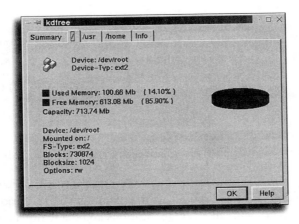

FIGURE 12.12
In addition to statistical information on the drive or partition, KDfree graphs disk usage. The reference to memory, by
the way, isn't RAM but instead storage space on the instant drive.

And if you happen to have a three-CD changer, I leave KSlot up to you to figure
out. You have compiled it. You can do anything!

KDE's Desktop Clipboard

Back in the old days it was not a simple thing to move a small amount of data from one program to another. Clipboard programs were memory-resident applets that were invoked by a hotkey combination. They were not particularly reliable, often got more or less information than you wanted from the source application, and pasted it weirdly into the target application; the whole thing was usually more trouble than it was worth.

Then came the graphical user interface (GUI), which usually provided a system-wide Clipboard that would let you copy and paste text from one native application to another. (The one in OS/2's later versions would even let you copy and paste graphics.) There were various add-ons offered, including programs that would keep more than one item in the Clipboard at a time, so you could go back and select something you copied or cut a while ago.

Surely you will not be surprised to learn that KDE includes such an application, Klipper. You start it by selecting **K Menu > Utilities > Cut & paste history (klipper)**. Once you have started it, you can leave it alone forever. It is swallowed by K Panel and restarts when you restart KDE.

To use it, you click on its icon in K Panel, and it produces a little menu (see Figure 12.13).

FIGURE 12.13

Klipper is employed by clicking the K Panel Clipboard icon. If the icon isn't there, you haven't started Klipper yet. It lists the items recently cut or copied by any application running under KDE.

Pick an item. It can be a little obscure, and there's no way to preview the contents. It becomes what will be inserted at the cursor location in an application when you click **Edit > Paste**. It works with all KDE applications and many others; some, such as Netscape, allow Klipper to receive data copied from the application, but will not paste material from Klipper into the application.

Klipper doesn't save its contents from session to session, so when you close KDE, they're gone.

Keep Your Eyes Open for More

New KDE utilities and front ends for Linux functions are avalable almost daily. It's a good idea to check the KDE Web page, www.kde.org, and its applications links for new and useful programs. These are available first in source tarball, but you know what to do with those.

Keeping Track of Your World with KOrganizer

In the DOSrivative world, they're called *PIMs (Personal Information Managers)*. If you see some of the advertisements by the companies that make PIMs, they assure that your path to affluence and influence is unencumbered by missed appointments or social *faux pas*.

KDE has a personal information manager named KOrganizer. It comes without such claims, but you'll see that it is as full-featured a product as are some of the expensive commercial products, and it is getting better with each new version. It does depart in many areas from KDE's conventions, making it a little harder to learn than some KDE applications. And while it is full-featured, it will not automatically order flowers and make dinner reservations on your wedding anniversary. It does, however, remind you that the anniversary is coming up and equips you with the names and numbers of the florist and the restaurant. Then again, if you have the email addresses of these establishments, it might just do those things, too. In short, it works.

KOrganizer is located at **K Menu > Applications > Organizer**, but many users make it one of the first applications they add to K Panel, as you learned to do in Chapter 7, "Making a Super K Panel." It employs as its native file format the ASCII text vCalendar protocol, which means that if you have been using a PIM in a different operating system, there is a good chance that some or all of your data can be exported to KOrganizer. It additionally offers tools for synchronization with the popular 3Com PalmPilot personal digital assistant. Its other features include

- A full calendar program with national holidays marked for your choice from among many nations.
- An appointment book with multiple levels of alarms that are triggered by a small, separate program so that KOrganizer doesn't need to run all the time.
- A running To Do list.
- A link to the KAddressbook applet.
- Group capability for use by more than one member of an organization, business, or family.
- The capability to mail appointments to others on the local network or even over the Internet.
- A wide choice of view options, from a simple calendar to a complex matrix of all KOrganizer's elements at once.

A program that offers all this is bound to be complicated, and in some respects KOrganizer is. It's nothing that you can't quickly get used to, but not everything works exactly as your first guess would suggest.

Which View Is Right for You?

When you start KOrganizer for the first time, you get a screen that looks like Figure 13.1 (except, of course, that it displays today's date).

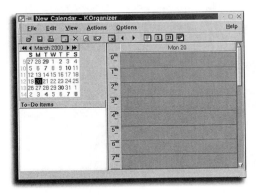

FIGURE 13.1
The default KOrganizer view features a small calendar of the current month, today's appointment list, and a To Do list that is not specific to the date. That which you put off yesterday you'll be reminded of today.

The divider that separates the calendar and To Do list from the appointment list can be dragged to the right to make more room for To Do items, though the calendar's size remains constant. Depending on the typefaces you have installed, some months and years may not fully display in the calendar's title.

The default is a good general view, particularly of use to people in business. For a better overview of how busy a week is likely to be, you might choose **View > Work Week**, as shown in Figure 13.2.

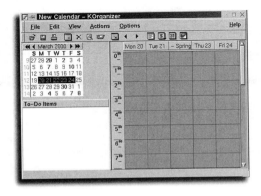

FIGURE 13.2
The work week view provides an overview of this week, a week in the past, or a week in the future. Double-clicking on a box highlights it; double-clicking again spawns a dialog box whereby you can enter an appointment.

An increasing number of people, especially those who telecommute or run their own businesses, consider the work week to be seven days long, and for them there is **View > Week** (see Figure 13.3.)

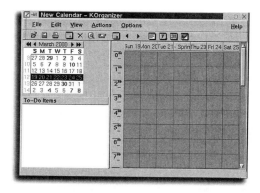

FIGURE 13.3

The week view has all the features of the work week view, but recognizes that there are seven days, not five, in a week. Clicking on a date on the calendar, by the way, switches KOrganizer to day view for the selected date.

Of more general use, perhaps, is **View > Month** (see Figure 13.4) where you can see a month's calendar at a glance.

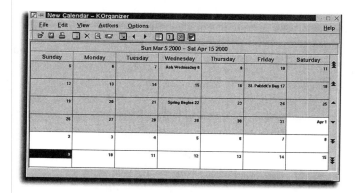

FIGURE 13.4

Month view displays an entire month, though not necessarily a calendar month. The small black triangles at the right let you navigate in time: The single triangles at center move the date a week at a time; the double triangles send you forward or back a month at a pop, and the triple triangles let you see what you did last year or what you will be doing next year.

Month view is particularly useful when trying to figure out such things as the day of the week on which an historical event took place. Using the stylized triangular arrows on the right, you can go a week, a month, or a year at a time, back to 1753, which is far enough for everyone except those who celebrate the Salem witch trials. You can also navigate far into the future. I stopped clicking when I got to the year 3029, which ought to be enough for even the most optimistic of us, though of course we cannot know if KOrganizer is Y3K compliant. There is a good likelihood you will have upgraded your software by then, anyway, which is another reason to be happy that KOrganizer's file format is portable.

The final view, though it is first in the **View** menu, is **List** (see Figure 13.5).

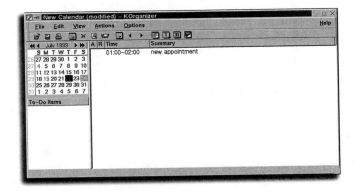

FIGURE 13.5
List view summarizes the day's activities. The columns let you know whether an alarm has been set for a particular item, whether it is a recurring event (such as a birthday or the date the mortgage payment is due), the time of the event, and a brief description of the item.

In List view, you can right-click on an item to produce a menu that allows a date column to be displayed in the list, the editing of the item (which also reveals details about it not seen in the summary), and deletion of the event.

Remember that these are all different views of the same data, and what you can see or modify in one you can see or modify in any of the others.

Some Configuration Options You Should Know About

KOrganizer does many things in ways that differ from other KDE applications. For this reason, you want to spend some time in the **Options > Edit Options** dialog box, the first page of which is seen in Figures 13.6 and 13.7.

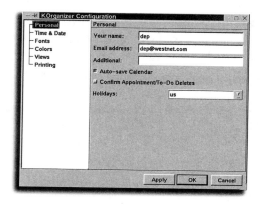

FIGURE 13.6
Instead of the tabbed pages design characteristic of KDE applications, KOrganizer is configured by way of an arrangement reminiscent of the KDE Control Panel. You would not typically change any of this page's defaults except perhaps the country whose holidays you would have KOrganizer show.

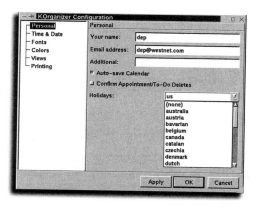

FIGURE 13.7
Holiday selection is via a drop-down list. No dual citizenship here. If you celebrate Thanksgiving, Boxing Day, and Bastille Day, you'll need to keep track of two of them some other way.

You will likely make some changes in the **Time & Date** page (see Figure 13.8). The choices are straightforward, but its defaults may not be to your liking. The Time Zone is the number of hours offset from Greenwich Mean Time, to which your Linux system is, or should be, set. If your appointments usually run more or less than one hour, you can change it here, as well as the alarm time. If you make appointments seven days per week, you'll want the **Week Starts on Monday** check box unchecked.

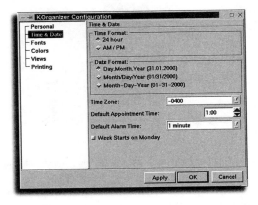

FIGURE 13.8
Another departure from KDE convention: You are not allowed to change the configuration to base your appointments on Internet beat time (see Chapter 5), for which your clients and associates can be grateful.

You are likely to want to make some changes on the **Fonts** page (see Figure 13.9) as well, if for no reason other than the fact that the default 5-point Helvetica used in Month view in some versions is not discernable on any known monitor. Clicking on the button next to each listed font produces a straightforward but non-standard font selection dialog box.

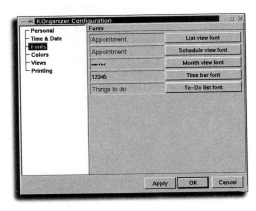

FIGURE 13.9
Can you read the default Month view font? Neither can anyone else. Here is where you change it.

The Colors page comes next (see Figure 13.10), and you can do as you wish, accept the defaults, or click on the **Use system default colors** check box.

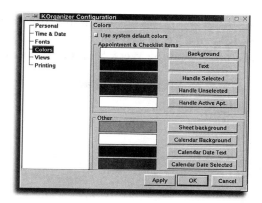

FIGURE 13.10
Clicking on the button next to an element produces, somewhat surprisingly, the standard KDE color selection dialog box.

The Views page (see Figure 13.11) presents its own small mystery. The Day Begins At: spin button lets you set an hour before which you do not make appointments, saving you from having to work your way from Midnight when setting appointments. And Show Events that Recur Daily in Date Navigator lets you decide whether the color of the date on the thumbnail calendar used in some views, which changes color on dates where you have appointments, changes for recurring events. The mystery is the slider that changes the Hour size in Schedule view. There isn't any Schedule view, and it doesn't seem to change anything in any other view. I can't find anyone who knows what it's for. So you can probably leave it at the default without much risk.

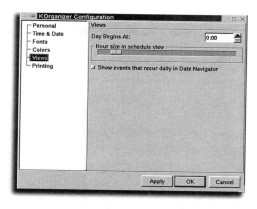

FIGURE 13.11
Okay, the icon on the KOrganizer toolbar for Work Week view is labeled Schedule View in the bubble help. But the slider has no effect on the size of the hours there. So you can ignore the slider.

Printing (see Figure 13.12) lets you set some options for the making of hard copies of your calendar. Like many of the other KOrganizer configuration pages, this one, too, is nonstandard, which is in part a good thing. It lets you set a paper size that is remembered from session to session and does not default to A4. You can choose which print spooler to use, and you can specify a print preview program (such as gv) if you like. If you don't, know that **File > Print Preview** does not work.

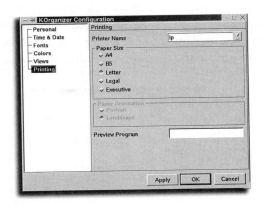

FIGURE 13.12
Paper Orientation is grayed out in the Printing menu because the shape of the window automatically determines the orientation.

From all that, you should be able to cobble together a configuration that is suited to your way of working.

A few more menu options are worthy of your attention, if only to prevent confusion. In the **File** menu are **Import from Ical**, which brings existing calendars created using the Linux Ical program into the current calendar, and **Merge Calendar**, which joins your choice of the calendar files in your ~/ directory with the current calendar. This is especially useful when KOrganizer is used as groupware.

Actions > Mail Appointment sends a copy of a specific appointment, with all its details, to any participants in that appointment for whom you have email addresses. This is how you can set up KOrganizer to contact the florist and restaurant, although it probably would be easier to just dial the phone yourself.

Appointment Handling

You can get to the screen where you set appointments in any of a number of different ways, and some depend on the view you are employing. The two ways that always work are to click **Actions** > **New Appointment** or **Actions** > **New Event**—the former being a "timed event," the latter not—and then click the icon that looks like a calendar but has no X or number on it. It is the one that's fourth from the right, to the right of the printer. This is an application where bubble help helps, because the icons do not provide instant clues. In Day view, quadruple-click on a time slot on the right to get the Edit Appointment dialog box (see Figure 13.13). The same holds true for Work Week and Week views. In Month view, double-clicking on a date produces the New Appointment dialog box (see Figure 13.14), which differs from the Edit Appointment dialog box. The New Appointment dialog lacks the capability to delete the appointment, because it doesn't yet exist.

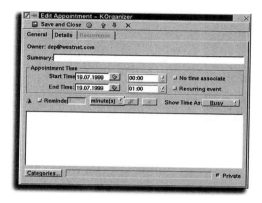

FIGURE 13.13

The Edit Appointment dialog box builds on the New Apppointment dialog box because with Edit Appointment you can click on the X and delete the appointment...

Both of these dialog boxes are busy places. They are so busy, in fact, that the only icon in the toolbar that you could probably identify without any help—the Save icon, as is true throughout KDE, is a representation of a floppy disk—is the only one that is labeled. The others—a circle with a vertical line (Cancel), an up arrow (Previous Event), a down arrow (Next Event), and an X (Delete this appointment)—require you to wait for bubble help. Then there is a line labeled Owner that lists your email address for some reason. The Summary line is where you write what will appear in the other views, particulary List view.

In the Appointment Time section, KOrganizer again goes on its own. What looks like a spin box listing labeled Start time is actually the date on which the event takes place (or begins, for those multiple-day events). Clicking on the associated widget produces a thumbnail calendar from which you can select a month, day, and year. Likewise, End time begins with the date. In fact, there is no place to enter the time at all unless you uncheck the No time associate check box, which is there to specify that this appointment doesn't take place at any special time. If the box is unchecked, you can then access drop boxes offering time in 15-minute increments (see Figure 13.15).

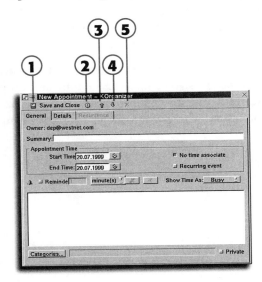

FIGURE 13.14
...while with New Appointment you can't.

(1) Save and close

(2) Cancel

(3) Previous event

(4) Next event

(5) Cancel this appointment

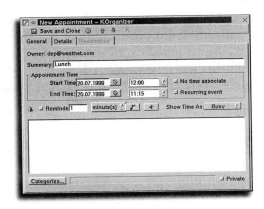

FIGURE 13.15
Beware! KOrganizer allows you to set an appointment that ends before it begins. If you save it in this state, it sets the start and stop times both to be the *later* of the two times selected. No warning is issued, so you risk being reminded only of the appointment you just missed.

Beneath the No time associate check box is another, Recurring event. This simultaneously removes the date portions of Start time and End time: and makes available the Recurrence tab page. (A nice feature is that you can still uncheck No time associate so that you can enable an alarm to remind you of the 3p.m. Wednesday meeting or your favorite television program.)

If you want to be alarmed about this event, check the **Reminder** check box and specify how many of the units you choose in the time unit drop box to have as warning before the event. You may choose the manner of your warning by clicking the musical symbol button, whereupon you get a listing of sounds (see Figure 13.16).

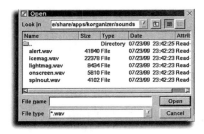

FIGURE 13.16
You can choose among the sounds provided or navigate with the Look in list to a sound you like. What does the sound sound like? You'll need to wait until the appointment to find out: there's no preview facility.

Next to the musical symbol button is a button that leads you to believe by its picture, a man running, that it must be where you choose a program that is to be run at the specified time. It renders the same dialog box, with the same contents, as does the musical symbol button. You can browse in search of the proper executable file for the program you'd like to have run, if you want, but smart money is on setting the alarm to go off well enough ahead of time that you can start the program yourself. Perhaps a later version will offer K Menu or a place to add command-line modifiers, such as a file to be loaded into the program, when you click this button, but not yet.

Next to all this is a drop box labeled Show time as:, with the choices being Busy and Free. And beneath all this is a large text box where you can enter details of the event. Beneath this is a button labeled Categories, which renders the dialog box shown in Figure 13.17.

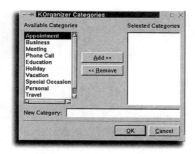

FIGURE 13.17
The KOrganizer Categories dialog box lets you characterize your appointments in unusual ways.

It is not immediately apparent, but here's what you do with the KOrganizer Categories dialog box:

1. Highlight a word in the list on the left that you want to have characterize this appointment.

2. Click the **Add** button. This adds the word to the list on the right. If there are several words you would like to use, repeat.

3. If you think better of it, you can use the **Remove** button to take away the word highlighted in the list on the left. Make certain that you get the words you want and none that you don't want *before* you click on **OK.** Once you have okayed your choices, reopening the KOrganizer Categories dialog box no longer lets you remove them except by replacing them with something else. You can't blank the line in the new appointment that follows the Categories button.

The Private check box keeps the appointment in your local calendar and does not share it with others who might be using the same calendar.

Clicking the **Details** tab provides additional possibilities to help you pass the time until the appointment takes place (see Figure 13.18).

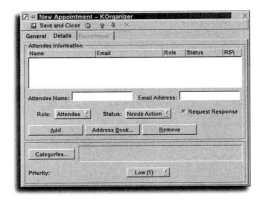

FIGURE 13.18
The Details tab lets you list everyone involved in the appointment and how important you think the appointment is.

Here you list all the people expected to be in attendance at the appointment, which is not a bad way for those in a group to check in and state their plans to attend. You can enter a name and email address in the appropriate text boxes. Then the status of the person can be established in the Role: drop box (see Figure 13.19).

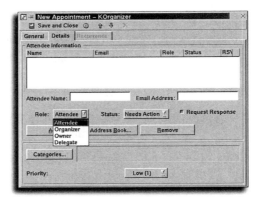

FIGURE 13.19
The Role drop box lets you assign a category to the participant.

Likewise, the Status drop box lets you choose what must be done, if anything, about this appointment or meeting (see Figure 13.20).

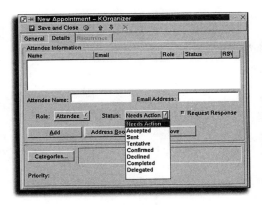

FIGURE 13.20
What to do? Status provides a reminder.

The name and email address can be filled out for you if the participant is listed in the Address Book (see Figure 13.21). When all is well, click **Add**, and the person is added to the list in the until-now blank text box labeled Attendee Information. If someone can't make it, you can click **Remove**, and the person highlighted in the Attendee Information box disappears.

SEE ALSO
➤ *The Address Book button is a link to KAddressbook, a KDE applet that is detailed in Chapter 15, "Multimedia: Music and Movies," on page 341.*

FIGURE 13.21
Address Book opens an address book applet where you can search for participants for your meeting.

Once again, you can assign Categories to your meeting, and now you can assign a Priority to the event with the drop box shown in Figure 13.22.

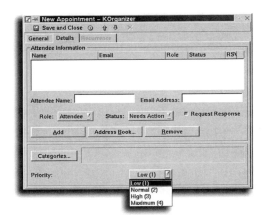

FIGURE 13.22
Choose the relative importance of this event with the Priority drop box.

If you are always forgetting the weekly meeting, or someone's birthday, or National Paper Clip Awareness Week, KOrganizer is for you. Go to the **Recurrence** tab page (see Figure 13.23).

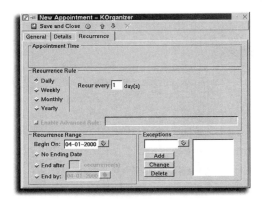

FIGURE 13.23
The Recurrence tab lets you enter just once an event that happens over and over. However, if you forgot to uncheck the No time associate box on the General page, you'll be able to narrow it down only to the day.

If you unchecked No time associate on the General page, you'll find a place that lets you select a time of day for the event; otherwise, no, which does limit the utility of daily reminders ("Still Alive" is just about it, and even that would one day be wrong).

Which is to say that you can set the reminder to go off at a given time every day: perhaps you need to take medicine or vitamins at the same time each day, or you need to call to make sure the kids got home safely from school. You can also set weekly, monthly, and even yearly reminders by checking the appropriate box.

The Recurrence Range section lets you stop being bothered by the alarm when the prescription runs out, the project for which the meetings are scheduled is completed, you've paid off the mortgage, or you break up with that special someone whose birthday you needed to be reminded of. If you are in prison, perhaps you can remind yourself of the number of days remaining in your sentence, or the regular schedule of parole hearings, if the screws let you have a computer.

The Exceptions section allows you to specify times when the alarm will not go off because the event will not take place. The Monday meeting might fall on a holiday and therefore be cancelled, or the Grinch might steal Christmas. You get the idea.

Organizing Your To-Do List

As complicated as setting an appointment can be, adding an item to the To-Do list is simple. Right-click on the list and select **New To-Do** from the resulting menu (see Figure 13.24).

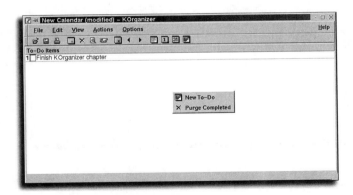

FIGURE 13.24
Right-clicking on the To-Do list lets you enter a new item and remove completed ones.

Having selected **New To-Do**, you are presented with a blank line in the list, which you can fill out as you wish. You should notice that it is preceded by the number 1 and an empty box. If you double-click on the number, you will be given a list of priorities for this item, from 1 to 5, as seen in Figure 13.25.

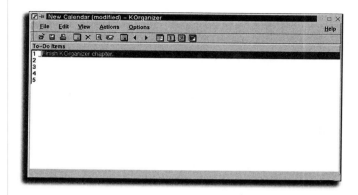

FIGURE 13.25
KDE standards are again flung down and danced upon in the selection of a priority for an item in the To Do list.
Double-click on the **1** to get a drop box of other numbers.

When an item has been completed, you can rid yourself of it. Double-click on the little box after the number, which enters a check mark there (see Figure 13.26). Then, using the right mouse button, draw forth the menu again and select **Purge Completed**. All items marked with the check mark are deleted.

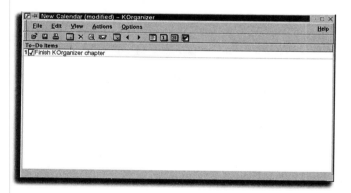

FIGURE 13.26
Mark an item as completed by double-clicking the box that follows the priority number.

An additional oddity is the RMB menu when you click on the item itself, as in Figure 13.27. This is a puzzler because it contains items that apply to more than the selected item. This is also where you can sort the entire list by the priority numbers you assigned to the specific items.

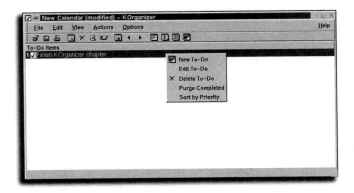

FIGURE 13.27
Clicking the RMB on an item in the To Do list produces a menu that offers general as well as specific choices.

The KOrganizer Alarm Daemon

When you started early versions of KOrganizer, an icon would appear on K Panel. It looked like a KOrganizer view icon, but it had a bell atop it. It was the alarm daemon, a small program that runs even when KOrganizer isn't running, to keep track of any alarms you have set. It ran even if you had no alarms set, and while it did not take up much processor time or memory, it did consume some, and it was very difficult to kill.

In recent versions, though, it runs only when you have actually set alarms while entering appointments. This is a big improvement, and it requires only that your computer be on with KDE running.

As you can see, while KOrganizer is still a little rough around the edges, it is also very powerful as calendar applications go. With a little practice, you'll wonder how you ever did anything else.

chapter 14

Programs that Make Your Everyday Work Easier

Most modern GUI desktops come with a set of accessory programs that are designed to let you learn the new system a little and that are useful in their own right. KDE is no exception. Indeed, the base KDE distribution contains a vast array of *applets* that perform a variety of tasks. These include multimedia programs, graphics viewers and editors, archive handlers and a tape-backup tool, games, a handful of screen toys, some screen utilities, configuration and system information tools, a full Internet suite, and a group of programs that ease administration of a local network. Each of these categories receives our consideration in its own chapter. This chapter is about the basic applications, including some you are likely to use every day (and some that, depending on the kind of computing you do, you may use every day or never). These are applications that you are likely to add to K Panel for instant access. The most fundamental, and essential, of these is a text editor, so that's where we'll begin.

KEdit for Text Files

If you have ever used a simple text editor under any operating system's GUI, you will have little problem with KEdit. It is, as they say, intuitive in all of its major functions and conforms admirably to general KDE standards. If you've mastered KEdit, you have mastered much in other KDE applications as well. It does offer a few nice little surprises, though, and we'll get to them after we've gone over the basics.

When you open KEdit for the first time (**Applications > Text Editor** from the K menu), it looks like Figure 14.1.

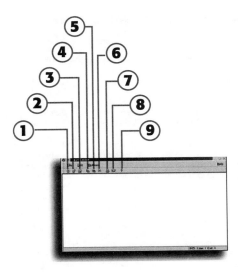

FIGURE 14.1
If you haven't looked at a KDE application before, KEdit is a good introduction. The menubar icons and many of the menu items are consistent in most KDE apps.

① New

② Open

③ Save

④ Copy

⑤ Paste

⑥ Cut

⑦ Print

⑧ Mail

⑨ Help

The toolbar is consistent with practically all other KDE applications, so let's look at the meaning of the icons from right to left:

- **New** creates a new file and is the default behavior of KEdit upon opening.

- **Open** gives you the standard KDE file selection dialog box, shown in Figure 14.2. You choose the file you want to open in KEdit.

FIGURE 14.2
The standard KDE file selection dialog box lets you choose a file to open in KEdit or almost any other KDE application. This window will become familiar to you, if it isn't already.

- **Save** saves the file to disk. You are given a dialog box, shown in Figure 14.3, identical to the **Open** dialog box except that you now have to select a location for the file and, of course, a filename.

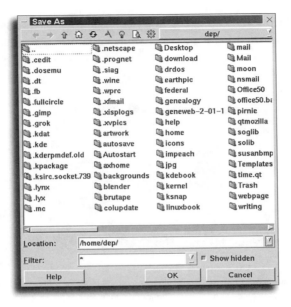

FIGURE 14.3
The file selection dialog box now lets you decide not which file to open, but where to save a file and under what name to save it. If you choose an existing filename, you are warned (see Figure 14.4) and, if you choose not to overwrite the existing file, are thrown back to the file selection dialog box to try again.

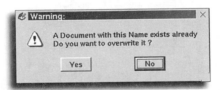

FIGURE 14.4
If you click an existing file while trying to save or type in the name of an existing file in the text box, you receive this warning.

- **Copy** loads the selected text into the Clipboard for reuse.
- **Paste** inserts the Clipboard's contents (or most recent contents, if you are using Klipper) at the current cursor location.
- **Cut** removes the selected text and holds it in the clipboard for reuse. If you make an additional cut, this material is purged, unless you are using Klipper. In this case, it is moved down one step in the clipboard order, and you need to go to Klipper if you want to retrieve it.

- **Print** produces the Print dialog box (see Figure 14.5). This is one area where KDE applications differ somewhat. Some applications, such as KFM (discussed in Chapter 10, "Navigating *Everything* with KFM"), offer a completely different dialog box.

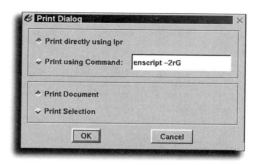

FIGURE 14.5
Print directly using lpr usually works; otherwise, you can enter whatever command is required by the print spooler you are using. You also have the choice of printing the entire document or just the selected (highlighted) section.

- **Mail** sends the document to the person specified in the mail dialog box, shown in Figure 14.6.

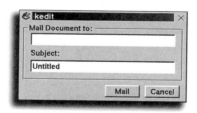

FIGURE 14.6
Enter an email address and a subject and, if you are online, your file wings its way to the specified recipient.

- **Help** opens the KEdit Help file. It's always useful to read, though you will notice that it is probably a few versions behind. This doesn't matter much because KEdit is a stable application and the few changes that get made from release to release are usually small, internal ones.

You won't see all these icons in every toolbar in every KDE application, but when you do see them their meaning remains constant. In this way, KDE can be both powerful and easy to use.

Configuring KEdit

For the huge majority of purposes, KEdit works just fine in its default configuration. But you're using Linux, so there's a good chance that you're easily dissatisfied with things as they are served to you and are eager to change things so that they suit your tastes and not someone else's. Good for you! You can do that with KEdit's **Options** menu.

The first item lets you select your screen **Font** and is illustrated in Figure 14.7.

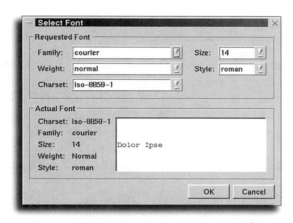

FIGURE 14.7
If you plan to use KEdit for system configuration files, it's a good idea to use a monospaced typeface, such as Courier, rather than a proportionally spaced one. Why? Because several Linux configuration files are tabular and will look awful and be difficult to follow when editing otherwise.

The **Colors** option lets you set foreground and background hues from the now-familiar KDE Select Color dialog box.

It's a poor idea to make any changes to the **Spellchecker** unless you plan to write using KEdit in a language that uses accented characters. If you do, change **Encoding** to Latin 1. Bear in mind that this doesn't provide the character set for such writing, but it simply keeps the spellchecker from thinking that words with accented characters are misspelled.

Options > KEdit Options renders the dialog box shown in Figure 14.8.

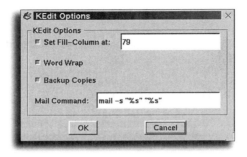

FIGURE 14.8
The KEdit Options dialog box offers choices unique to KEdit.

The **Set Fill-Column at** check box and text box and the **Word Wrap** check box are useful if you are using KEdit for non-programming purposes and don't want your paragraphs to appear as long, continuous lines. If you select **Backup Copies**, the next-to-last version of a file being edited is saved in the same location as the original, and with the same name but for its being followed by a tilde (~). **Mail Command** provides a place for you to enter the command that KEdit employs when you use it to mail files. There's no reason to change it unless the default fails to work.

Make Backups Automatically

I highly recommend that you enable the **Backup Copies** feature if you are using KEdit to alter configuration files. It's not as good as the sensible expedient of saving the original versions of configuration files as *filename*.orig, but it's better than nothing. And few people always remember to back up files before messing with them.

Auto Indent is a programmer's setting that sets the indent of a new line to that of the last line that contained anything but a carriage return. If you're not a programmer, you don't need it. You can **Hide Tool Bar** if you'd rather go to the menus, and you can **Hide Status Bar**, the bottom line that tells you whether you are in Insert or Overtype mode, your location in the file, and sometimes other information at the left part of the line, if you find its information of no use to you.

Any changes you make apply only to the current session unless you click **Options > Save Options**.

Special Functions of KEdit

It being inconceivable that you don't know the basics of using a simple text editor, we'll jump ahead to some functions that you may not have encountered with other text editors. These are found primarily in the **File** menu, though **Edit** has a couple of contributions to make, too.

File > Open Recent provides a list of files edited in the current KDE session (see Figure 14.9). You can click any of them to reopen it.

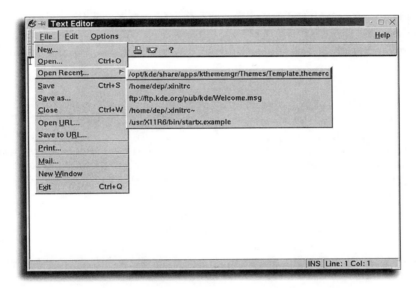

FIGURE 14.9
If you've ever tried various possibilities in fine-tuning a configuration file, only to have to climb up and down the directory tree over and over in search of the file you're working on, you'll appreciate the **File > Open Recent** menu item.

You can read, write, and save text files on the Internet with KEdit almost as easily as you can on your local machine. (If you have browsed to an ftp site and have clicked on a README file, you have seen this in action, at least the reading of remote files.) This is achieved using the **File > Open URL** and **File > Save to URL** menu items. Each opens a dialog box in which you need to specify the URL you have in mind. Of course, you do need write access to the Internet site to be able to save a file to a URL (and good thing, too).

Edit > Insert File renders the familiar KDE file selection dialog box. Here you can select a file for insertion at the current cursor position, so make sure the cursor is in the right place. If you want to add today's date to your file, choose **Edit > Insert**

<u>D</u>ate. **<u>E</u>dit > <u>G</u>oto Line** is a lot less useful if you don't have the **Status Bar** enabled, but it's still not useless. For instance, you could discover a problem in a program you have compiled. Accordingly, you might think it of sufficient import to email the program's author, who might in turn suggest that by substituting a value on a certain line in a certain file with a different value and recompiling, the problem will go away. You can jump directly to the line you need. Don't pooh-pooh this. It will happen.

Drag and Drop

KEdit subscribes to KDE's excellent drag and drop protocol. This means that you can drag a file from KFM and drop it onto a KEdit window, and KEdit opens the file. If you have KEdit as an icon on your desktop, you can drop the file on the icon with the same results.

Editing Root Files from Your Desktop

It is tiresome to log out and log back in as root if you want to edit a configuration file outside ~/, and it is tiresome, too, to have to climb up and down the directory tree if you use **K Menu > System > File manager (Super User Mode)**, especially when you could simply open a terminal, su root, and then type **kedit filename**. The problem is, on some if not all current Linux distributions, doing so produces an error:

```
Xlib: connection to ":0.0" refused by server
Xlib: Invalid MIT-MAGIC-COOKIE-1 key
kedit: cannot connect to X server :0.0
```

There is a solution. If before you su root you type

```
Xhost +local
```

and press **Enter**, you can run KEdit or any other X Window System editor you have installed and edit your configuration file as root. If you do this frequently, you might consider adding the line to the top of your ~/.xinitrc file, making it always available. Then, you don't need to type it in.

Beware, though, that doing this could pose a security risk to some extent, giving other users access to X. Like all security risks in Linux, it is a matter of convenience, and whether you think it likely that someone will fool around with your machine. The setting, when made in a terminal window, remains in effect for the rest of that KDE session.

If You're a Programmer or Want to Be: The Advanced Editor

From reading the KEdit information, you have probably recognized that programming requires different features of an editor than does simple text file editing. Beginning with KDE 1.1.1, an editor that is attuned to these special needs is included in the basic KDE package. It is the Advanced Editor, also known as KWrite. I mention it because many people moving from the DOSrivative world are likely to think that it is to KEdit as WordPad is to Notepad. That's not true...unless you're a programmer. Because we are here, it might be a good idea to highlight some of the differences. If you're a programmer, they will delight you. If you aren't, you'll learn why you probably want to stick with KEdit for most purposes.

K Menu > Applications > Advanced Editor brings KWrite to your screen. (If you think of it, the next time you're root and using kmenuedit, you might want to move KWrite to **K Menu > Development**, where it probably belongs.) And you will see (see Figure 14.10) that it looks a great deal like KEdit.

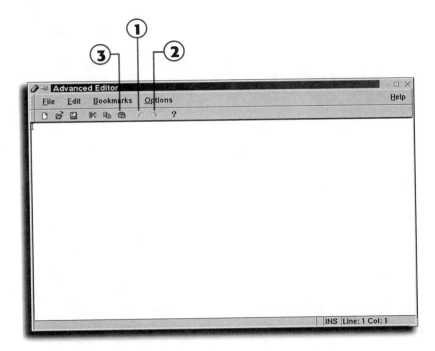

FIGURE 14.10
The apparent differences between KWrite and KEdit are the replacement of the **Printer** and **Mail** toolbar icons with **Undo** and **Redo**, and the addition of a **Bookmarks** menu.

① Undo

② Redo

③ Bookmarks menu

Notice the absence of a Printer icon? There is no Print command in the **File** menu, either. You cannot print from KWrite. (Nor can you mail directly from it, which is a difference that few will notice or care about.) The **File** menu does offer something new, namely **New View**, which opens a second window of the same file so that you can look at two sections of it at once.

The **Bookmarks** menu doesn't refer to a listing of Web sites and ftp locations, but instead to places that can be marked within the file being edited. When bookmarks are added, they are listed by line number in an addition at the bottom of the menu itself. This is useful to the programmer and, I suppose, others under certain circumstances.

It is, however, the **Options** menu that most vividly tells us that we're not in an ordinary text editor anymore. This is best illustrated by **Set Highlight** (see Figure 14.11).

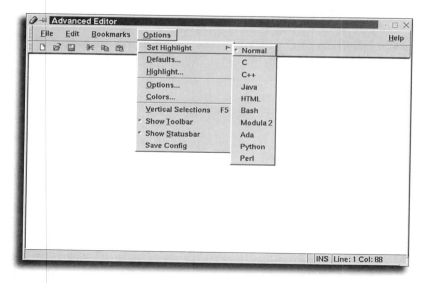

FIGURE 14.11
KWrite offers special highlighting options for each of 10 programming languages and scripting formats.

Another option of use chiefly to programmers is **Vertical Selections F5**, which when toggled lets you select blocks of text not just by line but by line and column.

If you are a programmer, these are welcome developments, so to speak, and if you aren't, you now know why KWrite is probably of limited use to you.

Hex Editor: If You *Really* Need to Look at Binaries

Since the earliest days of the Norton Utilities (and probably earlier than that), it has been deemed useful to have a binary file editor and viewer. I did not know why then, and I barely know why now, but KDE supplies one. You can find it at **K Menu > Utilities > Hex Editor**. I bring it up because you might see it and wonder what it is, and because you might be someone who hopes that such a thing exists. It does (see Figure 14.12).

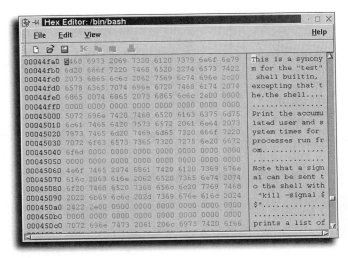

FIGURE 14.12
The **Hex Editor** is a powerful tool for those who know what to do with it, and a powerful way to really screw up your system for those who don't. If you don't believe me, make some random edits to an important binary file, save it, and watch what happens when you try to run the program. Better still, just believe me.

To those who know what to do with it: Hex Editor supports drag and drop, so you can drag your binary file from KFM to it and it will open.

To those who don't know what to do with it: If you want to go poking around in binary files, looking for cute comments made by programmers (and there are a lot of those in Linux), make sure that you limit your looking to files for which you don't have write permission. Then you can't break anything. To be extra sure—you really can't imagine the damage you could do—don't change anything and, when you close the program, if it asks you if you want to save changes, say **No**.

Prospecting with KFind

It has probably happened to you: You are looking for a file that you just know exists somewhere on your hard drive. The problem is you can't remember where, and Linux is a big place with lots of little subdirectories in which a file might hide.

For such occasions, there is **KFind** (see Figure 14.13). You open it by **K Menu > Find Files**.

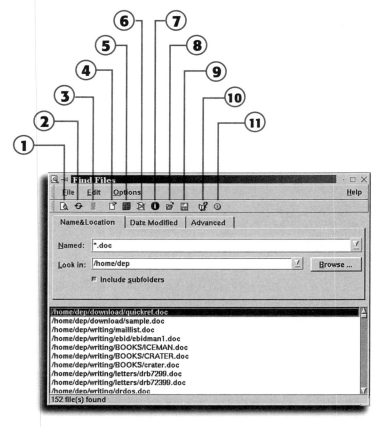

FIGURE 14.13
KFind is a front end to the Linux **Find** command, with lots of extra functionality.

① Start Search	⑤ Add to Archive	⑨ Save Search Results
② New Search	⑥ Delete	⑩ Help
③ Stop Search	⑦ Properties	⑪ Quit
④ Open	⑧ Open Containing Folder	

You can probably use KFind in a very basic way without the slightest bit of instruction, but its power isn't immediately visible on the surface. As we have done in a few other places, let's begin by running down the toolbar icons because they aren't necessarily intuitive and are certainly not consistent with the rest of KDE:

- The first icon, with the looking glass, is **Start Search**. As its name implies, it begins the search for whatever file you have asked it to seek.

- The two curved arrows, the second icon, is **New Search**, which removes the results of the previous search and the search parameters themselves so that you can begin to search for a different file.

- The third icon, a traffic light visible only when a search is underway, is **Stop Search**, and it stops the current search. It never turns green: You can't use it to restart the search.

- The fourth icon, a file with a little arrow making a right turn at its upper-right corner, is **Open**. If your target is a text file or file of a type to which a program has been attached, this opens the program in the text editor or other program respectively. If it is an executable program, it executes the program, making this button useless if the object of your search is a script that you want to look at and edit. (If the search turns up more than one file, you need to select it before you can use this or any of the other file-specific commands.)

- The next button, which looks like a gift-wrapped package with green ribbon, is **Add to Archive**. Clicking it opens the standard KDE file specification dialog box, where you can direct KFind to the .tar file to which you hope to add the selected file.

- The file icon with the red X across it is **Delete**. It erases the selected file. You are then prompted for confirmation. It doesn't just delete the file from the found list, it also deletes it from your drive.

- The universal information icon is your link to the **Properties** of the selected file, and clicking it produces the same dialog box as does right-clicking on the file in KFM and choosing **Properties** from the resulting menu.

- The open folder icon is **Open Containing Folder**. When clicked, it launches KFM at the location of the selected file.

- The save icon signifies the **Save Search Results** function. Depending on how it is configured, the search results are saved either to a text file or to an HTML file. The default is the latter. A confirmation message tells you the name of the file (see Figure 14.14). If the search is saved as HTML, the listing of files is in the form of links, and clicking one produces the same result you would have received using the **Open** command.

FIGURE 14.14
It's a good thing you're told the name of the file to which the search results were saved because, as you can see, it is a hidden file.

- The book with the question mark is the **Help** icon. As of KDE 1.2 the help file was several versions old, but don't worry: you have this book!

- The little circle with what looks like a letter *I* in its middle is **Quit**. Click it to close KFind.

The **File** menu duplicates the icon functions in a more intuitive way, while the **Edit** menu is largely grayed out, with the only functional item being **Copy**.

Configuring KFind

There's not much to configure in KFind and half of that is disabled as of KDE 1.2. You can find the lone item that does exist to configure by choosing **Options > Preferences** (see Figure 14.15). (Why a one-item menu? Who knows?)

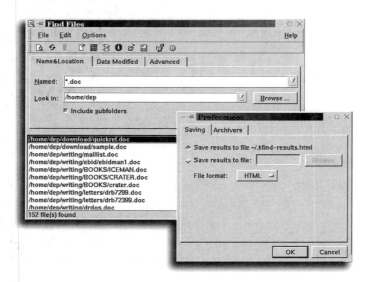

FIGURE 14.15
The **Saving** tab in **Preferences** lets you choose to save your results to a file of the default name in HTML format, or to a file whose name you specify, in either HTML or text. Don't bother to click the **Archivers** tab: there's nothing you can change there, anyway. Your choice is Tar, and that's that.

Conducting a Search

In its easiest form, a **KFind** search is done like this: Type in the name of the file for which you are looking, and if you like, narrow the search to a particular area of your Linux installation (see Figure 14.16). You may use the standard Linux wildcard operators if you like. Then click the first button in the toolbar.

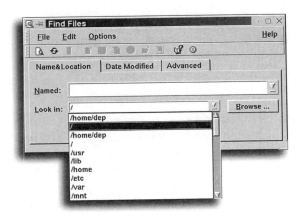

FIGURE 14.16
You can use the **Look In** drop box to narrow the places in which KFind will search. Or you can use the **Browse** to bring up a list of directories, beginning with your ~/. Narrowing the search reduces the time it takes to complete, which can be a minute or more if you have a very large drive or drives fill of files.

Another way to narrow the search is to use the **Date Modified** tab. If you remember working on the file in the last month or so or it is part of a program you just installed, you can enter a date or range of dates (see Figure 14.17), and KFind will only display files that meet those criteria as well as any you set on the **Name&Location** tab.

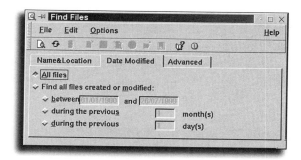

FIGURE 14.17
You can narrow your search by specifying a range of dates during which the file you seek was created or modified, or a period of recent time during which creation or modification took place.

The **Advanced** tab (see Figure 14.18), sad to say, doesn't work. If it did, it would search for files containing a specified text string, and a drop box would let you search as to file type. You could further narrow the search for file size and specify that the file is at least that size or no bigger than that size. As it stands, its use on three different computers produced the following results: On one, it worked as expected. On another, it located every file on the drive. On a third, it found nothing.

As of KDE 1.1.2, the **Advanced** tab works properly! Hurray!

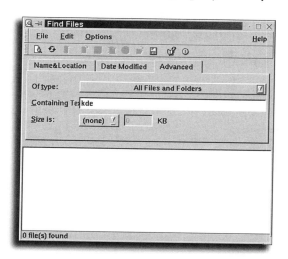

FIGURE 14.18
The **Advanced** pageworks in KDE 1.1.2, but it doesn't in earlier versions. Example: Its 1.1.1 iteration reports that there are no files on my hard drive containing the text string kde. In 1.1.2, it listed 75 such files in my home directory alone.

Despite its shortcomings, and they are few, you'll discover that KFind is a very useful utility. It saves you a lot of time.

kCalc for Calculations Anywhere

A calculator has become standard equipment with any graphical user interface, and in this regard KDE is no different. It offers kCalc, shown in Figure 14.19, and kCalc offers much. You can get to it through **K Menu > Utilities > Calculator**.

FIGURE 14.19
There's more to kCalc than meets the eye.

Though there's not much to configure in kCalc, what is there is important. Although you might not guess it at first, the little box containing the name of the application is the button that opens the KCalc Configuration dialog box, shown in Figure 14.20.

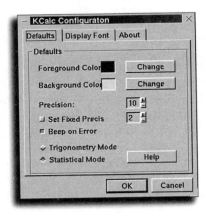

FIGURE 14.20
The **kCalc** button opens the configuration dialog box. It's pretty meaty, isn't it?

The changing of colors is simple: clicking the **Change** buttons produces the standard KDE **Select Color** dialog box. The **Precision** spin button lets you determine how many decimal places, up to 12, to carry your calculations. **Set Fixed Precision** determines how many decimal places will be reported in the result. For details on the **Statistical** and **Trigonometry** modes, consult the Help file, which, unlike many KDE application help files, is complete and thorough.

The **Display Font** tab page, shown in Figure 14.21, lets you open the usual KDE font tab.

FIGURE 14.21
The **Display Font** tab lets you change only the typeface and size of the numbers in the calculation text box.

KCalc supports the usual mathematical functions, plus some useful desktop functions. You can scroll among the results of calculations you have done by using your keyboard's up and down arrows. You can copy the results of a calculation by clicking the calculation text box, and if your clipboard contains a number, you can paste it into the calculator by clicking the right or center button there.

Everything else should be apparent to the mathematician. You can also add, subtract, multiply, and divide. It is very full-featured indeed.

Dashing Off Quick Notes: KJots and KNote

One of the leading annoyances of the non-paperless office is the proliferation of those little yellow sticky notes that people feel they have the right to stick anyplace in your office. In the world of the future, the paperless office must bring along its replacements for such things, and these include sticky little electronic yellow notes, or KNotes. At least they won't fall to the floor and get stuck to the bottom of your shoe. (They will, however, easily fall behind other applications on your desktop and don't appear in the taskbar, so they remain true to their physical-world model and can easily get lost until the end of the day when you close your other applications and see there, at the bottom, something you were supposed to do hours ago.)

To start KNote, go **K Menu > Utilities > KNote**. A little yellow pad icon appears on K Panel. To make use of the program, click this icon and select **New Knote**. You will get what you see in Figure 14.22.

FIGURE 14.22
A new KNote.

KNote is actually a fairly powerful program, not that you could tell from looking at it. Most of its features are somewhat buried. Actually, *all* of its features are *completely* buried unless you think to right-click a note. Then you get a menu (see Figure 14.23).

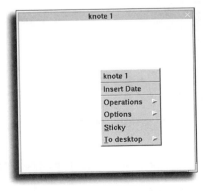

FIGURE 14.23
The RMB is the key to KNote's power.

The RMB menu offers three things that instantly affect the current note:

- **Insert Date**, which does so
- **Sticky**, which makes KNote appear on all your virtual desktops
- **To desktop**, which lets you banish the note to one of your virtual desktops

Everything else—and there is a lot—is found in **Operations**, (see Figure 14.24), or **Options** (see Figure 14.25).

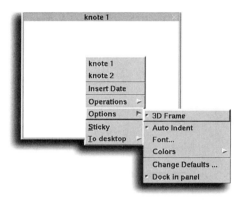

FIGURE 14.24
The **Operations** menu gives a hint that KNote packs a wallop.

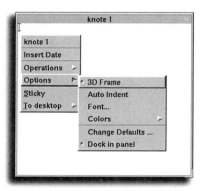

FIGURE 14.25
Changes you make anyplace other than **Change Defaults** apply only to the current note.

When you click the **KNote** icon in **K Panel**, a small menu appears, listing all your notes. This makes the **Rename Note** item in the **Operations** menu especially useful. It renders a little dialog box shown in Figure 14.26.

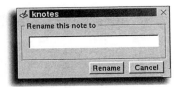

FIGURE 14.26
Giving your notes names more descriptive than **knote 1** will help you keep better track when you have several of them stacked up.

KNote can also serve as a useful reminder and calendar program for those who find KOrganizer the equivalent of killing a fly with a shotgun and who don't mind if the date isn't always assigned to the proper day of the week (see Figure 14.27). The calendar, as you see, has a rather serious bug.

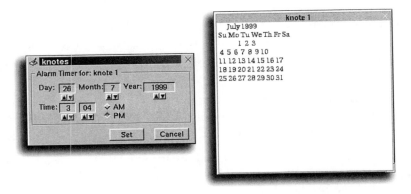

FIGURE 14.27
The Alarm Setting dialog box and calendar functions are illustrated. Setting the alarm is straightforward enough, but 1 July 1999 was on a Thursday and the month did not jump from Wednesday to Sunday. Perhaps it was wishful thinking: a longer holiday weekend that way!

As with KEdit, you can mail a KNote using the same dialog box found in KEdit. You can also print a KNote, if your printer has been set up in the **Options > Change Defaults** dialog box.

Indeed, the **Options** menu is largely unremarkable. **3D Frame** changes the appearance of the KNote window slightly, whereas **Auto Indent** can improve the appearance of To-Do lists and the like. But changes made here apply only to this note. To alter the behavior of KNote forevermore (or until you change it to something else), you need to visit the **Change Defaults** dialog box shown in Figure 14.28.

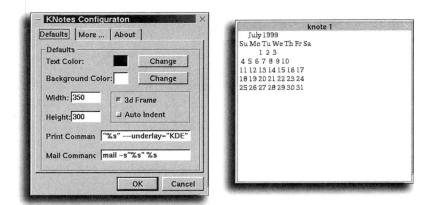

FIGURE 14.28
The dialog box produced by **Change Defaults** is simple enough. The **More** tab lets you change the default font.

To change the size of one particular note, hold the **Alt** key on your keyboard down while you use the right mouse button to resize the note. To change the size of all notes, type in the number of pixels in height and width you'd like the notes to be in **Change Defaults.**

KNote supports drag and drop, meaning that you can drop a text file on a note and it opens in that note. And if a note contains a URL, clicking it opens that link in a browser window, presuming that you are online.

Once started, KNote survives closing and restarting KDE, so there's no need to add it to your Autostart folder. You can kill it by right-clicking its **K Panel** icon and choosing **Exit Notes**, but if you do, any alarms you have set won't go off.

More promising in its way than KNote is a program called KJots, which is still part of the distribution even though it has not changed since late 1998 and therefore lacks the one feature that would make it truly useful. It seems as if development of this little applet has halted. The one feature that would have made it a winner is the capability to search among its notes, which would have transformed it into a free-form database not unlike the tremendously popular *Info Select* of the DOS days. It keeps notes in what it calls Books, and if the capability to search within books existed, it would be the perfect place to deposit all sorts of random information in a way that is readily accessible. It is pictured in Figure 14.29.

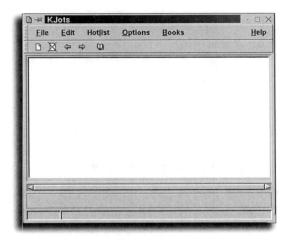

FIGURE 14.29
If KJots allowed searching, it would be the perfect note-taking application. We can only hope that its talented author or someone else continues its development, which has apparently halted.

The Start of Something Big: KAddressbook

One of the advantages of the unified desktop suite of applications is that it can prevent duplication by providing a central repository for data such as addresses, phone numbers, email addresses, reminder dates, and so on. A step in that direction is made by the KAddressbook applet. Ultimately, it could provide the information for mail merges in the under-development KOffice, addresses for KMail, even a cross reference that would pop up automatically with a caller ID application. Its potential, therefore, is very great.

Though still in its early stages, KAddressbook is already linked to KOrganizer (though deep within it) and is useful in its own right. **K Menu > Utilities > Address book** gives you a look at its current state (see Figure 14.30).

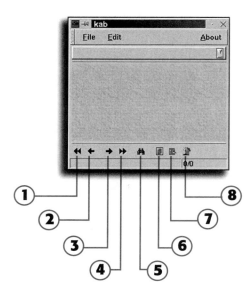

FIGURE 14.30
At first blush KAddressbook seems a little barren, but that all changes when you begin adding entries.

① Go to first entry   ⑤ Search among the entries

② Go to the previous entry   ⑥ Add an entry

③ Go to the next entry   ⑦ Edit an entry

④ Go to the last entry   ⑧ Delete the current entry

When you open it, KAddressbook allows you to do only two things: **File > Quit** and **Edit > Add Entry**. (Well, the **About** menu is entirely enabled, but you'll get little satisfaction there.) For our purposes, then, the only choice is **Edit > Add Entry**, which of course spawns a dialog box (see Figure 14.31).

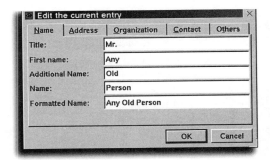

FIGURE 14.31
The first page of the entry editing dialog box is a little puzzling, but what it means for you to do is to provide a title (Mr., Mrs., Miss, President, Senator, His Royal Highness), followed by first name, middle name, last name, and then the whole thing on one line.

Go through the tabs in order, filling in the information as required, and as applies (see Figures 14.32 through 14.36).

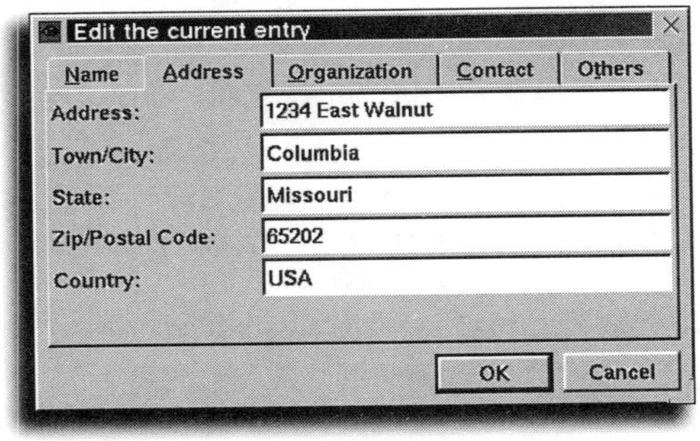

FIGURE 14.32
The **Address** tab wants the full street address on one line, with City, State, ZIP Code, and Country on separate lines.

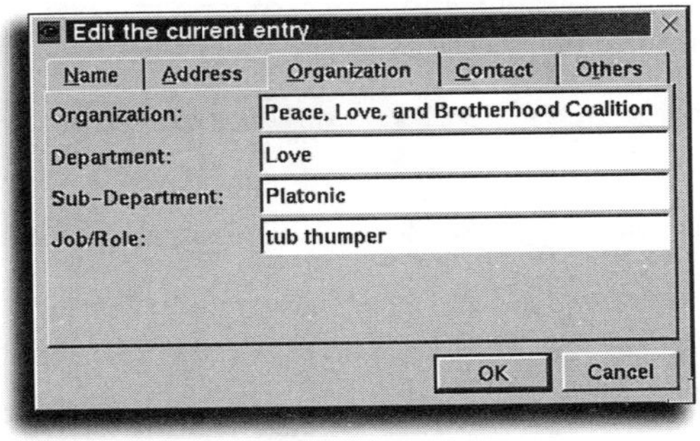

FIGURE 14.33
The **Organization** page is optional, but if you have the information, it will aid in later making use of KAddressbook in other applications.

FIGURE 14.34
The **Contact** page is a little unusual in that it offers subpages for the entry of email and online chat information.

FIGURE 14.35
The reason there is a sub-page for email addresses and talk addresses is that people frequently have more than one. This dialog box is slightly tricky in that you must click the X icon before you can add or modify an entry.

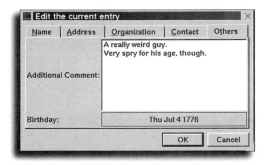

FIGURE 14.36
Others is where you add comments and birthdays. To add a birthday, double-click what looks like a text box and choose from the resulting calendar.

After you have done all this, click **OK**. The new entry now exists in your address book file (see Figure 14.37).

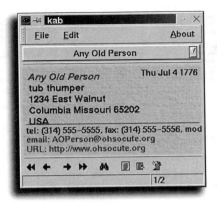

FIGURE 14.37
Now you can see the connection between the data you entered and how they are displayed.

A lot is going on here. You might think that you could resize the window to show more information, but you can't. Indeed, much of the information you entered is available from within KAddressbook only if you **Edit > Edit Entry**. But you can, if you are online, click the URL and a KFM browser window opens and takes you there (if it exists; in this example it doesn't). You can also send email by clicking the email address. Because we entered several addresses, clicking the email address renders a menu of these, from which you can choose one. Then the KMail window opens, ready for your message (see Figure 14.38).

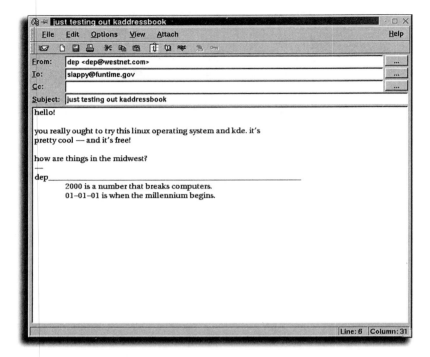

FIGURE 14.38
After you've selected the email address, the KMail message entry window opens. If you are online, your message is sent at once; otherwise, it is saved for the next time you are online and send a message or tell KMail (see Chapter 22) to send accumulated messages.

You can select the address you want by using the drop box at the top of the KAddressbook page. The icons on the toolbar near the bottom allow you to, in order

- Go to the beginning of the address book
- Go to the previous entry
- Go to the next entry
- Go to the last entry
- Search among the entries
- Add an entry
- Edit an entry
- Delete the current entry

The **File** menu allows you to save the address book, export it as an HTML table, search or print it, or, of course, **Quit**. The **Edit** menu provides all the usual functions and allows you to browse to the URL specified in the entry, send email, or open a talk session if you have entered such information.

KAddressbook, commonly called *kab*, demonstrates a great deal of functionality, and will provide even more when other KDE applications tap into it.

KDE in Your Pocket: KPilot

The U.S. Robotics (later 3Com) PalmPilot has proved to be a very popular Personal Digital Assistant, as these pocket-sized computers have come to be called. They are all the more useful if you can pass information back and forth between the PalmPilot and your desktop machine. KDE software exists (and is part of the standard distribution) that makes this possible. It is called KPilot, and it consists of a daemon and a front end. You get to it by **K Menu > Utilities > KPilot** and **KPilotDaemon**. The daemon makes the actual connection, and unless your PalmPilot is in its cradle and connected to your desktop machine, it will fail. But you can still run the KPilot program (see Figure 14.39) and load up all the things you want to send to your little electronic marvel.

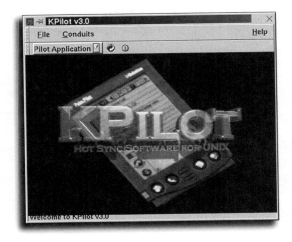

FIGURE 14.39
You can adjust KPilot's settings through the **File** menu, where the little computer's contents can also be backed up to your desktop drive (or network drive elsewhere) and restored. You can set up the connection through the single-item **Conduits** menu, whereas the three functions you can perform (Memos, Address Book, and File installer) are in the **Pilot Application** drop box.

KPilot is remarkably sophisticated. It is also, thankfully, well documented. If you have one of these little gadgets and would like to hook it up to your KDE desktop, the extensive **Help** file tells you how to do so.

chapter

15

Multimedia: Music and Movies

If you have a sound card and like to have your computer emit sounds other than beeps and the little system sounds that you may have enabled, this chapter is for you. If you don't meet these criteria, there's probably nothing here that will be of much interest, but you're invited to come along for the ride anyway. Maybe you'll get a sound card as a result.

KDE includes a modest suite of multimedia applications in the base distribution. Talented programmers are adding more applications all the time when they see a need and write a program to fill that need. You will find the newest applications at `ftp://ftp.kde.org/pub/unstable/apps/multimedia`. Don't let the "unstable" fool you: Although some of these applications are indeed unstable, many work perfectly. And none are likely to break anything, so an application that doesn't work won't take anything else down with it. You do need to compile these yourself, but this is usually a thing easily done. If you have the latest whiz-bang television card, radio tuner card or CD burner, there's a good likelihood that you'll find software for it there now or soon. At the end of the chapter we'll survey some of the incoming and upcoming KDE multimedia applications. For now, we'll look at what's on the plate already.

Playing Music CDs in KDE

There are several CD players for KDE, located in the ftp directory mentioned previously, but the one that comes with KDE is pretty good. You get to it via **K Menu > Multimedia > CD Player**. Its real name is kscd, though you are unlikely to see that name displayed anywhere, not even as depicted in Figure 15.1.

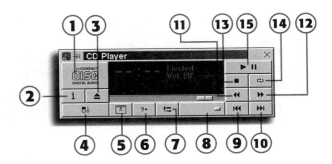

FIGURE 15.1
The CD Player adopts a control panel resembling its hi-fi system equivalent, but it's a good thing it has bubble help.

(1) Toggle Time Display

(2) Artist on the Web

(3) Eject

(4) Off

(5) CDDB dialog

(6) Random

(7) KSCD Configuration

(8) Track Selection list

(9) Previous Track

(10) Next Track

(11) Back 30 seconds

(12) Forward 30 seconds

(13) Stop

(14) Repeat CD

(15) Play/Pause

Everything on the CD Player that isn't on the central information screen is a button. Going counter-clockwise beginning with the button containing the CD logo:

- By default, **Toggle Time Display** shows the time played on the current track. Clicking on this button cycles you through the time remaining on the current track, total time played on the CD, and time remaining on the CD. It is in minutes and seconds. Internet beats isn't a choice...yet.

- The button with **i** on it is useful if you are online. It produces a menu from which it conducts searches as to performances by the artist on the current CD, where tickets and additional CDs may be purchased, and newsgroup items and Web items having to do with the artist on the current CD. It then puts the results of those searches in a KFM browser window. Its menu also contains a monstrous thing called KSCD Magic, about which you should read the following sidebar.

Danger!

KSCD Magic, when it works as it is supposed to, makes little psychedelic patterns in time with the music being played. It practically never works, and its malfunctions create conditions that bring your PC to its knees, literally slowing it to where things that usually take milliseconds now take minutes. The only way to fix it all is to kill the thing, and the only remotely easy way to do that is to right-click your mouse pointer on the taskbar where KSCD Magic is listed and then **Close** it.

- The button to the right of the **i** icon, with the triangle and the line, ejects the CD from the player. It is the graphical equivalent of typing `eject` at the command line and pressing **Enter**.

- Below the previous two buttons is the On/Off switch. Of course, it's actually the **Off** switch, in that if you can see it it's already on. It closes the CD Player.

- The icon that looks like the front of a file cabinet drawer is the button to open the CDDB dialog box.

About the CDDB Dialog

In the CDDB dialog box, you can enter the name of the artist and the title of the album, along with the names of all the tracks, or you can go online and see if someone has already typed them in and made them available for download. If no one has, and you type them in, there's a convenient upload button so that others now won't have to type it all in for that particular album. You might want to log on to **www.cddb.com** and look at all the things you can do there.

- The **?>** button doesn't open the help file but sets the current album to play in random order.

- The button with the hammer and screwdriver is where the actual CD player motif falls apart a little bit. (For absolute authenticity, it would say "No user serviceable parts inside.") It is the button that opens the KSCD Configuration dialog box. This lets you set colors and your email address for submissions to the CDDB server that you also select there, and it lets you modify the terrible and dangerous KSCD Magic feature.

- The broad button to the right of Configure KSCD is the **Track Selection** list. Click on it and, if your CD is in the database, you are treated to a list like that depicted in Figure 15.2.

FIGURE 15.2
Choose the track you'd like to hear from the list. On this album, the place to be is Track 5.

- Labeled I<< and >>I respectively are the **Previous Track** and **Next Track** buttons.

- Immediately above these are << and >> buttons, which jump backward or forward 30 seconds in the current track.

- Above << is a button containing a black box. It is the **Stop** button.

- To **Stop**'s right and above >> is a button with two arrows chasing themselves in an oval pattern. The Loop button, when clicked, plays the current CD over and over, forever, unless a housemate attacks the computer with an axe, which is likely after about the 15th consecutive play.

- And the big button atop it all is the **Play/Pause** button.

All these buttons are wrapped around a display that provides information about the music currently being played (see Figure 15.3).

FIGURE 15.3
KDE's fonts don't always fit in the space provided, but you probably know the name of the album you are playing.

The display features a large time readout of whatever you toggled the time display to be. To its right are the status of the current operation as well as the total length of the current CD. Below that is the volume level (which is meaningless) and the current track number and total number of tracks on the CD. Stretched across the whole width of the display is the name of the artist and the name of the album, if they will fit, which they often won't. Beneath this is the name of the current track, or part of the name, anyway.

Below that is a slider that you might think would control balance. It is actually the volume control, or would be if it worked. It does nothing but change the volume number in the display. Pick a number that you like.

1. Start KSCD.
2. Put a CD in the CD reader.
3. Give it a few seconds to get recognized. Click the Play button.
4. Listen.
5. If the volume is too low or two high, choose **K Menu**, **Multimedia**, **Sound Mixer Panel** to change it.

KSCD is extremely well documented, and if you are really interested in building a database of your CDs, you'll learn all you need to know there. Ah, but how do you get to this help file? That's right, there's no place on the application screen to get to the help file. Therefore, you must click on the **KSCD Configuration** button, which renders a dialog box that does have a **Help** button.

Playing MIDI Files

KDE provides an application (actually, two applications) capable of playing MIDI files in very high quality. The first of these is kmidi, which you can access by choosing **K Menu**, **Multimedia**, **Midi player** (see Figure 15.4).

FIGURE 15.4
Look familiar? kmidi's controls are identical to those of the CD player with three exceptions: the **Eject** and **i** buttons do different things, and the volume control works.

The quality of sound produced by kmidi depends upon the application of the timidity-patches files, which are available at just about all Linux file repositories and included in some Linux distributions. Look for a file called timidity-patches with the file extension appropriate to your system and C libraries. After the patches are installed, the sound is truly surprising. Timidity is something of a moving target. To find what you need and how to use it, visit the Timidity homepage at www.goice.co.jp/member/mo/timidity/.

The kmidi panel looks and works a lot like the CD Player's, but there are a few differences. You cannot eject a MIDI file, so the eject button is employed to create the play list, shown in Figure 15.5.

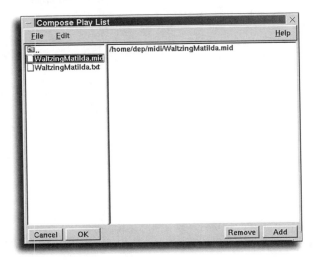

FIGURE 15.5
Clicking on a folder on the left opens it. Find the MIDI file you want, click to highlight it, and click on the **Add** button. If you grow weary of it, open the playlist again, highlight it in the right column, and click **Remove**.

The **i** button doesn't go searching for things on the Web, but instead provides information about the MIDI being played, as shown in Figure 15.6.

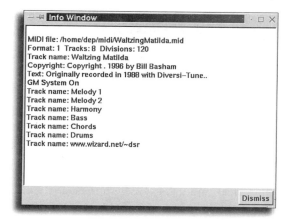

FIGURE 15.6
This is a relatively simple MIDI file, as the Info Window shows. It sounds nice, though. MIDI files can get much more complicated.

If the kmidi configuration window, shown in Figure 15.7, were any less complicated, it would be blank. Clicking on either **Change** button produces the standard KDE Select Color dialog box. If you want bubble help, check the appropriate box, and if you want **Help**, there's a button for it.

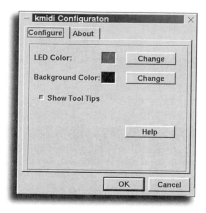

FIGURE 15.7
The blessedly simple kmidi configuration dialog box.

The kmidi Processor Hit

There is one little catch to kmidi, but in many, if not most, cases it won't matter and probably won't even be noticed. It achieves the high quality provided by some pretty hefty hardware additions without adding any hardware at all. (I get great quality from a trusty old ISA SoundBlaster 16.) But it does this by using the processor for functions normally tossed to a sound processor. The author of kmidi says that it can consume from 10 to 30 percent of the processor cycles. I tested this by conducting a little experiment. I opened kmidi, KSnapshot (to capture the results), and the Task Manager in **Performance Meter** mode. I let it run for a couple of minutes with no MIDI file playing to establish a baseline, and to let the system settle down from having loaded the programs. Then I played a MIDI file. The results are shown in Figure 15.8.

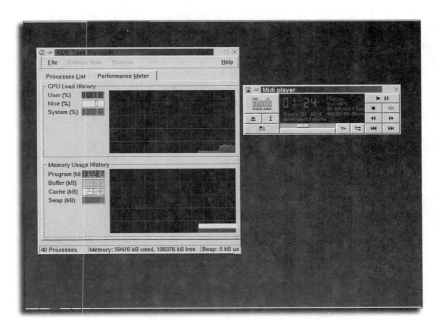

FIGURE 15.8

Is the processor 11 percent used, or 86 percent unused? You decide. Though it probably wouldn't be the best of ideas to play MIDI files while doing a long and complicated software compile, you probably wouldn't notice the difference at other times.

Besides being a good MIDI player, kmidi serves to demonstrate that high quality audio is available from Linux without costly hardware upgrades. This in turn is likely to spawn development of the kinds of music writing and sound development programs for Linux that are available now only in expensive commercial versions on other platforms.

The Other MIDI Player, KMid

The title by no means diminishes the second MIDI player that is part of the KDE core distribution because it has some very interesting features all its own and a help file that can be opened from the first screen. **K Menu**, **Multimedia > Midi/Karaoke Player** brings you **KMid**.

I have to admit that while KMid (see Figure 15.9) has some intriguing features, not all of those features work all the time. The Karaoke "sing to your computer" feature is interesting, but unless the file includes the lyrics—and many don't—that part of the fun will not exist. Indeed, I haven't found any files that include the lyrics, though I'm assured they exist.

FIGURE 15.9

A different design philosophy is employed in KMid, and it is loaded with features. For instance, you can change the speed at which the MIDI file is playing by clicking on the triangles on each side of the **Tempo** display.

One of the niftiest things about KMid comes to pass if you click on the little keyboard button. Then your desktop becomes a zillion player pianos (see Figures 15.10 and 15.11).

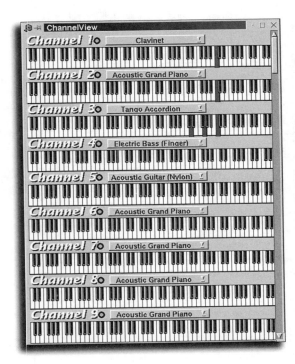

FIGURE 15.10
Each of the keyboards, obviously, represents an instrument, and those drop boxes mean something...

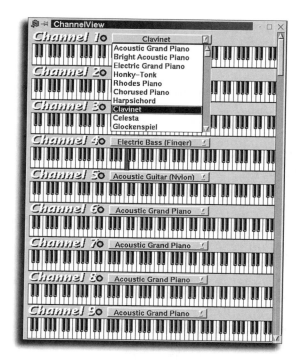

FIGURE 15.11
...You can fiddle around with the voice on each track.

In addition, KMid supports multiple playlists and drag and drop. Its help file goes into far greater detail than there is room for here, but it is well worth exploring, if making music with your computer appeals to you. You can also, of course, use **File > Open** to load a file. The standard configuration options (typefaces, colors, and so on) are supported on the menu of that name, and you can even use multiple MIDI maps and switch between multiple sound cards if you have more than one installed. This requires considerable knowledge, though, of both hardware configuration and midi map structure.

Playing .wav Files

KDE makes extensive use of .wav files, the system sounds that you can configure so your computer makes noise other than beep. To listen to them without making them system sounds, there is the KDE Media Player, which probably could have better been called the KDE Medium Player because the only medium it plays is the .wav file. (It plays .wav files well, so perhaps it could have been called the KDE Medium Well Player. Sorry.)

K Menu > Multimedia > Media Player brings it to you, as depicted in Figure 15.12.

FIGURE 15.12
Click **File, Open** to get the standard KDE file selection dialog box. Navigate to the .wav file you want to play and select it. Click the **Play** button. That's all you're likely to need to know.

Movies and More

Okay. I promised you movies. And there is an excellent little movie player for KDE, but it isn't part of the KDE distribution, and you probably have to compile it yourself. It's called aKtion, and you can get it at `www.geocities.com/SiliconValley/Haven/3864/`. It requires a program called Xanim to run, but there are links on the site mentioned that take you to that in source or, thanks to David Sweet, one of the KDEfolk, compiled binary form. Even if you don't think you need it, it comes in handy if you spend much time online because sooner or later you'll get to a link that's a QuickTime file. It is almost ridiculously easy to compile aKtion. Do it. Here's how:

1. Download the source tarball, and unarchive it into /usr/local/src.
2. As root, change into the resulting subdirectory of /usr/local/source.
3. At the command prompt, type `./configure`.
4. When the configure program has run, type `make all`.
5. When the make program has compiled the aKtion, type `make install`.

You are done in about the time it took to type this. In short, it's done in exactly the same way as KDE and every other KDE application.

On the KDE site cited at the beginning of this chapter are at least two programs in the /video subdirectory that allow television viewing on your computer. It was never clear to me why someone would want to turn an expensive and powerful computer into a fairly low quality television set. My mind was changed, though, when I was shown the delight grandparents received when their children hooked up the camcorder to the computer and made snapshots of the grandkids that could then be sent by email. If you have a television tuner card, you want to check these applications out. Again, you have to compile them yourself, which is consistent with the compilation instructions for aKtion. Your one concern is likely to be making sure that your TV card is compatible with Linux, which information you can get from the Web page of your Linux distributor. You may also have to recompile your Linux kernel to enable video for Linux. Information about that relatively complicated and certainly exacting procedure is supplied with the kernel source code, which came with your Linux distribution and which you can download from www.kernel.org or one of the mirror sites listed on that page.

Rolling Your Own

Look. You're running Linux. You're on the bleeding edge. You're not on the skinned knee edge. Sooner or later you are going to want some application very badly, and it will be available only in source code. You *will* compile programs.

I know. It sounds a little terrifying at first. It *is* a little terrifying at first, wondering if you got everything just right, didn't leave anything out, have everything installed that you need. It's real nail-biting time as the compilation takes place, with the occasional WARNING: message zipping by, possibly before you can read it. But then you'll type **make install** and you will have a new application! If it's a KDE app, chances are the next time you start KDE, it will be on K Menu.

The point is, you must not assume that because a thing needs to be compiled, it's over your head. Because it isn't. Millions of people who know no more than you do have done it. Join them and be free.

Playing MP3s

The current core KDE distribution contains no application for playing the newly popular MP3 music files, but the KDE ftp site has two good MP3 players. Yes, they need to be compiled, but they are worth the (small, in both cases) effort to do so.

The first is kmpg, which after you have compiled and installed it and restarted KDE appears at **K Menu > Multimedia > Mpeg Player** (and also in Figure 15.13).

FIGURE 15.13
The menus are where you tap into the power of kmpg, though it will probably work right out of the compiler with no configuration changes necessary, just by browsing to the MP3 cfile you want to play.

The other is KJukeBox, which after compiling and KDE restart finds its way to **K Menu > Multimedia, > KJukeBox**. It is shown, without benefit of playlist, in Figure 15.14. Like every other application mentioned in this chapter, you can download it at `ftp://ftp.kde.org/pub/unstable/apps/multimedia`, and you use the standard compilation and installation instructions, listed in the aKtion section earlier, to compile and install them.

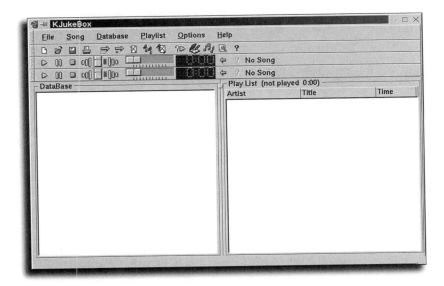

FIGURE 15.14
If you want to play the occasional MP3, KJukeBox isn't for you. If you are serious about playing music on your computer or are a Disc Jockey who wants to spin the tunes via computer, the very elaborate KJukeBox more than meets your needs.

KJukeBox is a serious program. The more I look at it, the more I marvel that it compiled so easily. It offers a world of features, including tracks sorting by genre, specialized playlists, and even the playing of two MP3 files at once. You wouldn't want to do the latter at home necessarily, but you would need to do this if you were a professional disc jockey who does weddings and parties, and who needed to be able to blend one song into the next. With it, you could program a whole night's music through a four-pound notebook computer (and, of course, external amplifier and speakers). It's an impressive application. Just don't forget the AC adapter for that notebook machine!

chapter 16

Image Creation, Editing, and Manipulation

If there were no need to edit graphics on the computer, no graphical user interfaces would exist.

Think about it: The GUI consumes resources and displays characters far less efficiently, and far more slowly, than plain old character mode does. Back in the days when people who owned PCs were running plain old DOS, companies like Microsoft and Digital Research licensed their GUIs (Windows and Gem, respectively) in runtime form to companies like Corel and Xerox, whose graphics and publishing programs needed a graphical front end. Licensing runtime versions saved those software vendors from having to write their own and saved users from carrying the overhead when running a program that didn't require graphics. (Remember that this was when memory could cost as much as $200 per megabyte and when many processors couldn't use more than 1MB anyway.)

Today, of course, rare is the character-mode machine in general computing. Like it or not, you are going to be supporting a GUI whether it's especially suited for what you are doing or not.

All of which makes it a special pleasure now to discuss the applications that unquestionably require a graphical user interface. The core KDE distribution includes several of these, which we'll consider in turn.

Two programs that are distributed as graphics programs, KSendFax and the KDE Fax Viewer, are discussed in Chapter 33, "Faxing from KDE." Two more, to view PostScript files and files in the TeX DVI format, are discussed in Chapter 19, "A World of Other KDE Applications" and 20, "KLyX: The Paradoxical Processor of Complex Documents," respectively.

It is worthwhile to note also that the other graphics programs for Linux work well under KDE, if you need some features that KDE applications don't yet provide.

KView to Look at Images

The most basic of graphics applications, and therefore the one we'll look at first, is KDE's image viewer, KView (see Figure 16.1). You find it in **K Menu > Graphics > Image Viewer**.

FIGURE 16.1
KView lets you look at a variety of bitmap graphics: JPG, BMP, GIF, and more.

There are several ways to display a file in KView:

- You can specify **kview** */path/filename* at the command prompt in a terminal window.
- You can right-click a graphics file and select **Image Viewer** from the resulting menu (see Figure 16.2).
- You can use the KView **File > Open** menu item.
- You can open KView and drag an image file to the blank KView window and release it there, whereupon it opens.
- If you have no other graphics programs installed that will intercept the command, you can click an image icon, and it is likely to open in KView.
- You can also make it part of a list, which we'll get to shortly.

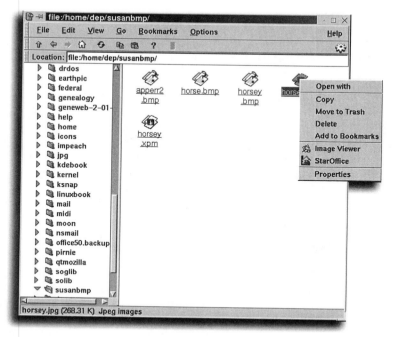

FIGURE 16.2
The RMB menu is just one of the ways you can open a file in KView. Some graphics files—BMPs, for instance—don't by default show KView. To open them, drop the icon from KFM into a KView window.

After you've opened a file in KView, look at the bottom and right side for scrollbars: the image doesn't necessarily display in its entirety. You can drag the edges of the KView window to show more of the image, or you can use the scrollbars to show different parts of the file.

The **Edit, Zoom,** and **Transform** menus are self–explanatory. Feel free to play with them.

If you like an effect you have created, use the **File > Save As** menu item to keep it.

To Desktop gives you the choice of instantly putting your file on the desktop as temporary wallpaper (see Figure 16.3). Temporary? Yes, it stays there only until the next time you close and start KDE. To make it permanent, you will need to use the Wallpaper dialog box in Display Properties in the desktop RMB menu.

INSERT 16.3
You can display your bitmap as the KDE desktop tiled, stretched to fit, or enlarged to fit, but it stays there for this session only.

The **Filter** menu lets you make some primitive alterations to your image. These let you alter the contrast and brightness of the image, turn a color picture into black and-white (but not change it back), and make it slightly out of focus, to eliminate blemishes, scratches, and dust spots.

It is the **Images** menu where you can set up slideshows or browse among image files. To do this, click on **Images > List**, which produces a dialog box (see Figure 16.4) into which you can drag and drop image files to create the list mentioned earlier as one of the ways to display images in KView. After the list is populated, the other controls in the menu let you travel to and from among the image files.

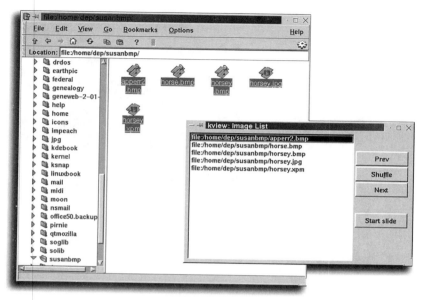

FIGURE 16.4
The easiest way to populate a **List** is to drag the files you want to view from KFM and drop them in the kview:Image List dialog box.

If you want to put together a Slideshow, you can change the length of time each image is shown, and whether it stops at the end or starts over at the beginning with the **Edit > Preferences** item, in the **Slideshow** section.

Kfract for Generation of Simple Fractals

Fractals are to computers as tie dye is to hippies, and it has become obligatory that an advanced desktop include a fractals generator. In KDE, that program is Kfract (see Figure 16.5).

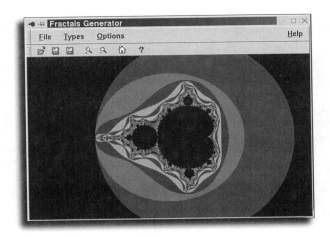

FIGURE 16.5
Among its other virtues, playing with Kfract can provide stress relief in a chaotic world.

Kfract, found at **K Menu > Graphics > Fractals Generator**, currently supports two **Types** of fractals, Mandelbrot, as seen in Figure 16.5, and Julia, shown in Figure 16.6.

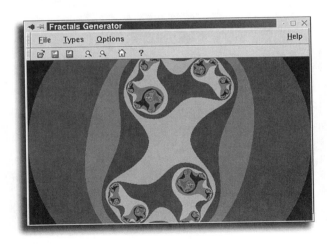

FIGURE 16.6
Switching to Julia fractals is as simple as clicking in the **Types** menu. You will be prompted for parameters, which you'll enjoy if you're a mathematician, or you can stick with the defaults.

To dive deeper into your fractal, you can drag a box with the mouse (see Figure 16.7) which, when you release the mouse button, repaints the Kfract window with your selection, shown in Figure 16.8.

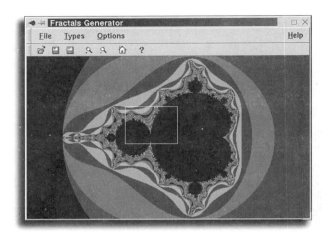

FIGURE 16.7
To generate a fractal based on part of the one you have, select a section with your mouse...

FIGURE 16.8
...which, when you release the mouse button, paints a new fractal based on your selection.

The **File** menu offers the opportunity to save not just the picture you've created, but the parameters you entered when choosing the kind of fractal you made. You can, of course, reload these parameters later if you want. This is why there are two identical **Save** icons on the taskbar. The first saves the parameters; the second saves the image.

Quick and Easy Screenshots

The KDE application I've used most in the course of putting together this book is KSnapshot. I have come to like it a great deal, and with one small improvement it would make my job far easier than it already has. That one small improvement would be the capability to save in .pcx format.

KSnapshot is seen in Figure 16.9 and is found at **K Menu > Graphics > Snapshot**.

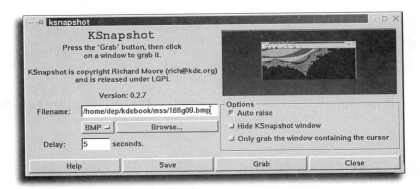

FIGURE 16.9
A **KSnapshot** self portrait. Normally, the **Hide KSnapshot Window** box would be checked. As you can see, the file is being saved in .bmp format; I'll need to use another program to convert it to a .pcx for publication. Too bad for me.

If You're Writing a Book for Que

I used the GIMP, a Linux graphics application that almost certainly came with your distribution, to make the conversion from a file format supported by Ksnapshot, in this case .bmp, to the PC Paintbrush format (.pcx) required by the publishers for the illustrations in this book. I made the snapshots as I wrote the chapters, opened the GIMP, opened each file one after another, and saved each file as a .pcx. That's all it took. Now you know, in case you're ever called on to produce .pcx images from Ksnapshot images.

KSnapshot does support multiple formats: JPEG, BMP, GIF, PS, and XBM, chosen by clicking on the list box that at the start says GIF. When saving a file, you can enter the full pathname and filename in the text box, or you can use the **Browse** button to select a location. The latter isn't the quickest, but you'll be sure to have all the pathname qualifications correctly entered. Often overlooked is the **Delay** text box. In my experience, this should be set to at least 3 because repainting everything on the KDE screen, if you have lots of icons or several applications open, can take two seconds or more, which means you might get only a partially painted screen, with blank menus and the like.

The **Auto raise** check box brings the selected application to the top of the pile if you have multiple applications open and are shooting only one. **Hide KSnapshot window** keeps KSnapshot from appearing in your full-screen screenshots (it doesn't even show up on the taskbar during the making of the picture). **Only grab the window containing the cursor** lets you make shots of individual windows instead of the full screen, which can reduce confusion and certainly saves storage space.

Confirming Your Catch

The preview image in the upper right corner of KSnapshot doesn't really tell you a lot, but clicking that image does because it expands the image to full size. Clicking on the full-size image returns you to the KSnapshot window.

It's simple, easy to master, and efficient. It works. I love it, and if you need to make screenshots, you will love it, too. But I sure wish it saved in .pcx!

Making Your Own Icons

KDE comes with a nice selection of icons. The problem is, most of them are for particular applications. The Appfinder, for instance, draws upon these when assigning icons to the programs it finds. To be useful, icons must be unique. If you have a row of identical icons, you need bubble help or a caption of some sort to remind you which is which. That defeats the purpose of icons (or already defeated, I think, or else we wouldn't need bubble help).

So now you have a new application and you intend to use it regularly. You would like an icon for it, but everything in the selection available is really for some other program.

Have no fear. There is **kiconedit**, shown in Figure 16.10. You can find it at **K Menu > Graphics > Icon Editor**. It is a simple and specialized paint program that lets you edit a pixel at a time.

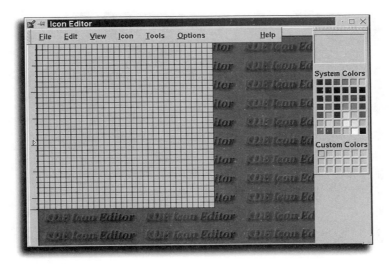

FIGURE 16.10
Here is your icon canvas. Fill in the little squares with the colors of your choice and the result is an icon.

It's simple to use, though it cannot provide graphic design talent, as I am about to prove. As I was writing this book, a miniature crisis erupted in the KDE world. It seemed that a well-known computer company had registered as trademarks the trashcan icon and the word "Trash" in association with that icon. KDE's developers go to great lengths to avoid stepping on other people's trademarks. They got into this to write good, free software, not to learn about civil lawsuits. I thought about it a little, opened the **Icon Editor**, and went to work (Figure 16.11).

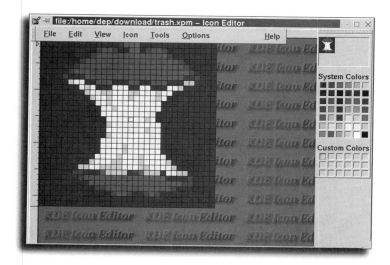

FIGURE 16.11
What would be a good, universal image of something to be discarded that doesn't involve a trashcan? You can't really make a compost heap into an icon, but you can surely make one of its ingredients into one.

Now, those little boxes can be very difficult to select individually for coloring, and for that reason there is the **View > Zoom in** menu item. You can use this over and over until you are happy with the size of the boxes (each of which represents one pixel, by the way). You can also **Zoom out** to make your image smaller on the screen, or you can go directly to the **View > Zoom factor** item and get there all at once.

Several menu items are unique to kiconedit. The **Icon** menu, for instance, allows you to change the size of the icon you are making. This is especially useful if you want to make a customized image for the opening screen of an application or some other purpose where a nonstandard size is needed. You can also remap your icon to shades of gray if for some reason this is useful to you.

The **Tools** menu (Figure 16.12), gives you access to a nice range of drawing implements. This sets kiconedit apart from a lot of icon editors that don't have much in the way of area tools.

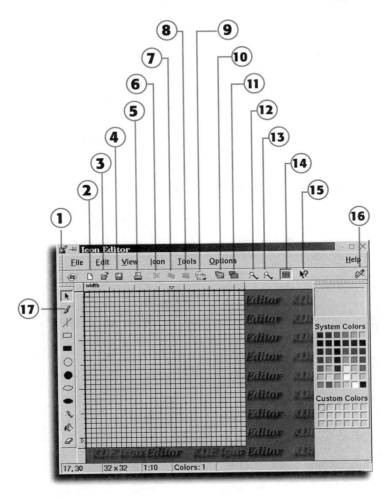

FIGURE 16.12
The only confusing item in the **Tools** menu is **Freehand**, which is a pixel-by-pixel tool. When it's selected, you can click on any pixel to change its color to the one chosen from the palette.

① Drag source

② New File

③ Open a file

④ Save the file

⑤ Print icon

⑥ Cut

⑦ Copy

⑧ Paste

⑨ Select area

⑩ Resize

⑪ GrayScale

⑫ Zoom out

⑬ Zoom in

⑭ Toggle grid

⑮ What is...?

⑯ New Window

⑰ Draw freehand tool

The **Options** menu allows you to toggle various screen elements and to make configuration choices that fit your preferences.

So then, how is kiconedit used? Simple. Select a color from the **System Colors** or, if you have made some, **Custom Colors** palette. Then choose your tool and start drawing. Remember that for a transparent background, you can use the eraser tool. Save your work. Then you can use it with an application or file type. In the case of the little icon I made, I used it to replace the trash icon in /opt/kde/share/icons. Here is the result (see Figure 16.13).

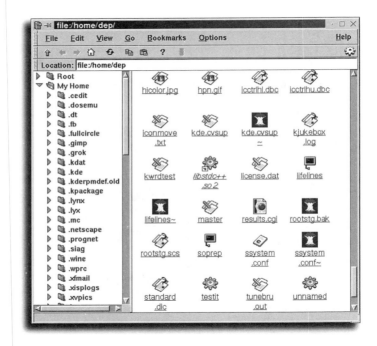

FIGURE 16.13
The newly minted icon, which gives a whole new meaning to the phrase "core dump", in use marking files that KDE lists as trash.

Editing Larger Images with KPaint

A paint program of some sort is standard with most GUIs, and KDE provides one that looks and acts in important ways like others with which you may be familiar. **K Menu > Graphics > Paint** brings it to you, as seen in Figure 16.14.

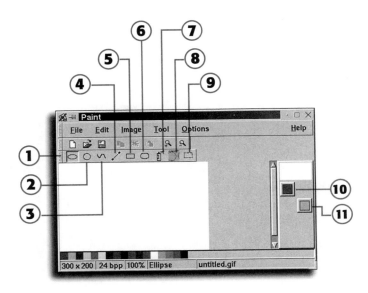

FIGURE 16.14
KPaint is a basic but versatile image editor.

(1) Ellipse

(2) Circle

(3) Pen

(4) Line

(5) Rectangle

(6) Roundangle

(7) Spray Can

(8) An arrow icon that becomes blank when an image is loaded and that does, apparently, nothing

(9) Area Selection

(10) Foreground color

(11) Background color

You can use the tools to create a file from scratch, or you can edit an existing graphic. This is brought about through the **File > Open Image** dialog box, which produces the standard KDE file selector, or **File > New Image**, which produces a small dialog box asking you the size in pixels of the image you want to make. You can open an image from a URL and, if you have write access to the site, save to a URL.

The controls are otherwise similar to those found in kiconedit.

chapter
17

Manipulating File Archives and Backing Up Your Drive

If one file format is common across all flavors of UNIX and therefore Linux, it is TAR, for Tape ARchive. It is the standard by which files or groups of files are stored and shipped. But unlike some archiving formats in other operating systems, TAR doesn't compress the files in a *tarball*, as TARred files are called. To reduce file size, an additional step must be undertaken. This usually involves a compression program called *gzip*, though another, more efficient program, *bzip2*, is gaining increased usage. This results in files that end in extensions like *.tar.gz*, *.tar.bz2*, or *.tgz*.

Using these file formats is quick and easy, if you've memorized a bowl of alphabet soup of command-line options. Linux users are quick to grab a few: `tar xvfz` to open a file ending in *.tgz* or *.tar.gz*, for instance, and `bzip2 -d` for files that end in *.bz2*, after which `tar xvf` must be run. Few of these users know all the options available to them, and man pages aren't always entirely clear. It certainly would be nice if there were an easy-to-use graphical front end for these files, wouldn't it?

Well, there is. Or, actually, are: There are several archive handlers for KDE, and a couple are included in the KDE core package. Still others can be readily downloaded, some precompiled, and all in source that you can easily build.

KFM: Your Invisible Friend

KFM, the KDE file manager, has impressive archive handling capabilities already built in. Click an archived file and see how transparently they work (see Figures 17.1 through 17.3).

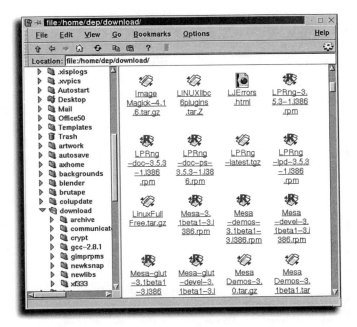

FIGURE 17.1
Here is a directory that contains a number of compressed tarballs. Clicking one of them...

FIGURE 17.2
...opens it as if it were a folder (which it would be, if extracted), and which, when clicked...

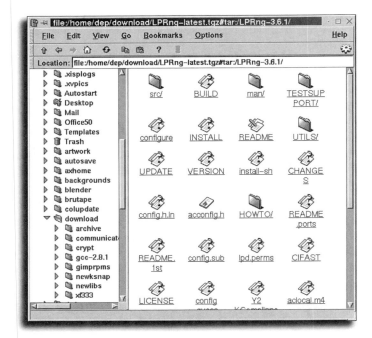

FIGURE 17.3
...shows the contents of the tarball. If you click the README file, it opens in your default editor.

This is wonderfully useful for a couple of reasons. Looking at a binary tarball lets you see how it is structured, which makes it easy to determine where it should be copied before unarchiving it. Looking at the README and INSTALL files in a source tarball lets you learn of anything special you need to do before you're ready to build the application. If you keep old documents archived and compressed, you can also have access to them without having to open the tarball and then close it back up again. This is a very nice feature, and it works for several kinds of archives.

Ark: Archive Builder and Extractor

Had you right-clicked instead of left-clicked that tarball or another archived and compressed file, you would have found **Archiver** among the choices in the menu. Had you made that choice, something like Figure 17.4 would result. Clicking the selected file opens it in your text editor (see Figure 17.5).

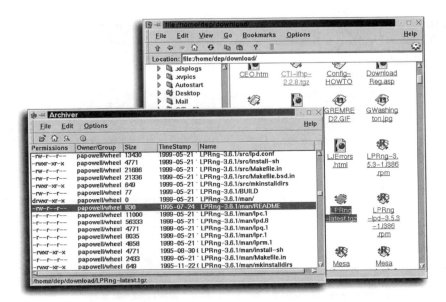

FIGURE 17.4
The view in ark is a little different than that achieved by clicking the left mouse button on an archive, but the results are the same.

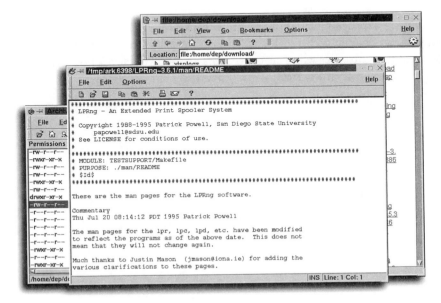

FIGURE 17.5
And clicking a text file opens it in your default editor.

If this were all that ark does, it would be nice enough. But it's not, by a long shot. Go **K Menu > Utilities > Archiver** to take a look at it in its empty form, shown in Figure 17.6.

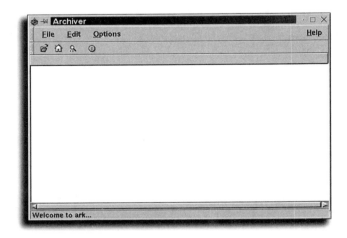

FIGURE 17.6
It looks like an editor, but it isn't. That white space is waiting for you to drag and drop an archive you want opened, or files you want made into an archive.

The big white space in ark should by now cause a lightbulb to flash on in your head. Yes, you can drag an archive file onto ark and it will open. Okay, big deal. You can also drag files into that white space to *create* an archive. Here's how I made the one shown "in process" in Figure 17.7:

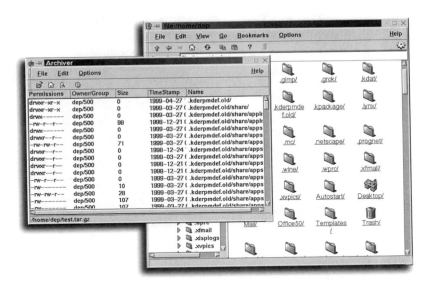

FIGURE 17.7
After creating an empty archive, simply drag the things you want to bundle up—in this case an old directory I'll probably never need again—to the ark window. Poof! They're in the archive.

1. Click **File > New**.
2. In the standard KDE file dialog box, give the new file a name. Its extension determines what kind of file is produced. (In this case, saving it with a .tar.gz extension produces a gzipped tarball of 16,835 bytes, whereas saving it as a .tar.bz2 makes a file of 14,303 bytes. The original directory, by the way, was 57,743 bytes in size.)
3. Drag the directory to be archived to the ark window.
4. Click **File > Close**.

That's it! Now I can delete the old directory and recover the disk space it's consuming, but if I discover I've broken something, I can open the file to restore it. (Of course, in that this was a bunch of old KDE configuration files, it's possible though not likely that I've taken away something that now will prevent KDE from opening. There are a few console prompt commands that a person should know, and `tar xvfz` *filename* is one of them.)

But wait, there's more. If you click **File > Extract To**, you get the dialog box shown in Figure 17.8.

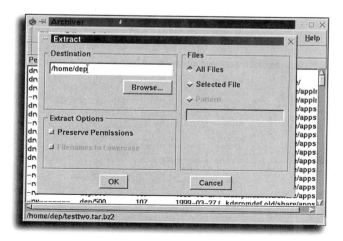

FIGURE 17.8
You can extract an archive to any location to which you have write access.

The Extract dialog box offers a whole selection of possibilities. You can, of course, specify a target for the extracted files, but you can also choose to preserve the permissions of the files that are extracted. This can be crucial if you've backed up a directory of scripts and other executable files and some of the other strange files to which only root has access. You can force the filenames to lowercase. Apparently, some operating systems believe that filenames carry more weight when they are SHOUTED. Linux doesn't. This option, then, is useful if you're opening a zipfile of data from someone less enlightened than yourself. But wait…there's still more. You can choose to extract the entire archive, or a selected file, or all files of a particular type. Robert Palmbos, the author of ark, wrote a right dandy little utility here.

The **Options** menu has a couple of tricks to offer, too. Chances are that you have one directory where you keep the archives you've downloaded and, now, the ones you make. **Options > Set Archive Directory** lets you point to that directory. Then when you click the little house icon in the toolbar, you'll be taken to that directory, making less navigation necessary when you want to open or create an archive. There's no need to change the TAR executable file, so you can leave that item alone. **Options > File Adding Options** gives you the little dialog box shown in Figure 17.9.

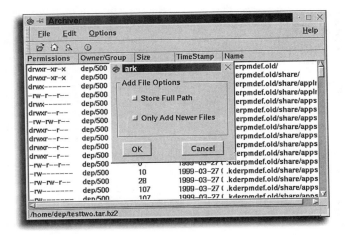

FIGURE 17.9
To store the file's entire path when you add it to an archive, check the appropriate check box. The **Only Add Newer Files** check box keeps you from replacing a file with itself or, worse, an older and perhaps incompatible version.

Everything else in ark works as you would expect it to work. It's just one of those little utilities that you will soon find irreplaceable.

An Essential Ark Task

As I was writing this very chapter, strange things happened. First, I couldn't save this file: I received the message that I didn't have write permission to it. Puzzled, I logged out and restarted KDE. All my customizations were gone. My K Panel arrangement was gone. Wallpaper I had not chosen was suddenly irremovably on my desktop, and I could not change any of it. I did a full reboot. No help.

I looked at the configuration files in ~/.kde. Fortunately, I have another machine that I keep configured very closely to this one. I was able to use ark to make a .tar.bz2 file of its ~/.kde directory, which I copied to floppy and then extracted to my ~/ directory. Pretty much everything came back. There are still a few anomalies, but it's recoverable.

It all would have been easier to fix had I copied my ~/.kde to a nice little archive kept in a safe place. You should do it, too. Now.

A Program to Handle RPM and DEB Files

Though it isn't part of the KDE core application set, KPackage is shipped with some Linux distributions that use KDE as their default desktop, so it is worth mentioning here if only briefly.

When opened from **K Menu > Utilities > KPackage**, the program looks like what you see in Figure 17.10.

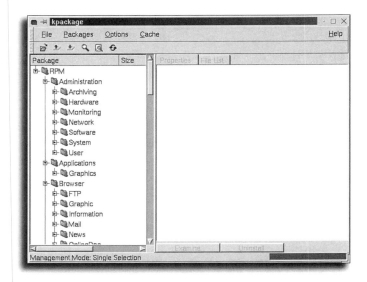

FIGURE 17.10
KPackage at start lists the installed RPM files (or DEBs on a Debian system) in a tree view.

By clicking on the little square to the left of each listing in KPackage's package tree, you can see what packages of that sort have been installed on your system. Clicking on one of the packages populates the right side of the window with information about the package (see Figure 17.11).

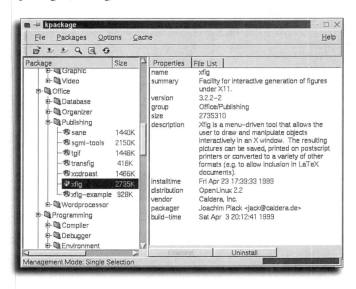

FIGURE 17.11
General information is displayed in the right pane. It includes who built the package, when, and possibly where you got it.

By clicking on the **File List** tab, you can see all the files contained in the package and where they were installed (see Figure 17.12).

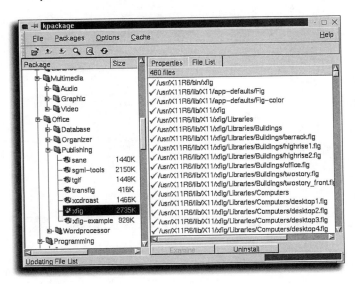

FIGURE 17.12

As time goes on, you'll have occasion to wonder whether a specific file was installed and, if so, the package to which it belongs. The **File List** is one way of gaining this information.

Clicking on an item in the **File List** opens it in your default editor, if it is a text file, or opens it in KFM, if it is a directory or HTML file. You'll notice the **Uninstall** button. It is of no use unless you are logged in as root.

As useful as this is, it's not how you are most likely to see KPackage. Instead, you'll be most likely to encounter it when you click on an RPM or DEB file, as shown in Figure 17.13.

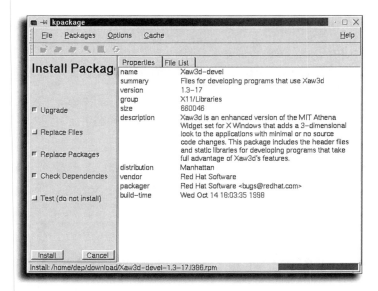

FIGURE 17.13
When KPackage is installed, clicking on an RPM or DEB file launches it in a mode to let you perform various functions, including integrity and dependency tests on the package and installation of the package if you are root.

The **File List** is somewhat more useful in this mode because often when a program fails to function, it complains of the lack of a particular file. This is a frequent reason for the acquisition and installation of RPM or DEB packages; with KPackage you can check before installing a package that might not solve the problem.

If you didn't get KPackage with your Linux distribution, it's worth downloading and compiling. You can find the latest version and its very simple compilation instructions, which are identical to the compilation instructions for every other KDE application, at `ftp://ftp.kde.org/pub/kde/stable/1.1.2/apps/admin/`.

Making Tape Backups Under KDE

The core KDE distribution has a fine little front end to the `tar` command in its original sense: tape archive. You'll find it at **K Menu > Utilities > Tape Backup Tool** (see Figure 17.14).

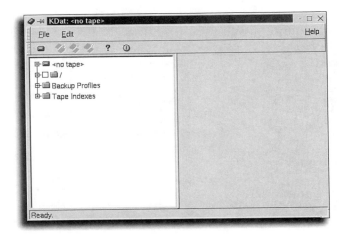

FIGURE 17.14
At first, **KDat** shows little. You can back up the entire system using Backup Profile 1, or you can create a profile for
your ~/directory.

For KDat to work, you need a Linux-compatible tape drive, which means one that
works in non-rewind mode. This is usually located at /dev/tape or /dev/ftape, if it
runs off a regular or enhanced floppy drive controller. SCSI tapes are listed as SCSI
devices. This likely involves a little experimentation. Because tape drives aren't usually enabled by default in Linux kernels except as modules, you will have learned
what yours is called when you installed the module for it or when you compiled support into the kernel. (As you may have gathered, most tape drives aren't easy projects
in Linux.) When you know what your tape is called, go to **Edit > Preferences** to tell
KDat where it is. Then it is simply a matter of, on the same screen, telling KDat the
uncompressed size of the tape itself. If you intend to back up the entire system, select
Backup Profile 1, and click the **Backup** icon, second from the left in the toolbar. If
you want to back up, say, just your ~/, go to **File > Create Backup Profile** and
select it as I did in Figure 17.15.

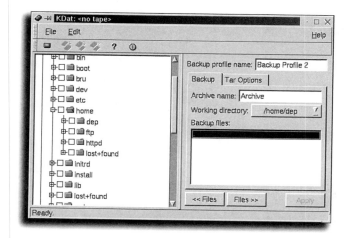

FIGURE 17.15

By clicking on my ~/ directory in the tree view at left, I created **Backup Profile 2**: my home directory. Now it's a matter of putting a tape in the drive and clicking the **Backup** icon.

After you've made your backup, you want to **Verify** that your files were written properly to tape. You do this by selecting the directory or directories that were backed up, and clicking the **Verify** icon (fourth from the left on the toolbar).

After you have made your backups, a second tree containing the contents of the tape is shown when the tape is mounted. Select the files or directories you want to **Restore**, and click the **Restore** icon, third from the left.

There are other tape backup programs for Linux, and most commercial distributions of Linux include a personal edition of a commercial program that uses a method that its makers say is more reliable than tar. This program (and other programs that, like Kdat, are freely distributed) work well under KDE, so you might want to investigate any that you might already have.

chapter
18

Games and Toys

In the beginning, there was Pong.

It's true: Many people's first computer experience involved dropping a quarter (or two, if a friend was playing) into the slot and hitting the little green spot back and forth for awhile. And many people's first computers were things that could be plugged into the television set so as to simultaneously play this game and permanently burn lines and score boxes into their TV screens.

Maybe it's a sign that old age is approaching ("Why, when I was a boy we had Pong and were happy with it."), but it doesn't seem all that long ago. Like everything else in computing, though, the quality and sophistication of games have grown exponentially. If you can find Pong at all anymore, it will be in a museum or played on a digital wristwatch or pocket calculator.

The games included with KDE demonstrate this. Many is the evening I spent dropping quarters into a machine whose *Asteroids* game was nowhere near as graphically elaborate as the one you get with KDE for free.

Yes, the book is *Practical KDE*, and the practicality of games can be argued, but who hasn't endured a long and boring phone call by a quick game of *Minesweeper* or *SameGame*? Stress release is an increasingly important part of life. If you insist on keeping your nose against the grindstone, hop on over to Chapter 19, "A World of Other KDE Applications," because this chapter is about having fun. And for the purposes of this chapter, fun is found in two places: **K Menu > Games** and **K Menu > Toys** (after you've moved them, using kmenuedit, from **K Menu > Utilities**).

KAbalone

KAbalone (see Figure 18.1) is a little board game, reminiscent of Chinese checkers.

The purpose of the game is to knock six of your opponent's 14 pieces off the board. It can be played by two people, by one person playing against the computer, or by the computer playing against itself. The last possibility is probably the best way to learn the game, though the Help file contains full instructions, too.

In the **File** menu, you can of course start a new game, but you can also save a game and then restore it later, make the computer stop searching for its best move and make the best move it's found so far, undo your last move, and get the computer to make your next move for you.

The **Options** menu lets you select a level of play, choose which side the computer plays or tell it to play against itself, turn animation on and off, and even "read the mind" of the computer as it contemplates your last move and its next one.

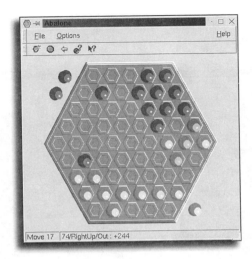

FIGURE 18.1
KAbalone opens as a tiny part of your screen, but you can drag it to a larger size.

KAsteroids

KAsteroids, one of the all-time great arcade games, has never looked better than it does in KDE (see Figure 18.2).

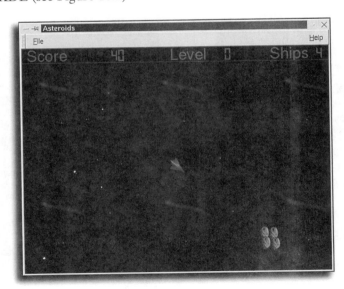

FIGURE 18.2
Use the arrow keys to point your spaceship at the asteroid, and use the spacebar to fire. Left and right arrows spin the ship, while up and down arrows send it zooming around.

Some games are good for stress relief, but KAsteroids is not one of them. Sometimes you win, and sometimes the asteroid does (see Figure 18.3).

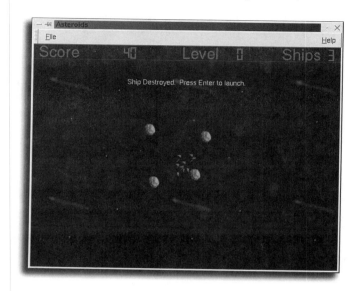

FIGURE 18.3

The spaceship can transform an asteroid into a pile of rocks. An asteroid can transform the spaceship into a flurry of sharp shards.

KAsteroids is remarkably simple to play because the choices are between playing and not playing. No options.

KBlackBox

There are people for whom KBlackBox (see Figure 18.4) is the most exciting thing in the world. My hat is off to them. I've tried, but I cannot figure the thing out, save to say that it is a logic game involving balls and lasers, or something. You get to it by **K Menu > Games > KblackBox**. It has a Help file which, given sufficient study, may equip you to play this challenging game.

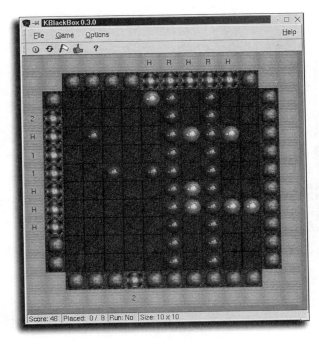

FIGURE 18.4
It looks nice, but half the game is figuring out how it's played.

For Budding Megalomaniacs: Konquest

If taking over the Universe is on your to-do list, Konquest provides a place to practice. After an impressive opening screen, shown in Figure 18.5, you and your friends—it requires at least two players—select your planets and go to war.

FIGURE 18.5
From the opening screen, click the **Recycle** icon at top left to begin a game.

After the game begins, each player selects a home planet (see Figure 18.6).

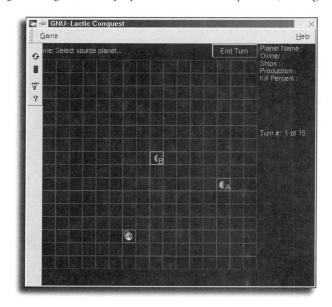

FIGURE 18.6
The farther your home planet is from other planets, the longer it will take your space ships to get there…and theirs to get to you.

After you've selected your planet and your opponents have selected theirs, you attack each other until someone has conquered the Universe. For full instructions, look at the Help file, which like other KDE help files is at **Help > Contents**.

Kmahjongg

It wasn't until I began writing this book that I discovered Kmahjongg and now I'm addicted to it. In fact, I'm going to pop out right now to do a little more research. See you in an hour or so. Meantime, you can look at Figure 18.7.

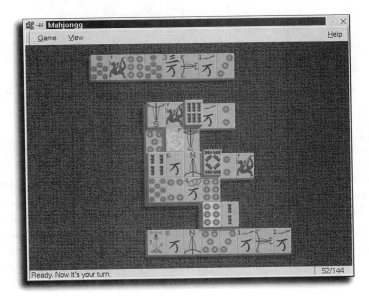

FIGURE 18.7
If there isn't a program at some clinic to treat Kmahjongg addiction, there ought to be.

Okay, I'm back. The purpose of Kmahjongg is to remove all the tiles from the board. You can achieve this by finding two that match and clicking on them, whereupon they disappear, but they need to be on the edge to be eligible for selection. It can be done (see Figure 18.8).

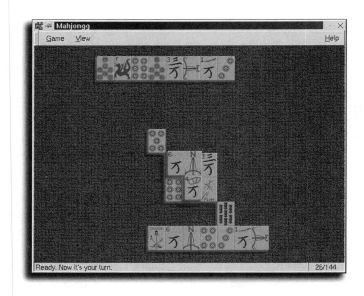

FIGURE 18.8
Moving down in the pile, with a goodly distance yet to go. The reward for clearing them all away? You'll have to find out for yourself.

Kmahjongg takes help to a whole new level, offering assistance on the next play from the **Game** menu, with its **Help me** item, and even a **Demo mode** that plays a game for you slowly enough to show how it's done. It also offers a number of different starting points, and lets you customize the background. A submenu under **Game >
Start new game** offers several levels of complexity, and the **View** menu lets you change the background from the default Astroturf to a bitmap image of your choice.

Minesweeper

If KDE were to ship with only one game, Minesweeper would be a good candidate. It exercises one's reasoning, but not to the extent that a simple writer can't win from time to time. In case you've never played it on Linux or some other operating system, it looks like Figures 18.9, 18.10, and 18.11.

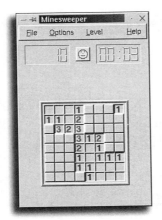

FIGURE 18.9
Kmines at its **Easy Level**. There are 64 boxes, of which 10 contain bombs.

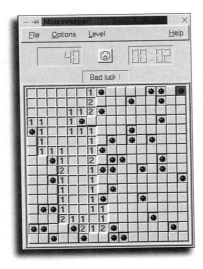

FIGURE 18.10
Kmines in **Normal Level**. Forty of the 256 boxes contain bombs.

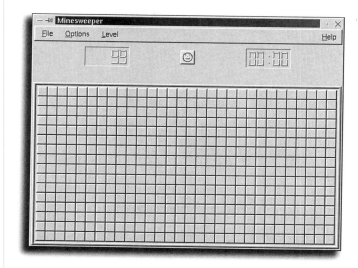

FIGURE 18.11
The **Expert Level**: 480 boxes, 99 bombs.

The object of the game is to expose every square that doesn't have a bomb underneath it. This is done by clicking the box. If you are lucky, a whole bunch of boxes will open. The ones bordering boxes containing bombs have numbers that signify how many of those bordering boxes contain bombs. Each box borders eight other boxes. The ones that touch at the corners count, too. This information is usually sufficient to let you figure out which boxes contain bombs. Right-clicking on boxes that you know contain bombs mark them with a flag; clicking again marks a box with a question mark, in case you're not sure; clicking yet again clears it and allows you to click the left button on it. Remember: The object isn't to mark all the bombs, it's to reveal all the boxes that don't contain bombs.

You are playing against the clock, as witness the **High scores** list in the **File** menu. To knock off a previous champion, clear the minefield quicker than he or she did.

If I had the power to make any improvement to this game, I suppose it would be for a more spectacular display to take place when you win...and one when you lose.

KPat: Solitaire and More

Solitaire has become a mainstay of GUI systems, and KDE's version is called KPat. It is a sort of Patience, the venerable X Window System suite of Solitaire games. Its default screen, Figure 18.12, is surely familiar to you.

FIGURE 18.12
The default Solitaire game plays in the standard fashion. You must move the cards to where they belong. Double-clicking them does nothing for you.

Like Patience, KPat offers a selection of games (see Figure 18.13). Its Help file will guide you through each game, if you need the help. Though Captain Kangaroo has been cancelled, cigarettes are bad for you, and the deck contains 52 cards, not 51; you may still find yourself playing it til dawn. Hey, it's something to do. Don't let anyone tell you otherwise.

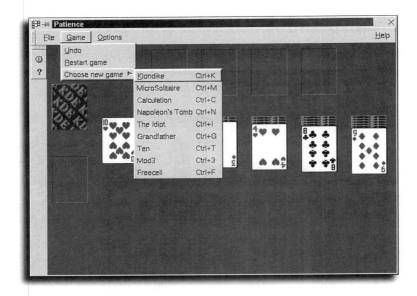

FIGURE 18.13
Choose your game from the menu and have at it.

From the **Options** menu, you can also make your choice from a selection of card backs, and turn the opening animation off if you have a slow machine or are in a hurry to play.

Kpoker: A Little Casino Game

Kpoker will not likely do much to hone your card playing skills. Still, it is an enjoyable way to make those boring phone calls go more quickly (if you turn off the sounds). It is a small game (see Figure 18.14).

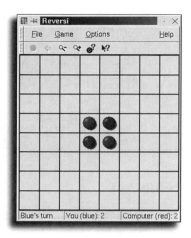

FIGURE 18.16
Blue moves first. If you don't know what to do, **Game > Get hint** helps you out.

Probably the best way to learn Reversi is to play against the computer for a while, which lets you figure out the rules (though they are listed in the **Help > Contents** file), which Figure 18.17 shows I have not done sufficiently.

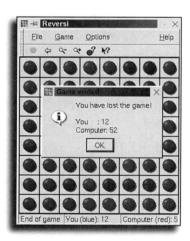

FIGURE 18.17
The computer plays Reversi better than inexperienced players do.

The **Options** let you change just about everything about the appearance of the gameboard.

SameGame

The first time I played SameGame I didn't know quite what to think of it. Now, maybe 500 games later, I still don't know what to think of it. The purpose is to make the colored balls, which rotate entertainingly when the cursor is rested on them, disappear. There are three colors of balls (see Figure 18.18).

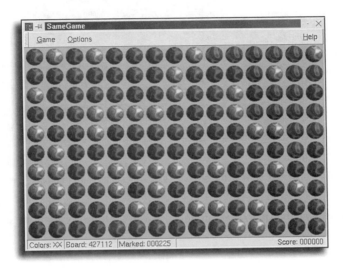

FIGURE 18.18
A hint on the Status Bar shows how many points you'll get for clicking right now.

The greater the number of same-color balls that are connected, the higher the score through some exponential formula. It's possible to start big with just one click (see Figure 18.19).

FIGURE 18.19
Move the mouse around to find out what will give you the biggest bang for the click. Here's a pretty good one-click score.

If you remove all the balls, you get an extra 1,000 points as a bonus (see Figure 18.20).

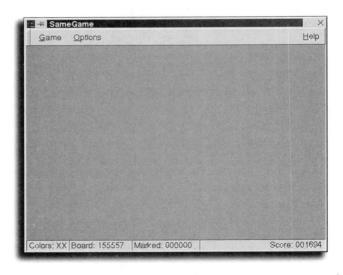

FIGURE 18.20
All the balls are gone, which requires a little planning, but this score is nothing to write home about.

The sole item on the **Options** menu randomizes the playing board.

Shisen-Sho

This is a game similar to Mahjongg, but played in only two dimensions (see Figure 18.21).

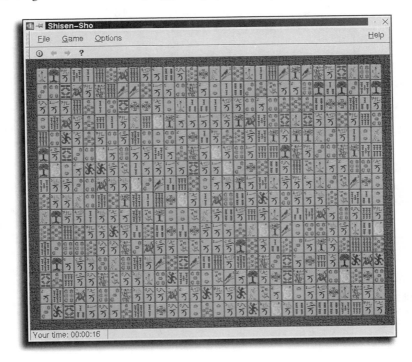

FIGURE 18.21
It's more difficult than it looks. Shisen-Sho is another tile-matching game. This is in its biggest, most difficult mode.
Size and difficulty are set separately.

Like Mahjongg, Shisen-Sho offers hints and has different layouts available. Unlike Mahjongg, Shisen-Sho times you and marks the Status Bar as Cheat Mode when you've asked for a hint. You can choose from multiple levels of difficulty as well.

The programmer of this game has a demonstrable mean streak: Some of the games can't be won. You can query it as to whether the current game can be solved, and you can set it to produce only solvable games. There is a cheat mode in which you click on a tile and, if there's a playable matching tile, it blinks at you. You can adjust the size of the board. Poke around the menus; half the fun is experimenting.

Sirtet

Ho ho. This is *Tetris* spelled backwards. This little game does not play backwards, however. You don't supervise the disassembly of row after row of tiles that fly out the top of the window. In fact, it plays exactly like Tetris, and looks the same (see Figure 18.22), too.

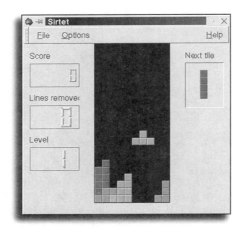

FIGURE 18.22
.sirteT ekil tsuj skool dna syalp tetriS

Among its features is a multiple player mode.

Smiletris

Smiletris (see Figure 18.23) is another Tetris knockoff, but it has pieces made up of three smiley faces or variations thereon.

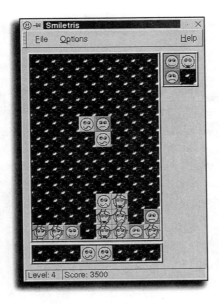

FIGURE 18.23
Fortunately, you can change the smiley faces into something else if you want.

Probably the coolest part of Smiletris is the arcade-style sound effects.

Snake Race

This game requires a remarkable degree of agility and probably shouldn't be played unless you have a spare keyboard: you're likely to break the arrow keys on the one you have. The opening screen, Figure 18.24, says it all.

FIGURE 18.24
The snakes eat the apples. The walls and bouncing balls kill the snakes, as do running into themselves or each other.

After the game begins, you have practically no time to set your vegetarian reptile off in search of apples to eat (see Figure 18.25). You need to be really quick with the arrow keys.

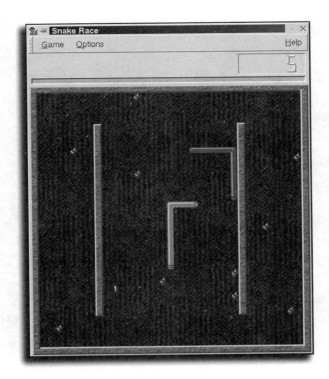

FIGURE 18.25
Bump into anything and the snake dies. Don't eat all the apples in time, and more apples appear. The object of the game is for your snake to eat all the apples.

Snake Race is tremendously configurable, as you'll find when you slither around its menus. You can adjust the number of snakes, the general degree of difficulty (from very hard to impossible), the number of bouncing balls, the background color (or bitmapped graphic), and even the keys that move your snake around.

Sokoban

Sokoban, shown in Figure 18.26, is a cute little game in which you are a warehouse worker who needs to move a number of items from one place to another. (It must be from an earlier day, because there are no government safety forms to fill out and no union monitor.)

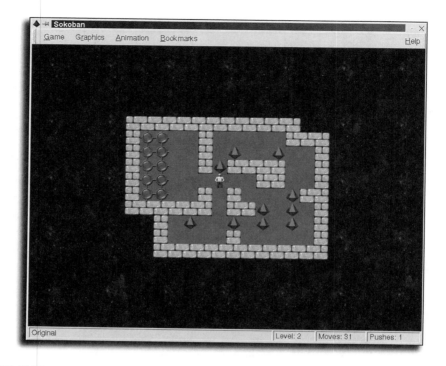

FIGURE 18.26
The little guy has to push the diamond things onto the circles, one at a time. He can't jump over them and if one gets into a corner there's no way to get it out.

It looks *so* simple. Which makes it all the more maddening when you get yourself literally in a corner. If you run into trouble, consult the help file or ask a child to assist you. The **Game > Level collection** menu item lets you try out a series of problems devised by various sadistic programmers. And if you need to stop in the middle of a game, you can "bookmark" where you are to return to it later. In fact, you can return to multiple games in this way.

Sokoban is a tremendously addictive game. The technical editor of this book tried it out and wasn't heard from again for weeks, except for eager (or anguished) email messages about the level most recently achieved or currently being attempted.

Toys

There is in the KDE distribution a file called kdetoys. What does it do? Where do they go? Good questions. It comprises three silly little programs that are worth mentioning anyway. And it installs them not in the **K Menu > Toys** submenu—silly you for thinking that that would make sense—but instead in **K Menu > Utilities**. Which makes sense if you think that a program that measures the distance your mouse pointer has moved is a utility. (Unless you have Caldera Open Linux 2.2 or later, you may not have a **K Menu > Toys** submenu at all.) You can (and probably should) use kmenuedit to create **Toys** and move them there, because **Utilities** is awfully full.

KMoonPhase

This little number, **K Menu > Utilities > Moon Phase**, puts a small yellow circle on your K Panel that more or less graphically shows the phase of the moon. If you rest your mouse pointer on it, it will tell you the age of the moon, a kind of computerized *Farmer's Almanac*. That's it. Oh, and one other thing: if you right-click it and click **Quit**, it can shut down your entire K Panel.

Mouspedometa

This masterpiece measures mouse movement (Figure 18.27). The **Help** file, accessed by right-clicking the application (as is everything else in connection with the program), says the next version will be useful. I can't imagine how.

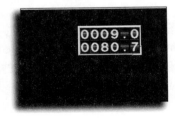

FIGURE 18.27
Mouspedometa provides the essential service of tallying mouse movement.

World Watch

This little thing (see Figure 18.28) is actually pretty cool, and one doesn't have to tax one's powers of rationalization to come up with a way that it might actually be almost good for something.

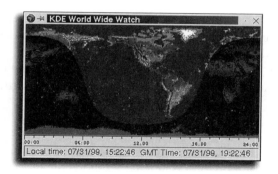

FIGURE 18.28
KDE World Watch starts out showing the local time and GMT, plus the state of the Sun's illumination of the Earth.

If you move the mouse to a point on the Earth map, it will show you the time there, more or less. I say more or less because the map isn't divided into time zones. Instead, the time shown is what it is for that exact location based on time as a zone-less continuum. One needn't run it for long before starting to wish for additional features: the capability to run the thing as the desktop, the capability to zoom into an area so you could determine where your location is located within the time zone, how many minutes the zone time is away from Sun time, and so on. A right-click produces a menu that lets you clutter the map with flags or speed up the illumination display to prove that Earth does spin on its axis as it revolves about the sun, producing seasons that you might otherwise not have noticed. Still, it's pretty cool as such things go. The only thing missing is a way to make it your KDE desktop. Then it would be *really* cool.

chapter 19

A World of Other KDE Applications

The KDE core distribution is by no means the whole show when it comes to KDE applications. This chapter pauses to survey some of what is available, bearing in mind that it is just a snapshot. By the time you read this, some applications may have been dropped, while others will have been combined and others added. Some of these applications are redundant, while others are unique.

The best way to find out what's available is to look in the Applications section at `http://www.kde.org`. Some of the applications listed there are on the KDE ftp site (`ftp://kde.org/pub/kde` and its mirrors), and there are links for those that aren't.

If, for instance, you have a CD reader capable of writing, you will find several CD burners on the KDE ftp site. If games are your reason for living, you'll find a multitude of them there.

Several of the applications already mentioned (KPackage, some of the multimedia stuff, kdu, among others) were obtained here. By the time you read this, new versions will be available. I mention several more in this chapter, and one, KLyX, has its own chapter.

SEE ALSO

➤ To learn more about KLyX, see Chapter 20, "KLyX: The Paradoxical Processor of Complex Documents," on page 425.

About KOffice

You cannot be around KDE for very long without hearing about something called *KOffice*. It is true that a group of crack code writers at kde.org have been at work for years fashioning and improving software of that name.

The KOffice suite was in fact developed for a long time under KDE 1.X, but in the spring of 1999 development efforts were moved to the KDE 2.0 project. The libraries involved with version 2.0 and some other new features were better suited to the kind of data interchangeability that the designers had in mind.

What this means is that there isn't, and probably never will be, a KOffice suite for KDE 1.1.1 or 1.2. Fortunately, other office suites run very well with KDE

What follows, then, is a listing of a few of the many KDE applications that are available. Bear in mind that KDE developers, like many Linux developers, hold to the "release early and often" philosophy. This means that an application will likely be released for testing and peer review as soon as a fundamental design is settled on and the major features work, at least to some extent. If you are accustomed to commercial software, this can evoke emotions ranging from puzzlement to terror. Relax. KDE applications, like most Linux applications, are in a constant state of development. Indeed, by its very nature Linux software invites you, the user, to make improvements to the code and to release your code to the world.

Source Code

All the applications listed here are available chiefly as source code tarballs. While compiling code has been made very easy, it isn't going to involve any animations, "wizards," or cutesy stuff that disguises the fact that it is doing what it wants to do and not what you want it to do.

I've compiled the applications depicted here. I found and downloaded them all in the space of an hour or so; compiling took less than 30 minutes for all the applications. *This is not difficult stuff.*

Without exception, the entire process involved exactly this:

1. Downloading the tarball and copying it to /usr/local/src.
2. As root (actually, su root in a konsole window), typing `tar xvfz` *`filename`*`.tar.gz` and pressing **Enter**.
3. Changing to the newly created /usr/local/src/*filename* directory and reading the INSTALL and README files.
4. Typing `./configure` `— prefix=/opt/kde` and pressing **Enter**. (If your KDE directory is elsewhere, use its actual location.)
5. Waiting for a minute or so while the configuration took place.
6. Typing `make all` (most would have compiled with just `make`, but `make all` does no harm and is sometimes needed) and pressing **Enter**.
7. Waiting for a few minutes while the application was compiled.
8. Typing `make install` and pressing **Enter**.
9. Restarting KDE so those applications that automatically put entries in K Menu would have those entries recognized.

That's it.

I've harped on this, and will continue to do so: If you're using Linux, you're cheating yourself if you're not compiling applications.

System Enhancements

As I browsed the list of applications in the works, again, available either at the KDE ftp site or linked on the KDE Web site, a couple of them appealed to me. Setting the system time in Linux is always a little bit of a pain, especially if you're limited to the somewhat obscure command-line programs. It was extremely pleasing, then, to see kcmclock (see Figure 19.1).

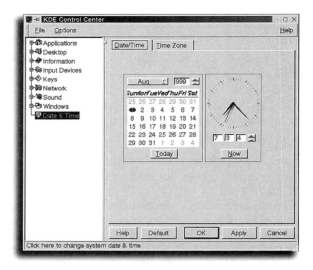

FIGURE 19.1
kcmclock adds timesetting functions to the KDE Control Panel. Here you set the date and time.

This small file (about 75K as a gzipped tarball) compiled in seconds and provides a second page that is not to be overlooked because Linux machines should be set to GMT (Greenwich Mean Time), as shown in Figure 19.2.

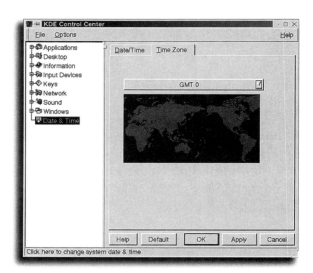

FIGURE 19.2
The drop box lists all the world's time zones as offsets from GMT. It covers the little world map. You pick the offset from GMT, which allows KDE to display correct local time on a machine whose clock is set to GMT, as it should be.

You can play with kcmclock while you are logged in as a user, but remember that only root can set the system time. Therefore, once you've figured it out, pop over to root and set your machine's time.

Similarly, there is kcmjoy, which is a KDE utility for setting up a joystick, if you have one.

A popular application for the desktop is KGoodStuff (see Figure 19.3).

FIGURE 19.3
Okay, it doesn't look like much at first, but KGoodStuff provides a floating icon bar from which you can launch your applications. It is fully documented, so setting it up is a piece of cake. The configuration dialog lets you create new buttons and assign applications to them.

KGoodStuff is the KDE equivalent for the Good Stuff program familiar to long-time Linux users. Its chief difference is that you don't have to edit an inscrutable text file to configure it. If you're not familiar with the concept, it is a floating icon bar into which you can place applications for launching. Given the multitude of ways to launch applications in KDE (desktop icons, K Menu, and K Panel), I can't see much point to KgoodStuff. But somebody thought that there was sufficient need for it that it was written, so perhaps somebody will feel the same need and use it. It's easy to configure and well documented.

Many other system-level applications and enhancements are available for KDE. Among them are Kapm, an automatic power management program, and Kcmlaptop, which provides several functions of special interest to people who use Linux and KDE on laptop and notebook computers. All the applications mentioned in this section are available at `ftp://ftp.kde.org/pub/kde/`.

SEE ALSO
➤ *I discuss Kapm and Kcmlaptop, in Chapter 37, "Using KDE on Notebook and Portable Computers," on page 651.*

Multimedia Applications

KDE programmers tend to be young and enthusiastic people who spend a lot of time slaving away over a hot computer, so it's no surprise that they have developed a number of applications that let them amuse themselves with music and other multimedia. Several multimedia applications are mentioned in Chapter 15, "Multimedia: Music and Movies," and I'll not go over them again here. Instead, I'll introduce a few more.

Krabber

One application that has drawn a lot of buzz in KDE circles is Krabber (see Figure 19.4).

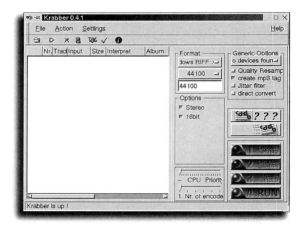

FIGURE 19.4
Krabber grabs audio tracks, converts audio tracks, and burns audio tracks onto CDs if you have a CD writer.

Besides being nicely designed, Krabber is quite versatile. If you are interested in the manipulation of audio files, it's well worth the download from the KDE ftp site mentioned earlier.

KRecord

KRecord (see Figure 19.5) lets you record to memory or a .wav file sounds from any source supported by the Sound Mixer Panel, one of the KDE core applications to which it is linked by a menu.

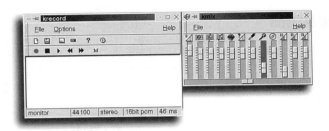

FIGURE 19.5
You can use the KDE Sound Mixer Panel to blend sounds that are then saved by KRecord.

If you have a little jingle or something that you would like to make into a system sound, KRecord is where you can do it. You can also record your own voice (or someone else's voice) as a .wav, and tie it to an event or use it in any other way you can use a .wav file. You can find KRecord at `www.in-berlin.de/User/kraxel/` `krecord.html`.

aRts

If you like to make your own music, you might want to check out aRts, which stands for *analog real-time synthesizer*. It's at `arts.linuxbox.com/`.

KmodBox

Another popular tool for manipulating audio files is KModBox, by the author of aKtion. Both are available from `www.geocities.com/SiliconValley/Haven/3864/` `mainframes.html`.

KHDRec

If you are really serious about sound recording, KHDRec makes digital recordings to a hard drive, as is used in most state-of-the-art sound studios. This thing is a sight to behold. Behold (and download) it at `verona.phys.chemie.tu-muenchen.de/people/` `lorenz/khdrec/`.

Communications

KDE has an abundance of applications designed to make your Internet experience more rewarding and more secure. It's always a good idea to look at the KDE ftp site for the latest and greatest. Here are some others, and where you can get them:

- **KICQ**—An icq client for KDE. `http://www.cn.ua:8100/~denis/kde/kicq.html`
- **kISDN**—ISDN front end, including advanced telephony features. `http://kisdn.headlight.de/kisdn.html`
- **kticker**—Downloads and displays news headlines. `http://www.ee.mu.oz.au/staff/paul/kde/kticker/`
- **K Instant Messenger**—An AOL Instant Messenger client. `http://www-ec.njit.edu/~adt6247/`
- **geheimnis**—A KDE front end for PGP. `http://members.home.com/cdwiegand/geheimnis/`
- **LinKT**—A packet radio program for KDE; not Internet but certainly useful if you're a HAM operator. `http://www.1409.org/projects/linkt/`

Graphics Applications

Image manipulation is an area of increasing development in KDE, with more and enhanced applications available all the time. Some are very specialized, whereas others are for more general use.

KFourier performs complex (and very processor-intensive) filtering of images, allowing them to be sharpened or softened, as well as transformed in other ways (see Figure 19.6)

FIGURE 19.6
If a bitmap is too sharp, or not sharp enough, KFourier puts things right.

You can download the latest version of KFourier from
`www.arrakis.es/~rlarrosa/kfourier.html`.

Kover allows you to design and print the label inserts for CD jewel boxes. That
seems a little *too* narrow a niche for an application until you consider the number of
CDs that come without jewel boxes at all. So you get the CD holders from the store,
and they all look alike, and… (see Figure 19.7).

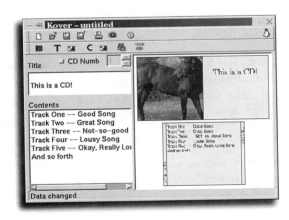

FIGURE 19.7
Kover does only one thing—it makes CD covers—but it does that job very well indeed.

The quality of the printer you're using determines the quality of Kover's product. A good color inkjet can produce very professional-looking results; an old dot-matrix printer cannot. Get Kover at `www.fischlustig.de/kover/`.

KuickShow is a slideshow program for KDE that lets you click through a whole directory of images at once, or set it to do the clicking for you so you can just watch. It's at the KDE ftp site.

KPlot puts your data into graphical form. This is useful especially for scientists and researchers (do you *really* want to know the average of your friends' phone numbers?), it's available from `www.glue.umd.edu/~dsweet/KDE/KPlotW/index.html`.

KScan is a KDE front end for SANE-compliant scanners, which is to say scanners that have adopted the SANE standard. If you have one of these, download it from `rf-hp.npi.msu.su/kscan.html`. To find out if your scanner is SANE-compliant, check your Linux distributor's list of compatible hardware.

Again, these are just a few of the graphics applications available. Take a look around. If there's a need, there's probably an application or an app under development.

Office Tools

Though the bulk of office application development is focused on KOffice and programs that tie into it in some way, you might find a few apps useful.

PeopleSpace is a KDE application under development, but usable in its current form, that emulates the interface of the popular ACT! business information manager. You can find the current version at `www.slac.com/mpilone/peoplespace_home/`.

KProject is project management software for KDE. Take a look at `rs45.bv.tu-berlin.de/JOCHEN/KPROJECT/kproject.php3`.

KPSQL is a query front end for the popular PostgresSql database engine for Linux. You can locate information about it and links to the source at `www.mutinybaysoftware.com/kpsql.html`.

I mention KSendFax (see Figure 19.8) again later on, but it's worth bringing up now, too. It and KHylaFax are front ends for Linux fax programs.

To learn about your fax options under Linux and the ones that integrate most happily with KDE, see Chapter 33, "Faxing from KDE."

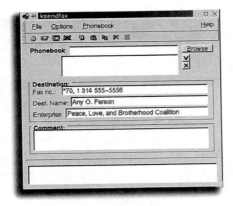

FIGURE 19.8
If you have any of several commonly used Linux fax programs, KSendFax lets you avoid having to learn complex command-line options in order to send faxes over your modem.

KHylaFax is similar, but it is especially attuned to the HylaFax fax server program. You can find both on the KDE ftp site.

Miscellaneous Programs You Might Not Be Able to Live Another Day Without

In KDE or anywhere else, among the most enjoyable applications are those that defy categorization. One of the reasons is that you probably don't have another program that does the same thing. Another is that the people who write such programs are often clever and sometimes delightfully quirky. There are many very clever people writing programs for KDE.

KWeather

KWeather is the answer to a question you may never have asked, but when you think about it, it's a good idea. It does not change the weather, but it lets you talk about it intelligently (see Figure 19.9).

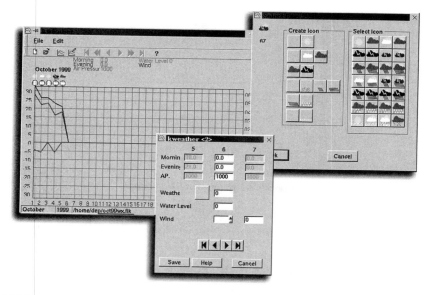

FIGURE 19.9
If you are interested in weather, or if you have reason to keep track of it, KWeather makes things easier. It lets you keep a running record of temperature, precipitation, and so on. Beware, though. It graphs temperature in Celsius, barometric pressure in Celsius, and rain in centimeters, so for the uninitiated, it can be a metric nightmare.

You keep a separate file for each month. If crops (or even a good-looking yard) are among your concerns, KWeather, available at `www.privat.kkf.net/ ~juergen.hochwald/linux/kweather/e_index.html`, is of interest to you.

KLab

I don't know quite what to make of KLab. I know that it comes from David Sweet, and if he sees a need for such a thing, you can rest assured that there *is* a need for such a thing. Here's what his page says about it:

"KLab is based on Rlab by Ian Searle. Rlab is a matrix math engine and high-level prototyping language interpreter. It provides plotting services through externally-defined functions (in .r files). This function base will be modified and extended as needed to interface with KLab. The plan is to provide a plot window, RLab command entry window, simplified matrix entry via a spreadsheet-like grid, point-and-click plot editing, drag-and-drop support (for raw data files), active UI controls, output to .ps, .gif, etc., and a proprietary format so that plots/variables may be reloaded."

If you understand all this, you can be sure that KLab will be good at doing it. Download KLab from www.chaos.umd.edu/~dsweet/KDE/KLab/.

KVideoList

KVideoList is a little database program that catalogs your videotapes. You can get it at www.bamberg.baynet.de/home/ba1005/kde/kvlist.html. There are other small, specialized databases available on the KDE site that can be adapted to keep track of other things, such as a record collection.

KFTE

KFTE is not one of those programs that defies categorization, and it duplicates some functions that you have in other applications. But if you are a programmer, KFTE (see Figure 19.10) is likely to become your favorite editor.

FIGURE 19.10
KFTE, a port of the highly regarded FTE programmer's editor, offers features that will excite programmers and put the rest of us in awe.

You can find KFTE on the KDE ftp site.

The Neatest Desktop Around

This is not, strictly speaking, a KDE application, but the developer went to considerable pains to make it KDE friendly, which is reason enough to include X Globe. It is a program that replaces the simple static colors or random wallpapers of your desktop with a real-time sunlit view of Earth from space. Take a look at Figure 19.11.

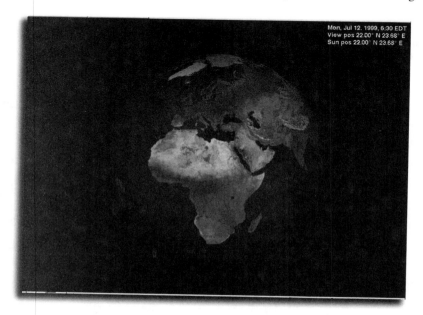

FIGURE 19.11
X Globe lets you choose actual high-resolution photographs taken from space to cover the globe that displays on your desktop and updates as frequently or infrequently as you like.

There is talk of porting X Globe to create a Moon version that would track the phases of the moon using a high-resolution lunar map. I know, because I have done most of the talking and have used the project to prove to the satisfaction of all that I am not a programmer. It may yet come to pass, and even if it doesn't, X Globe makes your desktop a lot more interesting. Get it at www.uni-karlsruhe.de/~uddn/xglobe.

Again, don't think that this brief listing is comprehensive or even exemplary. It includes only some applications that are mostly unmentioned elsewhere in this book that were available for download on the day this chapter was written. It is not even close to complete for today, nor is it intended to be. There is no way that it could list the new and wonderful things that have appeared between my today, as I write this, and your today, as you read it. So take a look at www.kde.org and follow the links to the application pages. You'll find something you like.

chapter
20

KLyX: The Paradoxical Processor of Complex Docments

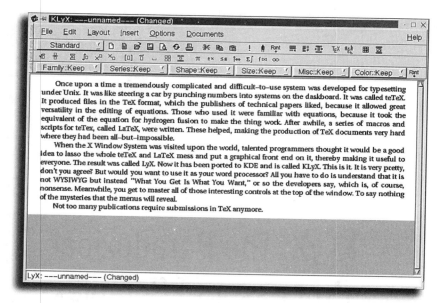

FIGURE 20.1
Read the text of this window to learn the history of KLyX.

It is impossible to see or use KLyX and not have a strong opinion about it. It is entirely possible, on the other hand, to have multiple conflicting strong opinions about it. It is certainly an attractive application, and it is the most elaborate and sophisticated of all the native KDE 1.X applications.

On the other hand, it is devilishly difficult to learn, and after you've learned it, what do you have? You have the ability to produce documents in a non-WYSIWYG, not-quite word processor that cranks out files in an obscure format that in some cases it cannot itself read. That's right: sometimes it cannot read its *own* files.

Still, many extremely talented and skillful people spent thousands of hours for which they were not paid putting KLyX and the underlying document processing code together. They must have had a reason, right?

It is my sad duty to inform you that I shall now devote many pages to KLyX, and at the end of those pages you are likely to be no closer to the answers to these questions than you are right now. The fact is, you love KLyX or you hate it...or both.

Getting and Installing KLyX

The latest version of KLyX is always available at the KDE Web site (www.kde.org) or ftp site (ftp://ftp.kde.org/pub/kde/) or the KLyX homepage (www.devel.lyx.org/~ettrich/klyx.html). Sometimes binaries are available, but your best bet is to download and compile it. In my experience it compiles uneventfully. (It's a good idea to specify your KDE directory as the --prefix= option when running ./configure.)

When you run KLyX for the first time, you're likely to be surprised by the big KOffice logo that splashes itself onto your screen with its picture of the little dumpling child. Don't worry: It will go away after a few seconds. You may also be treated to a dialog box saying that there is no Lyx directory in your home directory. If you are, let KLyX create one. It is where your configuration and data files will be stored. The default KLyX window size is too small to be of much use, but you can drag it to a larger size.

At first, the <u>H</u>elp menu is all but empty, and clicking on any of the items returns an error, saying that the help files could not be found. This is because the help files, unlike those of other KDE applications, are not HTML but .lyx format. To get to them, open /kde/share/apps/klyx/doc/Intro.lyx. Now the help file is populated with a wealth of documentation, though most of it is for LyX, of which KLyX is a rather more elegant port.

Necessities

The bottom item in the <u>H</u>elp menu is, actually, the first thing you should check. It contains the results of the search the compile-and-install process did for things that determine whether your system has everything necessary for KLyX to work. It is entirely possible to compile and install KLyX without support software on your machine, but you won't be able to do much of anything useful with it. This file also contains information as to where you can download the latest version of anything it wants that you don't have.

Here is what it wants:

- **teTeX**—The current distribution.
- **LaTeX**—The TeX macros that makes TeX (barely) bearable.
- **Linux Doc–sgml tools**—Files that support various formats under Linux. It is sometimes referred to as linuxdoc.

- **Standard LaTeX document classes**—The functional equivalent of templates in word processors, these are not things that you whip together yourself. They consist of
  - **article**—The basic document class
  - **report**—Similar to article, has a more rigid structure
  - **book**—Supports chapters
  - **letter**—For writing letters in English
  - **slides**—For preparing transparencies
  - **aa**—The format for articles to be submitted to the magazine *Astronomy and Astrophysics*
  - **amsart**—A variation on article, produces formatting that complies with American Mathematical Society standards
  - **dinbrief**—For writing letters in German
  - **foils**—A more elaborate and attractive alternative to slides
  - **paper**—An alternative to article, more elaborate
  - **REVTeX**—A document class that meets standards set by the American Physical Society, the American Institute of Physics, and the Optical Society of America
- **Paper size packages**—As you can imagine, support for paper of different sizes. These include
  - **a4**—The standard European paper size
  - **a4wide**—Like a4, but with wider margins
  - **geometry**—Lets you change paper size and margins at the cost of some of the program's typographical functions

Typefaces include

- **EC fonts**—Supports high-quality kerning and hyphenation
- **psnfss**—The 35 standard PostScript typefaces

Other packages include

- **algorithm**—To support some kinds of mathematical layouts
- **babel**—Handles automatic translation of some document elements into non-English languages
- **color**—Supports text in color

- **fancyhdr**—Supports alternative headers and footers when the fancy page style is selected

- **floatflt**—Allows text to wrap around a graphic or other object

- **graphics**—Allows the insertion of PostScript graphics

- **linuxdoc-sgml**—Allows the Linux Doc tools to process files generated by sgml tools

- **rotating**—Allows the orientation of some items to be changed

- **subfigure**—Allows the grouping of multiple figures with independent captions

- **setspace**—Necessary if you want control over line spacing

- **longtable**—For use if your article, letter, or book is to be more than one page long

Now, you are probably wondering why all this stuff is treated as if it were optional. One reason is that it was developed when memory and storage were precious commodities. (Indeed, if you look at your word processor, you'll find all manner of features and layouts that you've never used and never will. Why bother with them? Just in case?) Other layouts are being developed all the time, as well as other add-ons. You don't need all the preceding listed items, but you certainly need some of them if you are to do any useful work. Fortunately, the essential ones are included with most Linux distributions, and the **Help > LaTeX Configuration** menu item describes where the missing ones can be had. Once you have obtained and installed the missing items, if any, run **Options > Reconfigure** to run the search again, to make sure they are properly installed and recognized.

Using KLyX

KLyX, as you have figured out by now, is based on very strictly defined layouts that are not something you just toss off, as you might in a word processor. The layouts are collections of styles that you can apply to paragraphs. This relieves you of the burden of formatting your documents.

You may also have begun to suspect that you probably know absolutely nothing that will be of any use in KLyX, and if you have, you are very close to right.

Try this: Open a KLyX screen. You will notice that it is very attractive and has a familiar layout, with menus, rows of toolbars, a text entry box, and a status bar at bottom. Now, look a little closer and try to figure out how many of the toolbar items you recognize. Open some of the menus and look at some of the items there. Click a few.

Chances are that you are among those who install new software, open it up, and try to figure it out, resorting to the documentation only when you get stuck. With some packages, especially word processors, you may never get stuck. KLyX is very powerful and complicated, and it cannot be used right out of the compiler. It is not intuitive, and it adopts few of the de facto standards that have come to populate word processors, where your most difficult task initially might be figuring out how to turn off the annoying animated paper clip character. If you intend to use KLyX, you will need to study it first.

On the other hand, KLyX has some very cool features. Remember, structure and consistency are top priorities in KLyX, which is designed to prepare documents for places that would reject the formula for cold fusion if it were improperly formatted. In KLyX you must, for instance, change an attribute of an item by changing its style, and when you do, you change *all* instances of that style in that document. It is extremely strict. This is great for your doctoral dissertation, but less so for a freewheeling, informal letter to a friend. If extremely formal writing is what you do and you intend to produce files that are to be read by systems that can read .lyx or .tex files, KLyX is just the thing. But for other kinds of documents, it can be like swimming against a powerful current.

When you start KLyX, Figure 20.2 is what you see.

FIGURE 20.2
After a few seconds, dumpling boy goes away.

Then, fortunately, you see that which is depicted in Figure 20.3.

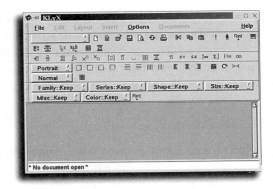

FIGURE 20.3
The default KLyX screen is tiny and puzzling. You can make it larger.

The first thing you want to do is stretch it out to a useful size, see Figure 20.4.

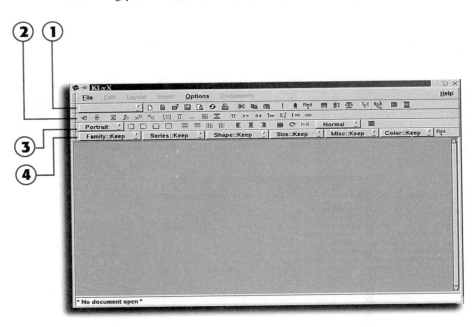

FIGURE 20.4
Once you make KLyX bigger, it starts to look at little more like an application with which you can come to terms.

1. General toolbar
2. Math toolbar
3. Table toolbar
4. Character toolbar

431

Now that you have something to look at, you can begin to sort it all out. You notice multiple levels of toolbars. You recognize some of the icons, but many of them are mysteries, and a lot of icons you are accustomed to seeing are absent. The screen is gray and what appears to be the main button on the top toolbar is blank. Most of the menus are grayed out. This is not a program that you fire up and just begin typing away. No, it is far more circumspect than that.

Before we go further, let's identify those toolbars:

- **General**—The top toolbar contains items you are likely to recognize.
- **Math**—The second toolbar contains items for use in equation editing. It is not entirely ridiculous to say that KLyX is an equation editor with some word-processing functions wrapped around it. Typical KLyX users also use this toolbar a lot.
- **Tables**—The third toolbar creates and manipulates tables in KLyX documents.
- **Character**—The fourth and final toolbar comprises drop boxes used to control the characters in the document.

You can control which, if any, of them appear via **Options > Screen Options > Toolbars**.

Before you can do anything, you need to create a **File > New** or **File > New from template** that prompts you for a filename and location, using the standard KDE file selection dialog box. If you chose **File > New**, the default layout is used. If you chose **File > New from template**, you are offered a choice of installed layouts (see Figure 20.5).

FIGURE 20.5
Choose your project from the layouts dialog box. Various document layouts are available; some publications provide their own.

After you have chosen a layout, the grayness of the screen diminishes a little, and the menus come to life. You can now begin to type. It looks perfectly normal, almost as if from a standard word processor (see Figure 20.6).

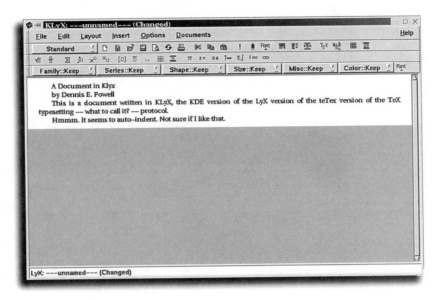

FIGURE 20.6
It auto-indents, but otherwise seems to be a well-behaved word processor.

This isn't how the final document ought to look, though, is it? It needs to be prettified, and if it is to be submitted for publication, it needs to be prettified according to the standards of the publication. How do you bring this about? There's no icon for centering the text, is there? Ah. Let's look under that formerly blank drop box, the one on the first toolbar, the one that now says **Standard**. Maybe the answer is there (see Figure 20.7).

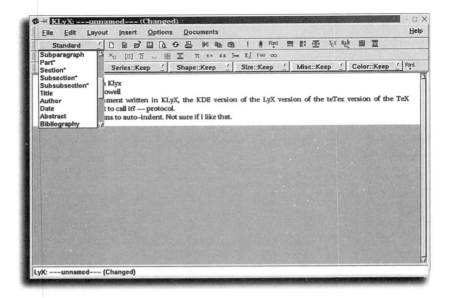

FIGURE 20.7
Here you find all the defined styles for the current document. Let's try out a few.

The title of the document should probably be of the Title style, so let's put the cursor somewhere in the title and click **Title** in the styles drop box (see Figure 20.8).

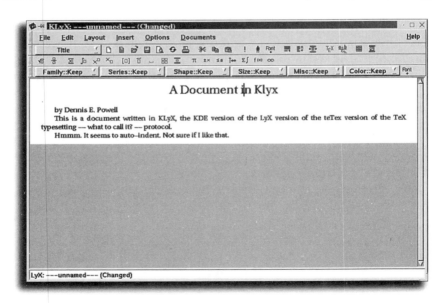

FIGURE 20.8
It worked! Putting the cursor somewhere, anywhere, in the title and clicking **Title** in the styles drop box formats the title.

But now my name is off to the left, kind of forlorn-looking. What shall we do about that? (See Figure 20.9.)

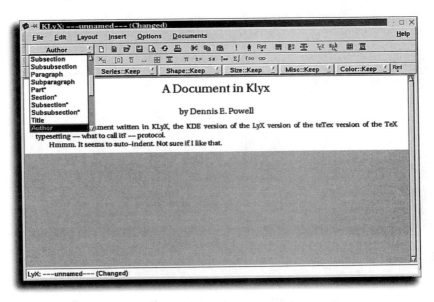

FIGURE 20.9
Is there anything here for the poor author? Yes, indeed.

Okay, so you know how to format paragraphs, at least a little. What else can you do?

Well, that depends entirely on the layout being used, and you won't find any of the changes where you might expect them. For instance, in this layout, clicking on the item labeled **Font** in the **Character** toolbar toggles the selected text from the current typeface, Utopia, to Courier (see Figure 20.10). This is not something that has to be, though. By changing the attributes in the drop boxes spread across the **Character** toolbar, you can make the Font button produce something entirely different (see Figure 20.11).

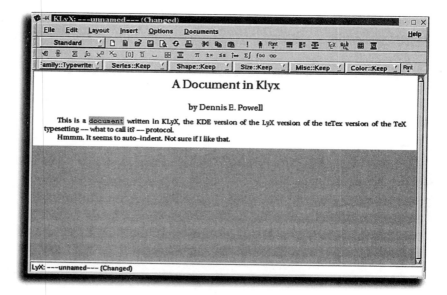

FIGURE 20.10
Clicking the **Font** button by default changes the selected text to Courier typeface.

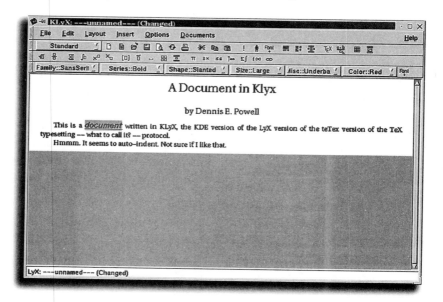

FIGURE 20.11
You can change the characteristics of the characters with the drop boxes in the **Character** menu.

You can change the user-defined characteristics on a per-use basis: You can have small caps in one place and slanted large red underline someplace else, if that sort of thing appeals to you. The exclamation mark on the General toolbar toggles the Emphasize characteristic as set by the layout, whereas the silhouette of the little man toggles the Noun style.

The Equation Editor

I am quite certain that I have never inserted an equation into a document in my life, and I feel confident in saying it's unlikely I ever will. But if you are someone who needs to produce documents in the formats that KLyX supports, you probably do it every day. You will therefore be pleased to note that it's easy in KLyX (see Figure 20.12).

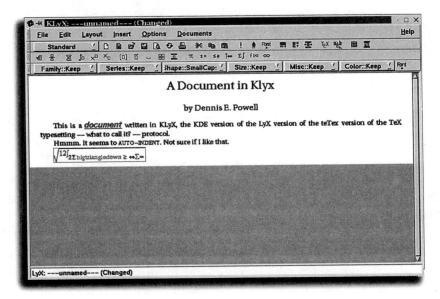

FIGURE 20.12
Clicking on a function produces that function in the equation editor, whereas clicking on a scientific character produces a dialog box whence the character you want can be selected.

The equation editor supports other KLyX functions. For instance, you can alter size and toggle it with the **Font** button (see Figure 12.13).

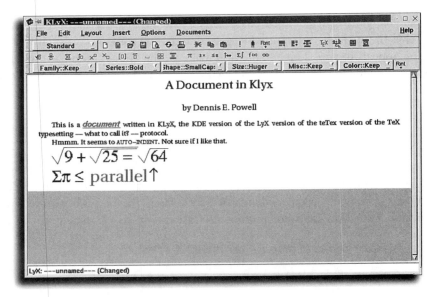

FIGURE 20.13
You can set the size of the equation in the user-defined character settings.

Additionally, there is an icon on the General toolbar that brings you into Math mode.

How to Really Learn KLyX

There is no way to describe KLyX adequately in a few pages or a few dozen. Indeed, full treatment of this strange and powerful program could easily fill a book the size of this one. To do so or anything close to it would be far outside the scope of this book.

Fortunately, vast documentation is available, and is part of KLyX itself. After you have opened the documentation index file for the first time, you will find that the Help menu provides frightening detail on the usage of KLyX (see Figure 20.14).

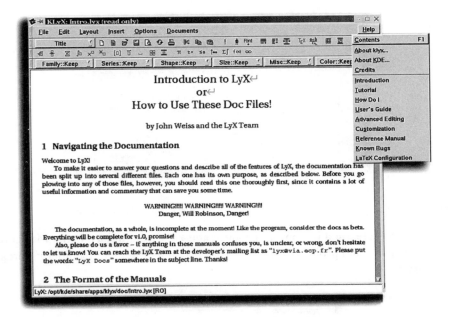

FIGURE 20.14
The extensive documentation provides a clear path for those willing to make the commitment necessary to learn KLyX.

Should you learn KLyX? It depends entirely on your needs. If you submit papers to scholarly journals that require TeX format, the choice is made for you. If you are intrigued by a completely different way of looking at text processing, KLyX will keep you amused for many a day, night, and weekend. Just sorting out the **Document layout** dialog box (see Figure 20.15) can take many hours, if true proficiency is the goal.

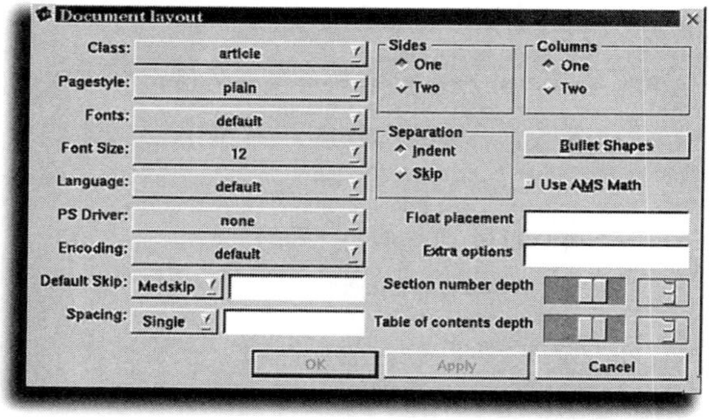

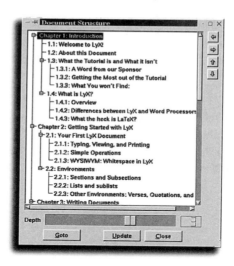

FIGURE 20.15

The Document layout dialog box goes into greater detail than many people would choose to use.

Once you have learned it, you can produce and zip through documents with considerable efficiency and produce work that would be more difficult in a different program (see Figure 20.16).

FIGURE 20.16

Table of Contents generation is automatic because it is built into the KLyX document.

If you are looking for an easy-to-use word processor that produces documents that look on paper as they do on the screen, KLyX is certain to be a disappointment.

Deciding for yourself is easy enough: Download KLyX and take a look. It costs nothing but the time you care to invest. No matter what you decide, you'll certainly be convinced that it is a remarkable program.

GOING ONLINE WITH KDE

Going Online with Kppp

Setting Up Kppp for Your Account

Using Kppp to Log In

Linux is a creature of the Internet. It was created there, it grows there, and a surprisingly large part of the Internet is based on it. So, too, with KDE (though there's really nothing of KDE on which to base any part of the Net). Were it not for programmers working together from all over the world via the Internet and users who download the thing via the Internet, there would be no KDE or anyone using it.

Of course, the majority of Internet users use the Internet through dial-up accounts through an Internet service provider (ISP). It therefore was necessary for KDE to include a native dialer application.

If You Like Your Dialer

Other X Window System dialers have been around for years now, the most popular being EZPPP and Xisp, both of which are quite good and will work under KDE. So if you have one of these and are attached to it, you're free to continue with it.

In putting together the dialer, **Kppp**, the KDE developers sought ease of setup and use, richness of features, and ready access to anything you are likely to need. You are likely to conclude that they succeeded on all counts.

This chapter helps you set up Kppp for your account. It does not go into the theory of ppp or the inner workings of Linux's use thereof. My goal here is to get you online with minimum fuss and bother.

Setting Up Kppp for Your Account

When you start Kppp, the first thing you need to do is set up a new account (see Figure 21.1).

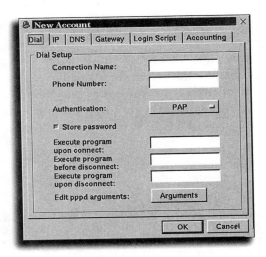

FIGURE 21.1
The New Account dialog box begins a fairly quick and easy configuration process.

The Dial page involves naming the account and providing the telephone number (don't forget the ***70,** to disable it, if you have call waiting). If your ISP has multiple phone numbers, you may separate them with colons, in which case a busy signal causes Kppp to dial the next number. You must then select the kind of login your ISP requires and choose it from the **Authentication** list box (see Figure 21.2).

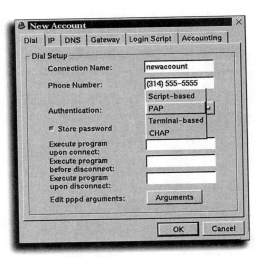

FIGURE 21.2
You may need to find out from your ISP the kind of authentication required. If all else fails, script-based authentication usually works.

If you are the only one who ever uses your machine or your Linux account, you can check the **Store password** box; otherwise, you must enter your ISP account's password each time you log on to the Internet. If you want to run any programs while online or immediately afterward, you may enter them here. And if your system, modem, or ISP requires that any arguments be passed to **pppd**, the *point-to-point protocol daemon*, you can enter them by clicking the button so labeled. Before you do this, you should make yourself familiar with pppd, which is beyond the scope of this book.

About pppd

In many cases, you may be able to get up and running without ever considering the Linux ppp daemon. But if you've among those who need to feed special parameters to this program, you can find help—and you'll need it—in a number of places. The first is the pppd man page. The second is the PPP HOWTO, which is likely to have come with your Linux distribution and probably resides on your machine.

It's always a good idea to have a good, comprehensive Linux manual. Among the best are *Special Edition Using Caldera OpenLinux* by Allan Smart, Erik Ratcliffe, Tim Bird, and David Bandel (Que, ISBN: 0-7897-2058-2) and *Running Linux*, Third Edition by Matt Welsh, Matthias Kalle Dalheimer, and Lar Kaufman (O'Reilly, ISBN: 1-56592-469-X).

In any case, you should take a lazy afternoon or evening sometime and explore the Linux HOWTOs. They're usually in /usr/doc/HOWTO, and they represent an enormity of information about your operating system and its applications.

The next tab page in your New Account setup is **IP** (see Figure 21.3).

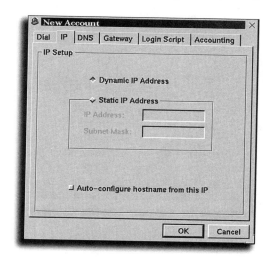

FIGURE 21.3

This is where you set your IP address. Try the defaults before fiddling with it.

Most ISPs provide dynamic IP addresses, though some issue static addresses, possibly for a fee. If in doubt, check with your ISP. Normally, you check the **Dynamic IP address** box. Unless you have a reason to do so, do not check the **Auto-configure hostname from this IP** box: in some cases it can prevent successful login.

The next page handles the Domain Name Server for your ISP (see Figure 21.4).

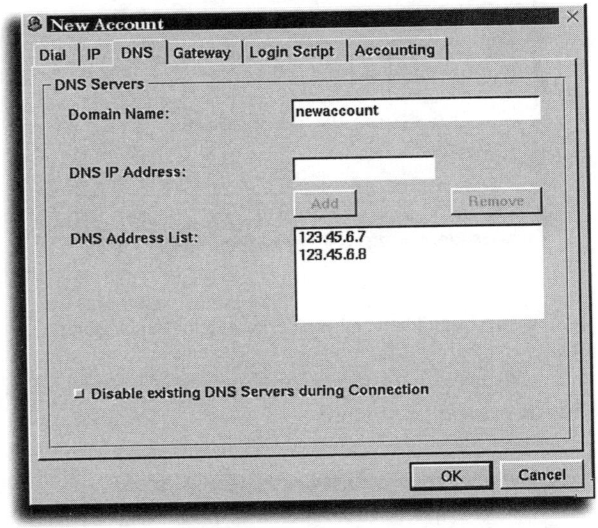

FIGURE 21.4
You definitely need to get the information for this page from your ISP.

Enter the domain name of your ISP, followed by the DNS IP address. Press Enter to add it to the list. Many ISPs provide more than one, so if yours is among them, repeat the process. Check the **Disable existing DNS Servers during Connection** box only if you have multiple DNS sessions running, which for a home machine not on a network is unlikely. Look in /etc/resolv.conf for a list of DNS entries that would be affected.

The **Gateway** page again requires information from your ISP, though the defaults (see Figure 21.5) work in most cases, probably in all cases unless you've paid your ISP extra money for a static IP. (If you don't understand any of this, you haven't.) You almost certainly want to leave the **Assign the Default Route to This Gateway** box checked.

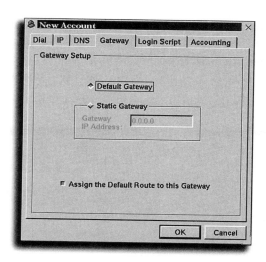

FIGURE 21.5
If your ISP provides a static gateway, enter it here; otherwise, leave the defaults intact.

You can leave the next page, **Login Script**, Figures. 21.6 and 21.7, blank unless you selected **script login** on the **Dial** page.

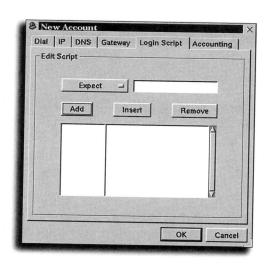

FIGURE 21.6
Even if your ISP offers no trick login procedure, you can automate the process by fashioning a script.

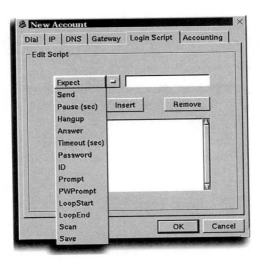

FIGURE 21.7
From the verb drop box choose the action and the word(s) on which the action is to be taken. If you don't know what to put there, wait: There's a way to find out that I'll get to in a few minutes.

Finally, there is the **Accounting** page (see Figure 21.8). This is chiefly of use outside the United States, where users are billed for all telephone use.

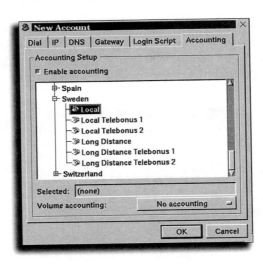

FIGURE 21.8
To keep a running total of your online costs, select **Enable accounting,** and then select your country and the nature of the telephone service you use to get access to the Internet.

Some phone services and Internet services charge based on the amount of data transferred. If yours is one of these, select the method used in **Volume accounting:**
(see Figure 21.9).

FIGURE 21.9
If you pay per byte, the Volume accounting drop box lets you select the method used by your provider.

After you have filled out all these pages, click **OK**, and you are returned to the Kppp
Configuration dialog box. Here, the running total of phone costs and data transferred are displayed, and you can edit or add accounts. We will continue our Kppp
setup (see Figure 21.10).

FIGURE 21.10
The rest of the Kppp setup applies to all accounts.

We've entered the information for the particular account, but that's only part of it. We need to make sure that Kppp can speak to our hardware.

We begin this on the **Device** page; see Figure 21.11.

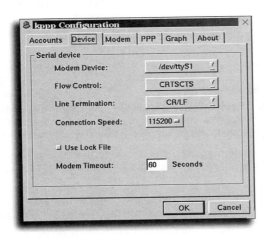

FIGURE 21.11
Some changes in recent versions of Linux make your choices here more critical than ever before.

Where's that Pesky Modem?

For the longest time, Linux used /dev/cuaX (where X was the number of the serial port, beginning with 0) to specify its serial ports, and many distributions made a symbolic link called /dev/modem that would point to the serial port containing the modem. Beginning with Linux 2.2, such a thing as /dev/cuaX no longer existed. It is now /dev/ttySX, where X is again a number beginning with 0. (Com1 in the DOSrivative world is /dev/ttyS0 in Linux.) And using /dev/modem was never a good idea. So in the **Modem Device** drop box, choose the actual location of your modem as /dev/ttySX—for most people it will be /dev/ttyS1—instead of anything else. The other stuff is included for backward compatibility.

Flow Control is where you choose hardware flow control (CRTSCTS), which is preferred; software flow control (Xon/XOFF), which is not preferred; or, perish the thought, none. Unless your modem doesn't support it, choose **CRTSCTS**.

Line Termination is almost always **CR/LF**. If your script doesn't run, this would be a good first place to make an adjustment.

You should set **Connection Speed** to the highest rate supported by your serial port, not by your modem. This means that if you have a 16550afn UART (a chip on the modem—your modem's documentation will tell you whether you have one, which most modern modems do), you can set it twice as high as your maximum modem speed, or more.

The **Use Lock File** check box creates a lock file that enables Kppp to work with some other programs, such as mgetty.

The **Modem Timeout** text box is where you enter the amount of time you're willing to let Kppp wait before it receives a CONNECT signal. You can adjust this as needed. If line negotiation takes a very long time because of poor phone lines, you may have to set this higher.

Those Horrible Windows-Only Modems

In the early 1990s the U.S. Robotics company, which makes some of the best modems in the world, introduced one of the worst, a thing called a *Winmodem*. This atrocity tossed some of the processing normally done by a modem to the CPU via what was called a *virtual device driver*. In the best of circumstances, it was a second-class modem.

Since then, many companies have produced modems using the same design philosophy, and computer manufacturers, looking to save a few bucks and practice on the naiveté of first-time computer buyers, stuffed them into their machines.

These modems work only with Microsoft Windows products, and not all of those. Unfortunately, the vast majority of *internal* modems made today are Windows-only modems: They do not work with Linux.

If you have one of these things, remove it from your machine and give it to someone you don't like. Then buy a good *external* modem. You'll be glad you did. They work with Linux and the information the LEDs on external modems provides is of great diagnostic use.

The next page (see Figure 21.12) is where you teach Kppp to speak to your modem. You will probably need to consult your modem manual for some of the settings.

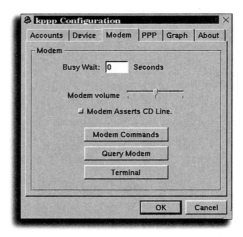

FIGURE 21.12
The **Modem** tab page can be very complicated or very simple. If yours is entirely Hayes compatible, it will be the latter.

The first setting is a text box in which you tell Kppp how long to wait before redialing after getting a busy signal. If your ISP has many lines, you can set this to 0 with a good likelihood of getting results on the second or third try.

The **Modem volume** slider is self explanatory. If your modem is too loud, turn it down here; if it's not loud enough, turn it up. Louder is to the right.

Clicking the **Modem Commands** button brings the dialog box shown in Figure 21.13.

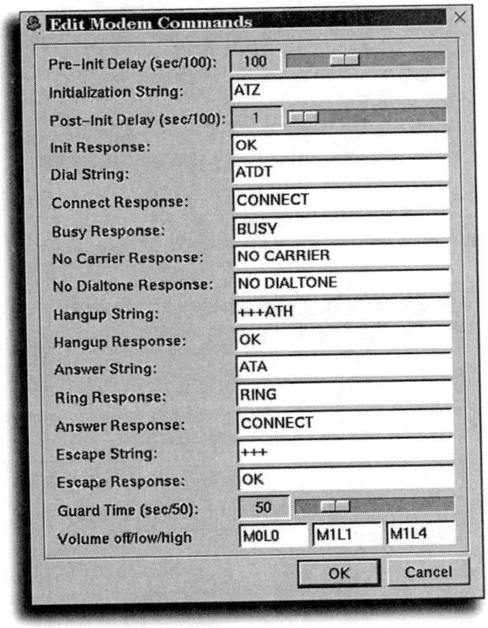

FIGURE 21.13
This is where your modem manual may come in handy, though the defaults are likely to work with most modems. If you have call waiting, you can insert the ***70**, here, after ATDT.

Clicking the **Query Modem** button causes Kppp to interrogate the modem about itself (see Figures 21.14 and 21.15).

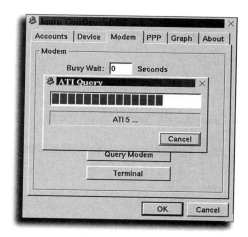

FIGURE 21.14
Querying the modem takes a few seconds; the bar graph shows the progress.

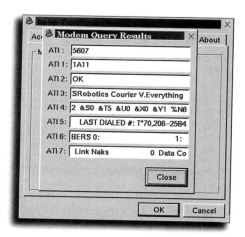

FIGURE 21.15
The results of the modem query may help you in setting up Kppp for your modem.

The **Terminal** button opens a little terminal window, shown in Figure 21.16, where you can dial your ISP and log in manually. Keep track of what you need to do to get logged in because you will use these things if you are planning to employ a script. Usually this involves a series of EXPECT and SEND commands, though there may be a place or two where a carriage return is necessary.

Logging In Manually

Logging in to your ISP manually through the Terminal window is easy if you know a few simple tricks.

The first is to set your modem to the factory initialization string by typing **ATZ** and pressing **Enter**. Then type **ATDT** (**ATDP** if you have pulse dialing instead of tone dialing) followed by the telephone number of your ISP's dial-up, and press **Enter**. If you have everything configured properly, you'll hear your modem dial, hear your ISP's modem answer, hear the modem screech as they negotiate the connection, and see the login prompt appear in the terminal window.

If you have call waiting service from the phone company, you should precede the ISP's phone number in the ATDT string above with the code that disables it, usually ***70** followed by a comma (**1170** if you have pulse dialing).

Now you can learn what is needed to create an automated login script.

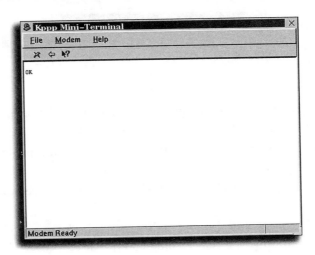

FIGURE 21.16
The Kppp Mini-Terminal window lets you dial manually.

The **PPP** page (see Figure 21.17) involves matters of personal preference.

FIGURE 21.17
This page lets you set preferences as to Kppp's behavior.

The choices on the PPP page cover a number of areas:

- **pppd Timeout**—Sets the amount of time Kppp lets the pppd daemon negotiate without getting a connection before Kppp gives up.
- **Dock into Panel on Connect**—If chosen, shrinks the Kppp window to an icon on K Panel when a connection is made.
- **Automatic Redial on Disconnect**—If chosen, tries to reestablish a dropped connection.
- **Show Clock on Caption**—If you click on its check box, displays in the Taskbar the amount of time you've been online in the current session.
- **Disconnect on X-server Shutdown**—Logs you off if you close KDE and go to a console.
- **Quit on Disconnect**—Closes Kppp when you click on the **Disconnect** button to terminate a modem session.
- **Minimize Window on Connect**—Sends the dialer to K Panel and the Taskbar and nowhere else once a connection is made.

The **Graph** page, see Figure 21.18, controls whether a graph of modem throughput will be available in the **Details** button on the Kppp dialer (more about that in a few paragraphs).

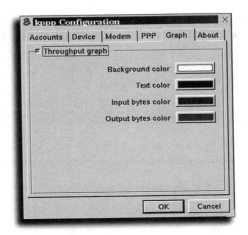

FIGURE 21.18
The colors are up to you, but you *do* want to enable the graph. Trust me.

Be sure to drop by the **About** page. These guys are some of the best programmers ever, and they, especially Harri Porten, have spent enormous amounts of time on the KDE Users mailing list helping users isolate problems and debug them. The result is a great piece of work. Hats off.

Now you are ready to give Kppp a try.

Using Kppp to Log In

It's easy. Click **K Menu > Internet > Kppp**. Select your account from the resulting window (see Figure 21.19).

FIGURE 21.19
Select your account and click **Connect**. If you are using a script and your script is not working, check the **Show Log Window** box to find out where it is breaking down. This will let you figure out what you may have left out of the script. It will certainly provide useful information if you need to talk about the problem with your ISP's tech support people.

After you click **Connect**, the Modem is initialized (see Figure 21.20) and the ISP is dialed. When a connection has been negotiated, you are logged in (see Figure 21.21).

FIGURE 21.20
The modem is initialized and dialing takes place. You will see your ISP's phone number as the dialing takes place.

FIGURE 21.21
After the connection has been established, Kppp negotiates to log you on to the Internet.

At any time after you have connected, you can click the little blinking modem lights icon on K Panel (which, by the way, blinks in reaction to real line conditions) to get information as to the duration of your call, to disconnect, and more (see Figure 21.22).

FIGURE 21.22
The Kppp window allows you to log off, and it shows some information of its own.

To learn a great deal about your current connection, though, you can click **Details**. It tells you everything you could possibly want to know about the connection, but more than that, it graphs the data transfer (see Figure 21.23).

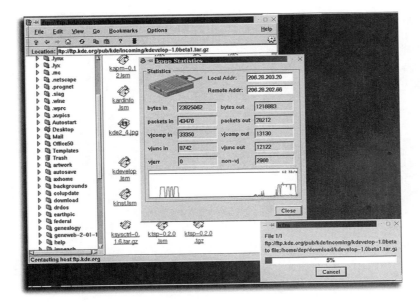

FIGURE 21.23
Remember that graph you enabled in setup? Here is where you'll find it. It stands in silent testimony of the poor phone lines around here on a hot summer's day.

Having gotten online, we'll next look at some of the things KDE helps you do there.

chapter
22

Kmail for Quick Communication

The ability to send and receive messages instantly, with files attached for action if needed, is possibly the single greatest effect of the online revolution. No suite of Internet applications would even think of shipping without a mail client of some sort. Often, these are just enough to get by.

KDE's mail client, Kmail, is fully featured and rivals the best standalone mail applications. It is part of the core KDE distribution, so you have it, and it didn't cost anything. Let's use it!

Configuring Kmail

When you start Kmail for the first time by going **K Menu > Internet > Mail Client**, your introduction to the program comes in the form of an error message that is, fortunately, not alarming (see Figure 22.1).

FIGURE 22.1
Click **OK** to create your mail directory. Each user must do this because mail is stored in the ~/Mail directory.

Once you have allowed Kmail to create a mail directory, you are treated to the opening screen, which resembles that in Figure 22.2.

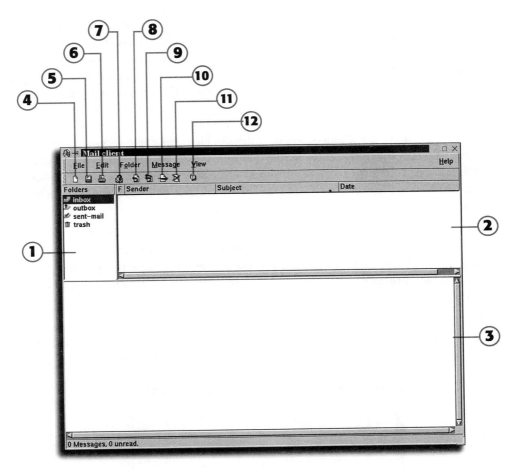

FIGURE 22.2
The box at upper left contains your mail folders; the bigger box at the top lists the messages in a particular folder.
The biggest box at the bottom previews the messages themselves.

① Mail folders

② Message list

③ Message preview

④ Compose new message

⑤ Save message to file

⑥ Print message

⑦ Get new mail

⑧ Reply to author

⑨ Reply to all recipients

⑩ Forward message

⑪ Delete message

⑫ Open address book

Before we go any further, let's take a look at the toolbar.

The first icon, a blank page, opens a blank message for you to compose and send. The second icon saves the message as a file. The third prints the current message (a little more about this later), whereas the fourth collects any mail that has accumulated at your ISP's server. The next one, with the curved arrow, replies to the current message. The one with a double curved arrow replies to everyone who received the message to which you are replying, and is how you arrive at those monstrosities that have 50 names in the To field and a dozen sawtooth rows of quote upon quote at the left. Just don't use it unless you're willing to clean up the mess you're about to create. The icon with the arrow across it is to Forward the current message; the icon with the red X through it deletes the current message. (If you press it by accident, you can get the message back from the Trash folder.) Finally, the last icon opens your address book.

One more thing: The heading bar atop the message list, when clicked, rearranges the messages. Click the **F** to arrange them by status, **Sender** to arrange them by sender, **Subject** to arrange them by subject, and **Date** to arrange them by date (the default). Clicking again reverses the order. This is especially useful if you're trying to follow a thread.

The first thing you need to do is tell Kmail who you are and where your mail is to be found. This is done by **File > Settings** (see Figure 22.3). If this is the first time you're using Kmail, the Settings dialog box may come up automatically.

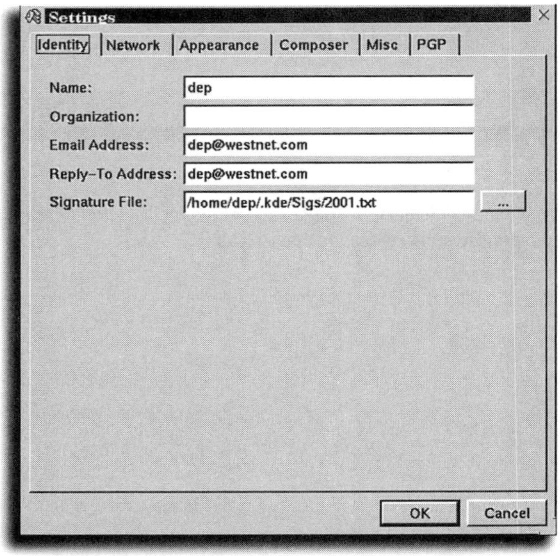

FIGURE 22.3
Fill in the blanks. The button next to the Signature File text box produces the standard KDE file selection dialog box. Any text file will do, though netiquette dictates that it be no more than four lines long unless there is a good reason for it.

The next task, and one a little more difficult, is telling Kmail where to look for your mail. Most people get their mail directly from their ISP without the intervention of a Mail Transfer Agent such as sendmail. Yes, this is true even if you have sendmail (or another MTA) installed, which you probably do and certainly should. How this is set up and whether you use your ISP directly or filter your mail through an MTA depends on the kind of network you are on. If there is doubt in your mind, ask your system administrator, and if you have no system administrator you can assume you're getting your mail from your ISP directly. In which case, you fill out the **File > Settings > Network** tab in much the same way it is filled out in Figure 22.4.

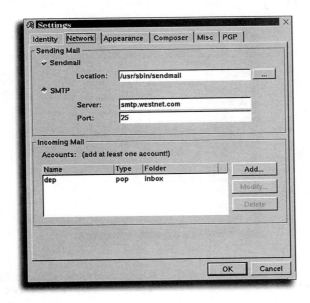

FIGURE 22.4
The mail Server information for outgoing mail is something you get from your ISP; Port 25 is standard. You must also click the **Add** button to provide information that lets you receive mail.

When you have filled out the information for outgoing mail, you need to click **Add** to set up an incoming mail account on your machine. This produces the dialog box seen in see Figure 22.5.

FIGURE 22.5
Select **POP3** if you're getting your mail directly from your ISP.

After you click **OK**, you receive another dialog box; see Figures 22.6 and 22.7.

FIGURE 22.6
Provide your name as you want it to appear. The Login field, however, must be the login name you use when logging in to your ISP. You need not store your password with the configuration file, but if you do you won't be prompted for it each time you seek new mail. You must get the Host information from your ISP, but Port 110 is standard.

FIGURE 22.7
This shows the Configure Account dialog box as I had it filled in for an account I had when writing this book. I've chosen to store my password so that I won't be prompted for it, to retrieve all the mail from my ISP, and to delete it from the server once it's on my local machine. I have decided not to have Kmail check for new mail every so often. This is because I often read mail offline, and because Kmail's threading is such that everything comes to a halt while it is checking for mail.

The next tab, **Appearance**, in my experience involves a little alchemy: some type-faces and sizes look good, whereas others look terrible (see Figure 22.8).

FIGURE 22.8
Clicking the button next to each choice produces the KDE font selection dialog box. Here, I've selected the **Long folder list** layout because I expect to have a dozen or so different mail folders, and I want to be able to see all of them all the time. Otherwise, scrollbars would be taking up screen space.

The **Composer** tab, shown in Figure 22.9, is where you determine the form and appearance of your outgoing mail.

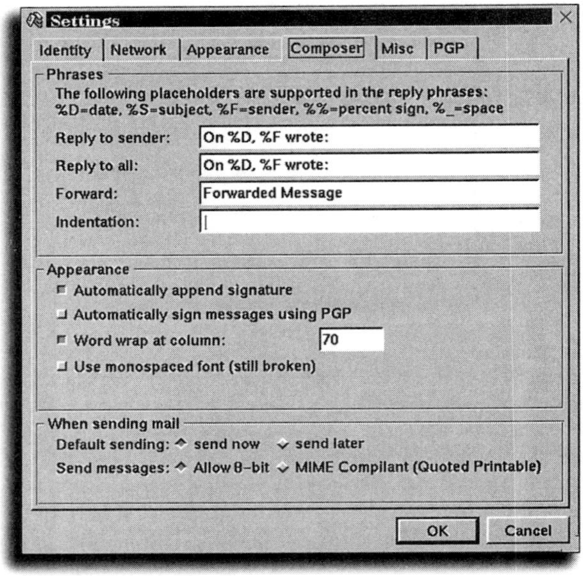

FIGURE 22.9
The first section, Phrases, lets you set the way in which messages are quoted in replies. The indentation character, which is usually >, is how quoted portions are set off from the rest of the message. I don't like the sawtooth effect, so I use the pipe character (**Shift **) instead.

You can check the box that automatically appends the signature to your messages, but do so *only* if you specified a signature on the Identity tab. If you use PGP (sorry, but why bother?), check that box and make sure your PGP is set up correctly. When entering a number at which word wrap kicks in, remember that your message is likely to be quoted, and perhaps requoted, so leave plenty of room—set the number fairly low—to avoid the ugly effect of long lines followed by very short lines that causes most people to press the Delete key. I cannot affirm that the monospaced font is still broken. I take their word for it. You should, too.

When sending mail you can choose to save the mail to **send later**, which avoids annoying error messages (that otherwise have no effect) when you are composing mail offline, though you need to remember to send it later via the **File > Send Queued** command, or you can put up with the error messages and choose **send now**. The 8-bit setting works well, though the MIME Compliant setting works well with a wider variety of recipient systems.

The **Misc** tab is where several important settings are found (see Figure 22.10).

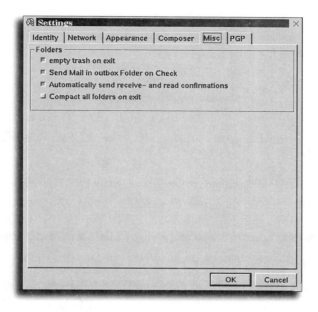

FIGURE 22.10
Unless you want your Kmail Trash folder to grow insanely large, you want to empty it when you exit the program.
Send Mail in outbox Folder on Check is a good idea if you have the **send later** option checked on the Composer page or ever write mail offline. **Automatically send receive- and read confirmations** is for those who believe their messages are so very important that they demand receipts. If you do not want to educate them as to their relative importance in the universe, just check it. **Compact all folders on exit** is a good idea, but can take a little while if you have many messages stored. It is an option first made available in KDE 1.1.2's Kmail.

The final tab, **PGP**, is for those who are afraid that others will pretend to be them and who want to saddle the rest of the world with long encryption keys at the end of each message. If you really need this—you're a secret agent, say—you should set it up. Otherwise, bear in mind that you are annoying people almost as much as if you sent mail in HTML format, a growing and irritating trend that causes many people to press the Delete key without even reading the message.

Using Kmail

Having configured Kmail, it's time now to see whether it works. To begin, you must close Kmail for reasons unclear: it does not want to fetch the mail if it is started before you are online. (This bug was introduced sometime between KDE 1.0 and 1.1.) If it works properly, the Retrieving messages window and bar graph appear, see Figure 22.11, though they do not take focus.

FIGURE 22.11
The Retrieving messages window tells you how many messages are on the server awaiting your attention, and the progress Kmail is making in downloading them for you.

Okay, you have your messages. What, now, can you do with them?

Well, for one thing, read them (see Figure 22.12).

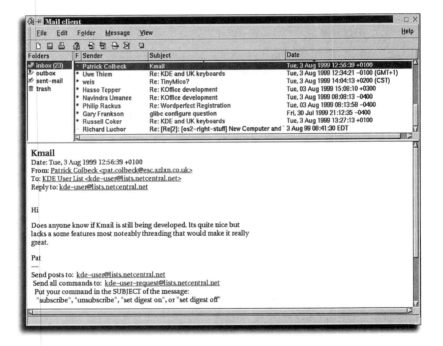

FIGURE 22.12
You can read messages in the preview pane at the bottom of your Kmail window, or you can double-click on the message in the list above to open a viewing window.

For another, you can reply to them (see Figures 22.13 and 22.14).

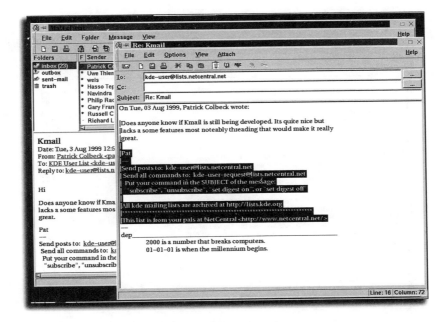

FIGURE 22.13
By going **Message > Reply** or by clicking the toolbar's **Reply** icon, you can open up an editing window containing the original message quotes as you specified in Kmail setup. Good manners dictate the deletion of material not necessary to the reply being understood, which is what is being done here: I've marked the material and am set to employ the Delete key.

Sometimes you may want to save messages but not have them clogging your Inbox. The way to do this is to create a folder for them. Of course, if you're going to do that, you might as well create several folders into which you can sort the saved messages. This is easy to do. Simply click **Folder > Create** and give the folder a name. (Alternatively, you can right-click on an existing folder and choose **Create** from the resulting menu.) Because I want to save messages that have to do with KDE, I'll create a folder for them. (You would be surprised at the peculiar coincidence between the deletion of messages and the problem they deal with appearing on the local machine.) I'll also create a folder for Personal messages.

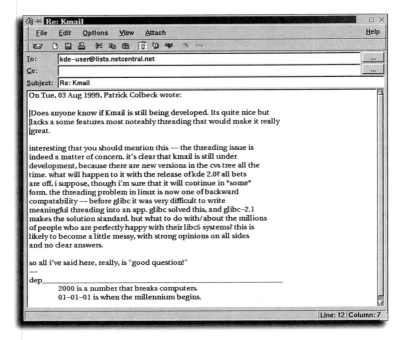

FIGURE 22.14
The reply is typed in and the **Send** icon (the first icon on the toolbar) is clicked. You could also click **File > Send** or **File > Send later**. The difference—I am offline—is in whether error messages telling me that Kmail can't connect with my ISP appear. Even if they do, it doesn't matter: The reply gets sent later either way.

Email Purgatory

As is the case with much of KDE in general, you can right-click a mail folder, and a menu will appear. This allows you to Create a new folder, Modify the one you clicked, Compact it (permanently removing and deleted messages and making the storage space needed smaller), Empty the folder (in which case the messages cannot be recovered, though they'll remain in ther folder's file until it is compacted), and Remove the folder and its contents entirely.

Messages that are deleted individually (or in a highlighted group, but not through the `empty` command) are put in the trash folder, where they remain until Kmail is closed (if you've configured it to empty the trash on exit) or until you manually empty it. At least during the current session, you can get to a message that has accidentally or erroneously been deleted. During a session, the Trash folder is like any other folder except that messages that are deleted go to it automatically.

Once you've created the folder, you have a couple of ways of transferring messages into it. One is to drag the message to the folder in the folder list and drop it there. Because the folder list is fairly compact, though, it is easy to drop a message into the wrong folder. A more certain way is to right-click the message in the message list, which produces a menu, from which you can click **Move** and get a list of your folders (see Figure 22.15).

FIGURE 22.15
When I click **OK**, the current message moves into the KDE folder.

You can create as many folders as you want, but if you create too many, some will not be visible and you'll need to use the scrollbar to get to them (see Figure 22.16). (You can avoid this by checking the **Long folder list** check box on the **File > Settings > Appearance** page, which produces what you see in Figure 22.17.)

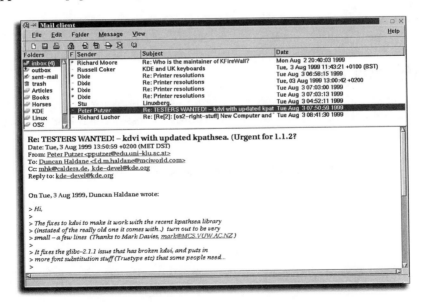

FIGURE 22.16
You may need to use the scrollbar to get to all your folders, unless...

FIGURE 22.17
...you've enabled the **Long folder list**.

The Address Book

On some bright, sunlit day there will be one address book for all of KDE, but that day has not arrived, so Kmail maintains its own address book. It begins empty (see Figures 22.18 and 22.19).

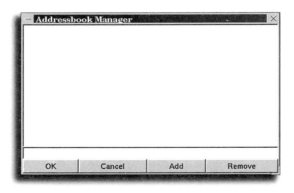

FIGURE 22.18
To add an address, type the name and email address (or just the email address, if from it you can divine the recipient's name) in the bottom text box, and then press **Add**.

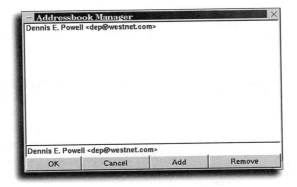

FIGURE 22.19
Clicking **Add** puts the name in the address list, but there are other ways of doing it, too, as you shall see.

If you regularly correspond with someone and want to put that person's name into your address book, you can right-click the name in a message, producing a menu whence you can add the name to the address book (see Figure 22.20).

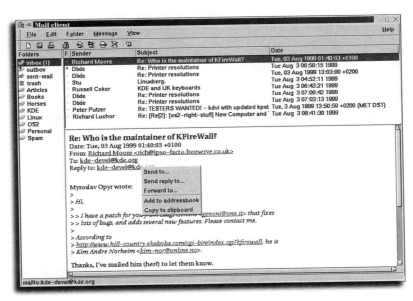

FIGURE 22.20
After you've added the name to the address book, you may want to open the address book and edit it, adding, for instance, a name.

When you have a name in the address book to whom you want to send email, click the **New** icon and when the window opens, click on the little button at the right end of the To field. The address book opens, as in Figure 22.21.

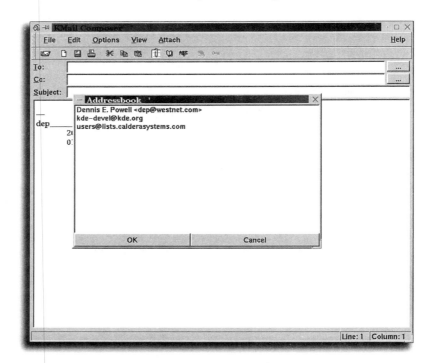

FIGURE 22.21
Click the name to put it in the To field; likewise, clicking the... button at the end of other fields opens the address book. And you can click it multiple times for multiple entries in any given field.

Sending and Receiving Files as Attachments

One of the great strengths of Kmail is the ease with which you can send files as attachments. Drag the file from the desktop or from KFM and drop it onto the message you are preparing to send. You receive a menu; see Figure 22.22.

FIGURE 22.22
To send a file as an attachment, just drop it onto the message to which you want to attach it. The menu that pops up is more for confirmation than anything else.

Once you've okayed the menu, the message is attached and is sent out with the message (see Figure 22.23).

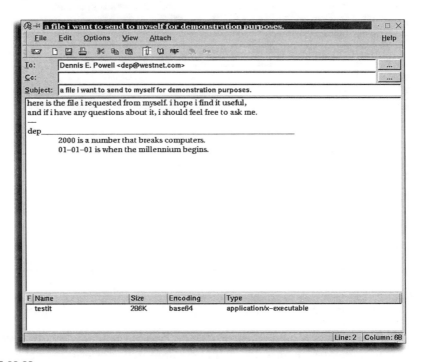

FIGURE 22.23
The attachment is now listed at the bottom of the message.

When you send messages, a small window opens (see Figure 22.24) that shows—inadequately, in my opinion, because it needs one of those nifty KDE bar graphs—the status of the messages being sent.

FIGURE 22.24
The small window at the bottom of the screen lets you know that your mail is being sent.

Okay, so you can send attachments. How do you receive them? In any of several ways. For instance, I just now received a humorous picture from a friend. It came up in Kmail, as shown in Figure 22.25.

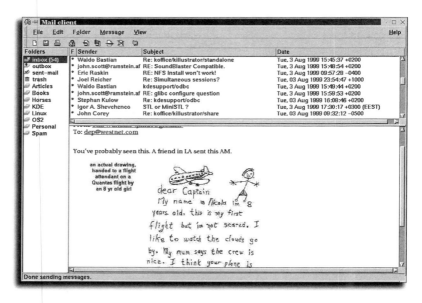

FIGURE 22.25
Some graphics formats display in the message body, and no, you may *not* see the rest of the message!

Still others may arrive as attachments at the bottom of the file, as the demonstration file I sent to myself (see Figure 22.26). (There are three choices for attachments in the **View** menu, but no matter whether you select Iconic, Smart, or Inline, what you get is Smart. This means that if the file will display well in the message body, it does so; otherwise, it is an icon at the bottom of the message.)

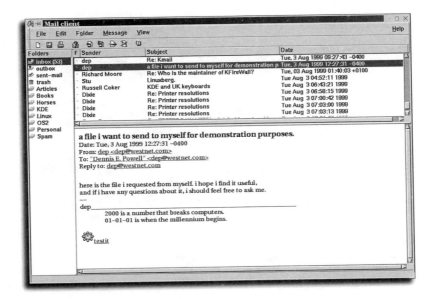

FIGURE 22.26
In this case, the attachment arrived as an attachment icon (as do those miserable HTML "cards" people feel free to use to double the size of their messages).

You can right-click the attachment and open it, save it (in which case the KDE file selection dialog box appears, so you can pick a name and location for it), or you can drag it from the message to a folder or the desktop.

Filtering Messages

This is really just a note because the subject of filtering messages is a complicated one and the results are never all that pleasing. Kmail does offer a message filtering procedure, **File > Filter**, that produces the dialog box shown in Figure 22.27.

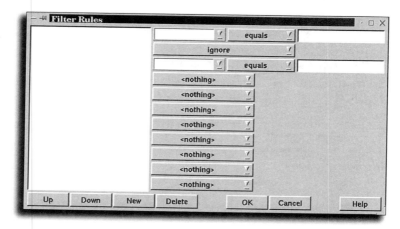

FIGURE 22.27
The Filter Rules dialog box provides many ways to torture messages.

Why might you want to filter messages? Well, you might subscribe to mailing lists, with a separate folder for each, and want the messages to be filed automatically. Or there might be persons from whom you do not want to receive messages, in which case you can direct their missives to the bit bucket, either via Trash or via /dev/null. There are a lot of reasons.

Unfortunately, filtering messages tends to get them lost in the shuffle. While Kmail's folders do, when they contain unread messages, have a little number next to them totaling the messages that you haven't looked at yet, they tend to be ignored for way too long. So it's easy to automate your mail sorting with filters and by so doing to miss mail that requires your immediate attention. In my experience, the Delete key is better than a filter for getting rid of unwanted messages, and moving messages to folders manually is a better way to archive them. Perhaps you are more disciplined than I am, though.

If you want to build filters, click the **Help** button on the Filter Rules page to learn how. I'll offer the example that it does, to give you a sense of it. Let's say that you've subscribed to the kde-user mailing list (which, by the way, you should; visit http://lists.kde.org to do so). Because it's a fairly active list, you might receive several dozen messages per day from this list, and you don't want them all mixed with your business and personal mail in your Inbox.

In Kmail, select **File > Filter** and click the **New** button. Because you don't have any filters yet, the list of filters that appears will contain only one item anyway, signified by a pair of angle brackets, <>. If you already had filters, you would need to select this one from the list.

Messages in the kde-user list always have the phrase "KDE User List" in the To field. So in the first blank drop box, select **To**. The second drop box defaults to **Contains**, so leave it as it is. In the text box on the same line, type `KDE User List`.

There is a stack of drop boxes down the center of the Filter Rules page, each of which is initially labeled **<nothing>**. Select the first of these, and from it choose **Transfer**. Another drop box, containing the names of all your existing folders, appears to the right on the same line. Select the folder into which you want your kde-user messages to go.

In the next drop box that contains **<nothing>**, choose **skip rest**. This isn't strictly needed in this example, but it's good practice. Its function is to make sure that no further filtering functions are performed on the message.

The results are shown in Figure 22.28.

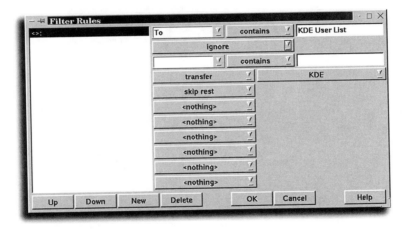

FIGURE 22.28
Here's how your filter to move kde-user list messages into the KDE folder should look.

Finally, click **OK**.

Now, as you have probably already figured out (and certainly have if you've played along on your real, live Kmail screen as we've explored filters here), the top three lines of the Filter Rules dialog allow you to enter one string and modify it for messages containing a second string. You can also put multiple criteria into the filter by using more than one of the drop boxes labeled **<nothing>**. For instance, if you are a regular recipient of spam from a particular address, you can filter mail from that address so as to forward it to your ISP's spam-control department and the Trash folder. You can make very elaborate filters.

Additional Features: Printing and Spellcheck

When you send a message, you can run the Linux spelling checker on it. At the top of the composition window is an **ABC** icon that opens the Spellcheck dialog box. It will find and fix any spelling errors, making you virtually alone in the email world in having messages in which attention was paid to spelling.

And you can print messages by clicking on the **Printer** icon. This opens the standard KDE Print dialog box, complete with A4 paper as the default size. There used to be a fairly easy way to hack the KDE code to set the default to letter, but this isn't as easy as it used to be. So you have to select it every time and hope the next version will let you store your settings.

chapter

23

Reading the Newsgroups

For much longer than there has been anything called the World Wide Web, there have been Usenet newsgroups. These were originally designed to allow the discussion of ideas and problems of a technical nature, and some of them still serve that purpose between the spam posts. Thousands upon thousands of newsgroups operate today on a variety of topics, some worth the trouble.

In order to participate, though, you need a news reader program. Such a program allows you to read the groups online, to post your own original messages, or to respond to messages from others. One is built into Netscape's Communicator product, of course, and various versions are available for Linux, with console-mode versions being among the most popular. The core KDE distribution includes one, too. It's called *KRN*, and you get to it by selecting **K Menu > Internet > News Client**. Unfortunately, the word count of the KRN documentation is approximately equivalent to the number of words in this chapter to this point, so what you learn about its use, you'll learn here. This is too bad because KRN is a dandy little program on which a lot of work was done; a few hours more and they could have told people how to use it. As it is, navigation is mostly by error message, like finding your way down a dark hall by bumping into the walls. So watch your nose, knees, toes, and elbows, and cross your fingers that there are no stairways heading down.

Setting Up KRN

Before you begin, you might have to configure KRN. (For some reason, some installations seem to work right out of the compiler, no configuration required, while others require the procedure listed here, which is quick and simple, so fear not.) All these items are available later in the **Options** menu.

The first thing to configure is **Identity**—see Figure 23.1.

FIGURE 23.1
You should need no help with this dialog box.

Then comes **NNTP Options**—see Figure 23.2.

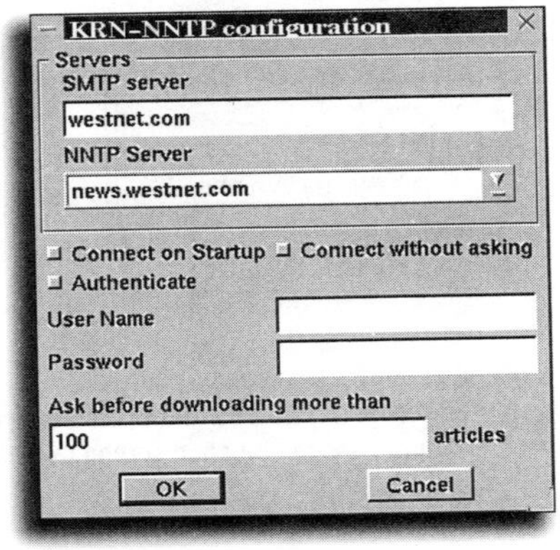

FIGURE 23.2
You may need to get some of the information from your ISP for this page. Mine works as pictured. If you want more than 100 messages at a time, you can set that number higher.

This should be enough to get you started, but while we're here, let's look at the other items in the **Options** menu. The next in the list is **Expire Options**—see Figure 23.3.

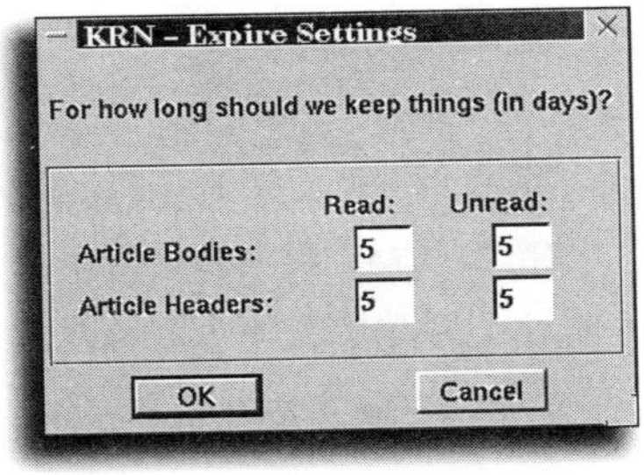

FIGURE 23.3
This dialog box lets you decide how long KRN retains the headers it has downloaded. If you read a number of groups, or read extensively in just a few, the amount of storage space needed for all this stuff can grow pretty quickly, so archiving it for very long can be a costly proposition. The defaults are pretty good.

Finally, we have **Printing Options**—see Figure 23.4.

FIGURE 23.4
Set these to suit your printer setup. My printer handles native PostScript, so these are my settings. You may want to experiment with some of the others. I wish you luck…not so much in setting up your printer but in finding things worth printing!

Subscribing to Newsgroups with KRN

When first you start KRN, you see a pretty sparse screen (see Figure 23.5).

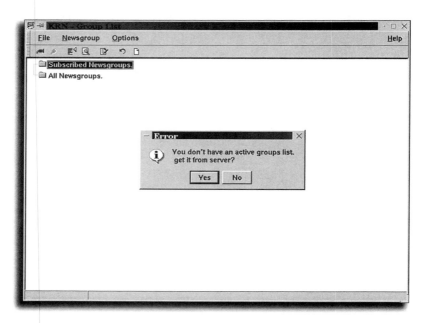

FIGURE 23.5
KRN, having noticed that you have no list of newsgroups from which to choose, invites you to let it fetch one.

And then, unless you are online, it gets a little touchy (see Figure 23.6).

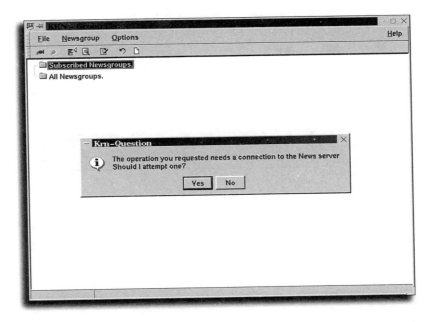

FIGURE 23.6
Now it as much as says, "Well, I can't very well get the list unless we're online, can I?"

And so you click **Yes**, and then if all is well, it downloads the list of newsgroups. You truly cannot imagine the sheer number of these things that exist. Fully half could be eliminated without anyone noticing, and half of the remainder could be eliminated with no loss to anyone. (Fortunately, one does not have to download a listing of sites in order to go onto the Web!) All this is to point out that you are going to download a megabyte or so of newsgroup names—not the contents of the groups, just a list of their names—and to give you something to ponder while this takes place. You will have an additional opportunity to ponder it as you go digging through the lists for groups worthy of your attention. After a while, the length of which depends on the speed of your modem, the quality of the connection, and the number of groups your ISP carries—not all ISPs carry all newsgroups. You will see something like that which is depicted in Figure 23.7.

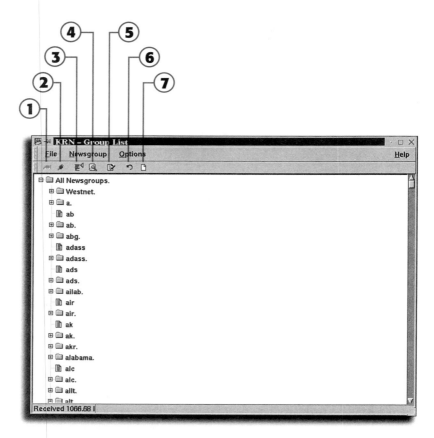

FIGURE 23.7
Each of those listings is merely a top-level grouping, like your home directory. They contain from a few to more than
a thousand subgroups and actual newsgroups, in hierarchical order, but at least you've downloaded them.

1. Connect to server
2. Disconnect from server
3. Get list of active groups
4. Find group
5. (Un)Subscribe
6. Check for Unread Articles
7. Post New Article

Now you get to go through the list, clicking on the plus signs next to the areas that
look promising and watching them drool down your screen. They have accumulated
over time, like singletons in the sock drawer, and like those lone socks serve little
purpose but to waste your time when you're looking for something. The good part is
that there is a newsgroup for every imaginable interest; the bad parts are that many
are flat-out offensive, and some of interest have very little if any traffic. Don't get me

wrong; when you find good newsgroups, they can be a wealth of information, but finding them is difficult. We'll look into that a little more in a bit.

When you find a group to which you would like to subscribe, click it, and click the (Un)Subscribe icon on the toolbar, the third from the right, which looks like a pen and paper. You'll notice that it now has an (Un)Subscribe icon next to it (see Figure 23.8), which looks like the icon that was next to it with a check mark of some sort added next to it.

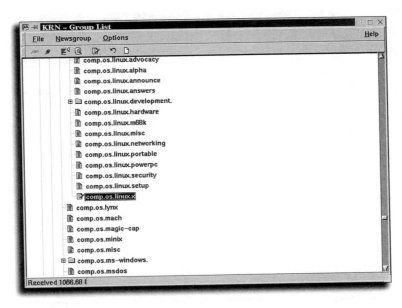

FIGURE 23.8
I cheated—I knew where to look—and found a newsgroup likely to deal with KDE. Then I went online and double-clicked the name of the newsgroup.

Now, there could be thousands or tens of thousands of messages in any given newsgroup. They do expire at some point, but they tend to sometimes hang around. When you double-click a newsgroup to which you have subscribed, a brief period of modem activity occurs. During this time, the status bar tells you that it is getting the article list, which is very much like the list of mail in Kmail. (The difference is that in KRN, the messages themselves aren't downloaded unless you specifically request it.) After a short time, KRN discovers that there are lots of messages on the list, and asks you how many headers to download. It will also ask you if you want the oldest ones or the newest. The 100 newest will usually do; you can always go back for more later if you want. Soon, you see the names of articles and the people who posted them, along with the date (day/month/year) they were posted. When you see one of interest, click it. The result will be something like Figure 23.9.

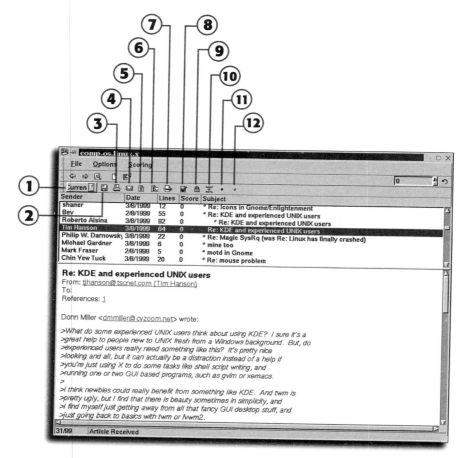

FIGURE 23.9

An article in a newsgroup. You can read it and, if you want, respond. When you've read a message, its header turns blue in the article headers window.

1. Display Selection drop box (determines which messages are displayed)

2. Save currently displayed article

3. Print currently displayed article

4. Reply to current article by email

5. Post a follow-up (reply) to current article in newsgroup

6. Post a follow-up and reply by email

7. Forward current article

8. Tag current article for later action

9. Lock current article in cache for easy retrieval

10. Decode current article (if UU encoded)

11. Mark current article as read

12. Mark current article as unread

Now, the scoring feature is something like the scoring of hits when you do a Web search. If you use KRN's minimal filtering, the column will return a score based on the relevance of the article to the search terms.

Posting to a Newsgroup

In the course of looking through the messages posted to the newsgroup, I found one to which I had the answer. Because the poster asked for a response by email as well as to the group, I selected the icon that provides for this. There are ones that post just to the newsgroup and that post just by email to the poster. Figure 23.10 shows the original post and the window in which I responded. You'll note the similarity to Kmail.

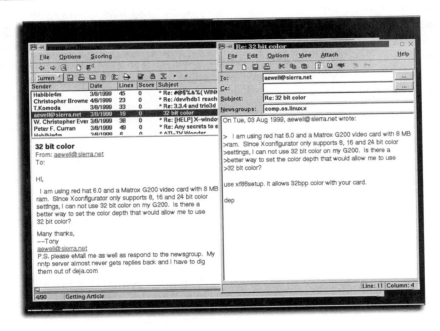

FIGURE 23.10
Posting to a newsgroup is as easy as sending an email message.

That's all it takes!

You can perform some basic search and filtering functions in KRN by setting the search terms in the **Scoring > Edit rules** dialog box. This is supposed to work similarly to the filtering system in Kmail, allowing you to "score" articles based on whether the search text is found in the selected article element (Sender, Subject,

Header, or Body). The Score column in the article list rates each article in the newsgroup based on your criterion (or criteria), in much the same way that a Web search engine rates hits as to the degree that they match the search term. I have spent hours playing with this function, though, and sadly have never been able to make it do anything at all. KRN is no longer being developed, so it is not likely that this function will be improved or repaired.

Finding Newsgroups That Interest You

It could take days to go through all the newsgroups in search of ones that cater to areas that you find interesting. The best way to find them is to ask around. There is a listing of a few that have to do with Linux and KDE in Appendix C, "Getting Help in a Hurry: The KDE Mailing Lists," but you might be interested in more than Linux. Often, publications and articles list newsgroups that deal with their topics; sometimes Web pages contain pointers to groups of interest. You can search for groups, and even old articles on a particular subject, at www.deja.com, which will help you find groups to which you might want to subscribe. They're a lot easier to find when you know their names.

chapter
24

Browsing and Other Things Internet

The majority of things people do on the Internet and more specifically the World Wide Web doesn't involve email or reading newsgroups. They "browse" the Web in search of information of one sort or another, or in search of files and software. Sometimes they have little chat sessions with each other.

These things are all possible with native KDE applications.

Browsing Under KDE

As is noted in Chapter 10, "Navigating *Everything* with KFM," KFM can work as a Web browser. When you click on a URL in Kmail, for instance, it is KFM that opens and displays the referenced page. There are those who quite reasonably wish it were possible to call a different browser, such as Netscape Navigator, instead, but it isn't. Whether this will change at some point in the future is unknown. What is known is that as of KDE 2.0, KFM is put to rest, replaced by something different. If you are browsing with KFM and click on a mailto link, Kmail opens whether it is your mailer of choice or not. This, too, cannot be changed without diving into the code and doing some hacking that is beyond the scope of this book (and the author's abilities).

This is not to say that KFM is a terrible browser because it isn't. However, it does lack some features to which you may have become accustomed (and in some cases accustomed to swearing at). Java implementation is basically nonexistent. Handling of forms is terrible when it works at all. Badly written HTML pages are shown with all their shortcomings in KFM; very badly written ones may not show up at all.

But for the wider variety of Web pages, KFM works just fine. To get to a page, simply type its URL in the **Location** text box, as shown in Figure 24.1.

FIGURE 24.1
And there it is, the KDE home page. To bookmark it, select **Bookmarks** > **Add Bookmark**.

The problems arise if the page you are using uses Java or if there is a form that you are required to fill out: neither works well if at all in KFM.

KFM is an excellent tool, though, for file transfer protocol downloads from a remote site. Simply type in `ftp://` followed by the ftp site. If anonymous access is not allowed, and you have a password, the syntax is

`ftp://username:password@hostname`

Obviously, you fill in the proper name of the ftp site.

We will go on to some other ftp possibilities with KDE, but before we do, we really need to address the browser question a little further. The shortcomings of KFM, and the fact that it's no longer being actively developed (which in my opinion is a pity), dictate that you make use of another browser as well.

Netscape Navigator and Communicator

Both Netscape Navigator, the browser, and Netscape Communicator, the suite of Internet tools, work well with KDE, but you ought to be aware of a few things.

The first is that KDE's Clipboard and Netscape's do not completely cooperate. If you copy text from a Web page in Netscape, it goes to Klipper very nicely, but the transfer is extremely quirky going the other way. I have never found a method, for instance, of pasting a URL from Kmail into Netscape's URL text box. This seems a minor matter unless, say, your sister gave you a birthday present and you were informed by email from the vendor, who now wants you to click on the very long URL and fill out the form so that it can ship the present to the right address. Clicking the URL takes you to the page, but in KFM the forms don't work. Trying to stack Netscape and Kmail in such a way as to copy the URL correctly is irritating. You can always print the message, open Netscape, and type in the URL, but this is taking the long way around, don't you agree? The solution would be to make the choice of browser started by Kmail configurable, but that is not going to happen, at least not in any 1.x version of KDE. Some people using particular mice have been able to exploit Linux's capability to paste using the middle mouse button (or both buttons of a two button mouse if "emulate three buttons" is enabled in Xfree86), but others report that this does not work reliably for them.

The second is that Netscape can behave strangely if in your desktop settings (**Display Settings > Style**) you have checked the box that applies fonts and colors to non-KDE applications. This can result in slightly odd to unusably weird changes in Netscape's display. For one thing, if you use Netscape for reading newsgroups, the distinction between read and unread articles is no longer visible. So if you use Netscape, which is free for individual use and which probably came with your KDE distribution, make sure that you haven't checked this box.

StarOffice

You can't paste a URL into StarOffice, either, unless you open a new text document and paste the URL there, and then double-click on it, in which case you'll be taken to the Web site. That having been said, the Web browser functions of StarOffice's excellent suite of applications (also free for individual use and also probably included with your Linux distribution), work wonderfully under KDE. Indeed, no commercial application integrates so nicely with the KDE desktop.

SEE ALSO
➤ *I will say more about StarOffice in Chapter 30, "Commercial Applications and KDE."*

FTP Transfers

FTP (file transfer protocol) is of course the standard way of uploading and downloading files over the Internet. And, as noted (and discussed in detail in Chapter 10), KFM is an excellent tool for bringing this about. With the addition of another native KDE application, though not one included in the core distribution, it becomes very nearly perfect.

The tool is called Caitoo (early versions were called KGet; the reason for the name change is unknown to me). It is an FTP tool that, in conjunction with KFM or another browser that supports drag and drop, makes downloads far easier and far less risky.

Getting and Building Caitoo

You'll find the latest Caitoo on the KDE ftp site: `ftp.kde.org/pub/kde/`. Once you've gotten the source tarball, as root, copy it into /usr/local/src, and use tar xvfz to open the source into its own directory.

Still as su root, change to the Caitoo source directory and type `./configure`. After that, type `make all`, followed by `make install`. That's all there is to it!

The current version is on the KDE ftp site. Yes, you have to compile it yourself, but it compiles easily and in conformity with the KDE standards. In short, it's easy to do. It may be possible to find a prebuilt binary someplace, but building it yourself ensures that it works on your machine and isn't terribly more difficult than is installing somebody else's binary.

When it is installed, you can find Caitoo at **K Menu > Internet > Caitoo**, and when clicked, it looks much like the window pictured in Figure 24.2.

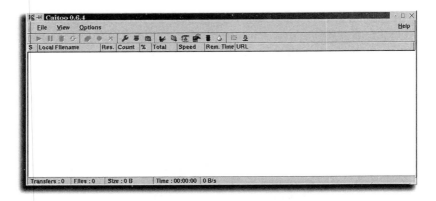

FIGURE 24.2
If Caitoo doesn't look like this when you start it, grab the edges with your mouse and stretch it out until it does.

What does Caitoo do for you? A lot, actually. If, for instance, you're seeking to download a huge file and don't get it all in one whack, upon the next connection Caitoo will interrogate the server to learn if resuming the download where you left off is possible, as it often is. You then can pick up where you left off, rather than starting all over again. You can also use it to schedule file transfers in the middle of the night. You can set it to make a transfer and log you off. You can set it to download different file extensions to different directories automatically. It is one cool tool.

It is also well documented, for very specialized configurations. For most purposes, though, what follows will be sufficient to get you working productively with Caitoo.

The fundamental use of Caitoo is this: Log on to the ftp site using, say, KFM. Select the files you want and drag them, either individually or in a group, to the Caitoo window (see Figure 24.3).

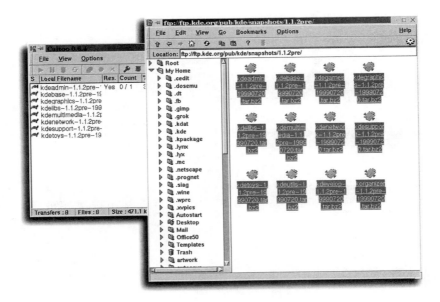

FIGURE 24.3
Caitoo queues the files for download. You can select in **Options > Preferences** how many files to try to download at
once and where to put them.

After the download has begun, you can close KFM, and Caitoo chugs merrily along,
administering your file transfer for you (see Figure 24.4). It is an extra layer of safety
and sophistication beyond simply dragging the files and dumping them on the local
directory within KFM.

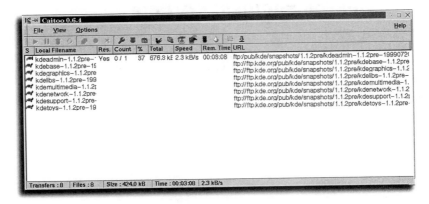

FIGURE 24.4
The status bar and list window give you a sense of the state of things. You can drag the column headings to make
them wider or narrower. You can also change the order in which files are downloaded, if you like.

Don't Get Stuck Online

A new version of Xfree86 had been released, and I sought to download it in all its many megabyte glory. It was late at night, and I didn't want to stay up to log off from my ISP when the transfer was done. Ah, but Caitoo has a setting, in **Options > Preferences > Automation**, to "Auto disconnect after done downloading." Great! So I checked this box and went to sleep, content that my connection would be shut down after the file transfer.

Imagine my surprise, then, when I returned to my machine eight hours later and saw from the LEDs on my modem that I was still online. I moved the mouse to remove the screensaver and was greeted by a dialog box that said "Are you sure you want to disconnect?"

Pretty much defeats the idea of an auto disconnect, doesn't it?

It turns out, **Options > Preferences > Advanced > Expert mode** must be checked if an unattended disconnect, without the "Are you crazy?" confirmation box, is to be achieved. I hope that this does not represent a trend in KDE development, the endless stream of confirmation dialog boxes. They are at minimum insulting, and at most, expensive.

If you have a permanent Internet connection (such as a cable modem or at T1 or DSL line), you can set up Caitoo to perform downloads in the middle of the night or some other off-peak time (though given the worldwide aspect of the Internet, it's always peak time someplace). You can do this by specifying a download time in the Transfer dialog box that appears when you drag a file to the Caitoo window.

Note that while it is possible to cobble together a shell script that starts Kppp and establishes a connection that would allow a non-permanent connection to be employed, nothing of this sort is included in the KDE distribution. Additionally, be sure that expert mode is turned on in **Options > Preferences > Advanced**, or all you will have automated is the appearance of a confirmation dialog box.

If you want to try to build a shell script to do some of this, you need to consult the documentation for the shell you are using.

Using FTP Search Engines: KArchie

All those nifty search engines that you can access to find Web pages are fine, but they very likely will not find for you a file or library you need to make a balking application work. For that, there is **KArchie** (see Figure 24.5). You get to it via **K Menu > Internet > Archie client**.

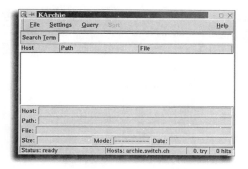

FIGURE 24.5
Type in the name of the file you seek (or a portion thereof), select the site which you want to have make the search, and the type of search you want to conduct. If you do all this correctly, and if it exists on an anonymous ftp site, **KArchie** will find it for you.

Let's see how it works. I think I'd like to find a copy of glibc compiled with crypt. This is required by many programs, but the U.S. government had barred its export, lest some foreign agent use it to steal our nuclear secrets without first making a political donation. As a result, it was freely available everyplace except the United States, where it could be tough to find compiled into glibc (the government barred Caldera, for instance, from including it in its Caldera Open Linux 2.2 distribution). The restriction was lifted in September 1999, so now I'm trying to bring my system up-to-date.

I know that the filename includes the words *glibc-crypt*, but that's all I know about it, so we'll try that. And Rutgers has a pretty good archie server, so we'll try that, too (see Figures 24.6 and 24.7).

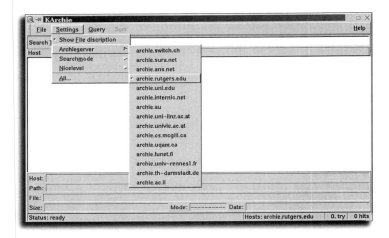

FIGURE 24.6
You can't see it, but I've typed in `glibc-crypt`, and now I'm selecting the Rutgers archie server.

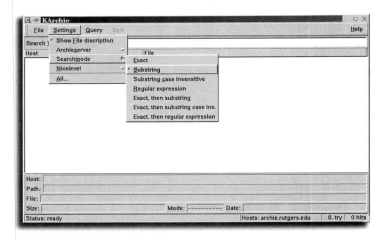

FIGURE 24.7
Because I don't know the exact filename, I'll look for something that contains the partial name I've typed.

After entering this information, KArchie chugs away for awhile, or, rather, sends my query to Rutgers (of course, you do need to be online to do this) which chugs along for a while. In a minute or so, I have my results (see Figure 24.8).

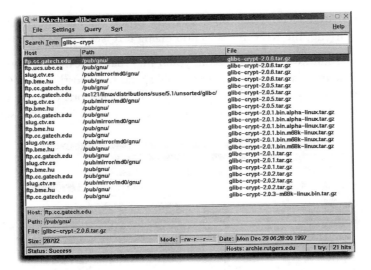

FIGURE 24.8
KArchie reports 21 locations where files including glibc-crypt as part of their name exist.

This is nice to know, but let's suppose that the reason I made the inquiry is that I happen to want the file for which I'm searching. Clicking on **File** helps me out (see Figure 24.9).

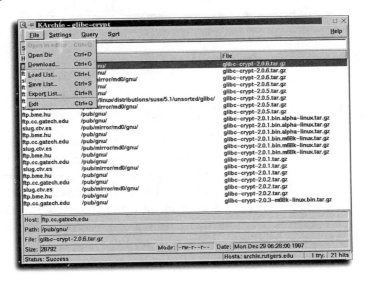

FIGURE 24.9
Clicking on **File**, **Download** starts the process of making the highlighted file my own.

Of course, KArchie would like to know where I want the file put, and as a result, we see our old friend, the KDE file selection dialog box (see Figure 24.10).

If you play around with KArchie a bit, you'll find that its search capabilities are very versatile. The more you use it, the less you'll spend time posting to newsgroups and mailing lists asking where to find a particular file. It's not one of those big time glamour applications, but it's an online utility that you will find very useful.

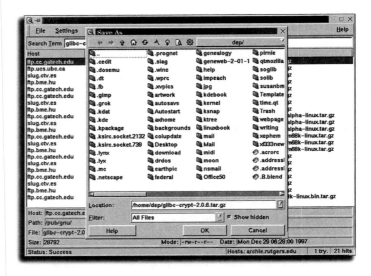

FIGURE 24.10
Select a location for the file to repose, and the download begins. That's all there is to it.

New Mail Notification: KBiff and Korn

Two little mail utilities are part of the core KDE distribution whose purpose is to let you know that you have new mail. The casual user, who logs on to the Internet through an ISP via a dial-up connection, may wonder what good they are. After all, when you open Kmail and download the mail, you can see easily enough whether you have any. If you have Kmail set to check for mail at intervals, there's every likelihood that you will check to see whether anything new has arrived before you log off. Even if you don't, Kmail will have gathered it anyway.

True.

But your ISP mailbox may not be the only place you get mail. For instance, your system may send you mail to let you know about certain system events (one case that comes to mind is if you are running HylaFax, which reports each day on the day's faxing activities). You would be informed of this new mail each time you boot your machine, but Linux users are accustomed to going for years without a reboot.

KBiff (found by choosing **K Menu > Internet > Biff**) is an application whose job is to monitor a mailbox, checking at specified intervals to see whether there's anything new. When it finds mail, it plays sounds, runs applications, or, actually, does just about anything you want it to do, for which you have the proper permissions set. If you really wanted to, you could set it to shut down your computer when mail appears. (You don't really want to do this; it's just to illustrate the breadth of possibilities.)

It normally lives docked to the K Panel, one instance per mailbox being monitored—if you're on a local network, this is not a bad idea, by the way. When you start it for the first time, you're treated to the setup screen, shown in Figure 24.11.

FIGURE 24.11

In its default livery, KBiff checks for mail once per minute, docks to K Panel, and keeps track of its settings from session to session. You may choose icons from a limited but useful set provided. Subsequent tab pages let you decide what happens when mail is detected, and which mailbox is being monitored. It's intelligently designed and straightforward.

Korn is the drag racer to KBiff's Formula I: It has more raw power, but is considerably rougher around the edges (see Figure 24.12). You will find it at **K Menu > Internet > Mail monitor**.

When you start this thing, you'll receive a dialog box asking you whether you want to set it up. There are no previews here: If you say no, it disappears and that's that. So, to provide information for you, I have clicked Yes.

What comes up is what you see, again, in Figure 24.12. You name your mailbox, give it a "caption," provide its location, and tell Korn how often to check for mail. The default is once every four minutes; the number you provide is in seconds. You also tell it what to do when it finds mail. It could, for instance, launch your mail program, or it could make a noise and then, when you click on its icon, launch your mail program. You can set up many mailboxes in Korn, but it lacks some of the little niceties of KBiff.

FIGURE 24.12
Korn is capable of monitoring multiple mailboxes. What it does when it finds mail is entirely up to you, and it makes no suggestions in that regard.

If you are among the growing number of people who are online all the time—through local network, cable modem, or DSL—one of these programs is likely to be useful to you. If your system is configured such that it is sending mail to you fairly regularly (through root's mail being forwarded to you, typically), the same holds true.

User Information: KFinger

There is something melancholy about the KFinger query I just ran on myself, shown in Figure 24.13. No mail. No plan. What could be sadder?

FIGURE 24.13
Alas, the author of KFinger is lonely, too: The last line of the Help file is "Mail me!!!!!"

You start Kfinger by executing **K Menu > Internet > User Information**. Kfinger goes by many names, Kfinger and User Information being two of them. It's also sometimes called KDE Finger. It obtains information about users on the local system or, if a username and the name of a remote system is supplied, it provides information about the user whose name and address have been entered (presuming, of course, that you're online). You can also use it as a talk client by selecting **File > Talk**.

Kfinger is of course a front end for the familiar `finger` command; if that command is not familiar to you yet, you can learn a lot by looking at the finger and chfn man pages. In my query I learned that I have no mail awaiting my attention and no `~/.plan` file.

Actually, KFinger gets information for users on the local system or a system that you specify in **Options > Setup**, where you can list as many systems as you like. It is of special use to the system administrator.

Network Utilities: GUI for Common Internet Functions

If you click on **K Menu > Internet > Network Utilities**, you are given a suite of commonly used network functions in a convenient central location (see Figure 24.14).

FIGURE 24.14
If you've been using Linux for long, the tab names will be familiar to you and so will their uses.

The Network Utilities, *KNU* for short, provide a graphical location for input and output of these network commands. Of special interest to me is Traceroute, but only because of the little program available in various places that maps the traces on the globe on your desktop, if you have XEarth or XGlobe running; it's pretty cool to watch. Of course, serious network folk have far more serious uses for all these utilities. Ping is a program every Linux user has used or will use; being told to "ping yourself" is not an insult, but instead a way of checking your system configuration.

Each of these, except for mtr and host resolution, has a man page that deals with the fundamentals. KDE merely provides a front end. The mtr choice will be blank unless you have installed the mtr package, which is a combined replacement for ping and traceroute with some enhancements that help determine the quality of a remote link. (For more on mtr, visit `www.bitwizard.nl/mtr/`.)

The functions comprising the Network Utilities are not exclusive to KDE or even to Linux. They are common to network and Internet platforms of all sorts. Here is a brief rundown of what they do.

Ping sends a dummy packet to a specific address and receives acknowledgment thereof; the transmission is timed. It is most frequently used in Linux to verify that the point-to-point protocol is set up correctly.

Traceroute requires by way of explanation a little about the way the Web works. When you log on to, say, a local computer bulletin board system (do any of these still exist?), the phone connection is from you to the BBS, and that's that. But the Internet is entirely different. You might have a Web page that someone at the next house in your neighborhood takes a look at. You might think that this would all take place on local lines. It might, but it's also possible that the transmission would go to England, Namibia, and then up to a satellite and down again in Japan and back up to another satellite, down again in California, and over several other stops before arriving at the house next to you. (Have you ever wondered where all the stuff on the Internet in, say, newsgroups, is stored? Keep wondering—there's no single answer!) Traceroute tells you where incoming information has been while on its way to you.

There's more: The information is sent in packets, so a Web page may jump all over the place on its journey to you, with the packets arriving out of order. The fact that it works is miraculous. I've had it all explained to me and have left such explanations convinced that it could not possibly work at all. But, somehow, it does.

Host resolution provides information similar to the Linux `host` and `nslookup` commands, both of which have man pages. It finds the Domain Name Server data on a specified host. It is most frequently used to learn the IP of a particular host. Do not be surprised if you never use this utility. If you run an ISP or do Internet detective work, it may well be of use to you.

Finger provides the functionality of the Kfinger program in a different location.

Okay, If We Must: Ksirc

There is probably a really good reason why some people use Internet Relay Chat, or *IRC*. I know people who swear they have done useful work more quickly because of it, and I don't doubt them. The fact that many—I think most—IRC "conversations" are of less than great import should not enter into it:

```
Turnip — what arre yew doin]
KingMaster — nothinn. just hangin out. finished my homework. history sucks.
Turnip — yeah. what are yew doin now.
KingMaster — nothin.
```

You'll also find inquiries of the proprietors of Web cams as to whether they intend to expose more of their bodies tonight, along with expressions of the wish that they do. Still, it's possible to be foolish with a word processor or telephone, and that fact says nothing much about the word processor or telephone. We have ksirc, and it is presumably useful. It's at **K Menu > Internet > Chat Client (ksirc)**, shown in Figure 24.15.

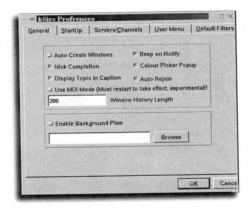

FIGURE 24.15
If Internet chat is your idea of a good time, or if you're actually breaking new ground and using chat for the furtherance of a project through an online meeting, you can set up Ksirc to do your bidding.

You configure it for the connection you want to make, give yourself a nickname, and you're off and running. If you've entered everything correctly, you'll soon learn about history, what people are doing now, and whether they intend to remain clothed.

part

V

KDE ON THE NETWORK

Running Your System Through KDE

User Administration

Setting Run Levels

Samba Management

Other Controls You May Want to Use

KDE does not yet provide all the tools necessary for the system administrator to live a fat and sassy life of never visiting the command prompt. Part of the reason for this, as you know if you are the system administrator in question, is that Linux is so inherently stable that once you've done your setup, it's mostly a matter of monitoring. And KDE does provide means for you to keep track of what's going on while playing Mahjongg or compiling applications for testing or having a high old time with Ksirc.

User Administration

One of the system administrator's tasks that KDE has made much easier is the administration of users. This is of particular importance if the system is a larger network involving dozens or scores, even hundreds, of users.

To gain access to this small marvel, go **K Menu > System > User Manager** *as root*, and feast your eyes on what you see in Figure 25.1.

FIGURE 25.1
KDE User Manager lets you add or delete users, assign them to groups, and a great deal more as you shall see.

To add a user, click **User > Add**, where you are prompted for a username. You are then treated to a dialog box beginning with the screen shown in Figure 25.2. (You can also get this dialog box by double-clicking an existing user, which is what is illustrated here.)

FIGURE 25.2
The details for the user are entered, beginning on the first page of the three-tab dialog box.

You specify the user number, the shell that the user will employ, the home directory for the new user, and a password for the new user (see Figure 25.3). You can add additional information, but it is not required.

FIGURE 25.3
The Password dialog box is where you assign a password to the new user.

If you are particularly security minded (and have a high annoyance threshold for user calls), you may want to set it so the password expires and must be changed periodically. You can also set the account to expire automatically, which is useful should you hire an outside contractor who meets deadlines. You can do all this on the **Extended** tab (see Figure 25.4).

FIGURE 25.4
The **Extended** tab gives you extensive automated control of the duration of passwords and accounts themselves.

You can also assign the users to **Groups** by clicking the appropriate tab. This is of course especially useful when you create groups to handle particular projects. You do this through a fairly standard dialog box, shown in Figure 25.5.

FIGURE 25.5
Each user must belong to a primary group and may be assigned to additional groups as well.

Of enormous importance is **File > Preferences** because it is here that much of what happens to new users is decided upon. Figure 25.6 shows the dialog box.

FIGURE 25.6
File > Preferences sets a default shell and location of the new user's ~/, and even if the user will have a ~/ at all, plus several other important things.

By checking the appropriate box, a *~/username* is created under /home, unless you change the location. Checking the box labeled **Copy skeleton to home dir** copies the contents of /etc/skel to the new user's ~/, thereby providing basic—or more than basic, if you've enlarged /etc/skel—configuration information for the new user. If you like, you can create a group comprising only the new user. That group will be deleted when the user is.

Just as you can double-click on a user to modify the account, so can you double-click on a group to add or remove users, as shown in Figure 25.7.

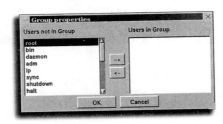

FIGURE 25.7
To add a user to the group, click on the username in the left column and the > button. To remove a user, click on the username in the right column (empty in this illustration) and click the < button.

You can add, edit, or delete both Users and Groups by choosing the appropriate menu, or by clicking on the labeled toolbar icons. Do be careful because playing around with the User Manager can really mess things up. If in doubt, click **Cancel**, close the application, and when prompted to save your changes choose **No**.

Setting Run Levels

Way back in the introduction to this book, you were shown a terrifying screen image (see Figure I.2 and, now, Figure 25.8) that probably made no sense to you, and you were promised an explanation. Here it comes.

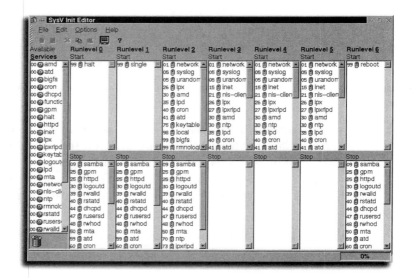

FIGURE 25.8
It's still scary looking, isn't it? And it's true: The SysV Init Editor is powerful and, if misused, can bring on wailing, anguish, and a world of hurt.

As you know, Linux offers a selection of "*run levels*," which are simply varying scripts that start applications or services at boot or when the run level is entered. These vary somewhat from distribution to distribution, but typically run level 1 is single-user mode, run level 3 is multiple-user console mode, run level 5 is multiple-user graphical mode, and run level 6 reboots the machine. The default run level is set in /etc/inittab in the lines near the top that look like this:

```
# Default runlevel.
id:3:initdefault:
```

The number following id: is the run level your Linux system adopts at boot. What this really means is that the scripts specified to start the particular services and applications for run level 3 will run when you boot your machine. Run level 3 is often the default.

The Right Default Run Level?

More and more Linux distributions install with a default run level 5, which is fine if everything always goes perfectly. Everything does not, however, always go perfectly.

Run level 5 is graphical mode: XFree86 is started (or a commercial X window system handler, if you've bought one of those), and the system boots to a graphical login manager, usually xdm or kdm. From there you log on to the machine and are passed directly to your window manager and desktop of choice. This is when all goes well.

But let's say that you get a new graphics card or that you've edited a configuration file and now your graphical desktop is, to use the technical term, all screwed up. You're effectively locked out of your machine.

Were your machine set to boot into run level 3, you could track down the problem and fix it. Now you're largely stuck. You can try booting into single user mode (at the LILO prompt press the **Tab** key to stop the process, then type **Linux single,** and press **Enter**), which may get you in to make repairs. Many people who have counted on this method have wished later that they hadn't.

The solution is to boot into run level 3 by default, which means changing the line in /etc/inittab from

```
id:5:initdefault:
```

to

```
id:3:initdefault:
```

Boot isn't quite as pretty, unless you are one of those who finds beauty in watching the processes in your machine start. If you're the system administrator, you are probably such a person; if you are not such a person, it's a taste worth cultivating.

When you start the SysV Init Editor (**K Menu > System > SysV Init Editor**—you need to be root to do this), it looks something like what is depicted in Figure 25.9.

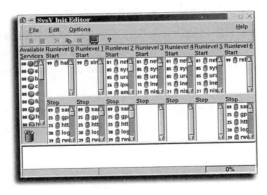

FIGURE 25.9
Nothing much useful here. Fortunately, you can grab a corner and resize **SysV Init Editor**.

After you resize it (see Figure 25.10), you can begin to get a sense of what it's all about.

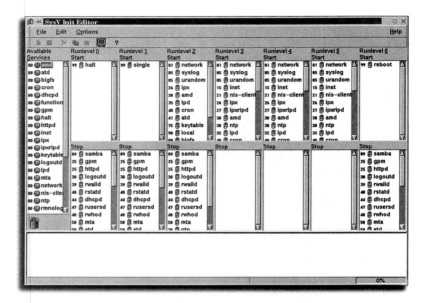

FIGURE 25.10

Now we can see. The various system services are in the column on the left, and the run levels that employ them are listed by numbered columns across the rest of the screen. Some run levels don't have much going on, whereas others run all sorts of things.

What can we learn from this? Well, one example is that even if you use gpm for console mode mouse support, it isn't running in single-user mode, run level 1. Likewise, network-related services are not in operation. (Also, you can drag the crossbar at the bottom of the lists down to make use of the white space.)

What does SysV Init Editor do? It assigns symbolic links from the services to the different run levels. On the chance that you're new to Linux, we'll take one of our little diversions away from the strictly KDE and into basic Linux because this is an area that is often ill understood.

In your /etc directory resides a subdirectory called /rc.d (if your distribution uses SysV initialization, which most modern distributions do). (If you're using BSD, you can skip all this because none of it applies to you.) Let's look inside (see Figure 25.11).

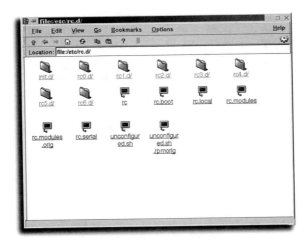

FIGURE 25.11
You will notice that each of the run levels has a subdirectory, but what is that init.d thing?

If you open /etc/rc.d/init.d, shown in Figure 25.12, you see all the services available. These may be assigned to none, one, or many run levels, but their mere presence in /etc/rc.d/init.d doesn't assign them to anything. There are a couple of symbolic links, one to the rc.local file which specifies programs that can run at startup, and one to the system's halt command.

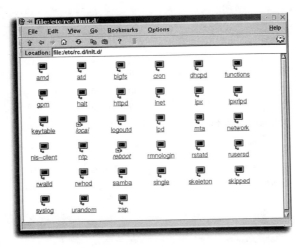

FIGURE 25.12
The icons in /etc/rc.d/init.d represent the services and programs that can be assigned to the various run levels.

Now, let's look inside one of the run level subdirectories, say /etc/rc.d/rc5.d (see Figure 25.13).

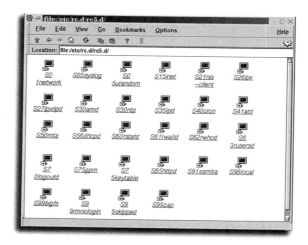

FIGURE 25.13
What is here in content is not as important as what is here in form: Notice that every icon represents not a program or service itself, but a symbolic link to that program or service.

Those S Numbers

You notice a number, beginning with a capital *S*, in front of each service. This is its sorting number, and to learn more about those, you'll need to consult a more comprehensive Linux book. May I suggest *Special Edition Using Caldera OpenLinux* by Allen Smart, Erik Ratcliffe, Tim Bird, and David Bandel (Que, ISBN: 0789720582) and *Running Linux, 3rd Edition* by Matt Welsh, Matthias Kalle Dalheimer, and Lar Kaufman (O'Reilly, ISBN: 156592469X).

As you have probably guessed, it would be a simple thing to create a symbolic link for a given service and put it in the run level's subdirectory. This is true with, say, KFM; less so from the command line, where you would do something like this for every service you need in every run level in which you need it:

```
ln -s > /etc/rc.d/init.d/<service> /etc/rc.d/<run level directory>/,Snn service>
```

You can see where this would grow old quickly and how the possibility for error would be huge. SysV Init Editor eases this by putting it all before you.

If You're Running Debian Linux

Some things vary among different Linux distributions, and one such variation is in the way Debian Linux handles run levels. My Debian guru tells me that the KDE SysV Init Editor isn't of much use with that distribution. The good news is that Debian has its own set of run level utilities.

To use it, drag and drop services from the left column to the column corresponding to the run level where you wish it to be offered. You'll find a few little caveats here as well.

If you drag and drop a service or program, you are moving it. In most cases, it is better to copy it (see Figure 25.14).

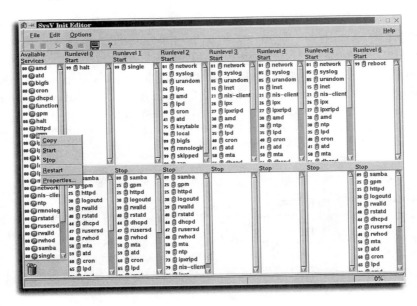

FIGURE 25.14
Right-clicking on an item allows you to copy it for pasting into a run level of your choice.

Likewise, right-clicking on an item already in a run level and selecting **Properties** renders a useful dialog box (see Figure 25.15).

FIGURE 25.15
The Properties dialog box shows what a service points to in /etc/rc.d/init.d. It also offers the option of changing the sorting order for the item, though it's best not to do this unless you know more about sorting orders than I explain here.

In SysV Init Editor, you can change the order of services and programs within a run level by dragging the item higher (or lower) in the list.

About that Trash can: Be very careful! An item dropped there is gone forever.

Samba Management

If you use a mixed network involving not just Linux machines but Windows machines as well, you'll probably employ SMB (Session Message Block) services to share drives, printers, and possibly other devices.

KDE does not provide a means for setting up such shares, but it does allow you to monitor those resources through a program, the Samba Status Monitor, found at **K Menu > Settings > Information > Samba Status**.

Samba is not an uncomplicated thing, and its administration is far beyond the scope of this book. While some documentation for Samba is included in your Linux distribution—the SMB Howto is a good place to start—you may want to get additional information from a more general Linux networking manual if you want to undertake setting up a Samba share system on your network.

The Linux Documentation Project

Much of this chapter deals with KDE front ends for Linux functions far, far beyond the scope of this book. If you want to delve deeper into these areas, you can find no better place to begin than the Linux Documentation Project. It offers a vast amount of information on practically every facet of Linux, including the famous Howtos, mini-Howtos, and even full book-length considerations of subjects from system administration to programming, all available for free download. You can find the LDP at `metalab.unc.edu/LDP`.

Other Controls You May Want to Use

Several KDE applications—and the number is growing all the time—are of great use to the system administrator but are not part of the core KDE distribution. These are available from or are linked to the KDE Web site, `www.kde.org`.

Here are a few and what they do.

KFirewall

This program helps administer the IP chains program, enabling a firewall between your local machine or network and the outside world. To use it, you need some familiarity with IP chains, which information you can get from any comprehensive and detailed Linux manual (which is to say, any one not shipped with a Linux distribution from a Linux vendor). KFirewall handles the administrative tasks from within KDE, graphically, if you are the root user.

KInst

This program makes the preparation of KDE applications for installation on machines throughout the network easier. You can make system-specific packages for use within your organization, thereby obviating the need for configuring machines individually.

KNetdump

This program lets you look at what is happening on your network connections, be they local or via dial-up connection.

kpm

Similar to Ktop but a little more stark, *kpm* (see Figure 25.16) stands for *k process manager*. When it has been built and installed, you'll find it at **K Menu > Utilities > Process management**.

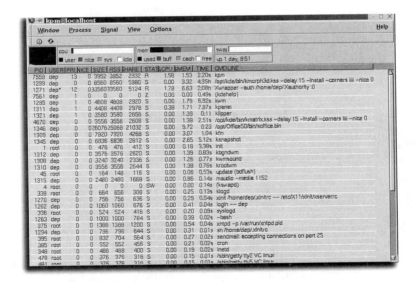

FIGURE 25.16
kpm offers, in a more compact form, everything you'll find in Ktop, the standard KDE process manager. The system administrator may, if desired, kill just about any process anywhere on the system. It's entirely menu-driven and easy to use.

KNetmon

This is a miniature suite of applications for keeping track of what is going on over a network using Samba shares, NFS, or both. It shows literally everything going on in a particular workgroup. The system administrator will find it well worth the download and brief time necessary to compile and install it.

Ktelnet

This dandy little program (see Figure 25.17) makes telnetting to another machine on the network a piece of cake. It acts as a front end not only for telnet but also for rlogin and secure shell. What it does is allow you to establish a session, either console or using the X Window system, on a remote machine with its output on your local screen. You can also use it to log in to a different session on your own machine. The telnet man page has a good, concise description of telnet.

FIGURE 25.17
Ktelnet puts a graphical face on the chore of telnetting from within a KDE desktop.

Kcmbind

This is a graphical front end for the bind command, which binds a specified name to a particular socket. For the short explanation of all this, if you don't know what it is, you don't have need for it. It provides lookup service for domain names, which is something your ISP already does for you. It's chiefly of use in local area networks but isn't always required even there.

KFStab

KFStab, shown in Figure 25.18, is one dandy little program. It makes easy the easy-to-screw-up process of editing /etc/fstab, which is the file system table that is used in determining what storage devices are mounted, how, and by whom.

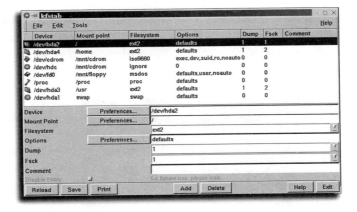

FIGURE 25.18
Non-root users can start KFStab , but they won't be able to change anything.

Ksysctrl

Again, new KDE applications are being developed constantly that will make the system administrator's job easier. One of the most promising is Ksysctrl, which is an attempt to put in one place all the things you need to identify and configure your hardware and peripherals. If you have used the most popular bundled operating system, you may be familiar with the way is looks (see Figure 25.19).

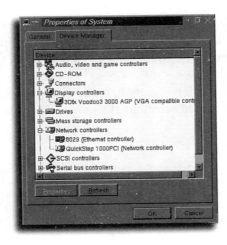

FIGURE 25.19
Ksysctrl lists the hardware in your system, providing one location where you can track down conflicts and look at your existing configuration. It promises to reduce the number of hardware issues in Linux by an order of magnitude.

This new utility joined the KDE core for the release of KDE 1.2, and is in my estimation by itself worth the trouble of upgrading. When you click on an item in the hardware list, you are given details about it and where in your system it resides (see Figure 25.20).

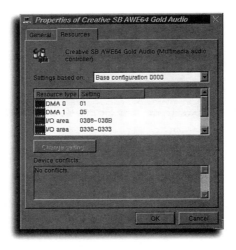

FIGURE 25.20
Whether a piece of hardware is properly installed, and whether kernel modules and software drivers are correctly pointed to it, has always been a matter of some alchemy in Linux, but Ksysctrl removes much of the mystery. This illustration shows what a sound card is up to, but imagine the help it will give you with network interface cards!

So it's to your benefit to check the KDE Web site frequently because it's very likely that the utility you want will be there in some stage of completion. The fact that an application is not completed is not necessarily a bad thing. You will have the opportunity to contribute, both ideas and code, and rare is the work in progress that is made available before it can do anything useful. Take a look, and if you've written something new, or improved something that exists, contribute it!

chapter

26

Supporting KDE in the Enterprise

One of the obstacles, perhaps the chief obstacle, preventing the adoption of Linux and KDE in the enterprise is the perceived lack of someone to turn to when things go wrong.

We can set aside the fact that things seldom go wrong in a properly set up and maintained Linux and KDE system even as we can set aside the fact that "someone to turn to when things go wrong" is as often as not a technical support number that, in exchange for a credit card number against which $100 or so will be charged, will tell you that they have no idea what the problem is either. The perception is there, and it is standing in the way.

This perception is, though, starting to be eroded a bit by the interest in Linux shown by leading computer companies and software vendors. Because the most widely used desktop for Linux is KDE, their interest extends to KDE as well. If you are running, or proposing to run, nibbleware Linux, put together from bits and pieces instead of from a full Linux distribution, your choices for third-party support are limited, but if you've put together such a system, it's also likely you'll need to go outside the company for support. (It's a good idea to keep records of how the system is configured. If you get squashed by a falling satellite on your way to work, you'll want your co-workers to be sad, not angry.)

Chances are you'll be using, or proposing to use, an existing distribution. There is much to be said for choosing a distribution that offers technical support. Almost all commercial distributions offer "90 days free installation support." This is, in a word, useless. You are looking for something a little more robust, which is to say something for which you pay and expect results.

In the United States, both Red Hat and Caldera offer a wide variety of support services. Both also offer programming and other training courses. (Caldera offers some distribution-independent courses as well.) There may be something in this regard available from the new Corel Linux, which features a heavily customized KDE as its front end.

It cannot go without notice that Lotus is offering its Domino server for Linux, and that its parent company, IBM, has taken a considerable stake in Linux. While much of the commercial interest in Linux focuses on the server side of things, there is no reason not to—and every reason to—carry this forward to the desktop, a thing made simple by KDE.

> **Security? Go Linux**
>
> In August 1999, the leading non-Linux operating system vendor set up a Web site with a challenge to crackers to try to hack it. It was down within hours, and the company said it was due to bad weather. At the same time, a Linux vendor in Wisconsin put up a site running the Apache Web server atop Linux, making the same challenge. More than 6,500 people tried to break in, but none succeeded. The site seemed invulnerable to the vagaries of weather as well. If your company has a Web site, there is really no alternative, though this isn't a KDE issue.

Providing Your Own Support

In a perfect world, a combination of stability of the system and competence of the system administrator would make technical support calls rare to the point of near extinction. Linux and KDE offer the former, and you can achieve the latter more easily than you probably imagine.

The phrase most commonly associated with Linux is "steep learning curve." It is also the phrase most unfairly associated with Linux. Yes, there is a steep learning curve, for those coming from the DOSrivative world. Linux is as unlike DOS and its successors as cantaloupes are unlike baseballs. A user accustomed to DOS-like systems (DOS, OS/2, and all versions of Windows) will be hindered at first by the belief that he or she knows something useful, but keyboard proficiency and the location of the on/off switch and back-panel connectors are about all that such a user can bring to Linux. What is steep in such a case is the *unlearning curve*. The Linux learning experience is no more difficult than it was for the computer user who started computing when computers arrived with blank hard drives and a box of DOS disks. (For the latter-day user, accustomed to buying a computer with everything preinstalled, the fact that there is *any* learning to be done may come as a surprise. It is up to you, the system administrator, to do the learning!)

But it is true: The Linux system administrator does need to know more than the tech support phone number and the tech support account number. You need to achieve a degree of competence.

There are many excellent books on Linux. There is also an enormity of online information available as well. If you can summon a little passion for the subject, you will have achieved a surprising degree of proficiency in very little time.

If your company is serious about Linux and if it is big enough that the MIS department is more than you, it may be a good idea to look into the courses offered by Caldera (www.calderasystems.com), which have the enterprise in mind, or by Red Hat (www.redhat.com), which is increasingly interested in the business use of Linux.

Caldera provides training and support through a series of partnership arrangements, whereas Red Hat offers these services at centralized locations.

However, if you are going to support it yourself, there is no way around learning the system. Fortunately, if you're interested in computing, learning Linux is a bracing challenge and a rewarding one. Learning KDE is sheer delight.

Outsourcing Support

In addition to the Linux distributors, there are some excellent third-party support sources. If you are in Canada, Starnix should be your first stop (`www.starnix.com`). It offers everything from turnkey systems to training to custom software and comes highly recommended.

In the United States, LinuxCare is a popular choice (`www.linuxcare.com`). It provides a wide range of general and custom support services, and its KDE knowledge is extensive.

Of course, the support services offered by your Linux distributor are worth investigating. A certification course of study is additionally under development that would be available to both consultants and to in-house MIS professionals. Again, your Linux provider is the first stop for details, though Caldera seems to be farthest along in this regard.

The fact is that KDE has become so much a factor in Linux that the Linux consultant who does not know KDE risks being left behind. Thus, any reputable Linux consultant can probably support KDE as well.

Hybrid Support

Unfortunately, much of KDE support is unlikely to achieve the "CEO stamp of approval," because it is...free. It is also accurate and fast. It is something on the order of combining in-house support with a degree of outsourcing, and it takes place online.

There are several mailing lists to which any KDE administrator, corporate or otherwise, should subscribe. These are similar to newsgroups but typically have a much better signal-to-noise ratio than do newsgroups. Additionally, archives of them are usually available. In that it is not very likely that you are the first person to encounter a particular problem, doing a search of the archives often provides an answer in minutes.

These mailing lists include, first and foremost, the KDE mailing lists, which you can join at www.kde.org/contact.html. You can find the archives for these lists at lists.kde.org/. The search engine there is very good. I recommend subscribing to kde, kde-announce, and kde-user. You may of course subscribe to others, too, as your interests suggest. Rare is the question you ask there that won't receive a prompt and accurate answer. You must be prepared, however, to provide a detailed description of the problem, what equipment and Linux version you are using, what you've done to try to fix it, and the circumstances under which it can be reproduced. "I just tried to run Kmail, but it doesn't work" is not enough to get you any useful results. If you do uncover a previously unknown bug, there is great likelihood that you will hear from the developer of the application, who will work with you to resolve it for one and all.

You would also be well advised to subscribe to the mailing lists sponsored by the publisher of your Linux distribution. These are not formal technical support avenues, but are quick, efficient, and free ways of getting help from other users. I have yet to encounter the problem that could not be solved by a well-worded question to either the distribution list, the KDE list, or both.

Of course, the newsgroups are a traditional source of information; if you're thick-skinned and don't mind wading through spam and sometimes endless digressions, there is often considerable knowledge available there.

And it is possible to directly email the author of a particular application. This frequently results in useful information. (The author's email address is usually found in the **Help > About** menu entry for the application on question.)

In all cases, bear in mind that your attitude plays a big part in the likelihood of a response and the quality of response. None of these people are being paid to look after you, and none of them owes you anything. The help they provide is from the goodness of their hearts, the desire to help others, the fact that they were probably helped in much the same way, and yes, the desire to display their proficiency. Questions politely asked are far more likely to receive solutions than are demands for help.

Gurus

This applies more to Linux in general than to KDE, but it is always a good idea to know a Linux expert. I can say with certainty that my progress in Linux would have been an order of magnitude slower had I not had a Linux guru who was willing to drop real work in order to help me climb out of some hole I'd dug for myself. If you can find a guru, your life will become easier. And it can be done. How?

If there is a Linux user group in your area, join it. If there isn't, ask around and see if you can organize one. Check with the computer science department at the local college: Chances are that the best of the best are working with Linux. These students can be a good source of part-time consultancy at reasonable prices. They get to build a résumé, and you get the help you need. And lest you pooh-pooh this idea, remember: Linux was written by computer students; so was KDE. These young hotshots are really, really good.

chapter 27

Managing Databases with KDE

The Big Guys •

Industrial Strength and (Usually) Free •

KDE Front Ends •

Its name is *SQL*, for *Structured Query Language*. Computer consultants like to call it "sequel" because that is a word that contains all three letters. There is another word that contains all three letters that in my experience might be more appropriate: *squeal*. Database development is not a mild thing.

Nevertheless, SQL databases are the meat and potatoes of modern business, and an operating system and desktop that can't make use of them isn't going to make it far in the enterprise. KDE can.

Needed: A Good Flat-File Database

There are all sorts of little, specialized databases for KDE, applications that are limited to keeping track of your videotapes or phonograph records, and there are several high-powered SQL servers and clients. Unfortunately, the middle ground, the flat-file, free-form, completely configurable database is unrepresented, so the user is left with a figurative choice of bicycle or jet airplane, but no car.

There being dozens of volumes the size of the Manhattan phone book on database management, there is no way even to sum it up in a single chapter. Database managers are in any case bound to know far more about their profession than I do or ever will. Instead, this is an overview of some of the industrial-strength databases that are available for use with Linux and KDE, and some special considerations as they apply to KDE.

The Big Guys

There are still a few independent, high-quality commercial database applications that haven't been consumed by some other company. Two of these are available for Linux, with the possibility of more on the way as time goes on: Informix and Oracle.

Informix

The Informix Corporation (www.informix.com) offers a broad range of Linux products, from an elaborate server to the Informix SE program that is available for free download. There is an Informix developer network, and the company offers free downloads and 30-day trial periods for even its high-end Linux products. The Informix commitment to Linux seems to be strong, and Linux database managers speak well of the company and its products.

Oracle

Linus Torvalds himself was widely quoted as saying that when Oracle released a Linux version, it was difficult for businesses not to take Linux seriously. In August 1999, the company announced a greater commitment to Linux, with a WebDB product in addition to its Application Server and Database products for Linux.

Oracle (`www.oracle.com`) is continually making announcements about availability and special offers.

Industrial Strength and (Usually) Free

Two databases have pretty much become standards in Linux: PostgreSQL and MySQL. Each has its adherents; indeed, each is as devoutly loved as is any religion with the possible exception of the Emacs text editor. Both are available for download, and both have licenses that let most users make free use of the program without paying a licensing fee.

PostgreSQL (`www.postgress.org`) and MySQL (`www.mysql.com`) are possessed of multiple applications, client programs, servers, and so on. It is on the use of these under KDE that the rest of this chapter will concentrate.

KDE Front Ends

Any of these databases works from a console window. The idea is to end up with a way that an office worker who is not a database expert can add, delete, search for, and otherwise make use of the data that are stored in a particular database. And there has been movement toward bringing easy-to-use front ends to MySQL, PostgreSQL, and, lately, even Oracle, with native KDE front ends.

KMySQL

The prettiest and potentially easiest-to-use of the KDE front ends for databases is KMySQL (see Figure 27.1). Don't let the name fool you: it employs modules between itself and the database application, so it works with PostgreSQL and MiniSQL as well as MySQL (though it is optimized for the latter).

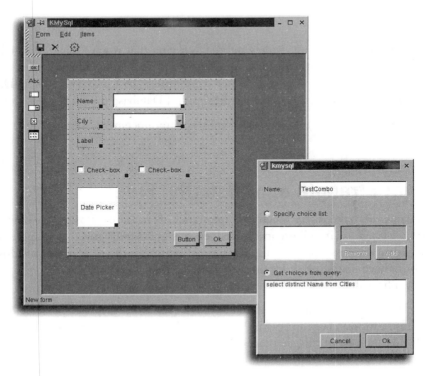

FIGURE 27.1
Among KMySQL's fine qualities are a table editor, shown, and a form editor. This eliminates a lot of text-mode programming of database applications for business.

When you first open it after compilation, KMySQL is attractive but a little mysti-fying (see Figure 27.2). This is easily tended to.

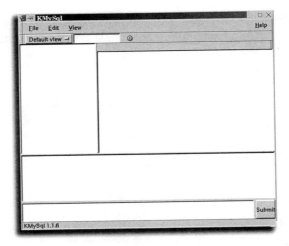

FIGURE 27.2
KMySQL shows what's in your database, but first, you need to tell it which database application and data file to use.

First, select **File > Modules**. This renders a dialog box, shown in Figure 27.3, that will probably be empty, even if you have compiled the KMySQL plug-ins.

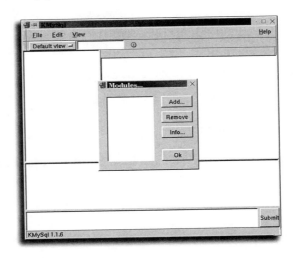

FIGURE 27.3
The first step in getting to your database is selecting the appropriate module or plug-in. Click **Add** to bring this about.

Clicking **Add** opens the standard KDE file selection dialog box. There are many clicks between your home directory and your /kde/share/apps/kmysql/plugins directory, but when you get there you can click on the plug-in you want, whereupon it is added to the Modules list (see Figure 27.4).

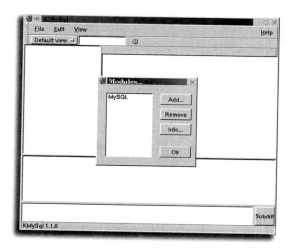

FIGURE 27.4
Even if there's just one module listed, click on it to highlight it before clicking **OK**, or you'll have to do the whole thing over again.

The plug-ins needed for the respective database applications are

kmp_mysql	MySQL
kmp_psql	PostgreSQL
kmp_msql	MiniSQL

After you've loaded the appropriate module, click **File > Add server** and face another dialog box (see Figure 27.5).

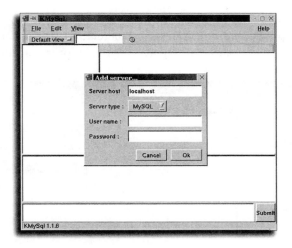

FIGURE 27.5
Pick the database application you seek, provide the username and password (which, depending on how you have the application configured, may be different from your usual username and password), and click **OK**.

Now the database application appears in your main KMySQL screen in the left column, shown in Figure 27.6.

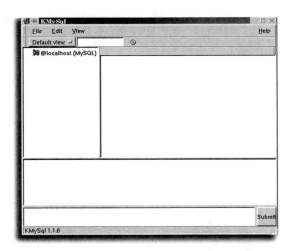

FIGURE 27.6
When data files are associated with the database, a plus sign appears in a box to the left of the database application name. Click on it to open the data tree.

After you have loaded your data, you can have your way with it, which is between you, your database application, your data structure, and the documentation of KMySQL, though you can see in Figure 27.7 that a lot is available to you.

FIGURE 27.7
KMySQL lets you manipulate your data in a multitude of ways.

KMySQLAdmin

A somewhat different, more classical database approach is taken with KMySQLAdmin (see Figure 27.8).

FIGURE 27.8
KMySQLAdmin works only with MySQL, but it performs a number of tasks that the database administrator needs to perform.

This application does not employ modules to connect it to the database application, so it works only with MySQL. It offers a wide variety of features, from administering user base access to the database to on-the-spot queries and table design (see Figure 27.9).

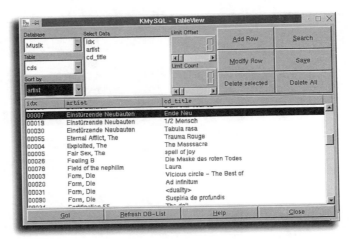

FIGURE 27.9
In addition to its database administration functions, KMySQLAdmin offers full access to and manipulation of the databases themselves.

KOra

A new arrival in the category, KOra is designed to produce a fully functioning front end for Oracle database products. As this is written, KOra is in its very early stages of development, but it looks promising and is well worth investigating if you have or are considering Oracle. As of late autumn 1999, it was at unstable version 0.3, though a good code hacker could probably make it do useful things and contribute to the effort as well.

part

VI

USING NON-KDE
APPLICATIONS WITH KDE

chapter

28

Console Applications on the Desktop

I've talked about how you can open a terminal and run a console application. It is entirely possible that you would like to set up a menu item or desktop icon that automatically starts a console program in a terminal window.

For demonstration purposes, I'll use Midnight Commander, the popular console-based file manager, but very nearly any console application will do.

SEE ALSO

➤ *I sing the praises of Midnight Commander in Chapter 34, on page 617.*

The simplest way, of course, to start this application is to open a terminal window and type the command that starts it (see Figure 28.1).

Getting Midnight Commander

Midnight Commander used to be a staple of many Linux distributions. For some reason, it isn't included as frequently as it once was. To get it, go to www.gnome.org/mc/ and grab the latest version.

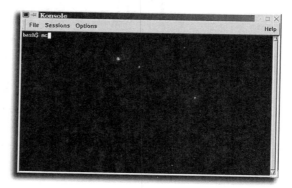

FIGURE 28.1

The standard way to start occasionally used applications is to type the command in a terminal and press **Enter**. To start Midnight Commander, the command is mc.

After pressing **Enter**, the application appears (see Figure 28.2).

FIGURE 28.2
In Midnight Commander, there is mouse support in a terminal window, which is not true of many console applications.

Putting Your Console Application on a Menu

How can all of this be automated? Actually, there are several ways. The method I prefer makes a menu item rather than a desktop icon for the application (which I show you how to do in the next section). To do so, you return to our old friend KMenuEdit, **K Menu > Panel > Edit Menus**. Right-click pretty much anywhere, and select **New** (see Figure 28.3).

FIGURE 28.3
You can right-click anywhere in your menu to get the KMenuEdit submenu.

This renders a blank dialog box, shown in Figure 28.4, which you now employ to build your menu item.

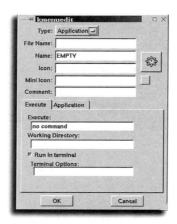

FIGURE 28.4
It's all a matter of filling in the blanks at this point.

The type of menu item is **Application**, of course, and the File Name is **mc.** You want the menu item to say **Midnight Commander.** The command line (**Execute**) is **mc,** and—this is where console applications are different from X-based applications—you *must* **Run in terminal** (see Figure 28.5).

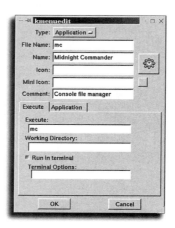

FIGURE 28.5
The critical thing that is easily forgotten here is checking the **Run in terminal** check box.

I don't want a menu full of the little KDE gear icons, so I'll need to find a new icon, which is done by clicking on the gear. As of KDE 1.2, there are new high-color icons available, though the selection still is pretty dismal. This is an invitation for you to get to work with the Icon Editor and make your own (and when you are happy with it, upload it to kde.org, so others may make use of it, too). But for now I'll look at what's available (see Figures 28.6 and 28.7).

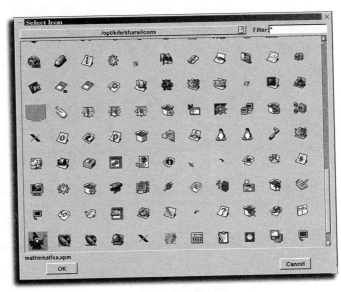

FIGURE 28.6
Alas, Midnight Commander does not have a specific icon, but I have a number of third-party icons in my ~/.kde/share/icons directory. Using the list box at the top of the Select Icon dialog box, I'll look there.

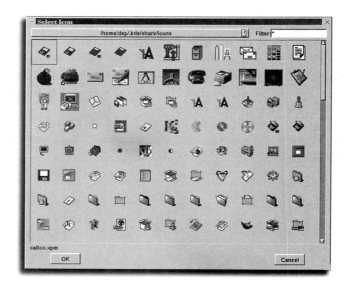

FIGURE 28.7
Many of the icons in the systemwide directory are here also, plus some others. Again, there's nothing that's Midnight Commander-specific, but at least there's a chance of finding something KDE hasn't reserved for a different application.

I happen to like the Escher-like ball that somebody painted for AfterStep very much, so I'll use it (see Figure 28.8).

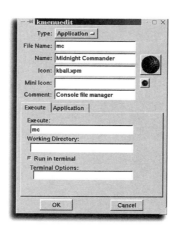

FIGURE 28.8
Clicking on the icon I want, followed by **OK**, closes the dialog box and returns us to the kmenuedit dialog box.

After this, I click **OK** and voilá, a new menu item (see Figure 28.9).

FIGURE 28.9
Now all I need to do is save my new menu, and Midnight Commander is just a couple of clicks away.

Making Console Applications into Desktop Icons

Now that you have tuned your settings for Midnight Commander, you might want to have access to it without having to click your way through menus. Doing this is astonishingly easy.

First, open your ~/.kde/share/applnk directory with KFM (see Figure 28.10). You'll find the icon for MC there.

FIGURE 28.10
When you used kmenuedit, you created an applnk for MC.

Although you could drag a template from the Templates folder and fill in everything there, there's an easier way. Just drag the MC icon to the Desktop directory, as shown in Figure 28.11. (If you don't have tree view enabled, you can drag it open from the left side of KFM.)

FIGURE 28.11

To keep the item on both the K Menu and the desktop, select **Copy**. To put it on the desktop only, select **Move**.

After you've done this, your application is on your KDE desktop (see Figure 28.12).

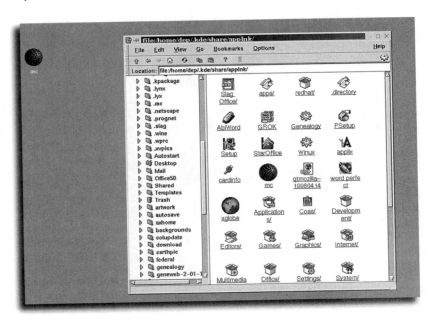

FIGURE 28.12
And there it is!

Moving applnk files, by the way, works both ways: You can open your Desktop directory and move desktop icons to the ~/.kde/share/applnk directory, or even to a subdirectory under it, which is, of course, a submenu. To make the menu item appear systemwide, as root move the applnk from the home directory's /.kde/share/applnk directory to the one in the systemwide /kde/share/applnk directory, whence anyone who wants to do so can copy it to the desktop.

Console Session Settings

There are a couple of places where you can make your iconized (or menuized) console applications more useful or enjoyable to use. These are in the settings for Konsole itself (which you really should be using; kvt is on its way out).

As you can see in Figure 28.13, if the settings aren't set properly, you will face a postage stamp-sized application if you're running at any resolution over standard VGA.

FIGURE 28.13
The window is too small. The font is too small. The mouse cursor remains the same size. Wouldn't you hate to have to manage files in this view of Midnight Commander?

Fortunately, you are not stuck with this state of affairs. The **Options** menu contains two controls, one for window size and the other for font size. I'll look at the former first (see Figure 28.14).

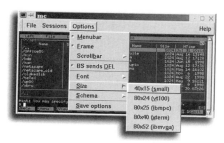

FIGURE 28.14
You can change the size of the Konsole—the numbers are columns first, then rows—but beware: You can make a Konsole that droops clear off the screen.

Now there is the matter of font size. Konsole does not give you the standard KDE typeface and size selection dialog box, but instead a menu of prebuilt choices (see Figure 28.25).

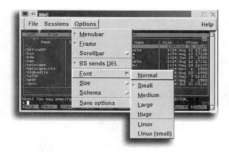

FIGURE 28.15
<u>Small</u>, here, was what you saw in Figure 28.13, too. **Huge** is not gigantic, but it's too big for many purposes. **Linux** is actually just about right.

What might be a good choice? I tried **Huge** and the 80×25 size, and got Figure 28.16.

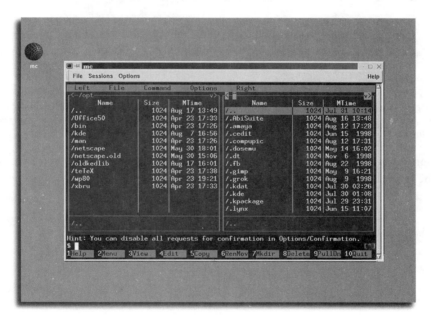

FIGURE 28.16
<u>Huge</u> actually works here, but pause for a moment to consider how much space is being consumed by relatively little information.

You have to experiment to determine what works best for you. While playing around, I discovered that with the **Small** font, the 80×40 all fit on the screen. With a lot of sizes it doesn't, but in Figure 28.17 it does.

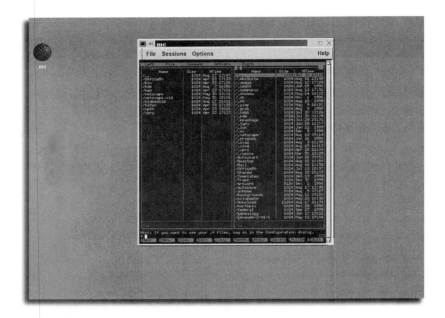

FIGURE 28.17
It's all there, but too tiny to be of much use. If I were at a very high resolution, instead of 1,024×768, perhaps all the fonts would work. It depends on the screen resolution you are using, the X server you are using, and the typefaces you have installed for use with Xfree86.

Some fiddling produced an ugly but workable combination, as shown in Figure 28.18. The setup is 80×40 with **Linux** typeface.

FIGURE 28.18
It all fits, but some of the graphics have been replaced by other characters. It still works, though.

After you have everything just the way you like it, don't forget to click on **Options >
Save options**, or the settings will be good for this window in this session only.

A Caveat and a Confession

There is a problem, though: The settings you make and save in Konsole apply to
every Konsole session, no matter what the application running (or if it's a plain
terminal window) thereafter. It would be nice to have different sizes for different
applications, but you can't get them this way.

My little confession: Yes, I know that Midnight Commander is also a Konsole menu
item, so making an icon and menu item for it are at least redundant. I chose it
anyway because it illustrates the principle better than just about any application. I
thought about using the popular Mutt mail program, which is installed on just about
every Linux machine, but most people run it in a color Xterm, not Konsole, and
color Xterms, though they run just fine atop KDE, are outside the scope of this
book. A color Xterm is a non-KDE terminal application, one of a multitude available
for running under Xfree86. You probably have Xterm installed on your machine.
Typing `man xterm` at a command prompt provides details.

Using Non-KDE X Window System Applications

The question is asked all the time: Will my Gnome/XForms/Tk/whatever application run under KDE?

The answer is yes, well, a conditional yes.

If you have the libraries and supporting files necessary to compile the program or to run the binary, it will run as well in KDE as it does anyplace else. How can you tell? Well, if you download a compiled binary in RPM form and, when you use the RPM command (or KPackage) to install it, it returns no errors, the chances are excellent that it will work perfectly well. If, on the other hand, you get dependency errors, you'd best make note of them if the program is important to you because you have some downloading to do.

Also, if you compile from source and get configure or build errors due to the lack of a particular file, you need to get and install the package of which that file is part.

Error Messages During Compilation

I would like to go on record here and now in condemning the sorry state of error messages during compilation. It's all well and good if foobar.h can't be found, but it's cruel punishment to make you go searching for it without any idea as to what package contains foobar.h. If a program requires something not universal to Linux distributions, the application developer should say so and tell the prospective user where to find it.

Having said all that, it's the rare application indeed that cannot be *made* to run under KDE. Exhibit One is Figure 29.1.

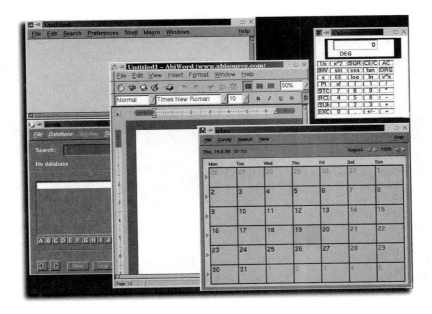

FIGURE 29.1
Clockwise from top left: Nedit, Xcalc, Plan, Grok, and, at center, AbiWord. None is KDE-native, but all run perfectly well under KDE.

There are some considerations, of course. Some of these applications make use of the KDE Clipboard, whereas others don't. Some use it in one direction but not the other. In many cases, KDE restores its own applications following an intentional or unintentional shutdown. It won't do this for non-KDE applications.

But getting them running in the first place can be a bit of trouble if you believe that you just download them, unpack them, and fire away.

Application Options: When Static Is Good

As I mentioned previously, you have several ways of making applications that are not KDE-native work under KDE. These include tracking down and installing supporting libraries, but you may have a way around this.

If you are getting compiled binaries from the publisher of the program, be it an individual or an organization, and if the binaries just won't work due to the lack of a library or two, you needn't necessarily go looking for the libraries.

Finding (Out) What You Need

Even if a program seems to have installed perfectly, it might not run. The first thing you do after installing a program is, of course, open a terminal window and type whatever you believe it is that will start the program. You may be surprised at the error messages.

For instance, you may need to set an environment variable before the program run.

You may discover that Linux doesn't believe the file exists. This could be because it has plopped itself down in a directory off the /etc/profile path. Or it could be that you don't have permission to run it, in which case you, as root, need to change the permissions.

Or you may discover that it needs a library that you don't have.

Go back to the place where you downloaded the program. If you obtained it from a general repository of Linux programs, next to the file you grabbed is very likely a file with the extension .lsm. Click on it. It is the Linux Software Map file, a text file, and it will be displayed on your browser or in a text editor spawned by your browser (KFM does the latter). It may well list the packages required for the application to work.

If you acquired it from its author, the page that had the original file may contain the needed libraries or links to them. Or it may contain something else: the program in binary form, statically linked.

What does *statically linked* mean? It means that it includes everything it needs from whatever libraries it calls upon. It also means that the program is somewhat bigger and uses somewhat more memory. It will not be as big as the program plus the libraries, though, so if you're short of storage space, you needn't necessarily rule out statically linked programs: They may save you space in the long run. (Of course, if you have a dozen programs statically linked to the same libraries, you are wasting both drive space and memory.) The opposite of a statically linked program is a *dynamically linked* one, which shares libraries with other applications.

If none of this works—there are neither links, nor static binaries, nor useful .lsm entries—you can always read the README file that was probably included with the program. (You should read this *first*, but for some reason few people do.) Also, the name of the program may prove helpful. The dandy little XFMail program, for instance, announces by its name that it uses XForms; Xisp, the fine Internet dialer, less so. Of course, you have Kmail and Kppp anyway.

If all else fails, you can ask on a mailing list or newsgroup. You will find the answer.

Incorporating Other Apps into KDE

A non-KDE application will never be a full KDE application unless you want to rewrite the source code to adapt it to the QT libraries (about which there is more in Chapter 36, "Programming for KDE"). But you can certainly invite it to the party, and much of the time you won't notice that it's not a native KDE program.

For demonstration purposes, I'll use AbiWord, a slick-looking but incomplete Gnomish word processor. Just so you know, I downloaded the source (didn't compile) dynamically linked (wouldn't run) and, finally, the static version. Though by now it may seem old hat to you fine readers who began on page 1 and have read every word until you got here, we'll go through the menu process for those who are using this as a reference, and for those of you who didn't memorize—shame on you!—every word.

You begin by knowing that if you open a terminal window and type **abiword**, the program appears. Good. That means that it or a symbolic link to it lives somewhere in your PATH statement. You are now prepared to go to **K Menu > Panel > Edit Menus**.

Right-click on any menu entry on the left side of the Menu Editor window. This produces the menu shown in Figure 29.2.

FIGURE 29.2
In that you're making a new entry, click **New**.

You're quickly at the dialog box wherein you configure a new menu item (see Figure 29.3).

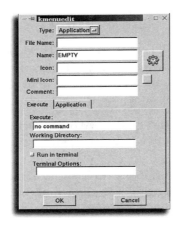

FIGURE 29.3
Here it's just fill-in-the-blanks to make a new menu item.

AbiWord is an application, so you needn't fiddle with that drop box. The filename of the program is *abiword*, but I want it listed on the menu as *AbiWord*. While there is a great icon for AbiWord, the installation didn't deposit it in the icons directory, and it looks a little like the Acroread icon. I don't have Acroread on my machine (though it's a fine program), so I'll adopt the icon for AbiWord. The command, as we know, is abiword, so that's what goes into the **Execute** box. And I won't be starting a terminal (had I checked that box, a terminal with no real purpose would have started alongside AbiWord).

We're done. Click **OK** and it's on the menu, tentatively. Click **File > Save** in the Menu Editor and it's official. Now it's a menu item (see Figure 29.4).

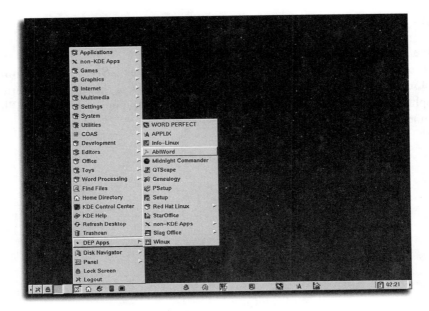

FIGURE 29.4
There it is, almost as if it had been born there.

But does it work? Let's see Figure 29.5.

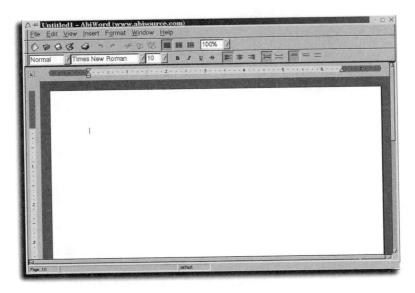

FIGURE 29.5
It has all come together. A totally alien program, using libraries that have nothing at all to do with KDE and that are not a part of many distributions of Linux, is running under KDE.

A KDE Configuration Consideration

One KDE setting can make life miserable for some non-KDE applications and for those who try to use them. It is the **Display properties > Style > Apply fonts and colors to non-KDE apps** setting. Although the effect of this check box varies from application to application, if you use a lot of non-KDE apps, you're best off leaving it unchecked.

chapter 30

Commercial Applications and KDE

StarOffice •

ApplixWare •

WordPerfect •

Other Commercial Applications •

Not long ago my father-in-law, a computer professional since the days when there was no such thing as a microcomputer, in response to mention of Linux said, "But what do you do for software?" It was a good question because unless you are in the midst of things Linux, the prevailing notion is that Linux exists pretty much for its own sake, with no applications software to allow users to do anything except tend the old Linux box.

Not many years ago, such a notion had a germ of truth to it. First were console applications, usually ports of mainstream UNIX applications: editors, mail programs, and the like. Then came the one-off graphical applications, not tied to any particular desktop. Sadly, it seems as if this kind of development is dying off somewhat. The applications optimized for a particular X Window System desktop came next. And now, more and more, we have industrial-strength commercial applications (not that the noncommercial applications are unfit for industry because in many, if not most cases, they are).

A lot of the software is network-based. For instance, in the summer of 1999, Lotus Development announced the trial version of its flagship Notes product for Linux (www.notes.net/linux/). There are, as previously noted, commercial database servers and clients for Linux. But what about the mere user, the home or small office Linux advocate who is looking for something between, say, the 25 or so half-finished word processors for the X Window System and some super high-powered network thing that has features that its own developers have probably forgotten about?

Such applications actually exist. In fact, the chances are better than even that you have one or more of them if you bought a commercial Linux distribution. They include a couple of office suites and an impressive standalone word processor that is likely to gain suitemates before long. We'll begin with the office suites.

StarOffice

I'm writing this book on the word processor in StarOffice 5.0 (and, after this chapter, StarOffice 5.1). It's a good thing that I like it because I really had no choice: StarOffice is the only application, as of this writing, that comes even close to supporting the Word for Windows format now so popular (for no apparent reason) throughout the world. The fact that I can apply the styles my publisher wants and save the whole thing in WinWord format saves some, perhaps a lot of, hair tearing.

StarOffice is, in fact, a wonderfully high-powered suite of applications, incorporating a full-featured word processor, spreadsheet, graphics and presentation graphics applications, and a useful Internet subsuite of Web browser, newsreader, and email programs. It is included with many Linux distributions, integrates wonderfully with KDE, and is free for personal noncommercial use.

Sounds just about perfect, doesn't it? Surely there is a catch, right? Well, actually, there are a few. StarOffice for the longest time suffered from tremendous instability problems. It was wont to crash without notice. This was not its fault, really: it was (and as of this writing still is) built on glibc-2.0.7. That would be no problem in and of itself but for the fact that there never has been an official release of glibc-2.0.7. There was a fairly general set of specifications on which many people extemporized. This meant that if you were running a system based on glibc-2.0.7 and you installed StarOffice, the libraries would be enough alike to allow the installation, but problems would arise later. This was less of a concern on the Linux distributions that were based on libc5 because StarOffice then installed its own glibc-2.0.7 and through a wrapper program managed to run, at least part of the time.

When Caldera Open Linux 2.2 was released in the spring of 1999, it came with a version of StarOffice 5.0 that actually worked and is nearly bulletproof. It is still running glibc-2.0.7 (while COL 2.2 is glibc-2.1 based), and I don't know how they did it, but they made it work and work well. A newer version, StarOffice 5.1, is out, but I was hesitant for a long time to tinker with the perfect balance achieved by whomever at Caldera or Star Division brought about the 5.0 miracle. I thought I'd wait until there was a StarOffice fully based on the standardized glibc-2.1, as opposed to 2.0.7 with some kind of hack applied. But then...

One Saturday night I decided to throw caution to the wind, a little bit at least, and install 5.1. (I kept my existing StarOffice 5.0 intact: a luxury I had enough drive space to afford. StarOffice 5.1 can take up more than 150MB of storage.) A few error messages were thrown, which, based on newsgroup postings I had read, was expected, chiefly having to do with the lack of encryption in the glibc-2.1 shipped with Caldera Open Linux 2.2. I chose to ignore them and proceed. Soon thereafter I had a StarOffice 5.1 installation that has not failed in the slightest way to this day, though I still haven't deleted my 5.0.

Not long thereafter, Sun Microsystems purchased Star Division, the somewhat quirky company that produced StarOffice. Sun made StarOffice completely free (no registration required) for not only Linux but also Windows, Sparc Solaris/Intel, and OS/2. Sun also announced that there will be a Web-based version of the product, which would allow users to perform office suite tasks without having StarOffice on the local system or network. There have also long been plans for a Java-based StarOffice.

StarOffice is now available from www.sun.com/dot-com/staroffice.html. Also on that page are links to FAQ lists and support newsgroups.

There is also the fact that StarOffice is not like most other programs or suites. It is said to resemble Microsoft Office, but I don't see it. Take a look at Figure 30.1 and decide for yourself.

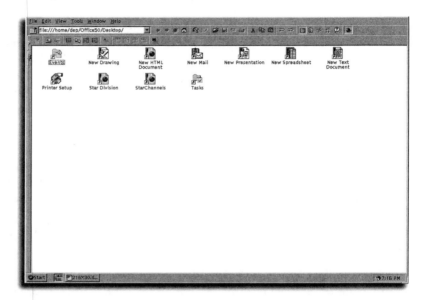

FIGURE 30.1
In its Windows incarnation, StarOffice actually replaces the Windows desktop; perhaps there is a way to do this in Linux as well. As we will see, it adopts many of KDE's processes as if they were its own, but I don't think it looks like Microsoft Office.

The whole StarOffice desktop is a browser, and it includes a number of features that are a mystery to those who do not study it. (That having been said, and I have by no means mastered the thing, time spent studying the workings of StarOffice is well spent because wonder after wonder is revealed. You get the sense that if you really knew this thing, you could probably manage much of the world from its desktop.) But it can be daunting, as Figure 30.2 illustrates.

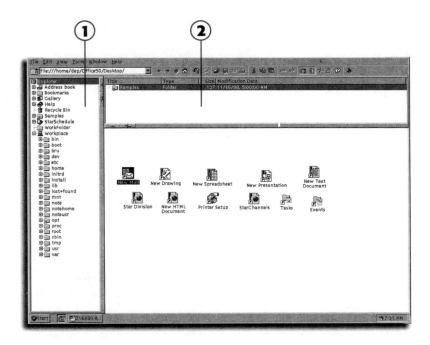

FIGURE 30.2
The column at the left is called the *Explorer*. The box across most of the top is called the *Beamer*. Can you guess what they do?

① Explorer   ② Beamer

One good thing is that you can be productive with StarOffice without mastering all its nooks and crannies. The word processor, for instance, is gorgeously full-featured, as the self-referential (in the Linux tradition) Figure 30.3 demonstrates.

FIGURE 30.3
Don't bother fishing out the magnifying glass to see what is on the screen because it's all right here in the caption, in easy-to-read, full-size print!

Even so, you expect some areas where tasks should be simple, but they aren't. Creating a simple letterhead, with a layout that begins page numbers with the number 2 on page two is a simple thing in most non-Linux word processors. I have yet to see one for Linux, commercial or otherwise, that makes this anything less than a struggle, and StarOffice's word processor is no different. Perhaps in today's fast-paced, email-driven world, pages and therefore page numbers are obsolete. I hope not. In any case, it's difficult to do in StarOffice and other Linux word processors.

StarOffice also includes a full-featured spreadsheet program that can read and write most popular spreadsheet formats (see Figure 30.4).

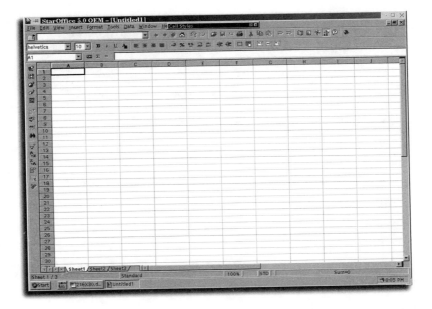

FIGURE 30.4
The StarOffice spreadsheet program does pretty much everything that spreadsheets do. If you have embedded macros in a file from another spreadsheet program, though, they may not survive the translation.

In addition, the spreadsheet imports, reads, and writes a number of popular database formats (see Figure 30.5).

But the real database power—as well as much of the rest of the power of StarOffice—comes from its **File > AutoPilot** prebuilt applications. These guide you through a wide selection of documents, queries, reports, even Web page designs.

The drawing program in StarOffice is excellent. A friend, the computer genius and new pilot Kari Jackson, sat down at a StarDraw desktop and went to work (see Figure 30.6).

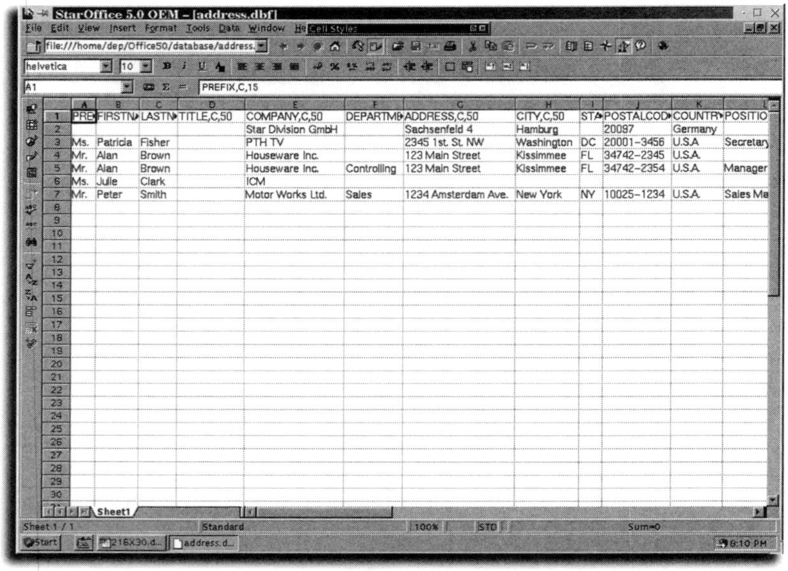

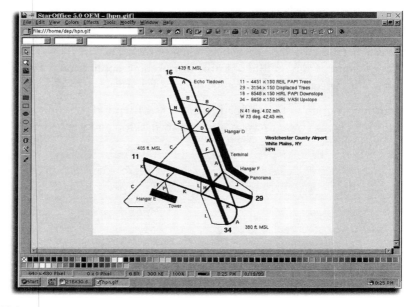

FIGURE 30.5
While it is not in forms view, it is a database. StarOffice includes its own programming language and tools so that if you want to develop something more formal, you can. Typically, importing data from another application's database requires importing the data into StarCalc, saving it as a StarOffice file, and opening it as a StarOffice-native database.

FIGURE 30.6
In her first use of the program, my friend Kari Jackson mapped the White Plains, New York, airport. StarDraw is full-featured and easy to use. It also supports many graphics file formats.

It goes on and on. The HTML editor in StarOffice is quite good, as are the Web browser, newsgroup, and email programs, but one of the niftiest features is its integration with KDE.

At the lower-left corner of the StarOffice desktop is a button labeled Start. This button, when clicked, opens a menu. In the Settings submenu, you will find, of all things, the KDE Control Center. More than that, **Start > Programs** renders something familiar to KDE users (see Figure 30.7).

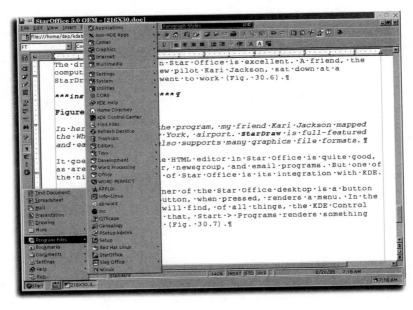

FIGURE 30.7
Yes, indeed, StarOffice includes the contents of K Menu in its own Start menu.

Of course, if you have K Panel and the taskbar set to autohide, StarOffice makes room for their few rows of pixels at top and bottom so that you have access to them as well. All in all, there's really not much excuse not to have StarOffice on your KDE machine, and for personal use, the price is certainly right!

ApplixWare

A very popular and attractive office suite is ApplixWare, available in stores and from some Linux vendors via the Applix Web site (www.applix.com) and included with Caldera OpenLinux version 2.3.

ApplixWare's suite includes a word processor, graphics program, presentation program, spreadsheet, file manager, and email program. It offers HTML editing and a development language for producing customized Applix applications.

When you start ApplixWare, it renders a button bar to the screen, shown in Figure 30.8.

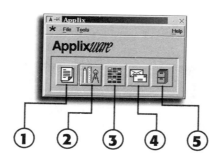

FIGURE 30.8
The ApplixWare button bar fits in very nicely, from a stylistic point of view, with the KDE desktop.

① Word processor

② Graphics program

③ Spreadsheet

④ Email program

⑤ Directory Displayer

Clicking on the word processor button (or on **Words** in the menu that is opened by clicking the huge asterisk at upper left) opens the word processor, which is straightforward though perhaps somewhat limited (see Figure 30.9). For instance, the array of possible font sizes is not as great as is found in other word processors, but it is probably sufficient for most users.

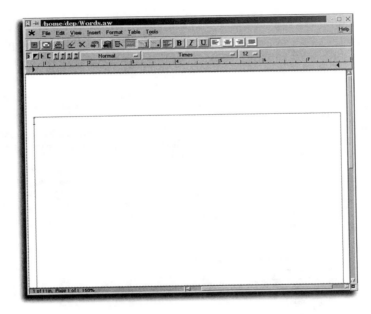

FIGURE 30.9
Applix Words works pretty much as you would expect. It reads and writes a variety of formats with varying degrees of success.

As is the case with StarOffice, ApplixWare has excellent internal support for the insertion of documents made by its own applications into other documents. This is, of course, especially useful when you seek to insert homemade graphics into your word processor documents.

The graphics program, when its button is clicked, opens a startup dialog box (see Figure 30.10).

FIGURE 30.10
You can look at this dialog box each time you start the graphics program, or you can set its default behavior to start one of the graphics applications.

The Grafix program (see Figure 30.11) itself is cleanly designed and relatively easy to use, though it is in desperate need of bubble help until you are completely familiar with the tool icons. It supports a variety of file formats, including several of its own.

The File Format Problem

Has anyone else noticed, or is it just me: don't we already have just about all the proprietary file formats we need for word processors and graphics files? Spend a while trying to get a written document or image from one application to another via an interim third application sometime.

Even worse is the email message storage mess. Most email programs establish a proprietary format for keeping email messages and such attachments as they may contain. Other email programs can't read these. The result is that if you upgrade or change your mail program, you have to keep the old one around if you have any messages archived. Oh, for some agreement on a common mail storage format!

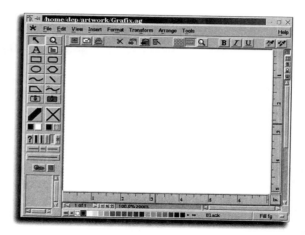

FIGURE 30.11
The Grafix screen is attractive, but some of those icons defy the person trying to guess what they are. Intuitive they're not. Fortunately, the Help system identifies each and what it's for.

The Applix spreadsheet program, shown in Figure 30.12, looks and acts like spreadsheet programs the world over.

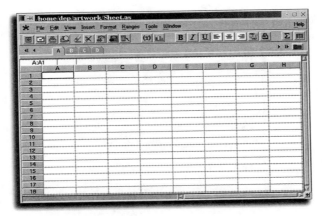

FIGURE 30.12
It's a spreadsheet, and it allows embedding of all or part of itself into other Applix documents.

The email program in Applix (see Figure 30.13) is both attractive and intriguing. It comprises a series of frames, listing the folders, messages in the selected folder, contents of the message, and any attachments the selected message may contain.

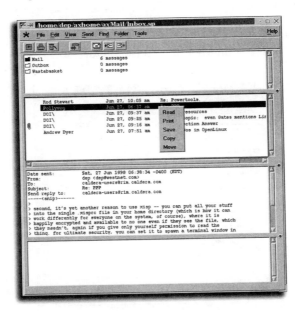

FIGURE 30.13
You can act upon each message by right-clicking it. Oddly, **Reply** is not among the choices. For that, you need to sort out the toolbar icons or click **Send > Reply**.

Replying to a message in the Applix email program is a little more complicated-looking than it is in most other email applications for Linux (see Figure 30.14).

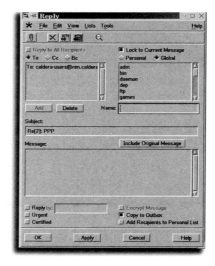

FIGURE 30.14
All I wanted to do was send a reply! The original message is not automatically quoted: for that you need to click the Include Original Message button. If you change your mind, you need to delete the contents of the original message by hand: Clicking the button a second time copies the contents of the original message a second time.

The file manager in Applix, the Directory Displayer, is, like the rest of the suite, very pleasing to the eye and somewhat limited (see Figure 30.15).

FIGURE 30.15
Directory Displayer does indeed display directories and files, though it doesn't show hidden directories or files by default. If you double-click on a file to open it, it comes up read-only. It is indeed a displayer, not a manager.

The real strength in Applix comes in its nonthreatening appearance—it looks as if it might be part of KDE itself—and the fact that users new to Linux and KDE will find much of its use familiar. It also offers developers an opportunity to create systemwide applications and macros, a plus if ApplixWare is to be deployed in the enterprise. Beware the import-export filters, however. They are spotty.

WordPerfect

If the dinosaurs had computers and sent letters to each other, they would have used WordPerfect to write them. WordPerfect, it seems, has been around forever, as has the UNIX version of the venerable word processor.

It is impossible, it seems, to use WordPerfect without developing a very strong opinion of it. It inspires tremendous affection…or tremendous hatred. It is certainly very powerful and, depending on something (genetic? as a result of upbringing?) is either easy to use and intuitive or difficult to use and impossibly inscrutable. WordPerfect does not do things the same way that other word processors do. It never has.

Like ApplixWare, WordPerfect at startup spawns two windows (see Figure 30.16).

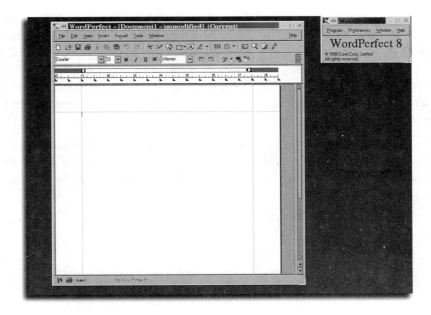

FIGURE 30.16
The small window at upper right offers access to settings and controls, along with a list of recently edited files. The main window is, of course, where you do business with WordPerfect.

WordPerfect is now available in a slightly limited version (you cannot, for instance, add typefaces to it) for download, with most Linux distributions, and elsewhere (in Europe, it was on a CD distributed with magazines). It is also offered for sale, with a thick and impossibly inscrutable manual and the promise of lots of clip art and 130 typefaces. (The typefaces, though, seem to have been left out in many copies, and you have to phone Corel, WordPerfect's publisher to get them.)

If WordPerfect is your cup of tea, run, don't walk, to the bookstore and get *Special Edition Using WordPerfect for Linux* by Rod Smith. Rod really knows the program, and I know from personal experience that he can explain its intricacies in such a clear way that you're left feeling that nothing could be more obvious. But not even he can bring sense to the import-export filters in WordPerfect. If you believe that your life is too serene, you can quickly cure it by trying to move a formatted file written in WordPerfect to, say, StarOffice.

Corel, which now publishes WordPerfect, is producing its own KDE-based Linux distribution, so it seems very likely that WordPerfect will soon be joined by the other applications that are found in the WordPerfect Suite on other platforms.

Other Commercial Applications

It is not possible here to list all the commercial applications available for Linux that run perfectly well under KDE. The list would be long and instantly obsolete, so rapid is the stream of new Linux apps. Some of these are niche products, some are "vertical apps" designed for a particular industry, some, like the Blender animation program (www.blender.nl) are developing so rapidly it's breathtaking. One thing you're likely to discover is that the prices for commercial applications under Linux are less than the prices of the same programs for other platforms.

It's a good idea to subscribe to one of the Linux magazines or to spend time in the Linux hangouts online (Freshmeat, Slashdot, JustLinux) to keep up to date on the new commercial developments. For instance, I learned of CompuPic for Linux (linux.compupic.com) entirely by accident (see Figure 30.17).

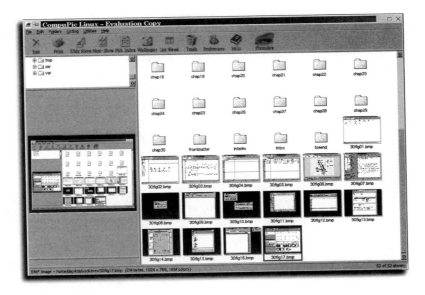

FIGURE 30.17
CompuPic, from Photodex, offers a multitude of graphics manipulation features, such as batch conversions. It also displays the images in a directory, with the selected thumbnail previewed at left in a larger size. Here, for instance, are the illustrations in this chapter, including this one.

The important thing to remember is that if it runs under Linux, it runs under KDE. To add an application to your desktop (if its installation program doesn't do it automatically), you can run **K Menu > System > Appfinder**, which adds the most well-known commercial applications to your K Menu if it finds them. To do it by hand, use the instructions given earlier for adding noncommercial apps to your K Menu or desktop. That's all there is to it!

chapter
31

Using DOS Applications Under KDE with dosemu

There is a possibility, even a likelihood, that if you're a refugee from the DOSrivative world, there is a DOS application, maybe two, that you really wish you could run under Linux and KDE.

Well, through a program called dosemu, you can.

This chapter does not dive into the vagaries of dosemu. In fact, we won't even get our toes wet. Suffice it to say that when properly set up, dosemu can run just about any DOS application (indeed, there are those who have gotten OS/2's version of Windows 3, Win-OS/2, to run well under dosemu). Instead, we'll discuss how you can set up applications in dosemu to work seamlessly under KDE.

To start dosemu in a terminal, you type **dos** and press **Enter**. The result (see Figure 31.1) is a DOS command prompt.

FIGURE 31.1
The dosemu command prompt looks just like the one you've used in other operating systems and accepts the same commands. The version that shipped with Caldera OpenLinux 2.2, shown here, includes Caldera's excellent improvement on plain old DOS.

It is, of course, a simple thing to create a link that automatically starts dosemu. You simply open KMenuEdit and create a new menu entry, as shown in Figure 31.2.

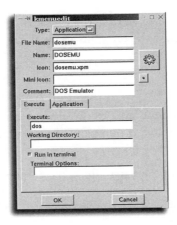

FIGURE 31.2
Don't forget to check the **Run in terminal** check box!

Now, when you click on the **dosemu** menu item, you get a terminal running DOS.

If you want, you can get really cute with this. For instance, I have a good friend who believes the sun rises and sets on The SemWare Editor Junior, previously known as Qedit, a wonderful programming editor. It runs nicely under dosemu, as shown in Figure 31.3.

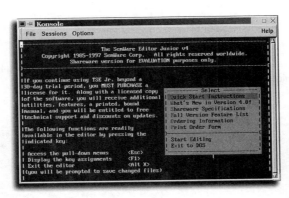

FIGURE 31.3
Qedit, a.k.a the SemWare Editor Junior, is happy in dosemu, but can we make a link that starts it automatically? We'll see.

When running dosemu, you need to know where your Linux files are listed. This is typically drive L:. So to start the program automatically, we need to create a batch file, which we'll call q.bat:

```
L:
\home\dep\download\qedit\q.exe
```

This batch file is saved in dosemu's C:\ directory. Now, to start TSE, you simply type **q** at the dosemu command prompt and press Enter. Good, but we can do better. Back to KMenuEdit.

This time, add the name of the batch file to the command (see Figure 31.4).

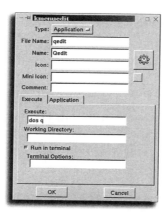

FIGURE 31.4
We make a new menu entry adding the executable file as a command variable, and, miraculously, it works. What happens now when we click on the new menu item? Let's see Figure 31.5.

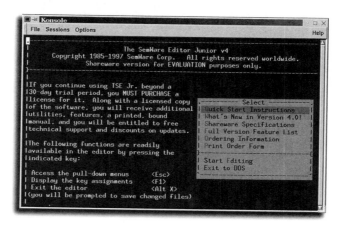

FIGURE 31.5
And here it is, as if it were any Linux console app!

You can do this with a wide variety of DOS applications and games, though I should note that it's a kludge, and the best course is to wean yourself to nice, safe, Linux applications.

If you really want to visit barely charted territory, there is reportedly a way of getting IBM's OS/2 version of Windows 3.x to run under dosemu. The framework for doing this is described in Chapter 32, "Running Windows Applications with KDE."

chapter
32

Running Windows Applications with KDE

It's easy to feel left out when you're running Linux and KDE. The newscasts are always running stories about these virus programs that destroy computers, but your machine never gets infected. In fact, you don't even have a virus scanner. In fact, you don't even know if there *is* a virus scanner for Linux. People you know complain about their computers crashing and having to be rebooted several times each day, but the last time you booted your machine was when you installed a new kernel. No, it was when you went on vacation…or was it? Well, it was a long time ago, anyway.

You feel underprivileged, like everybody gets to be a victim but you, as if you have nothing to talk about anymore.

Relax; you can now crash and burn with the best of them. You can run Windows and Windows applications under Linux and KDE.

WINE

WINE is supposed to stand, in its recursive Linux fashion, for *WINE Is Not an Emulator*. I think they chose the words just to be able to spell something because it certainly *is* an emulator. It emulates Windows, all flavors. I think they should call it *Winux*.

And you can use it to run windows applications under KDE, seamlessly, as demonstrated in Figure 32.1.

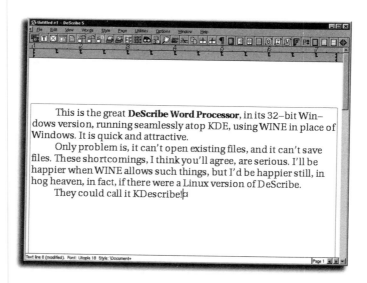

FIGURE 32.1
There is no application more lamented than the out-of-production DeScribe Word Processor, which many, including me, think was the best word processor ever written. It gets a few last gasps, though, under WINE.

You do need to be a little bit of a glutton for punishment to install and use WINE. The chief reason for this is that it is in development and when you download it (from www.winehq.com), you are warned that it will be a wonder if it works at all. With some fiddling, though, you can make it work to some extent, and if you have Windows applications that do not require you to save anything to disk, you can run them, and without a line of Microsoft code.

It is possible to go on at length about WINE, but this isn't really the place to do it. What I say about WINE now wouldn't necessarily be accurate when you read it—a couple of versions of WINE are released each month. If you do get it running on your machine, though, you might want to make icons for your favorite Windows applications. I've gone into the production of menu items and icons exhaustively already, so here's all you need to know that can be said with any certainty. The command **wine** followed by the name of the program you want to run, as in *describe*, will start the application. WINE has no desktop or file manager of its own: it's a command line application. If you have not put the fully qualified path name of the application in the PATH statement in your WINE configuration file, you will need to put it on the command line (such as `wine c:\describe32\describe` where c:\ is how you have the drives mapped in your WINE configuration file). If you don't understand any of this now, you certainly will by the time you have WINE running. The point is that the wine executable file accepts other executable files as command line options, and if you do it that way your Windows applications start seamlessly on your desktop.

The WINE configuration files are wine.conf and wine.ini and are typically located in /usr/local/etc. Like most Linux configuration files, they are plain text. Because the WINE code changes so frequently, the best help I can offer is that you need to read the documentation that comes with the version you download or received on your Linux distribution CD.

VMware: The Bad Stuff

In the summer of 1999, a company called VMware (www.vmware.com) brought out an interesting line of products that allow you to install many operating systems to run as very large, resource-gobbling applications under many other operating systems. If you have been bitten by an infected mosquito and are in the throes of delirium, you can purchase a product that will run Linux in a window in Windows. If the mosquito merely made you a little crazy, you can buy a product that allows you to run Windows—not just Windows applications, but your favorite flavor of Windows itself—in a window under Linux and the X Window System or, if you want, full screen.

> **The VMware X Server**
>
> If you are running a version of XFree86 earlier than 3.3.4 and you want to use a VMware virtual machine full screen, you need to download the XFree86 server for your video card from the VMware Web site and install it. If you are running XFree86-3.3.4 or later, you can run full-screen without the special server.

It does work. If you're willing to spring a hundred bucks for VMware (personal edition; for commercial use, it's three times that amount), and another hundred or two for Windows (price depending, of course, on version), and another hundred or so for a hard drive onto which the Windows stuff is to be placed (unless you have oodles of drive space to spare or a Windows installation already), and another hundred or so for extra memory (it grabs 32 megs for itself right off the bat and won't even talk to you if you have less than 64 megs), you can witness the admittedly amusing sight of a window on your KDE desktop, with Windows booting inside it, running a while, and, more often than anyone likes, crashing all on its own. Oh yeah, and according to VMware, if you don't have at least a 266mHz CPU, you'll need to upgrade that, too. For about the same money, you can buy a computer that already has Windows on it at a discount house. For a few dollars more you can buy a couple of network cards and a hub, and make yourself a little Samba network. You can also set up a partition and dual boot between your Linux and Windows installations. If you have a drive with Windows on it, dual booting is free.

It isn't perfect, but here is how it looks (see Figure 32.2).

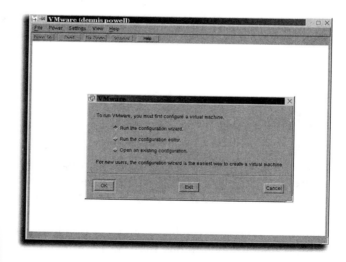

FIGURE 32.2
VMware allows you to set up virtual machines for DOS and all flavors of Windows. It offers a "Wizard," otherwise known as a sesup program, to help you configure things.

When you have a configuration done, you click the **Power On** button and watch what looks for all the world like your computer's Power-On Self Test (see Figure 32.3).

FIGURE 32.3
You can watch it check the memory it is taking from your Linux system and the rest of the boot process.

It's an amusing exercise, especially when Windows crashes and you use the **Power On** button, now the **Power Off** button, to "reboot."

To set the whole thing up, you need to download VMware, its tools, and a key that unlocks the whole affair. You get to try it out for 30 days for free. After you install VMware, you install the operating system of your choice on the virtual machine it has created. Then you can use that "machine" to install and run your Windows software.

VMware installs a daemon that starts itself when you boot Linux, so it's taking some memory even when you're not running VMware. But it does do what it is advertised to do, and seeing the famous "blue screen of death" in a window with your Linux system happily chugging right along, is something to behold. The question is whether it is worth the cost in money and system resources.

To run its sessions full screen with acceptable performance, you also need to install VMware's replacement for your XF86 server.

If you decide that it might be for you, you can install any of a number of operating systems to run under it. Because my lone Windows 95 CD had no boot disk with it, I had to install DOS and CD drivers, and then I could get to the Windows 95 setup program, but it was interesting, as you can imagine (see Figure 32.4).

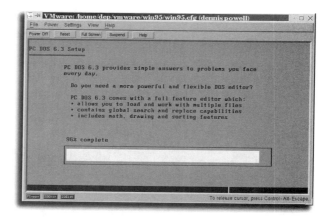

FIGURE 32.4

Watching DOS install itself into a window is a strange and amusing sight. After that came the drivers for my CD reader. Before DOS could be installed, I had to run fdisk and format from the dos floppy on what it believed to be the C: drive—a chilling event, even though I had been assured it would wipe out only the virtual drive, not my actual physical drive, which turned out to be true.

In due course, I was watching Windows 95 being installed (see Figure 32.5).

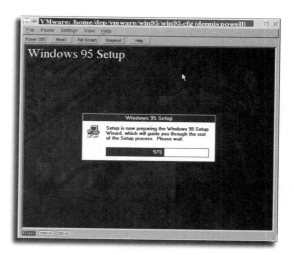

FIGURE 32.5

Note the mouse pointer. VMware has one pointer inside the window, and there is no escaping it. Nor can you use it outside that window. To do other work, you must press **Alt+Ctrl+Esc** (which normally kills an application in the X Window System), which freezes the Windows pointer and restores your Linux one. Or you can install VMware tools, which eliminate many of the initial annoyances, but don't work with anything less than Windows 95.

While VMware does allow you to run Windows in your Linux box, it will not perform miracles (see Figures 32.6 and 32.7).

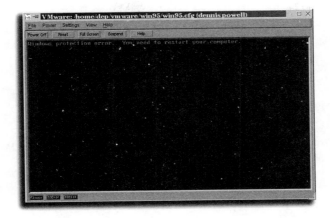

FIGURE 32.6
Windows will be Windows. Of course, Linux kept running smoothly. The VMware virtual machine needed to be rebooted, by the old Alt+Ctrl+Del.

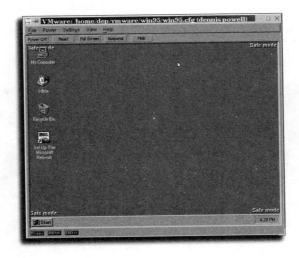

FIGURE 32.7
And when it rebooted, it was in "Safe Mode." I changed nothing, just shut it down.

After another reboot, Windows 95 seemed to be operating as advertised. Time to see whether it would install and run actual applications. Microsoft Office 97 seemed a good choice, and it did indeed install (see Figure 32.8).

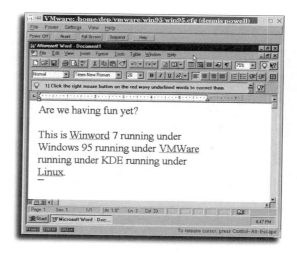

FIGURE 32.8

WinWord ran, noting that its own name as well as that—surprise!—of Linux are misspelled. But there are so many controls and things that there's scarcely any room to do any work! With a modified XF86 server, though, or the MNware tools, you can run the sessions full screen, albeit somewhat slowly, but it really gobbles up processor cycles.

There is room for comparison and amusement (see Figure 32.9).

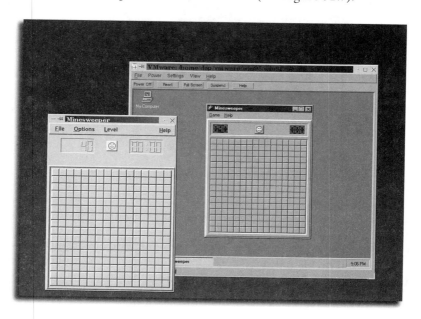

FIGURE 32.9

Your mine or mine? Both KDE and Windows 95 under VMware allow you to play Minesweeper; however, Windows definitely has a superior Solitaire game.

Depending on how elaborate you want to get into configuring the thing, it is possible to create a "network" from your VMware "machine" to the rest of your Linux system. Otherwise, to move data from the VMware system to the Linux system involves copying to floppy…or emailing yourself. Linux users tend to be very security conscious and may well balk at giving the Windows virtual machine access to much else, though there are no security problems that I've heard about.

The Windows boot is so sufficiently isolated that even its screensavers come up (see Figure 32.10).

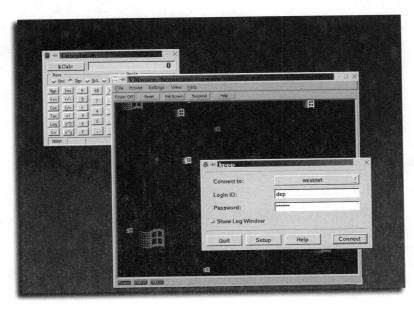

FIGURE 32.10
The Windows screensavers work, but if you leave focus in your VMware window, your KDE screensavers won't.

There *are* occasions when VMware comes in handy. We're considering a little bit of home improvement, and for that I turn to eBid 98, the industry standard construction cost estimating program, which runs only under Windows. (In the interests of full disclosure, I helped document the program, and if you run out and buy it, which I heartily recommend that you do, I get some money.) Though I didn't have the clipboard available to me, I was able to run calculations and get a sense of what some things are going to cost. (Maybe you'd better buy *two* copies of eBid, and copies of this book for everyone you know. They both make fine gifts!) It worked well (see Figure 32.11).

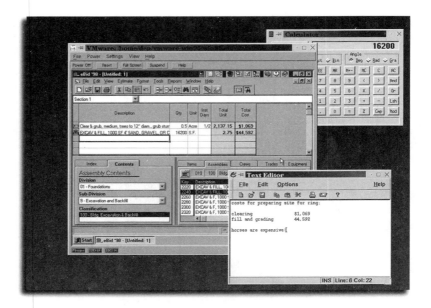

FIGURE 32.11
eBid made its calculations, and I was informed if not happy. If I were to use it regularly, though, I would probably install it with Windows 3.1 under VMware, to save system resources.

I should note that VMware and Windows 95 really take a bite out of your processor. I'm running a 400mHz processor with 1MB of L2 cache and 256MB RAM, and everything slowed more than noticeably. KTop reports that the processor is pegged. It really can be thought of as being for occasional use, only as directed. Side effects may include sluggishness, irritability, and headache.

VMware: The Good Stuff

I absolutely guarantee you that spending a day or two with VMware will cause you to think all the negative thoughts expressed previously, and all the factual statements are true. But if you hang in there and work with it a little, you'll find VMware pretty rewarding. In that respect, it's like Linux itself. And once you begin to explore its potential, VMware can knock your socks off, while leaving your boots intact. (Yes, the pun was deliberate.)

The Right Tools for the Job

First, go back to the VMware Web site (www.vmware.com) and download something called VMware Tools. Be sure to get the Windows version because you are going to install this into your Windows virtual machine (if running Windows 95 or 98, among the DOS-based versions of Windows—it won't work with Windows 3.x, NT, or 2000). At once about half your complaints will disappear. This point, I think, is not made strongly enough on the VMware page.

What do these give you? A great deal. First, your mouse pointer can now move from the VMware virtual machine to the desktop and back again. This isn't quite as smooth as it would be among native X Window System applications, but it is usable. Second, the tools include a very effective emulation of a Windows SVGA driver, meaning that you are no longer stuck with plain old VGA and can run your VMware Windows boot at any screen resolution and color depth supported by your Linux hardware (as shown in Figure 32.12).

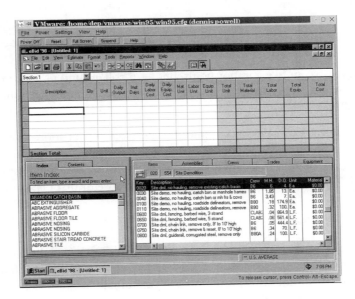

FIGURE 32.12
If you look at the portions of the Windows 95 screen visible in Figure 32.11, where VMware was running at 640×480 pixels, and compare it to the same application running here at 800×600, you'll see one of the values in installing the free VMware tools.

But I've saved the best for last: with VMware tools you can copy and paste among Linux and Windows applications and between different Windows virtual machines. When you copy something in a Windows application, it appears in Klipper. This is very cool.

Even cooler is the fact that you can create different VMware virtual machines for different operating systems. And you can even run them all at once! For instance, I made virtual machines for Windows 95, Windows 3.1, and PC-DOS 6.3.

What Won't VMware Do?

If you have all kinds of Windows games that run exciting 3D graphics, you'll have to run them in native Windows because those aren't supported in VMware yet. If you have one of those cheapo Windows-only modems or printers, VMware won't let you run them under Linux. It's a machine emulator, not software to make up for substandard hardware.

And for some reason I've been unable to figure out, it will not make a virtual machine with the otherwise excellent Caldera Open DOS (formerly DR-DOS). On two test machines it installed just fine but wouldn't boot. Too bad.

You can't run OS/2 as a guest operating system under VMware yet. But a version that supports OS/2 is in the works.

Now, this may seem like a minor point, but let it roll around in your mind for a while, as you might swirl a taste of expensive wine around on your tongue. Think of the possibilities.

Let's say that you're a Windows application developer. Your tools work perfectly well in a VMware boot, so you can write code there with no problem, and then you can test it on several different Windows platforms, all from the same machine, all without rebooting. Try *that* in native Windows! If one or more of them crashes, so what?

Maximum Safety

There's something even cooler. You can set disks (either virtual disks created in VMware or actual disks accessed through VMware) to be persistent, non-persistent, or undoable. What does this mean? A *persistent* volume behaves like a normal disk drive: you can change anything on it. You can write to it and you can delete files on it. A *non-persistent* volume behaves just like a persistent one, but no changes survive the current session. This means that if you must use one of those strange Windows mail programs that uses a proprietary format and automatically runs any executable file that is attached to a message, you can safely do so in non-persistent mode. Even if it contains a macro virus, it will do no permanent harm. Obviously, this is the con-figuration to have for examining suspect files. *Undoable mode* is like non-persistent mode except that at the end of the session you are asked if you want to save the changes made to the disk. This is a great mode for software testing: again, a way in which Linux running VMware is an ideal platform for Windows application developers.

Ever Hear of a One-Man Band? Here's a One-Machine Network

A great strength (and in some cases weakness) of VMware is the isolation of the operating systems and applications run thereunder. When you have, say, Windows 95 running in a VMware virtual machine, it is completely unaware that it is running under Linux, and Linux is unaware of it. This prevents anything that takes place in the Windows boot from corrupting the Linux file system. It's like a dangerous snake being held safely away with a long snake hook, or a scorpion in a bottle. You can, though, set up Samba shares or other networking so that you have a virtual network running on your desktop.

Making the Most of the Virtual Network

Having multiple virtual machines running at once requires more than the minimum hardware if you want decent performance (and you do). In addition to a fast processor, you need loads of memory and a big monitor and good video card. I've successfully run multiple machines with 256MB of RAM, and I wouldn't recommend anything really elaborate with much less. The reason for the hot video setup is that to have a bunch of virtual machines all chugging merrily along on your desktop and interacting over the "network" with each other, you want to run at high resolution, so that you can see all or much of the virtual machines all at once. I run at 1,024×768 pixels, which I think is just about a bare minimum.

What else can you do with VMware? You can set up a virtual machine to run an entire second version of Linux, which is a useful thing to do if you are a kernel hacker or Linux developer. The people at VMware say that a future version will accept OS/2 as a guest operating system, which will delight a multitude of users of that worthy but endangered operating system.

So yes, all those irritations mentioned in the first part of our consideration of VMware are true, but they don't eliminate the other facts: that it works at all is a demonstration of programming virtuosity. More than that, though, it allows a degree of versatility that allows it to perform functions available absolutely nowhere else. If you need to run Windows applications reliably, it actually offers improvements over a native Windows boot. If you have the horsepower to run it on your machine, it's well worth the download, but if you download it, plan on giving it a couple of days to prove itself to you. You may well decide, as I have, to keep it. Where else, after all, could you do this (see Figure 32.13)?

FIGURE 32.13

Lookee here! The late, lamented Textra word processor in a VMware DOS boot, a Windows 95 boot with applications running, and even that epitome of advanced user interface design, Microsoft Bob, in a Windows 3.1 virtual machine—all running at the same time atop KDE in a Caldera OpenLinux session. The sheer nerd value boggles the mind!

Running a Windows application under VMware involves getting VMware started—type **vmware** in a console window and select the virtual machine you want to use—after which VMware boots the version of DOS or Windows you selected in a window. From there, you start and use the application in exactly the same way that you would use it on a standalone Windows machine.

Windows Under dosemu

Users have been able to run the OS/2 version of Windows 3.0 or 3.1, Win-OS/2, under dosemu. This requires that you have Win-OS/2, and that it be installed on a drive you can read from dosemu. You can then change to the drive containing Win-OS/2 and, by typing **win** or **win.com**, start a Windows session whence you can run your applications. This is said to work fairly reliably. If you can do it at all, you can do it in a terminal window under KDE.

To get Win-OS/2, you need to purchase a copy of OS/2, if you can find one, and install it on a drive partition to which you have at least read access under your Linux kernel. You can then copy the contents of your Win-OS/2 directory to your Linux drive, to the virtual C: of your dosemu setup, or, if you have compiled FAT read-write support into your kernel and have installed OS/2 onto a FAT partition, you won't need to copy it at all. You must remember to mount that partition, either through an /etc/fstab entry for automounting or manually. If you have done this and are lucky, you will be able to start dosemu, give the fully qualified path and command to the Win-OS/2 directory, and run win.com. This is to say that all this is experimental and, to use a common newsgroup term, *YMMV:* your mileage may vary.

All in all, it generally makes sense to run Linux applications under KDE, and if Windows applications appeal to you, to run Windows for them, and to return to Linux and KDE when security and stability are paramount. It really is easy to set up a dual-boot system, and if you need to run both at once, then two computers, networked or not, are the sensible solution, at least until WINE is much further along.

Unless, of course, you merely want to look once again at an old and beloved application and sigh over what might have been.

part

VII

PROGRAMS THAT EXTEND THE POWER OF KDE

chapter

33

Faxing from KDE

When even an experienced computer user comes to Linux and KDE, one of the areas of greatest culture shock occurs when that person realizes that he can accomplish relatively few commonplace tasks by the quick downloading and installation of a program. Setting up a printer, for instance, can be relatively simple or it can be an anguishing and frustrating expenditure of hours. It is certainly not like anything with which the user is familiar, unless the user remembers fondly the days in which computers arrived with blank hard drives and a box of DOS disks (which, actually, I do). If there are "wizards" involved, they are the user and those online to whom the user turns for help.

This little prologue is especially appropriate when it comes to fax programs. You will not be downloading a fax program, installing it, and five minutes later be sending and receiving faxes. It does not, alas, work that way or even close to it.

This is not to say that faxing from Linux is impossible or even very difficult, but it is a complicated process to set up. Like most things Linux, though, once you set it up, it is easy to use and all but bulletproof.

Let's begin with a quick survey of the three most popular fax programs for Linux, and then look at the ways in which you can integrate them into KDE.

Efax: An Easy Standalone Program

If you are running one machine with one modem, no network, no bells and whistles, Efax is well worth your attention. You can get it at casas.ee.ubc.ca/efax/ in source. Additionally, many Linux distributors have binaries in either their standard distributions or in the /contrib directories at their ftp sites. You can get at it through a shell script, fax, that sends and receives facsimile transmissions from Class 1, Class 2, and Class 2.0 fax modems. (Yes, there is a difference, and an important one, between Class 2 and Class 2.0.) When you install it, it is a command-line program into which you type such information as the files to be faxed and the telephone number to which they are to be faxed.

Mgetty+Sendfax: You May Already Have It

If you have, say, Caldera OpenLinux, you have mgetty+sendfax, a combination of programs that allows the sending and receiving of facsimile transmissions through a Class 2 fax modem. If it was not automatically installed when you installed the distribution, you might want to search the CD thoroughly to see if it's there because it probably is.

What you may not have is a Class 2 fax modem. Many, indeed most, fax modems support Class 1, and U.S. Robotics (now 3Com) Courier modems support Class 2.0 (and Class 1), but not Class 2. (Class 1 offloads much of the work to the main processor, and a fax modem that doesn't support Class 1 uses some proprietary format. Good luck in finding Linux software for it because it might as well be a Winmodem for fax purposes.)

If you have a Class 2 fax modem, which is possible, and you have the software, which is likely, you can use mgetty+sendfax for the faxing duties of all users on your machine. It, too, is a command line program.

Hylafax: Industrial-Strength Faxing

If there is a Linux standard fax program, a big gun in the Linux fax world, it is Hylafax, which you can get in source and compiled binaries at www.hylafax.org. It is a monster program in the good sense of the word: if you have 100 machines set up, all networked together, with a dedicated fax server, Hylafax is the program you want. But if you have one machine and send and receive a lot of faxes over a single modem that you use for other things such as collecting email and snagging the latest KDE apps off the Web or an ftp site, Hylafax is not ridiculous overkill.

I must note that I have never been able to get Hylafax to compile on my machine, so when I've used it, it's been through the good work of someone whose competence exceeds my own and who was kind enough to compile it and make the package available. I mention this not out of a desire to confess this particular shortcoming but instead to warn away those who are new to building software from source. Hylafax is not the best possible first project. (If you want a first project, look at all the things earlier in this book that are easy to compile.) Chances are that you can download an RPM or DEB of the current Hylafax from the ftp site of your Linux distributor.

It supports all three fax modem classes, and, like the others, it is a command-line program.

Using These Fax Apps Under KDE

Why would a book about KDE have a chapter that begins with a couple of pages about console fax programs? I thought you would never ask. Because KDE has a way to free you from the command line with all three of these, silly!

That method is KSendFax. You can find it at the KDE ftp site or any of its mirrors, in the /unstable/apps/comm directory. In my experience it's perfectly stable, but the KDE folk are exceptionally discriminating in this regard. Yes, you will have to compile it yourself, but doing so is easy. Full instructions are in the tarball, and if you've ever compiled another KDE application, the instructions are pretty much the same.

SEE ALSO

➤ *Those instructions are detailed as well on page 413.*

KSendFax is really neat because it acts as a graphical front end to all of the command line console applications mentioned above. (If it excites you to do so, you can run any of them from a Konsole or kvt window as well.) It also offers some little niceties like a phone book, so you don't have to type in the phone number every time (and listen to some poor person say "Hello? Hello?" to fax screech if you make a typo in the number).

When you have compiled KSendFax, installed it, and started it, you should see a dialog box like the one in Figure 33.1.

FIGURE 33.1
It seems a little familiar and a little obscure, but once you get the hang of KSendFax, it's easy.

To begin, you need to make sure that the commands that KSendFax issues are correct for your fax program. You do this through **Options**, **Preferences** (see Figure 33.2).

FIGURE 33.2
Crucial to successful operation of KSendFax is Send Fax, a command line appropriate for your fax software.

Fortunately, in the course of installing your fax program, you are likely to have tested it. The line you used to get it to work from the command line is the line you should use here, with the variables as specified. Command lines that work and are a good place to start are

Hylafax `sendfax -n -h '@@Host' -c '@@Comment' -x '@@Enterprise' -d '@@Name'@'@@Phone' '@@FName'`

mgetty+sendfax `faxspool -F 'My Name' '@@Phone' '@@FName'`

Efax `fax send '@@Phone' '@@FName'`

These are enough to get you going, but you then have to enter all the information for each call in the KSendFax screen each time you use it. It would be helpful to have a phonebook of frequently used fax numbers. You can make one, but it is a little tricky. By default, KSendFax creates a ~/.phonebook file, but nothing is in it.

If, however, you enter the information in KSendFax and click on **Phonebook**, **Add**, the information is stored there and then displayed in the Phonebook window at the bottom of the KSendFax screen, shown in Figure 33.3.

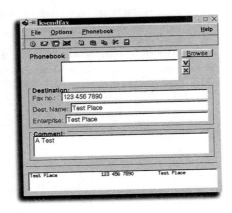

FIGURE 33.3
When you enter information about a particular fax destination and select **Phonebook**, **Add**, it's added to the phonebook and appears in the phonebook list (in this illustration containing just the one item) at the bottom of the dialog box.

Now, when it comes to sending faxes, KSendFax can be most confusing, which is something that is likely to change in later versions. To select a file to fax, use the **Browse** button or open a KFM window and drag the file to the nameless box beneath the Phonebook text box. It now appears in the Phonebook text box. If you click on the downward-pointing arrow button beneath the **Browse** button, it is added to the list of files to be faxed. It does not become the phonebook (see Figure 33.4).

FIGURE 33.4
To add a file to be faxed, **Browse** for it or drag and drop it from a KFM window and click the down arrow beneath the **Browse** button. To remove a file from the fax queue, highlight it and click the **X** button.

Additional features are associated with the individual fax programs that you can enable in KSendFax. To do this, consult the fax program's documentation and the KSendFax documentation, which is likely to be a later version than the one illustrated here because it is very much a work in progress.

In the version current at the time of writing, you select the file(s) to be faxed, select or type in the phone number, and click on **File > Send**. That's all there is to it, once you've configured it for your fax application.

chapter 34

Two Non-KDE Programs You Must Have

A Good Text Editor

Midnight Commander

Other Console Things You Should Know

You need to learn two things right now. The first is that only if you are the luckiest person in the world will you never be in a situation where you need to resort to Linux's console mode to solve some problem. The second is that you are not the luckiest person in the world.

Console mode does you no good if you don't have a couple of essential programs that allow you to fix things that may be broken. They are a good text editor with which you are totally proficient and Midnight Commander, the console file manager.

There will be a few illustrations in this chapter, but they won't be entirely accurate. In order to make the screenshots, it's necessary to run the programs in a terminal window, but when you have to resort to these programs, it will be in a full-screen, text-mode console session. Things won't be quite as pretty, and you will very likely be under considerable stress. It's important that you already know how to use these applications. Take a little time to learn them. The GUI proponents notwithstanding, text mode is not a mysterious and terrible place. You'll be surprised at just how comfortable and easy to use the console can be.

A Good Text Editor

If you are very dedicated, you will learn a program called vi. It is a text editor. Many people love it, and (I suspect) even more hate it. It is not intuitive and easy to use. Everyone agrees on one thing that vi has in its favor: it is installed on just about every Linux machine in the world (the lone exception that I know about is my production machine). If you are in a position where you will be helping others with their Linux installations, you have no choice other than to learn vi because sooner or later you will need to use it. So if you have the time, the thing to do is learn vi. (And if you know someone who is a vi whiz, have that person over, pay for the pizza and beer, and get a vi lesson. It's probably the best way to learn it.)

Are there alternatives to vi? You betcha!

After vi, the text editor that is probably most commonly found on Linux machines is pico. It is the editor typically used in the pine console mode mail program and is even included in some pine packages. There is a good chance that you already have pico installed. To find out, open a console window, type `pico`, and press **Enter**. If it's there, you'll see what you see in Figure 34.1. If you don't, log on to www.freshmeat.org and do a search for the current version, download and install it, and be happy.

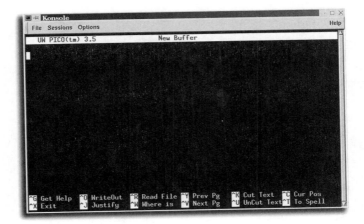

FIGURE 34.1
If you used computer BBS systems back in the good old days, you probably remember this interface because pico was the message editor on many of them.

Using pico is pretty simple. To edit a file, simply type `pico` followed by the filename (fully qualified if you're not in the directory containing the file) and press **Enter**. If you are editing a system configuration file, which is what you'll be doing when you resort to it for emergency use, chances are you'll need to log in as root (or su root) first because otherwise you won't be able to save the changes you make. This is something obvious now, but easily overlooked in time of panic. How might you use pico in an emergency? Well, you might have just upgraded your kernel but forgotten to add the new kernel to /etc/lilo.conf and run /sbin/lilo. So you boot into single user mode to make the repair (see Figure 34.2). (Consult your Linux distribution's documentation for the means of booting in to single-user mode. Often, it's by typing `linux-single` at the boot prompt at startup.)

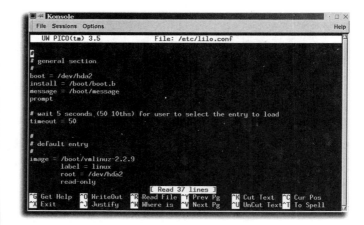

FIGURE 34.2
To fix /etc/lilo.conf, just type **pico   /etc/lilo.conf** (as root) at the command line and press **Enter**. To save your changes, press **Ctrl+O**. To exit the program, press **Ctrl+X**.

Likewise, you can fix an errant /etc/XF86Config and a multitude of other configuration files. The time to learn what you need to know about pico (or vi, if that's your choice), though, is now, when you have time to get comfortable with it.

You may well choose another text editor. Emacs is a popular choice, though I have noted that Emacs is a religion, so fervently is it argued about.. If you want to use it, take a month off and learn it. Bear in mind that the Emacs you get at the command line looks nothing at all like the XEmacs you typically get when you type **emacs** at a terminal command line (see Figure 34.3).

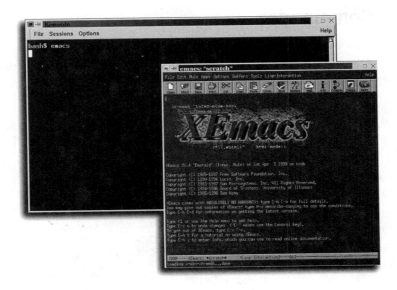

FIGURE 34.3
If you're comfortable using XEmacs, you may be surprised and perhaps terrified when you type **emacs** at a non-graphical text console and get something that looks entirely different. Typing **emacs** at a console window command line starts not Emacs but XEmacs if you have it installed. XEmacs has menus and icons; Emacs is much starker.

You can use several Linux text editors from the command line. If you don't have one you like, feel free to poke around the Web and find one that pleases you…or write one yourself. Bear in mind that if you get one that runs only under the X Window System, you have not accomplished your goal. Whichever editor you choose, learn it thoroughly *before* you need it. Almost all Linux problems are the result of misconfiguration, and sooner or later your text editor will save you. Learn how to load a configuration file into your editor of choice, how to edit it, and how to save the changes. This, of course, means that you have to learn some things about Linux so you'll know which configuration file is the likely suspect if something goes wrong.

Midnight Commander

Running Linux without having Midnight Commander installed is walking a tight-rope without a net. It is such an essential program that KDE's Konsole actually lists it as a menu item. But it is at the command line where it will rescue you in time of need.

First thing, let's find out whether you already have it installed. Open a terminal window and, at the prompt, type mc and press **Enter**. If it's installed, you'll see what is shown in Figure 34.4.

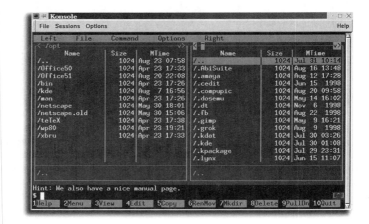

FIGURE 34.4

There's not much you can do with Midnight Commander that you can't do from the command line, if you've memorized the Linux file manipulation command-line options, which few people have. It doesn't hurt to learn them, though, unless you use them all the time it's difficult to maintain proficiency. I certainly don't.

Midnight Commander offers a command line at the next line to the bottom of its screen, but it's those numbered functions on the bottom line that give it its power. The numbers are for the function keys on your keyboard, so to exit you press **F10** instead of typing 10. If you have gpm installed for console-mode mouse support, Midnight Commander utilizes point-and-click even in a pure console. If not, you use the arrow keys and the **Enter** key to navigate, and the **Tab** key to switch from one side to the other.

When do you need Midnight Commander? One area where I use it all the time is in making a backup of KDE when I'm upgrading. As root, I copy my entire KDE direc-tory to a nice, safe place elsewhere. Then if the upgrade blows up, as sometimes happens, and I can't start the new KDE, I can log in to the console as root, start Midnight Commander, use it to delete the new KDE and to copy back the old one. I will go into this at length in the next chapter.

The reason Midnight Commander is so good for this—and the reason KFM isn't—is that Midnight Commander preserves permissions on the files it copies. KFM doesn't always, and that means a KDE that when copied back will work only if you're root. KDE contains hundreds of files, and you have no idea what the permissions are for them. Backing up and restoring KDE with KFM is a useless exercise.

All you need to do is pick the source file or directory in the left listing and the target directory in the right listing, and then press **F5**. A dialog box appears that makes sure you have made both selections properly. The file or directory is copied.

If you do not have Midnight Commander, get it. Your Linux distribution probably contains it somewhere on its CD; if it doesn't, check the /contrib directory of your Linux distributor's ftp site. If it's not there, go to `ftp://ftp.gnome.org/pub/` `GNOME/sources/mc/`. No, I do not know how Midnight Commander became associated with the Gnome project, but I do know that Midnight Commander is very easy to compile for your system, in the event that you cannot find a binary that works. The source tarball contains instructions.

Midnight Commander can perform a multitude of other tasks, though its management of files in a console session makes it an essential application. No other console application comes close to its utility and ease of use.

Other Console Things You Should Know

Albert Einstein supposedly remarked that he never memorized anything that he could find in a book. I do not know that he ever said this, but if he did it was not the brightest of observations: instead of remembering the information, he had to remember the book in which the information was located. There are times when you don't want to go poking around in books looking for a command line option that will get you out of the trouble that you have just created for yourself. There are a few command-line commands and options that it is a *very* good idea for you to memorize. Each of these command-line utilities has a man page, so if you remember the name of the command, you can get instructions for it even in a full console session by typing `man` *command*. To get out of the man session, type `q`.

RPM

There are times when you install an RPM package and, after doing so, you discover that you've broken something, either the program you've upgraded or another program (or programs) that rely on it. How do you uninstall the new RPM and restore things to their previous state? If you know the RPM command line options, you'll be able to bring this all about, if the previous installation of whatever you upgraded was from an RPM. In any case, knowing how to handle an RPM from the command line is an important skill. (The same holds true for the DEB file manipulation tool, dpkg, if you are using Debian Linux.)

TAR

The command-line options for the Tape ARchive command (which usually has nothing to do with tapes at all) will be critically important to you sooner or later. Learn them, and keep proficiency by using them from time to time.

GZIP, GUNZIP, and BZIP2

You'll regularly encounter these compression programs in Linux. The one problem with all the nice package managers that exist is that they can insulate you from having to learn these commands, which is fine unless you're in a bind and need to dig into something from the command line.

What's "Uncompress"?

From time to time you will encounter a program that in the course of compiling or some other operation will fail with the announcement that it could not find a file called "uncompress". `uncompress` is a UNIX command that is not usually used in Linux. What do you do?

Well, you're in luck. Gunzip, which you do have installed, is compatible with uncompress. Of course, the program that just blew up doesn't know that, so you need to give it some help.

Perhaps you can dive into the script or source that is calling `uncompress` and change it to `gunzip`, but that is a lot of trouble and only works for this one application. There's an easier and better way: Make a symbolic link from /bin/gunzip to /bin/uncompress. Then you'll never see this error message again.

A quick and easy way to make a link is to open KFM and drag gunzip into its directory, the equivalent of copying it onto itself. You'll be asked what you'd like to do, which is make a link named uncompress.

Alternatively, at the command line, change to /bin and do the following:

```
ln -s gunzip uncompress
```

It is not, of course, possible to know too many Linux command-line commands and options. If anyone in the world knows them all, I have not heard of that person. But if you learn the few listed above plus the few needed for maneuvering in the file system—plus maintain proficiency with your text editor and Midnight Commander— you can feel confident that you're well equipped for the majority of situations you're likely to encounter.

ON THE LEADING EDGE
WITH KDE

chapter

35

Upgrading to the Latest KDE Version

Unlike most other GUIs for the PC, and like most Linux applications, KDE is constantly being improved. To upgrade, though, you do not install a "fix pack" or something incremental; you have to install a whole new version if you want to upgrade the core distribution or the applications it contains. You can, of course, upgrade individual applications not part of the core package without updating the whole shebang. That is, unless the app you can't live without requires a new KDE, which can be found in the documentation of the application's source code. You should always read that documentation anyway, though many of us have fallen into the bad habit of doing so only if a program fails to compile or run.

The most time-consuming part of this is often the download. All of the KDE packages, together, can run to 20MB or more. Downloading can take a while.

Then, depending on the form in which you got your new KDE, upgrading is easy and can be quick. (If you roll your own, compiling can take several hours.)

We are now in an era, though, in which upgrading KDE is a little more complicated than it has ever been before, and can be perilous. For the first time, it's possible to really make a mess of things—believe me, because I've done it—unless you know exactly what you're doing. After you've read this chapter, you will.

Getting the Right Version

There now exist various incarnations of two major versions of KDE. Unless you are reading this late in 2000 or later, your distribution came with a variation of KDE Version 1. The final version in this series is KDE 1.2. KDE is built atop the QT libraries (www.troll.no/). All 1.X versions of KDE work with QT-1.42 or QT-1.44. Unfortunately, QT-1.4X is becoming more difficult to find. If you have QT-1.44, hang onto it!

But KDE 2.0 is beginning to exist (as I write this, and the situation will get worse, which is to say more complicated for the upgrader). KDE 2.0 is in many respects incompatible with KDE 1.X. KDE 2.0 requires QT-2.0 or better; KDE 1.X will *not* work with QT-2.0 or better. (Recipes under development will allow applications based on QT-1.4x to run on a system running KDE-2.0 and QT-2.x. These are subtle, not unlike the ways of allowing a Linux system to run both libc5 and glibc applications. Once a solid KDE-2.0 distribution is finalized, a document is certain to be made available to make the peaceful coexistence of both QTs easier.)

This means that you can now download and compile things that absolutely refuse to live together. Life used to be simpler.

If you want merely to upgrade your KDE 1.X to the latest KDE 1.X, as long as you make sure you're downloading the right KDE distribution, you're in good shape. You probably don't have to upgrade your QT unless you have a very old Linux installation, in which case you want QT-1.44 as well.

For the next little while, we are proceeding as if this is what you have in mind; we'll get to fiddling around with KDE 2.0 in a page or two.

Back Up Your Existing KDE, If You Can

Any time you're upgrading something as big and complicated as KDE, there is a chance that something will go wrong. If it were a big package that wasn't at the very heart of your system, StarOffice, say, you could always go online and try to get help sorting it out. If your KDE installation blows up, you're left without a way to get online to try to figure it out. (This is unless you're very good at the Linux console. We mustn't forget that people were going online with Linux long before there were X Window System tools for that purpose, but a trashed KDE installation isn't the best circumstance under which to begin this course of study). So before you do anything, back up your existing KDE.

If You're Running Red Hat Linux

Time to vent a little anger here. The Red Hat Linux 6.0 distribution plops KDE down in /usr. The things one would find in, say, /opt/kde/lib in another installation are in plain old /usr/lib in Red Hat 6.0. The things normally found in /opt/kde/bin are, in Red Hat 6.0, in /usr/bin.

Why does this matter? Because if you have Red Hat 6.0, there is no way to back up your current installation. If something goes wrong, you're out of luck or forced to use Gnome, which, if your KDE installation is really trashed, may actually be more reliable. I've heard all the supposed reasons for putting KDE in /usr, and none of 'em trumps the fact that an ability to back up your desktop is very important, and they've made it so that you can't. If you are a Red Hat 6.0 user and you have not extensively modified your KDE (by, for instance, compiling and adding new programs), I heartily recommend that you download new RPMS from `ftp://ftp.kde.org`. After you've done that, remove all the Red Hat-supplied KDE RPMs, and then install the ones you downloaded. KDE is now in /opt/kde where it belongs.

Now, for this to work, you need to change the KDE path listed in /etc/profile.d/kde.sh. Then you can operate like everybody else and back up your KDE when you upgrade. It's worth the trouble. Otherwise, you can fall back on the power of prayer, which has been effective many times over thousands of years, though in no KDE installations that I know of.

Making your backup is easy…if you use Midnight Commander. *Do not use KFM!* KFM changes the permissions on the KDE files, and you end up with a backup that's good for nothing except the consumption of storage space. Midnight Commander preserves permissions.

Here's how you do it.

As root, or su root, start Midnight Commander (by typing mc), which at this point you can do in a Konsole window if you want. Navigate so that the left column lists your KDE directory and the right column lists the directory into which you want to copy it (see Figure 35.1).

FIGURE 35.1
Notice that the KDE directory is highlighted; in this case, I'll copy it to /usr/local.

Now, press **F5** and you'll be treated to the dialog box shown in Figure 35.2.

FIGURE 35.2
Make sure that the paths are correct and make doubly sure that the box labeled **preserve Attributes** is checked. Then click **OK**, or press the letter **O**.

Soon, your entire KDE directory is being copied (see Figure 35.3).

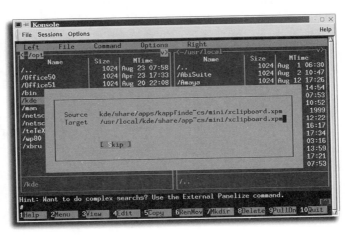

FIGURE 35.3
As you watch the copying process, you're likely to marvel at the complexity of KDE. A lot of people have done a lot of work to make this desktop available.

And after a minute or two, your copy is safely tucked away (see Figure 35.4).

FIGURE 35.4

And there it is, safe in /usr/local. It's a good idea to keep the last version backed up pretty much all the time, just in case a problem arises after the new version has been used for a while. If you want to save disk space, you can always make a tarball and either gzip or bzip2 it, and delete the original backup directory.

How can you have two full copies of it without the system becoming confused? Easy: your KDE environment variable is still set to the original installation. Now, if something goes wrong, you can either delete the corrupted KDE directory—this time using Midnight Commander as root in a full console screen—or change your KDE environment variable to point to the one in /usr/local. Then you can sort out what went wrong. Pretty nifty, eh?

The question of course arises: Why bother? KDE comes in tarballs or RPM or DEB packages, so replacing an installation is easy, even if you didn't save to the old one, right?

Well, no, as Figure 35.5 demonstrates.

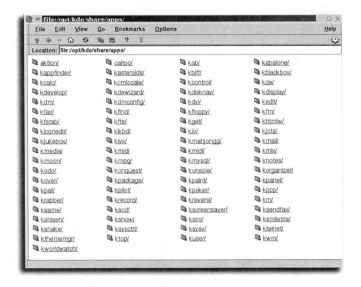

FIGURE 35.5
Compare this /opt/kde/share/apps directory to one after a fresh KDE install. You'll notice that many, many applications not in the KDE core distribution are installed into the KDE directory. Installing them all over again would be no fun at all. That's why backing up your working KDE installation is so important.

After you have everything backed up, you can safely begin your upgrade.

Making the (Up)Grade

Now it's simply a matter of installing your new KDE as described in Chapter 1, "Installing KDE." You can safely install over an existing installation, so long as the major version number is the same: any 1.X installs safely over an older 1.X. Your user configuration is undisturbed, though when you start again as a user, KDE may ask you if you want new template files, which you do. (If it doesn't, it only means that they haven't changed them in the new version.)

It may be a while before you notice the changes. For instance, in KDE 1.2, a number of pretty high-color icons have been added, which provide a pleasant surprise when you get an attachment in KMail, often the first place they get discovered.

Going to KDE 2.0

Upgrading to KDE 2.0 is not as simple a task because your configuration files, QT, and, really, everything change. As I write this, KDE 2.0 hasn't been released, but it is well enough along that some people are using it productively. As you read this, it is something worth looking at, especially if you like living on the bleeding edge.

As before, it's a good idea to make a backup of your existing KDE. You also want to make a backup of your ~/.kde directory (which is actually a good thing to do anyway, lest a wayward theme or something cause it to become corrupted). Don't erase your old QT source, RPMs, or DEBs just yet, either.

For KDE 2.0 you certainly need to install a new version of Mico (2.2.7 or better), which you can get at `http://diamant.vsb.cs.uni-frankfurt.de/~mico/`. And you need, of course, to install the new QT. I highly recommend installing everything QT of the version you select: development and doc packages, any sample or demonstration packages, the works. These are essential if you plan on doing any KDE development, and they are very helpful as new applications appear that may require some of what they contain. It's instructive, too, to look in the /examples subdirectory of your QT directory, no matter what version you have, to get a sense of the blocks from which KDE is built.

Beyond that, I can offer no help at this point. Fortunately, you don't really need my help. Instructions for handling the latest KDE version can be found at `www.kde.org`. At the same time, you can give the latest code of KOffice a try.

Snapshots

Each day, the latest code for the latest version of KDE (code that in many cases was altered that very day) is available for download in the /unstable/snapshots directory of your nearby KDE ftp mirror. This is unsupported source code, but it doesn't take much to get the hang of compiling and installing it. Back up your working KDE, even if it's just yesterday's snapshots, first. And bear in mind that these are for KDE 2.0 (or, after the 2.0 release, 2.01), so if you are using KDE 1.X you have to make some nontrivial upgrades that will break your existing installation.

Speaking of snapshots...

Just to whet your appetite, here is a screenshot of a very early version of KDE 2.0 (see Figure 35.6). The shot was posted to the KDE Web site, and I think it's the prettiest thing I ever did see on a computer screen.

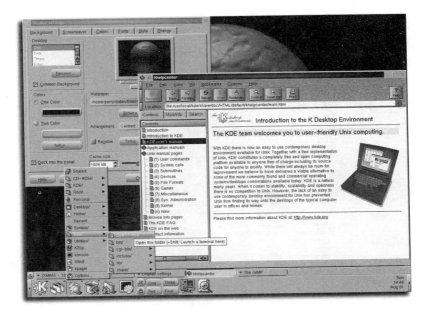

FIGURE 35.6
The shape of things to come (to me, as I write this) and already available (to you, as you read it). This isn't to say that you should drop everything and upgrade. Make sure you can do everything in 2.0 that you're doing in the stable and robust KDE 1.X first.

And as long as we're here, let's take a peek at KWord, the word processor in KOffice (see Figure 35.7).

So even if upgrading isn't something you feel up to just yet, you can see that sooner or later the urge will be overpowering. As long as you're prepared and have made arrangements to back out in case of disaster, go right ahead!

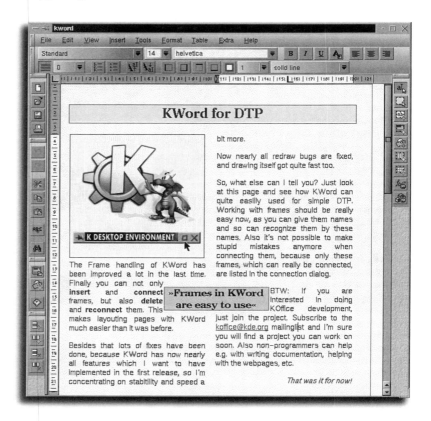

FIGURE 35.7
It's just a screenshot, but KWord looks as if it will offer a lot of power and flexibility. KOffice development includes a spreadsheet, presentation and graphics programs, and more—and all designed to be able to communicate with each other.

chapter
36

Programming for KDE

This chapter may seem a little bit confused, but it is because we're at a slightly confusing time in the course of KDE development. The installed base of KDE is of 1.0, 1.1, 1.1.1, and 1.1.2, but KDE 2.0 will take an increasing bite as time goes on, which isn't to say that the 1.X base will disappear anytime soon. Something that solid doesn't just dry up and blow away, and in some respects the two versions are incompatible.

What's more, one of the coolest applications for KDE, an Integrated Development Environment called KDevelop, is and for the foreseeable future shall remain a KDE 1.X application, using the QT-1.4X libraries and associated files. Meanwhile, there is the KDE software development kit, kdesdk, which requires QT-2.0 and therefore KDE 2.0. What to do?

If you're an experienced C++ developer, you do whatever you feel like doing, using your favorite tools and not relying on me for any advice. (And if you're an experienced C++ developer, I recommend that you ignore any advice I may offer because you know more about it than I do!)

The best information is that if you have both the QT-1.4X and the QT-2.0 libraries installed, as well as the KDE libraries for both 1.x and 2.x, and you have your library paths properly configured, you can continue to use KDE 1.X applications under KDE 2.0. This is likely to be the state of affairs for some time, perhaps forever: Some very useful little KDE 1.X applications will probably never be ported to KDE 2.0. As this all gets sorted out, you can find instructions on the KDE home page, www.kde.org.

In any event, this chapter is not designed to teach you how to write KDE applications. Instead, it is aimed at encouraging you to do so, at showing you where to get the tools you need, and (in case you don't plan on writing your own code) at demonstrating how even we mere users can dive right in and apply the occasional hack, fix, or test code.

Making a Simple Hack in Code

The most fundamental "development project" you might undertake as a user is in response to some little problem that arises and a proffered fix. Let me give you an example.

In KDE 1.X, the default paper size in printing is A4, which is the European standard. This is fine in Europe, but in places where Letter (8 1/2" × 11") is the standard size, it's another setting you need to make every time you want to print. Saving settings in, say, KFM does not save this particular setting: You need to hard-code it. This means that somewhere in the vastness of the KDE source code a value must be changed to make Letter the default. But where?

Learning C++ and going through the code line by line would be one possibility, but this is like trying to figure out who owns a phone number by reading down the numbers column in the phone book. Being fundamentally lazy, I posted a question on the KDE list and, within a day, had this answer from Stephan Goetter, one of the KDE developers:

"The function must be called before `printer.setup(0)`. So now, (kde-1.1.2-cvs 3 days old) it's line 1330. But it's possible this changes, up to 1.1.2-Release." It didn't.

```
void KHTMLWidget::print()
{
float scalers[] = { 1.1, 1.0, 0.9, 0.75, 0.6, 0.4 };
QPrinter printer;
---------->printer.setPageSize(QPrinter::Letter);
if ( printer.setup( 0 ) ) "
```

This is useful information because, in earlier correspondence, I had learned that the file in which this is set is kdelibs/khtmlw/html.cpp. This is, mind you, in the source code. So, opening the latest source in an editor, I went to line 1330 (see Figure 36.1).

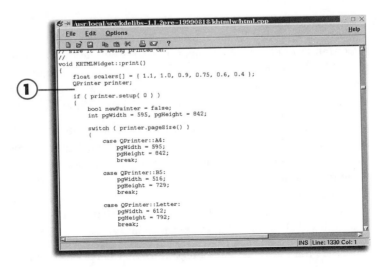

FIGURE 36.1
Looking at the source code, I can see what Stephan means. The lines he quoted are all there, except the one toward which he made the little arrow in his note to me.

① Line 1330 is blank.

As I look at the source, I see that most of the lines he quoted to me already exist, and that line 1330 is blank. So I insert the missing line there (see Figure 36.2).

```
// size it is being printed on.
//
void KHTMLWidget::print()
{
    float scalers[] = { 1.1, 1.0, 0.9, 0.75, 0.6, 0.4 };
    QPrinter printer;
    printer.setPageSize(QPrinter::Letter);
    if ( printer.setup( 0 ) )
    {
        bool newPainter = false;
        int pgWidth = 595, pgHeight = 842;

        switch ( printer.pageSize() )
        {
            case QPrinter::A4:
                pgWidth = 595;
                pgHeight = 842;
                break;

            case QPrinter::B5:
                pgWidth = 516;
                pgHeight = 729;
                break;

            case QPrinter::Letter:
                pgWidth = 612;
                pgHeight = 792;
                break;
```

FIGURE 36.2
The new line is added. Now all I need to do is recompile and reinstall the kdelibs/khtmlw/ subdirectory, though for safety I'll recompile all of kdelibs.

① Line 1330, with Stephan's suggestion added.

After this, as root (and in full console mode, not with KDE running) I change to /usr/local/src/kdelibs. Because I've already made the libs once, I type `make clean` to remove the previously compiled files, `make all` to rebuild the files, and `make install` to install them in my KDE directory. (I didn't need to run `./configure` again.)

Now, Stephan could have simply told me to insert the appropriate line at 1330 in the source file, but, as he noted, line 1330 is where the change needed to be made in the daily source snapshot of a given date, and could change. By providing the lines before and after the one to be added, he gave me—and now, you—enough information that it's possible to do a text search and find the right place, even if the line numbers changed before the release of the final code. This means that even if it's changed in some later version, I will always be able to set the default paper size to Letter.

It is really even easier than it looks here, and I think that here it looks pretty easy. Suffice it to say that it took more time to describe than it did to do. Of course, the most sensible thing of all is to make the change when upgrading KDE, so you only have to compile the whole business once.

There are variations on this theme. By looking in the code in that part of the file, you can learn what paper sizes are supported so that if, for instance, you want Legal to be the default paper size, you can learn what it's called by the program and change it so that the default is Legal.

After you've done this, you can rightly call yourself a hacker. Okay, not all that much of a hacker, but you have hacked source code to bring about a desired effect. And yes, it's a pretty good feeling, and it's a start. You have gained a valuable skill. If there's a problem, you post a question about it ,and you are offered a hack to try out, now you can. This skill is useful not just to you because sometimes the developer is asking you to test code to solve a problem that others may have encountered as well. When you can test the code and report back that it solved or failed to solve the problem, you're doing a service to the whole KDE project. If the hack works and fixes a malfunction, there's a good chance it will be included in the next release of KDE.

Hackers Are Good

If you listen to the television news, where studied ignorance of computers is displayed daily, you may think that "hacker" is a pejorative term. If you get your knowledge from within the computer world, though, you'll know that it's not. A "hack" used to be the term at Massachusetts Institute of Technology for a really clever practical joke. It was adopted at the MIT computer science department as a really clever modification of computer code, which is what it is, and all that it is. Those who can do this are *hackers*. People who break into other people's computers are *criminals*. There will probably be a term, too, for broadcast reporters who cover the computer world competently, should the need ever arise.

From here, it's just one step, albeit a long one, to finding and fixing problems all on your own. This isn't an easy step to make, but KDE does make it easier through a wonderful program that has just joined the KDE core distribution.

KDevelop

Beginning with KDE 1.1.2, an Integrated Development Environment, KDevelop, is included in the basic KDE distribution. It can make your life easier in a number of ways (see Figure 36.3).

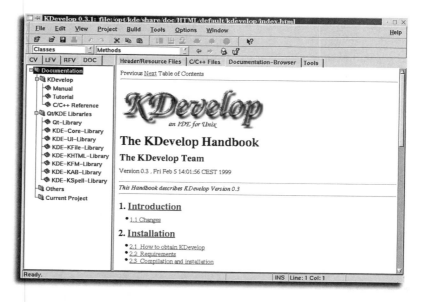

FIGURE 36.3
KDevelop makes writing applications not easy but easier, in much the same way that a word processor makes writing prose not easy but easier.

Now, even if you do not write code and have no plans to write code, KDevelop is still a good thing to have around because it allows you to learn a great deal about KDE, about how applications are written for Linux, and about programming in general. It is heavily documented, and there is even greater documentation available for download, including a long and detailed manual on the C and C++ programming languages (see Figure 36.4).

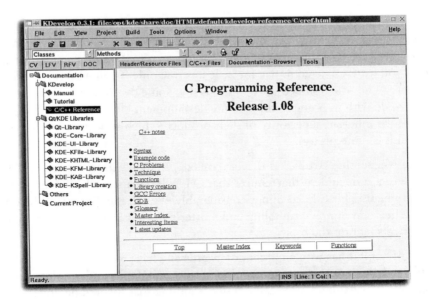

FIGURE 36.4
If learning, or learning about, C and C++ programming interests you, you can do it in KDevelop.

KDevelop offers quick access to the development tools on your computer, and a place to write, compile, and test code. It has its own mailing list, to which you can subscribe from the link on the KDE home page. KDevelop is a slick place to get started in programming or even in learning how programs work.

For those who are not yet using KDE 1.1.2, there are versions of KDevelop that you can download and compile. (Though I highly recommend upgrading your entire KDE distribution.)

Of course, KDevelop does not replace, say, a degree in computer science. If you become heavily involved in programming, you will no doubt seek other references and information. Even so, you are unlikely to outgrow KDevelop anytime soon.

The QT Toolkit

KDE is built using *QT*, a set of libraries and development tools produced by Troll Tech, a Norwegian company that developed it for use in producing Linux and other UNIX applications (and even Windows applications) with relative ease. It includes libraries, widget sets, screen controls, extensions for 3D and other development, and more. It serves where in other places a different toolkit, such as the commercial Motif, would be employed.

It also caused one of those little brushfires that so often erupt on the Linux world because it was not "free" as some free software advocates (or zealots, depending on your point of view) would have liked. If you used it to develop commercial applications, you were expected to pay for it. It was free only if you used it to develop free software. The situation became so furious that some distributors refused to have anything to do with it. Some in the Gnome development effort said that the QT license proved the inherent superiority of their product (which still isn't as stable as KDE, though it is quite pretty).

In due course, the "Trolls," as they are called, came up with something called the *QPL license*, a document that assures that QT will remain available for free software development. This calmed things considerably, though the Trolls and the Gnomes can be heard even now grumbling and muttering about it. Rumplestiltskin has remained silent on the topic.

The QT toolkit has won a number of awards and has proved over time to be both stable and efficient. As a demonstration project, the Trolls undertook to port Netscape Navigator's source code to QT, claiming that it could be done in one man month. They succeeded (see Figure 36.5).

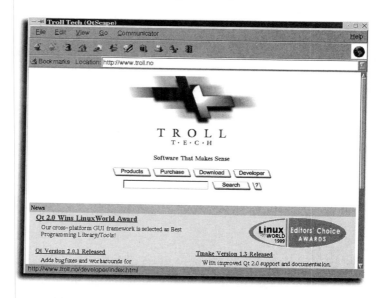

FIGURE 36.5
Five guys working for four days ported Netscape source code to QT, producing QTScape.

The Mozilla project, which has undertaken the huge task of a full Netscape port, offers a QT-based build if you download and build the source code (beware: it is an 18MB file). You can find out more about this at www.mozilla.org.

And the highly regarded commercial Opera Web browser is being built using QT (see Figure 36.6).

FIGURE 36.6
This pre-release shot of Opera for Linux nevertheless illustrates a certain KDE-like appearance, due to their common ancestry.

In that this chapter is about how you can develop for KDE, it's important to note that if you plan to do this, you need to download all packages offered by your Linux distributor or by Troll Tech. These include QT, QT-devel, QT-doc, and possibly others, including the OpenGL packages and such example packages as might be available. (This, as you can tell, varies from distributor to distributor.)

After you've done all this, it's worthwhile to poke around among the /examples subdirectory items in your /qt directory. You will see some pre-built suggestions (see Figures 36.7 and 36.8).

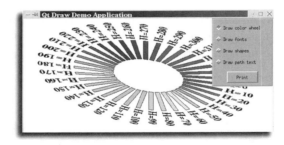

FIGURE 36.7
The Draw example renders this.

FIGURE 36.8
The Layout example gives a sense of some of the screen elements available to the programmer. You'll find more than a dozen little examples and even a couple of applications and games.

A tremendous amount of information is available about QT on the Troll Tech Web site at www.troll.no.

Observing KDE's Programming Rules

In order to present a consistent face to the world, specific programming rules (and some guidelines as well) enable the development of high-quality KDE applications.

You can find out more than you ever imagined was available by visiting http://developer.kde.org/documentation/standards/kde/index.html. This documentation should help you organize and design your project, protect you from having to reinvent the wheel, and make sure that anyone who knows how to use KDE will know how to use your application, at least to the extent that it doesn't add features unique to itself. Even then, the style guides will help you figure out how to implement new features and functions in a logical, easy-to-use way.

Joining the KDE Developer Network

In the course of using KDE, you may find a bug you know how to fix or a feature you would like to implement. As it happens, you're cordially invited to do so.

Generally, though, it's a good idea for there to be some organization to things. If you hack the code on your own machine and it works for you, great. It didn't break anything that you use, but it might have broken something that other KDE users use, so you don't just plop new code into the system. Instead, you get involved with KDE development. The recipe for doing this is at `http://developer.kde.org` (see Figure 36.9).

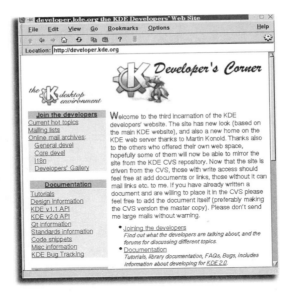

FIGURE 36.9
The KDE Developer Web page provides all the information you need to join in the effort. It also provides links to the developer mailing list, which is where those involved in KDE development discuss issues major and minor, where patches are tested, and people are recruited for projects. It's a strong and talented group of people with way too much work to do. They can use your help.

You don't have to be a world-class code writer to do your part. If you're a graphic artist, there are always icons and the like to be designed. If your experience is in public relations, there are things to be done in that field. If you're a teacher, you can demonstrate KDE to local computer user groups. And so on. But the place to start is on the developer page.

chapter 37

Using KDE on Notebook and Portable Computers

KCMLaptop

KAPM

If you can get Linux and the X Window System working on your laptop or note-book computer, you can use KDE there. I know...thanks a lot!

Actually, you can outfit most portable computers with Linux and the X Window System fairly readily. Not long ago the person who hoped to use Linux on such a machine was forced to be a pioneer. You haven't really experienced configuration until you've calculated your own XFree86 video chip and LCD screen settings.

But life is sweeter now, thanks to a Web site. It's the Linux on Laptops page, which you can find at `www.cs.utexas.edu/users/kharker/linux-laptop/`. Kenneth E. Harker at the University of Texas, Austin, Department of Computer Science has constructed a page that has onsite or by link just about everything having to do with the deployment of Linux on portable computers. This includes a repository of XF86Config files for most known notebook chipsets and LCD panels for many popular makes and models of laptop and notebook computers. It also offers a listing of Web pages where you can receive instructions for the installation of Linux on particular models, software, and newsgroups of interest to the notebook user. If you plan to put Linux on a notebook machine, it's just plain foolish not to gather and use the information on the Linux on Laptops page.

Guerilla Installation

On some machines, just how far you're willing to go can govern your success. For instance, on my little Toshiba Portégé 300CT, I had to remove the hard drive (easy, actually) and pop it into the desktop machine to put Linux on it. In that the drive provided with the machine was a tad small, I took the opportunity to get a bigger, faster one. (If you decide to upgrade a notebook hard drive, make certain that you get one that physically fits into your portable.) This involved buying, for about $10, an adapter that allowed the little drive to be hooked up to the IDE cable in my desktop computer. It also allowed me to copy data files and configurations so that I didn't have to reconfigure a lot of applications and download and install the proper XF86Config file for the Toshiba's unusual 1,024×600 pixel display. Those who use the little Toshiba Libretto—imagine a UNIX box that weighs under two pounds!—have to calculate special strategies because the little PCMCIA floppy drive included with that machine isn't supported in Linux. If you have a CD reader built into your notebook machine and you can boot from it, installation will likely be a lot easier.

After you get Linux on your portable computer, you want to do some things to take advantage of some of the machine's advanced features. The first and most obvious is to enable Automatic Power Management in the kernel, which usually doesn't require you to recompile the kernel, but it can.

Building a Kernel

Sounds frightening, doesn't it? The very audacity of recompiling your Linux kernel. Relax. It's easy if you follow the instructions *exactly*. They are included in the kernel source.

Generally, it's a good idea to download and install the latest *stable* kernel source, which is put into /usr/src. Before you build a new kernel, though, make sure that you look in the /Documentation/Changes file in the kernel source directory to make sure you have the versions of everything you need.

Then have at it. The people at `kernel.org` could not have made it any easier. You can create a module that supports the sound capabilities of your system, the automatic power management features, and so on. You want to take time with this—uninterrupted time—so that you can carefully tailor the new kernel to your needs.

The Kernel How-to, which probably resides on your hard drive in /usr/doc, but which in any case you can get at the Linux Documentation Project (`www.linuxdoc.org`), tells you all you need to know. Pay close attention to it and follow its instructions *exactly*.

You also need to make sure that you have the latest PCMCIA-CS package installed. This allows your machine to recognize and use PCMCIA cards and to hot swap them. (Sadly, as more and more notebook manufacturers build the execrable Windows-only modems into their machines, you become more and more likely to need a PCMCIA modem, which will reduce battery life to some extent. On the good side, you can upgrade PCMCIA modems, and overall system performance is better with one, even under Windows, than with a Windows-only modem. When you get a PCMCIA modem, make sure it's not one of those Windows-only things, which are fit only to shim up that uneven leg on your desk.)

PCMCIA cards are the modem, network, or other peripheral devices that stick in a slot in the side of your notebook computer. *PCMCIA-CS* is the PCMCIA Card Services package, which is downloaded and compiled after the kernel. *Hot swapping* is the capability to remove one card and replace it with another while the machine is running, and to have both cards properly recognized.

With that admittedly truncated description of getting Linux (and therefore KDE) onto your machine, I shall jump into the areas in which KDE has made notebook use easier.

KCMLaptop

One of the neatest little KDE applications, and an absolute must if you are using KDE on your notebook machine, is KCMLaptop. This combines the functions of PCMCIA card monitoring and automatic power management administration. You can find its source code in the /stable/apps/utils directory of your KDE ftp mirror.

After you have started it, a tiny battery icon appears on the K Panel. Resting your mouse pointer there produces a little help bubble that quantifies the current state of your machine's battery; if you're plugged into the wall, it tells you that too.

Right-clicking on the icon allows you to look at the setup of KCMLaptop in more detail, and to change that setup, beginning with the **Battery** status (see Figure 37.1).

FIGURE 37.1

This page lets you determine how (or whether) you want the battery status display to appear. You can even change the icons if you want, by clicking on each of the icons in turn and selecting a replacement icon. You also determine how frequently the system checks the battery's state.

The next tab, shown in Figure 37.2, is a simple listing of the occupants of your PCMCIA slot(s).

FIGURE 37.2

As you insert and remove PCMCIA cards, the values on this tab change automatically. You don't actually do anything here, but it lets you keep track of what's there.

Now we get into some serious configuration that can determine how efficiently your computer uses its battery charge. Many notebook machines offer more than On and Off, with built-in power saving features. These may include the following:

- **Standby mode**, where some things are powered down but the computer remains on and ready for nearly instant use.

- **Suspend mode**, which is close to Off but not quite. The contents of the current session are usually copied to your hard drive so that when you resume computing, you're right where you left off.

KCMLaptop allows you to configure these features (if they are supported) in a way that KCMLaptop expects (see Figure 37.3).

FIGURE 37.3
The **Power** tab is divided, offering settings for battery and mains power. You set the behavior of your machine after a period of inactivity that you specify on the left side, whereas you make the corresponding configuration on the right to tell the machine what to do when it's plugged in.

The **Warning** page prevents those embarrassing situations where your entire Masters thesis is lost because you forgot to save it and then the battery went dead, which is the cyber-age equivalent of "the dog ate my homework." If it isn't configured sensibly, though, it can produce embarrassing situations all its own (see Figure 37.4).

FIGURE 37.4

When your battery is about to run out of electricity KCMLaptop causes a warning to pop up on your screen. If you really want to, you can cause it to scream "Help! I'm dying" from your notebook's tiny little speaker (you would have to record the message yourself; it's not included) or run a program, any program, before the battery goes dead. It also provides a system beep, which is itself plenty annoying and embarrassing if you do library research or make notes in meetings. Fortunately, you can turn off the beep. You can even set it to force your machine into Suspend or Standby mode.

The **Critical** page is when KCMLaptop tells you it's not kidding, the situation is really serious, and you'd better do something right now or you can kiss that Masters thesis goodbye. You get the idea (see Figure 37.5).

FIGURE 37.5

This page mirrors the **Warning** page, but determines what happens when your battery is running on fumes.

KCMLaptop is simply one of the niftiest little utilities around, replacing the non-Linux thing that probably came with your machine. I wouldn't leave home without it.

KAPM

If for some reason you don't have, don't want, or can't compile KCMLaptop, there is always KAPM, which monitors your battery status (see Figure 37.6).

FIGURE 37.6
Though not as elaborate as KDCLaptop, KAPM does keep you informed of your battery's charge.

KAPM, too, docks itself into your K Panel, and right-clicking on it produces a menu (see Figure 37.7).

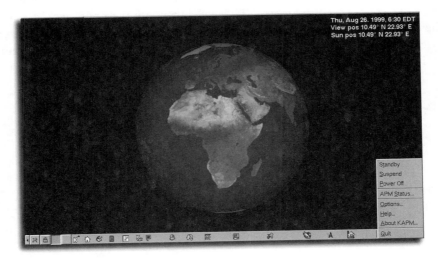

FIGURE 37.7
Tiny icons on an autohidden K Panel, easy access to power controls on the screen, a nifty live application as a desktop, and a nice, wide screen. What more could a notebook user want. Well, for one thing, a nice, warm bed at 6:30 a.m.!

Like KCMLaptop (I hate to keep making the comparison, but it's unavoidable), KAPM offers a warning when your battery is low; unlike KCMLaptop, it also warns you when your battery is charged. This isn't necessarily a bad thing: you can ruin some laptop batteries by overcharging. You can set when you want to be warned in both cases (see Figure 37.8).

FIGURE 37.8

You certainly want to be warned when your battery is almost discharged, and on some machines you want to be warned when your battery is recharged. You can set both in KAPM.

As is true of almost everything in the Linux world, developers are adding new features all the time, so it's a good idea to check from time to time for new versions of these utilities and new utilities that enrich—What would the marketers say?—your "portable computing experience." The fact is that with these tools you're ready to hit the road, and with them you can enjoy the supreme satisfaction of turning on your machine and booting up Linux and KDE, earning the right to look down your nose at the mere mortals with their lesser systems who surround you.

chapter 38

Joining the KDE Developer Network

To know where you're going, it's helpful to know where you are. In KDE, in the open software—movement? industry?—world in general, it is impossible to determine whether we are climbing toward something glorious or are even now at the pinnacle, whence we shall now make our descent.

In KDE, we have seen the work of hundreds of young, energetic programmers, producing great software for the sheer love of it. The joke is that "KDE is a wonderful desktop produced by dozens of people named Stephan and Matthias." But the joke, while amusing to all of us who have watched KDE come into being, shortchanges a lot of people. I think of Harri Porten, who has spent lots of his own time helping me figure out how to solve a problem with Kppp, ages ago (well, months, but that's ages in the Linux world), with me just one of a thousand users posting to a KDE mailing list. How many others did he help? I have no idea. He communicated with me by private mail, after I'd posted my question publicly. I think of Reggie Stadlbauer, who always has had a minute to talk about KOffice via email, long before I was writing a book. And as I write this today I have gotten from one of the Stephans, this one Stephan Goetter, information about the hack in a file in kdelibs that will change the default paper size, which will now be put into Chapter 36, "Programming for KDE." These things are the equivalent of calling Microsoft technical support—if there were a free avenue for such—and having the phone answered by Bill Gates, or calling IBM to ask about OS/2 and having Lou Gerstner express an interest in your opinions. It extends beyond the formal KDE folk to people like Jordan Grignon, who built a set of QT RPMs for me when I'd screwed up my compiler, for no reason other than we're all in this boat together. I doubt that there are many KDE users who, having posted politely to the KDE lists, lack such stories. These guys really care. They want users to be happy because it is a point of professional honor with them. The world would be a much better place if everyone took such pride.

These *guys*? Yes, indeed. While this is anything but a political screed, the lack of women cranking out KDE applications is noticeable, writing code in general, actually. There's no real reason for this that I can find, so, women, get to it!

The Future

No, we can't know where we're going until we know where we are. Where is that?

Open software is by definition a little bit anarchistic. At the same time, it is more highly organized than any institution that springs to mind. People in the open software movement—and in this use it *is* a movement—devote hours to arguing the fine points of some vague licensing issue. Wars break out within the movement from people who claim to be freer than others. This sort of thing plagued the early days of KDE, which was built against QT, which is or isn't a commercial product, depending on what you do with it. On the other hand, people in spite of it all come together to produce software like the GIMP, like all the free compiling tools that work so beautifully together, like KDE. There's no anarchy at the code level.

Eric S. Raymond, who is as perceptive a guy as you're likely to find, proffered in his landmark "The Cathedral and the Bazaar" that programmers write to scratch an itch. That does not explain, though, the groups of programmers who have produced things like KDE, indeed like Linux itself. Group itches? Does this mean that Linux is becoming less bazaar and more cathedral? Occasionally one might think so.

Already, the number of applications being developed by just one programmer not to any particular desktop project seems to be on the decline. The excellent XFMail program seems to have pretty much stopped with a mid-1998 version, and there is no new version of Nedit or any of a number of programs that were once Linux mainstays. Perhaps it is due to redundancy, but it is sad to see development centered around large projects.

But we are seeing increasing interest from bigger corporations: IBM and its Lotus subsidiary; Corel; Compaq; and Hewlett-Packard. This is encouraging in many ways, especially if you are hoping to base your business's computing on Linux and KDE, but we must be careful not to read too much into this. Linux has of its own volition drawn a great deal of attention, and the amounts being invested in it by the big companies, though huge by many standards, are a small part of what the companies spend each year, and are a small hedge against being left behind. Many of us remember the commitment IBM made to OS/2, only to back off from the standalone and desktop user. And I'm still awaiting the CorelDRAW! 3.0 that an officer in the company told me would be introduced for OS/2 "by the end of the year." That was in the summer of 1993. (I also remember the OS/2 Warp rollout in which company after company pledged to ship preloaded OS/2, and port their applications to that system. Few ever did.) The point is that a lot of big corporate money guarantees, really, nothing. If you plan to base your business computing on Linux and KDE, it's important to pay attention to the trends in Linux and KDE. It's very unlikely that either will become a dead end. I'm not a professional seer, though, and the lone thing the professional prognosticators in the computer industry have in common is that they have been consistently, completely wrong.

Paradoxically, applications such as VMware could provide an interesting niche for Linux (and KDE). VMware allows developers of Windows applications to run multiple versions of that user interface on one machine at once, which is a real boon for prototyping and testing. Because of its various modes, VMware prevents file system corruption and offers features that native Windows by itself simply cannot. It won't be long before Windows application developers notice this.

We have seen Linux distributors make public offerings of stock and suddenly become big business. Good for them. I am writing this book—in part—in hope that it will enrich me financially; indeed, in the hope that it and the ones that follow will allow me to elevate myself to the extent that money ceases to be a concern and I, too, can pursue loftier goals. You paid for the book (I hope, and so does the publisher), and you did it with money you earned doing something.

The vast majority of the people writing the code that led to this book, and to the stock offerings, did so for free. A time might just come when they wish that some of the wealth being generated by their work accrue to them.

Perhaps there will be new generations of young, hungry code writers, eager to show their stuff. Maybe this is how it will all progress. I don't know. Neither do you. We don't know where we are. This makes it harder to know where we're going.

Then again, perhaps as we're paid to do things, to develop code or to sort out some other aspect of computing, we'll make our tithe, contribute something, be it lines of code or online support, whatever, to the common good. We just don't know, do we?

Once, some years ago, a good friend told me of two neighbors who had a driveway in common for much of its length. How, he had asked them, did they manage to maintain it without dispute? "Easy," he was told. "We each do more than our share." I am not a preacher—though this book is dedicated to one—but I will sermonize to this extent: Find a way in which you can contribute, and then do it.

An Apology

In the course of this book I have criticized, whined, and complained here and there. I think those things were justified, but I do not for a moment want my complaints to be taken as criticisms of the people who spent time writing the code. GUI design is a tough thing to do. (Writing books is a tough thing to do, and this one has its weak points, I'm sure.) But in writing a book, one has a loyalty owed to a group other than the book's subjects: you, its readers. There is no greater KDE advocate in the world than me, but this isn't a cheerleading book. It's about how to use KDE.

(A few years ago I criticized something my not-yet-wife had written, and she was not happy about it. That night, I sent her an email: "If I cannot say what I think when I have criticism," I said, "how can you believe my praise?" Minutes later came the response: "Nice try." But she married me anyway.)

So my criticism (except for that ridiculous Internet beat thing) has been among friends, and if it has seemed otherwise, I apologize. KDE is at the center of my professional life, not just in this book but in things I write that have nothing to do with computing. If it weren't the best thing around, I wouldn't use it.

But it is; otherwise, it wouldn't be practical.

part

IX

APPENDIXES

Finding the Latest KDE and Its Applications

What the Core KDE Packages Contain

The center of the KDE universe is www.kde.org. Don't just bookmark this location, *memorize* it!

You can find the latest KDE news there, but stopping by the home page won't keep you up to date on the applications that are available for your testing and use. To stay on the bleeding edge, you need to dig a little deeper.

Here are some sites that let you get the code before the electrons have had a chance to settle:

- www.kde.org/wop.html—The "work-in-progress" page, this is the very sharpest part of the cutting edge. It lists applications in the works, some with home pages where you can obtain early code.

- www.kde.org/apphomepages.html—This is a page containing links to such KDE applications that have home pages. Many of the home pages, in turn, allow you to develop the latest developmental code, much of which works surprisingly well.

- www.kde.org/applications.html—This page lists all the applications that reside on the KDE ftp site. Again, there are links to home pages where you can find descriptions of the applications and, perhaps, newer code.

Bear in mind that in every case listed here, you will need to compile the source code yourself (again I say: it really isn't all that difficult), and in some cases you still may not end up with a working application. But you will frequently enough that it's worth the effort, and sometimes a failure to compile is something that the program's author will thank you for a note about. (Please be specific as to how the compilation failed, including the final error message, and do not inform the developer that he is in your opinion doing a lousy job. Be helpful. We're all in this together.)

Downloading the latest KDE itself is done via one of the KDE ftp mirrors. You find these at www.kde.org/mirrors.html. If you select a site near you, you will avoid congestion on the main KDE ftp site and probably get a faster download.

What the Core KDE Packages Contain

It can be useful to know which of the dozen or so packages in the KDE core contain which applications. This is especially true if you have somehow erased or corrupted a file essential to just one program. You can reinstall or recompile that package. (If you've left your KDE compilation intact in /usr/local/src, you can go to the proper directory and type **make install** to get your files back.) It's a poor idea, though, to update just one or two packages because the packages rely on each other, especially on kdelibs.

Four packages in the core KDE distribution are not listed here. kdelibs contains no applications. kdesupport is material essential to the proper compilation and use of KDE, but it contains no KDE applications. korganizer and kdevelop are standalone applications that are part of the core KDE distribution, but they contain no applications other than themselves.

KDEBASE

- **kaudio**—Audio server for use under KDE
- **kbgndwm**—Background manager for KWM
- **kcontrol**—Central control panel
- **kdehelp**—Help browser
- **kdm**—KDE login manager
- **kfind**—File find tool
- **kfm**—File manager with integrated Web browser
- **kfontmanager**—Tool for managing typefaces and sizes
- **kmenuedit**—Editor for menu entries in K Menu and K Panel
- **konsole**—An advanced virtual console terminal
- **kpanel**—Desktop panel and application launcher
- **kpager**—Pager module for KWM; previews virtual desktops
- **krootwm**—KWM module for root window handling
- **kscreensaver**—Screensaver package
- **kstart**—A tiny utility to launch legacy applications with special KDE features
- **kthememgr**—Utility to manage desktop themes
- **kvt**—A terminal emulator similar to Konsole
- **kwm**—The KDE window manager
- **kwmcom**—Communication tool for KWM
- **kwmpager**—Pager module for KWM

KDEADMIN

- **kdat**—Tar-based tape archive application
- **ksysv**—Run level editor for SysV-style initialization
- **kuser**—A user administration tool

KDEGAMES

- **kabalone**—Like Chinese checkers
- **kasteroids**—Asteroids game
- **kblackbox**—Logic game
- **kmahjongg**—Mahjongg game with great graphics
- **kmines**—Minesweeper
- **konquest**—Multiplayer game of galaxy domination
- **kpat**—A suite of Solitaire games
- **kpoker**—Poker game
- **kreversi**—Reversi (Othello)
- **ksame**—Same game (remove the colored balls)
- **kshisen**—Shisen-Sho, a Mahjongg-like game
- **ksmiletris**—Tetris-like game with smiley faces
- **ksnake**—Snake game
- **ksirtet**—Tetris spelled backwards, played forwards
- **ksokoban**—Help the little man store his jewels

KDEGRAPHICS

- **kdvi**—TeX DVI file viewer
- **kfax**—Fax file viewer
- **kfract**—Fractals generator
- **kghostview**—PostScript viewer
- **kiconedit**—Icon editor
- **kpaint**—Paint program
- **ksnapshot**—Makes screenshots of the whole desktop or a single window
- **kview**—Multiformat image viewer

KDEMULTIMEDIA

- **kmedia**—Mediatool compliant media player
- **kmid**—Midi/karaoke file player using external synth, fm, awe, and gus devices

- **kmidi**—MIDI player
- **kmix**—Sound device mixer
- **kscd**—Simple CD player

KDENETWORK

- **karchie**—Archie client
- **kbiff**—Biff utility for mail notification
- **kfinger**—Finger client
- **kmail**—Email client
- **knu**—Front end for several network utilities
- **korn**—Multiple-Mailbox mail notification program
- **kppp**—A dialer and front end to pppd
- **krn**—Usenet news reader
- **ksirc**—Chat client
- **ktalkd**—Enhanced UNIX talk daemon

KDETOYS

- **kmoon**—Displays phases of the moon on the K Panel
- **kworldwatch**—Displays a clock showing the time anywhere in the world
- **mouspedometa**—Measures your pointing device's desktop mileage

KDEUTILS

- **ark**—Archive utility
- **kab**—Address book
- **karm**—Time-management utility
- **kcalc**—Scientific calculator
- **kedit**—Simple text editor
- **kfloppy**—A floppy disk formatter
- **khexdit**—Simple hex editor
- **kjots**—Note-taking program
- **klipper**—KDE clipboard

- **kljettool**—Configuration tool for some HP LaserJet printers
- **klpq**—Printer queue front end
- **kpm**—Process status manager
- **knotes**—Note-taking application resembling sticky notes
- **ktop**—System monitor
- **kwrite**—Advanced text editor

Appendix

B

Distributions that Include KDE

First, let me note that sometimes it seems as if anyone who owns a CD burner is now a KDE distributor, so this list (Table B.1) is certainly incomplete. But it does give a sense of the leading and recently announced Linux distributions that include KDE and anything special you need to know about the particular distribution.

Table B.1 KDE Permutations Throughout Main Linux Distributions

Distributor	Version	KDE Version	Web site	Notes
Caldera OpenLinux	2.3	1.1.1	www.calderasystems.com	
Corel Linux		Custom	www.corel.com	Result of a collaboration among Corel, KDE, and Debian
Definite Linux	6.1	1.1.1	www.dlsl.demon.co.uk/definite.html	
Mandrake Linux	6.0	1.1.1 (enhanced)	www.linux-mandrake.com	Based on Red Linux Hat; puts KDE in /usr
Phat Linux			www.phatlinux.com	New distribution designed to run on a FAT drive containing additional operating systems
RedHat Linux	6.0	1.1.1pre2	www.redhat.com	Puts KDE in /usr, uses beta of KDE 1.1.1
Slackware	4.0	1.1.1	www.slackware.com	
Stormix			www.stormix.com	Based on Debian Linux
SuSE Linux	6.2	1.1.1	www.suse.de www.suse.com	
TurboLinux	3.6		www.turbolinux.com	

Note: Where version information is not provided, it either does not apply (as in Corel Linux) or has not been settled on as this was written.

Appendix
C

Getting Help in a Hurry:
The KDE Mailing Lists

It is possible that your Linux distributor has done something flaky with KDE so that you will need to handle problems you encounter at that level, either through the distributor's technical support or through its own mailing lists. (New Linux users should subscribe to their distribution's mailing lists, anyway. You'll find the means to do so on the distributor's Web page someplace.)

There are also many KDE-sponsored mailing lists, which are great places for information, problem solutions, news of new KDE developments, and so on. These resemble usenet newsgroups in many ways, but they arrive in your mailbox instead of requiring you to open a newsreader to find them. If you have a specific problem or question, it's a good idea to check the mailing list archives (http://lists.kde.org/) first, to see whether your question is answered there, as it very likely is. The search engine there is remarkably good. You'll probably find your answer quickly.

To subscribe to one or more of the KDE lists, go to www.kde.org/contact.html. Full information on subscribing (and unsubscribing) is available there.

The KDE mailing lists include the following:

- **kde**—General discussion of KDE-related issues
- **kde-announce**—Announcements of new KDE applications
- **kde-user**—Users help each other (making it the first list to search in the archives, too)
- **kde-devel**—For application developers (both applications in core KDE and contributed applications, but not the place to report bugs, wishes, or complaints)
- **kde-core-devel**—For developers of core KDE applications and support
- **kfm-devel**—For developers interested in issues related to KDE's file manager
- **koffice**—For developers interested in KOffice
- **kde-licensing**—Discussion of licensing issues
- **kde-look**—Discussing look and feel issues
- **kde-artists**—Discussion of icons and other artwork
- **kde-pim**—For developers of personal information managers, mail clients, calendars, and organizers

Note: Do not post HTML-formatted messages on the KDE (or, really, any Linux) mailing lists. Many of the subscribers pay by the unit, either of time or of transfer, for their Internet service, and doubling the size of the download so you can amuse yourself with blue text or a trick typeface is not likely to bring the results you seek.

Additionally, many use console-based mail applications, and HTML looks really silly in these applications and is customarily deleted without being read. HTML suggests that you don't know what you're doing.

Here are some observations and recommendations about the KDE lists. First, they are not for general Linux questions and posting general Linux questions there will very likely get you slapped down, depending on the mood of the other participants that day.

Second, you probably want to subscribe at least to kde-announce. This is where the availability of new KDE applications and new versions of KDE itself are made.

The general KDE list makes for interesting reading, while kde-user is where you get down and dirty in sorting out configuration issues and the like. Netiquette requires that you look in the archives for an answer to your question before posting it to the group, but this rule is usually observed by flagrant disregard. Subscribing to kde-devel is a fine thing to do if you're interested in knowing the thinking of the developers and if you're interested in hacking the code yourself. It is not, however, the place to ask configuration questions. (The exception is if you are beta testing either full beta releases or daily "snapshots" of KDE, in which case you can, of course, point out when a build fails for the lack of a file or something of that order.)

Though the KDE mailing lists involve people from dozens of countries, they are officially in English.

Appendix

D

KDE on Other Platforms

KDE is typically a Linux desktop, and any processor that runs Linux will run KDE.

But it will run in various iterations of the X Window System on other operating systems as well:

- Solaris
- FreeBSD
- OpenBSD
- NetBSD
- IRIX
- HP-UX
- UNIXWare
- SCO OpenServer

There are reports of KDE running with minor modifications on other flavors of UNIX as well. With considerable hacking you could install the OS/2 version of the X Window System and port KDE to that platform. (I don't know why you'd want to, but it could theoretically be done.)

Generally, you can find binaries for the operating systems listed earlier available for download. If you have gcc compiling tools installed, you should be able to compile the binaries locally as well.

INDEX

The IT site
you asked for...

It's Here!

InformIT is a complete online library delivering
information, technology, reference, training, news
and opinion to IT professionals, students
and corporate users.

Find IT Solutions Here!

www.informit.com

Get **FREE** books and more...when you register this book online for our Personal Bookshelf Program

http://register.quecorp.com/

 Register online and you can sign up for our *FREE Personal Bookshelf Program*...unlimited access to the electronic version of more than 200 complete computer books—immediately! That means you'll have 100,000 pages of valuable information onscreen, at your fingertips!

 Plus, you can access product support, including complimentary downloads, technical support files, book-focused links, companion Web sites, author sites, and more!

 And you'll be automatically registered to receive a *FREE subscription to a weekly email newsletter* to help you stay current with news, announcements, sample book chapters, and special events, including sweepstakes, contests, and various product giveaways!

 We value your comments! Best of all, the entire registration process takes only a few minutes to complete, so go online and get the greatest value going—absolutely FREE!

Don't Miss Out On This Great Opportunity!

QUE® is a brand of Macmillan USA.

For more information, please visit *www.mcp.com*

Other Related Titles

WELCOME TO THE REVOLUTION

LINUX
MAGAZINE
THE CHRONICLE OF THE REVOLUTION

DON'T MISS AN ISSUE!

Linux Magazine is the monthly information source for the whole Linux community. Whether you are a system administrato developer, or simply a Linux enthusiast, *Linux Magazine* delivers the information and insight you need month after month.

Our feature stories, in-depth interviews, and reviews will help you navigate and thrive in the ever-changing world of Linux an Open Source Software. What does Microsoft really think of Linux? What's the best way to build a Linux machine from scratch? How can you integrate Linux into a Windows-based network? Whatever you are looking for, *Linux Magazine* is where you will find it.

With regular columns from such Open Source luminaries as Alan Cox, Paul 'Rusty' Russell, Randal Schwartz, and Larry Augustin you know you can't go wrong…

So don't miss an issue — Subscribe today to *Linux Magazine*, "The Chronicle of the Revolution."

Check out our website at www.linux-mag.com